INSTRUCTIONAL REGULATION AND CONTROL

cybernetics,
algorithmization
and heuristics
in education

INSTRUCTIONAL REGULATION AND CONTROL

cybernetics, algorithmization and heuristics in education

L.N. Landa

Institute of General and Educational Psychology
Academy of the Pedagogical Sciences
Moscow, USSR

Felix F. Kopstein
Scientific Editor

Samuel Desch
Translator

Educational Technology Publications
Englewood Cliffs, New Jersey 07632

Library of Congress Cataloging in Publication Data

Landa, Lev Nakhmanovich.
    Instructional regulation and control.

    Bibliography: p.
    Includes index.
    1. Programmed instruction. 2. Cybernetics.
I. Title.
LB1028.5.L37   371.39'442   75-44383
ISBN 0-87778-087-0

Printed in the United States of America.

Library of Congress Catalog Card Number:
75-44383

International Standard Book Number:
0-87778-087-0.

First Printing: February, 1976.

Editor's Preface

In this volume L.N. Landa elaborates on a number of themes introduced in his earlier book, *Algorithmization in Learning and Instruction*. Some of the issues treated in the present book were barely discussed earlier or were only implied. Each of them had occasioned a paper published in Russian over the past decade. Taken together these papers do much to clarify the conceptual framework of Prof. Landa's cybernetic and psychological approach to cognition, to learning, to thinking and problem-solving, and to the technology of instruction.

While some of the earlier publications assembled for this volume had become somewhat obsolete, the issues they addressed remain as timely as ever. At our request Prof. Landa revised all of the material incorporated in this book. The revisions involved deletions of all obsolete material as well as additions of original material. Thus, every chapter has been brought up to date, except for the references, which are the author's original sources.

Clear, rational thought—especially when couched in logical formulations—requires extreme precision of language. Often fine nuances of denotative as well as connotative meaning assume a critical importance. At the same time the lexical and grammatical content of different languages such as Russian and English are not entirely identical. While every effort has been made in this volume to render the author's intended meaning precisely, the success inevitably is one of degree. Hence, there is a need to make certain editorial decisions explicit, so as to allow the reader some latitude of judgment about what was meant originally.

Whereas the distinguishing characteristics of objects or situations, i.e., those indicative of membership in a given class, were called "indicative features" in *Algorithmization in Learning and Instruction*, they are herein simply called "attributes." This usage is consistent with that of modern logic. Consistency of terminology between the two books was sacrificed to greater uniformity and precision of expression as the author's intent and meaning emerged more and more clearly. While "indicative features" is suited to explaining, e.g., the grammatical categories of various kinds of sentences to teen-aged students, the term "attribute" has a rigorous definition in logic, so that the generality of various propositions set forth in the present book will be more readily appreciated.

A similar consideration relates to the use of "cognition," "cognitive processes," and so forth. The word recurrently used in the original Russian manuscript can be literally rendered as "mental"; however, it does not carry a mentalistic connotation as does the English. Previously the somewhat narrower rendering of "intellectual" (as in intellectual operations, intellectual efforts, etc.) was regarded as a good substitute. However, as the full scope of the author's intent became progressively clearer, the broader term "cognitive" seemed the more accurate one.

Several other terminological issues also require some comment. There is frequent mention of the way in which, e.g., operations follow upon each other. Sometimes the word "order" has been used, and on occasion the word "sequence." The intent was to distinguish between loose and only partially constrained orderings (partial orders) and strictly determined sequences (linear orders). The term "mistake" was used in preference to "error," since discrete rather than continuous functions are involved. In many chapters mention is made of the "isolation of attributes." This phraseology seemed best suited to suggesting that all of the relevant attributes within a larger, more inclusive set are identified and "set aside." Algorithms, in the Russian original, are "constructed" (analogous to construction in geometry), but at various times "designed" or "devised" seemed to be the better English equivalents. These algorithms are (literally) "actualized" in students (e.g., by situational factors), and—depending on context—this has been rendered either as "recalled" or as "elicited." Similarly, algorithms are "realized" (i.e., made real or given a material existence), which suggested "implementation" as the best rendition. Lastly, in Russian there is but a single word (*obuchenii*) for the English words "learning," "teaching" or "instruction," and "education"; it is to be hoped that the correct choices were made here in each instance from the author's context.

Finally, some elucidating comments seem desirable regarding two important phrases which occur repeatedly throughout this book. There is repeated reference to actions or operations within a "system of operations," e.g., algorithms. The phrase means this: a relation (or plural) is defined on the set of operations, for example, a precedence relation. In other words, no particular operation can be taken in isolation, independently of all others within the specified framework. The meaning might be envisioned graphically as a net in which the points (nodes) represent the operations and the lines (arcs) the relation(s) linking them. This, incidentally, is the case in a flowchart representation of an algorithm.

Throughout all of the chapters in this book "programmed instruction" is used in various contexts. At times the intended meaning is literal, i.e., instruction in printed, or similar, material form, in a succession of small steps (segments) and presented in a book or via some device. At other times, however, the phrase "programmed instruction" has a broader meaning and refers to instructional programs or presentations of any kind which are based on instructional objectives specified in advance, which follow a careful design, which incorporate diagnostic achievement tests, etc. (often referred to as "instructional technology" in the U.S.A.). In some cases this has been indicated, but it would have been impossible to rephrase or circumscribe the original text totally without obscuring more than would have been illuminated. Readers will have to decide for themselves the intended meaning in each instance. The purpose is here to alert them to this necessity.

In conclusion I must record my gratitude to E.H. Kingsley,

who advised me concerning accepted, current usage in formal logic and who helped me to guard against the introduction of mistakes (and errors) in logical formulae into the final, typset copy of this book.

Felix F. Kopstein

Strafford, Pa.
November, 1975

Author's Preface

This volume reflects the author's approach to certain aspects of the instructional process. It does not provide a complete, systematic exposition of the problems with which it deals. There is, however, one idea which runs through and connects all of the chapters—that of control of the cognitive activity of the student during the instructional process.

The word "control" as applied to education has for many an odious connotation. It is often thought that to control, for example, the development of the student's personality or thinking means to exercise a dictatorial influence over him and to regulate all of his behavior and cognitive activity.

It is, of course, possible to exert control of this sort. But the concept of control in its current *scientific* sense does not at all correspond to such a rigid approach. Control is understood in modern science as any influence exerted by one system on another (e.g., by one machine on another, by a human being on a machine, a human being on another human being, etc.) in order to achieve a specific goal. Control is considered efficient as well as effective, if this influence achieves the goal in the easiest possible way, with the least expenditure of time, energy, and money. Effective control is usually adaptive, which means that it entails constant analysis of the state of the system which is being influenced, and dynamic adaptation of the controlling influences to these states.

All forms of education or instruction presuppose a specific goal: to transmit to the student a particular body of knowledge, or to develop in him specific skills, habits, abilities, motives, character traits, etc. All forms of education or instruction consist of specific influences exerted by the teacher* on the student (no other means has yet been invented), and in this sense all forms of education or instruction leading to a specific goal are control processes. The only question is whether the instructional influences always lead to the goal, i.e., whether they truly control the mind and behavior of the student, and, if they do, then to what degree of effectiveness.

If the teacher (or parent) desiring, for example, to develop in the child the qualities of honesty and kindness, exerts specific educational influences on him for this purpose, but achieves not honesty and kindness, but dishonesty and cruelty, then it may be said that these influences did not constitute control of the development of these qualities. The child's development with regard to these qualities proceeded as an *uncontrolled* process.

If, on the other hand, the desired qualities did develop, but not to a sufficient degree or with deviations, with various incidental and poorly controlled factors exerting an unduly strong influence, then it could be said that the developmental process was *incomplete* or even *poorly controlled*. In many instances the goal of the educational or instructional process is achieved and the desired qualities develop. But if the teacher influenced the child in such a way that achieving the goal was "expensive," requiring significantly more time, effort, and money than would have been required using other means of influencing the child, then the control of the development of the desired qualities was *inefficient*.

Thus, the scientific concept of control (in education and child rearing) is defined not by the means used to influence the student (whether rigorous or not, dictatorial or nondictatorial), but by the attainment of a specific goal. Control occurs if the goal is achieved, and fails to occur if it is not achieved.

Control is more efficient if the goal is achieved with a lesser expenditure of time, effort, and resources, and less efficient when

---

*The original Russian here might be more properly translated as "teaching agent" or "instructional agency." In other words, the "teacher" need not be a person; it could be a book, film, teaching device, etc. (*Editor.*)

a greater expenditure of time, effort, and resources is required to achieve it.

The means for attaining the goal (the means of instructional control) may be extremely varied, ranging from dictatorial to the most liberal forms, depending on the goals of the educational or child rearing process, the educational philosophical conceptions of the teacher or parent, and his or her educational abilities. For example, if the teacher/parent sets the goal of developing creative initiative and independence in the child, and so gives him at some points in the instructional process complete freedom in solving problems which he is required to solve, or even suggests to him that he make up his own problems, limiting teacher/parent involvement to evaluation of the child's solutions, and, if necessary, consultation, then this approach to teaching—providing that it achieves the goal—also constitutes a means for controlling the student. It satisfies the criterion of control defined above—the application of educational influences which achieve the goal of the instructional process. Whether such a means of control is in all instances adequate and efficient, and whether there are means by which the goal might be achieved more quickly, easily, and reliably, is another question. It has to do not with the problem of whether control is taking place—it *is* taking place, *if the goal is achieved*—but with the problem of how complete and effective such control is. In the extreme case control might entail the absence of any particular instructional influence, if this approach would achieve the goal. After all, in some circumstances the absence of influence can have a considerable effect, and can even prove stronger than other, more positive methods.

The most important objective of control in the area of education and upbringing, i.e., of educational control, is the development in the student of the capacity for *self-control*, i.e., the capacity for independent regulation of *his own* mental processes and behavior. This capacity underlies all forms of human independence: independence of thought, feelings, will, and action. The psychological mechanisms of self-control and self-regulation underlying the human capacity for independence guarantee freedom of thought and action, since with them a person is able, *without any external direction*, to make and carry out decisions. On the other hand, to the extent that these mechanisms are poorly developed, the more a person is dependent on external direction, the less he is free—in the psychological sense.

The capacity for self-control and self-regulation is not, however, an inborn characteristic; its development too must be controlled; so that it, too, must be taught. It is evident, moreover, that this is more difficult to teach than to control anything else, especially when the goal is to develop the processes of self-regulation which underly creative activity. The problem of developing the qualities of independence, of creativity, and of freedom (in the psychological sense) not only does not obviate the necessity for control in the course of the educational and upbringing process, but indeed requires control of a particularly skillful and complete sort.

It is true that the criteria by which the quality of this type of control may be judged are somewhat unusual. Educational control directed toward the development of the capacity for self-control is the more effective the sooner it proves unnecessary and is abandoned, but this is possible only when it has developed the subtle and "difficult" mechanisms of self-control which are capable of assuming the control functions.

The objectives of control in education may be of many different types, and control methods which are appropriate to the objectives must be used to achieve them.

Thus, an important instructional objective is the development in the student of rigorous habits for the performance of specific types of activity (reading, writing, arithmetic calculation, the solution of various types of intellectual and practical problems). Clearly, rigorous habits can be developed only under rigorous conditions, for which rigorous control methods are required. A goal of no less importance, however, is the development of heuristic search processes, creative fantasy, the ability to go beyond habitual and automatic ways of acting, etc. It is clear that it is possible to develop these "non-rigorous" processes only by applying "non-rigorous" methods of instructional control.

To establish as absolute one particular instructional goal and thereby one particular method of control (which is often done in various educational theories) would be a serious error. The more varied the objectives of the instructional process and the methods of control used to achieve them, the more effective instruction will be. "Rigorous" and "non-rigorous" control methods should complement rather than exclude one another. They should be adequate to the tasks which education and upbringing are called upon to perform.

A characteristic feature of contemporary education, in spite of all its achievements, is the fact that it still proceeds as a *poorly controlled process*. Much necessary knowledge and many necessary skills, abilities, character traits, etc., are not developed in the student, or developed incompletely, slowly, or at the cost of excessive expenditure of time, energy, and financial resources. These shortcomings are due in part to the fact that the control methods used in instruction are imperfect.

It should be noted at this point that although the concept of control began to be used in psychology and education primarily in connection with the development of cybernetics and the use of cybernetic methods in the instructional process, the basic problems of educational psychology and education were, in fact, always associated with control processes, and one or another approach to their solution was always directed toward the elaboration of this concept. The author began his own research in this field in the early 1950's.

The problem of teaching the student to think has always existed for psychology and education, and the wisdom accumulated by these sciences and in educational practice throughout their long history should not be underrated. Nevertheless, a general and powerful theory, and reliable methods for teaching the ability to think, have never been developed. This is due, in turn, to the fact that thinking either is not considered to be a specific device or mechanism,* consisting of specific components, each performing a particular function and connected and interacting

*A device or mechanism in the sense of a dynamic process in which information is extracted (gained) or transformed. (*Editor.*)

with other components in a particular way, or is not fully understood in this way. For example, images connected to one another by the laws of association are sometimes isolated as components of this device or mechanism, while the cognitive (internal) actions or operations by which these images and their interconnections may be acted upon, changed, transformed, restructured, etc., are not taken into account. The comprehensive theory of components of the thinking process as an *active* rather than a *passive* mechanism which transforms external and internal information and which is in this way capable of generating new information has not been created. The most important defect of the description of thought processes in terms of associationist, Gestalt, and certain other theories is that such description does not indicate how to develop these processes and how to design them, or else the recommendations deriving from these theories are inadequate in this regard. It might be said that these theories are more descriptive than constructive.

To approach thinking as a specific device or mechanism consisting of specific, interconnected, and interacting components does not, of course, imply that this device or mechanism is regarded as mechanical. However, the characterization of thinking as a psychological and, therefore, *specific* device or mechanism should not overshadow the fact (as has often been the case in the history of psychology) that thinking may, and from a certain point of view must, be regarded as a device or mechanism which not only may be explained through the functioning of its components (although it cannot be reduced to the functioning of its components, since a whole cannot be reduced to the sum of its parts), but also may be "manufactured" by developing, through the instructional process, the individual components and their interconnections.

An impression may arise that viewing a thought as a specific type of device or mechanism excludes consideration of such important components of thinking processes—or, more precisely, factors included in thinking processes and influencing their flow—as motives, emotions, different kinds of personality, attitudes, assessments, and the like. Such a view would be intellectualistic.

What is important in the framework of the approach being described is the fact that these factors also can be viewed as specific types of mechanisms, but mechanisms of an essentially different nature whose analysis is a specific topic. These mechanisms alone are not able to ensure the flow of thinking processes, but they are prerequisites for them, they are necessary but not sufficient conditions. In this book we will pay major attention to the knowledge-operations aspects of thinking processes, since precisely these aspects ensure the direct processing of information being transformed in the process of thinking. It should be borne in mind, however, that isolation of this aspect for consideration is only a consequence of the usual scientific abstraction which is necessary for detailed scientific analysis of particular aspects of phenomena studied. The comprehensive consideration of thinking processes presupposes taking into account all factors influencing the flow of thinking processes, including—and perhaps first of all—personality factors. The cognitive activity of a person is one of the functions of his personality, and many properties of thinking processes (first of all, the operations within the thinking processes which we mentioned above) can not be understood without viewing thinking activity as a specific manifestation of the activity of the personality as a whole.

Let us term *constructive* the approach to thinking (and, in general, to any psychological process) as a device or mechanism each component of which as well as the interconnections among components may be discovered and "manufactured" ("designed and constructed") in the course of the instructional process, as it is in the case of the constructive approach or the constructive principle (compare, e.g., the constructive trend in mathematics). The constructive principle in psychology regards both thought and its development as specific *generative processes*. The construction not only of descriptive but also of generative models of psychological and educative processes assumes a correspondingly important role in the implementation of this principle.

Since the constructive approach is based on the discovery not only of the components of the corresponding "psychological device or mechanism" but also of their internal interconnections, i.e., their structure, and requires that the apparatus be regarded as a specific system consisting of these components, it is also a *structural-systems approach*. It should be noted, however, that the structural-systems approach is not necessarily constructive. It may also be used in the descriptive analysis of psychological and educational phenomena, i.e., in the course of a generally descriptive approach. Our approach, which combines the constructive principle and the principle of structural-systems analysis, may therefore be termed more precisely a *constructive structural-systems approach*.

On a specifically psychological level this approach is closely associated with the conception of thinking as a unification of reflection and activity. This conception of thinking was successfully evolved in Russian psychology beginning in the 1930's. It follows from this view that, if thinking is not only a form of reflection but also a form of activity, then it is necessary to discover the actions (operations) of which it is composed, if these actions (operations) are to be deliberately and efficiently taught. However, this is not a simple task and not every approach to the discovery of operations permits the elaboration of a constructivist method of developing them. Thus, the isolation of only such traditional operations of thought as analysis, synthesis, generalization, differentiation, etc., does not directly lead to constructivist means for developing them. This is due to the fact that the terms analysis, synthesis, generalization, etc., do not denote particular cognitive actions, but are rather general designations for entire sets (classes) of actions. For example, analysis denotes among other things the division of the image of an object into parts, the isolation of its properties, the recognition of the relations existing among its components, etc. Although all this is called analysis, it is evident that in each case fundamentally different cognitive operations are being referred to. The same may be said of synthesis, generalization, and other cognitive operations.

It is obvious, for example, that it is impossible to teach analysis in general—it is possible to teach only those specific operations which constitute and manifest the analysis. If we teach someone, for example, to analyze the form of an object into parts, it does not at all follow that he will be able to isolate its attributes. The problem arises here of isolating the specific cognitive operations which can be taught ("constructed" in the student's mind) in a rigorous manner.

In order to implement a constructive approach of this sort, we chose to investigate the thinking procedures used by students in proving geometric propositions. The difficulties which teachers encounter when they attempt to teach the ability to prove theorems are well known, and this is due to the fact that teachers (and, therefore, also students) often do not know what to do in order to prove a theorem, i.e., the operations and the order of operations required for this purpose. It is reasonable to suppose that isolating these operations and combining them into a specific system will permit formulation of specific instructions as to what to do and how to do it in order to prove a theorem. These instructions will constitute a program of the cognitive activity of the student. The availability of such programs will permit, in turn, the design of instructional programs which will develop in the student the processes involved in proving theorems in an expedient, consistent, and reliable manner.

In setting as a research objective the problem of discovering the operations which must be performed in order to prove a geometric theorem, we had to keep in mind that these operations had to be, on the one hand, sufficiently specific (so that they could be systematically taught), and on the other hand, sufficiently general to be usable in solving a wide range of problems, rather than only a few particular problems. In other words, this system of operations had to be one which could serve as a basis for developing in the student a *sufficiently general method* for solving problems involving proof or, equivalently, a sufficiently general method of thinking (reasoning) during the solution of such problems.

In 1955 the research in question was completed and defended as a candidate's (i.e., doctoral, *Ed.*) dissertation. The operations of which the process of proving geometrical theorems is composed were determined and a set of instructions indicating how to proceed in order to arrive at a proof was compiled. A procedure for developing the relevant operations in the student step-by-step was evolved and an experiment was performed which demonstrated that teaching these operations according to this procedure caused students who had been unable to prove theorems, or who had done so poorly, to develop this ability in a relatively short time, although they had previously studied geometry in school unsuccessfully for one to three years. This experiment likewise demonstrated the correctness of the method and the efficacy of the instructional methodology on which it was based. The acquisition of a method of thinking for proving theorems had become a controlled process. Some of the results of this research are described in Chapters Eight and Nine.

As we noted in the preface to our earlier book, *Algorithmization in Learning and Instruction* (Landa, 1974), during the 1950's in the United States work was begun which was in some respects analogous to ours, but which had an entirely different objective— the writing of programs for proving logical and geometric theorems by computer (Newell, Shaw, and Simon, 1957; Gelernter and Rochester, 1958). In order for a computer to be able to prove theorems, it must be given a precise program of operations to perform, and this requires that the process of proving a theorem be analyzed into elementary operations and that the system (network, *Ed.*) formed by these operations be determined. This problem was solved by the authors of the programs. However, the first publication by American authors dealing with this problem appeared after our dissertation had been finished and defended. This was unfortunate, since a comparison of the "machine" and "human" approaches to the proving of geometric propositions as it had been displayed in our experiments might have permitted a more precise formulation of certain problems regarding both the general and specific features of how humans and machines think while proving theorems.

The research of P.Y. Gal'perin (e.g., Gal'perin 1956, 1957) and his co-workers, which was based on the theory of the stage-by-stage formation of cognitive operations and which began in the Soviet Union at about this time, should also be mentioned in this regard. This research, like ours, dealt with the problem of discovering the operations of which various forms of cognitive activity are composed. The two lines of research differed in direction and in the problems chosen for investigation.

The theory of stage-wise formation of cognitive operations attempted to determine the stages of development of the unitary operation (from the material or materialized stage through the externally and internally vocalized stages to the stage of functioning on the cognitive plane). The first step in this direction was the examination of elementary forms of cognitive activity, as expressed in the conceptualization of an object. The fundamental objective of our work, as contrasted to the stage-by-stage theory, was to expose the structure and mode of interconnection (i.e., the ways in which they are organized into systems) of the operations underlying complex forms of cognitive activity during problem-solving of a relatively high level of difficulty. The result of this effort was the formulation of sufficiently general thinking procedures for use in solving problems of this sort. It goes without saying that there is no contradiction whatsoever between these two approaches; in fact, they complement one another. Discovery of the stages of formation of an individual operation yields no information regarding the systems of operations underlying the process of solving a given type of problem, and the stage-by-stage teaching of individual operations does not in itself guarantee the development of their systems. On the other hand, effective teaching of systems of operations is possible only when there exist effective means of teaching the individual operations deriving, in particular, from the theory of the stage-by-stage formation of cognitive operations.

After a thinking procedure for proving geometric propositions had been formulated, the question arose as to the applicability of this procedure to problems in areas other than mathematics (geometry), i.e., as to its degree of generality. If it proved to be generalizable, then it would be possible to transfer the method from one subject-matter area to another and to develop more general cognitive abilities (it is reasonable to suppose that knowledge of general thinking procedures underlies general cognitive abilities).

In order to answer this question it was decided to investigate the thinking procedures used in solving other, nonmathematical problems. The thinking procedures used in solving grammatical problems were selected as the objects of this investigation. These were analyzed in the same way as in the case of problems in geometric proof. It proved to be the case that the difficulties encountered by students in attempting to solve grammatical problems had the same basic causes as those encountered by students in attempting to prove geometric propositions, namely that they do not know the cognitive operations which constitute the problem-solving process, or do not know them thoroughly.

The systems of operations underlying the solution of grammatical problems were analyzed and used to construct a general method for solving problems of this type. A psycho-educational experiment in which students were taught this method showed that it was even more effective than the previously formulated method for proving geometric propositions.

Although these methods have some features in common, there is one essential difference between them. The method for solving grammatical problems fully determines the actions of the student (as problem-solver, *Ed.*), while the method for proving geometric propositions does not.

This distinction can be expressed in a more precise way. It is well known that by the late 1950's, the ideas of cybernetics had become widely disseminated and had attracted the attention of researchers working in many fields, including some in the field of instruction. Among them was the author of this book, who began in the early 1960's to develop the principles of a cybernetic approach to instruction. His study of the concepts of cybernetics and mathematical logic showed that the method for solving grammatical problems was algorithmic, and the method for proving geometric propositions was nonalgorithmic, or heuristic, in nature.

Methods of both types have long been used in education, but neither a precise scientific classification of these methods, nor a theory describing how to generate them for the purpose of achieving instructional objectives, had ever been proposed. Moreover, a theory of how to teach such methods had never been developed. Of greatest importance, however, was the fact that the range of application of algorithmic methods in instruction was severely limited. Such methods were used primarily in mathematics, and were based for the most part on computational algorithms which were transformational in nature.

The effectiveness of our experiment in the teaching of algorithms, especially identification or recognition algorithms (algorithms for solving grammatical problems are of this sort), raised a large number of questions which had never been raised previously in psychology and education. How do algorithms in the rigorous mathematical sense of the term differ from instructional algorithms? What are the psycho-educational characteristics of the various types of algorithms used in education? How should they be written and taught? How can maximally effective algorithms be constructed, and how can the efficiency of different algorithms be evaluated? How do algorithmic methods compare with nonalgorithmic methods? What is the role of each type of method in instruction? An entirely new branch of psychology and education, "algorithmization in instruction," developed.

The author's first publication dealing explicitly with an algorithmic approach to instruction appeared in 1959, although some of the basic ideas contained in it were expressed in various earlier publications (without use of the term "algorithm," however). In 1966 the original Russian edition of *Algorithmization in Learning and Instruction* was published, in which the author attempted to formulate the problems in this area in a more complete and systematic fashion.

Several of the chapters included in this book deal with these issues, including the problem of the relation between algorithmic and heuristic processes. A number of other issues are not discussed in this book, but are considered only in *Algorithmization in Learning and Instruction* (Landa, 1974).

The usefulness of conceptualizing control of the student's cognitive activity during the instructional process in cybernetic terms stimulated the author to examine some more general problems in educational theory and practice from this same point of view. The cybernetic approach to instruction was more than simply "in the air" at this time. The English psychologist and cyberneticist, Gordon Pask, had formulated some ideas in this area quite precisely, and, moreover, had taken specific steps toward their practical implementation by designing an adaptive teaching machine. However, Pask's work was not then known in the USSR (or the US, *Ed.*), and the principles of the cybernetic approach to instruction were formulated here independently and specifically as a result of the attempt to introduce cybernetic ideas into education. The author's task consisted of examining the general problems in this area from the cybernetic point of view.

This book includes a chapter entitled "The Cybernetic Approach to the Theory of Instruction," in which the author attempts to consider instruction from the point of view of general control theory and to interpret the instructional process as a special case of the control process. This interpretation has enabled him to determine those aspects of the instructional process to which general control principles could be applied, and to determine the degree to which they satisfy the requirements for effective control as formulated by cybernetics.

None of these requirements is fulfilled in contemporary classroom instruction and new approaches and methods are needed in this area in order to eliminate existing shortcomings.

Practical means for eliminating some of these shortcomings were indicated by the theory of programmed instruction, which first became known and recognized in the Soviet Union in the early 1960's. Thus, the ideas of the algorithmic and cybernetic approaches to education and of programmed instruction entered the Soviet Union at the same time and converged, and the chapter in question, i.e., "The Cybernetic Approach to the Theory of Instruction" reflects this convergence.

The synthesis of these three approaches is a characteristic feature of their development in the USSR. This was not the case, or not quite the case, in other countries. For example, programmed instruction developed in the United States out of a particular psychological theory of learning (that of Skinner), and was not directly associated at its inception with the cybernetic approach to instruction or with the ideas of algorithmization. In the Federal Republic of Germany, the cybernetic approach to instruction, termed "cybernetic pedagogy" (by H. Frank and others), arose out of an information theoretic approach to psychology and at first was not closely associated either with general control theory or with programmed instruction. The application of the theory of algorithms in instruction initially involved only algorithms governing the teacher's activity (teaching algorithms), and not algorithms governing the student's activity (the teaching of algorithms). The design of teaching (or instructional) algorithms, however, should to a significant degree be based on the particular cognitive and other "mental" processes which need to be developed in the student and on the algorithms governing these processes (provided that they are algorithmic in nature).

Consideration of the instructional process from the point of view of general control theory and with regard to the problems of algorithmization immediately gave rise to a number of issues requiring theoretical resolution. Among these was the question of the necessity of distinguishing the "teaching *of* algorithms" from "teaching (or instructional) algorithms." If algorithms governing the student's activity and algorithms governing the teacher's activity are not identical, then what is the relation between them? How do they influence and determine one another?

In addition, questions of the following sort arose: Is it possible to algorithmize all aspects of the student's and the teacher's activity, and if not, why not? Is it worthwhile to algorithmize everything that can be algorithmized, and if not, what should be algorithmized? How should instructional algorithms be written, what properties should they possess? If programmed instruction constitutes algorithmization of the teacher's activity and does not necessarily entail algorithmization of the student's activity (i.e., the teaching of algorithms), then how should an instructional system handle those cases in which a teaching algorithm for some reason does not "click"?

An approach to the solution of these and other problems is described in the chapter entitled "Algorithms and Programmed

Instruction: The Theory and Methodology of Programming."

A separate but very important question, and one which is of special significance with regard to the problem of increasing the adaptivity of control in the instructional process, is that of diagnosis of the psychological causes of students' mistakes.

The problem of diagnostics in psychology and education is not new. The rapid development of psychometrics bears witness to the considerable attention which has been devoted to it. But there are a number of aspects to this problem. It is possible, for example, to diagnose the state of the student's knowledge, skills, and habits, the nature of his abilities, character, behavior, etc. This is the diagnosis of the student's *state* at a given moment (*state* is understood here in the cybernetic sense, as the set of values assumed by all variables at a given instant). It is also possible, however, to diagnose the internal structures and characteristics of "mental" activity which gives rise to these states. This is a diagnosis of the psychological mechanisms that underlie states, as well as the psychological causes of particular actions. Most of the tests in use at the present time are directed toward discovery and evaluation of the student's states. Does he know or does he not know, and if he knows, then how well does he know? Is he able to perform a given activity or is he unable to perform it, and if he is able to perform it, then how well? Does he possess certain abilities or character traits or does he not possess them, etc.? But in order to teach effectively, the teacher must know not only the character of the student's knowledge, skills, and habits, his abilities, personality characteristics, etc., but also how to control them by influencing their underlying psychological mechanisms. In order to do this he must be able to diagnose these mechanisms. In order to determine how to respond to a student's mistake, the teacher must know why he made it (because he does not know the rule in question, or because he is unable to apply it, or because the rule for him lacks the required automaticity, etc.). It is clear that the nature of the response to a mistake should be a function not only of the character of the mistake itself, but also of its psychological cause.

This problem is especially important in programmed instruction. In current linear programs, responses to mistakes fail to take into account not only the psychological causes of the mistakes, but even the character of the mistakes themselves, and in the most common branched programs only the character of the mistake is considered. In the latter case, of course, responses to mistakes are determined by the probable causes of the mistakes, but only the probable causes, not the actual ones, since as a rule no diagnosis of the psychological causes of the individual student's mistakes is performed.

It cannot be said that psychology has ignored the problem of the psychological causes of students' mistakes. A significant amount of effort has been devoted to this problem. In many instances, however, the causes to which mistakes are attributed are of a general and undifferentiated character (for example, "the operation of analysis has not been developed in the student," "the student's conceptual operations are insufficiently generalized," "the student is unable to switch operations," etc.), and do not indicate a specific and constructive means of responding to the mistakes.

The situation changes when analysis of the student's mechanisms of cognitive activity is directed toward elucidation of the specific cognitive actions (operations) determining the character of the student's solution to a problem. In this case it is often possible to elucidate a complete system of specific operations which must be performed in order to solve problems of a particular type, and to describe this system of operations algorithmically.

If the teacher or program author knows an algorithm for solving problems of a particular class, i.e., a system of operations which the student must perform in order to solve these problems, he will be able, when he encounters a mistake on the part of the student, to diagnose precisely which operations failed to "click in the student's head." An inventory of operations, after all, is at the same time an inventory of possible sources of mistakes at the operational level. The teacher or program author is then able, on the basis of a diagnostic procedure, to determine precisely which operation or complex of operations has "failed." It is evident that this task is analogous to that of searching for the causes of disease in medical diagnostics (searching for that which has "failed" in the patient's organism) or to the problem of searching for a malfunction in electronic or automotive diagnostics. It is this analogy with various types of diagnostics that we wish to suggest in terming the psychological cause of a mistake a "psychological malfunction."

The problem of diagnostics in the sense in which we have used it above is discussed in the chapter entitled "Diagnostics and Programmed Instruction." This chapter describes the principles of an approach to the problem of diagnosing the psychological causes of mistakes as well as one possible specific method for accomplishing such diagnosis. The chapter discusses how to design algorithms for solving specific problems (such algorithms are the outlines of the corresponding diagnostic procedures), as well as how to define means for designing the diagnostic algorithms themselves, since diagnosis of the psychological causes of students' mistakes in the course of programmed instruction is possible only on the basis of diagnostic algorithms. The ultimate goal here is to be able to establish not only computer-aided medical but psychological diagnoses as well.

The method described in this chapter is not, of course, universal; it is applicable only to algorithmic problems, and does not guarantee a diagnosis in all cases. In our opinion, however, it is not only, and perhaps not so much, the method itself which is important; rather, it is the principles in accordance with which it is designed, and, more generally, the approach embodied in it to the psychological diagnosis of the causes of mistakes in the context of the problems of adaptive instruction which are significant.

Another interesting question is that of the possibility of using programmed texts for adaptive instruction guided by a psychological diagnosis of the causes of mistakes. This has indeed proved to be possible. Our colleague, O.N. Yudina, recently developed a diagnostic instructional program for teaching Russian and, in collaboration with G.G. Granik, implemented it in the form of a diagnostic programmed text. The diagnostic procedures are performed by the text itself. Before responding to a mistake on the part of the student, it establishes the psychological cause, and can therefore respond in various ways to a given mistake as a function of its psychological cause.

In conclusion, I would like to express my gratitude to my co-workers and colleagues, who have constantly aided me in clarifying and sometimes generating the ideas expressed in this book. My foreign, including American, colleagues have also played a significant role in this regard, and my meetings with them have always raised new questions and generated new ideas.

The translation and editing of this material was not an easy task. I would, therefore, like to express my sincere gratitude to Mr. Samuel Desch, the translator, and to Dr. Felix F. Kopstein, the scientific editor, who have worked so hard to bring the ideas expressed in the following chapters to English-speaking readers. I would like, also, to thank Mr. L. Lipsitz, the publisher, whose constant interest in the problems and issues dealt with by the author has been instrumental in the completion of this task.

L.N. Landa

Moscow, USSR
April, 1975

Table of Contents

INSTRUCTIONAL REGULATION AND CONTROL

cybernetics, algorithmization and heuristics in education

Chapter One

The Cybernetic Approach
to the Theory of Instruction

The rapid development of science continually increases the volume of knowledge accumulated by man. Human ability to assimilate this knowledge, however, remains limited; memory capacity and time available for education, in particular, cannot be expanded to any significant degree. This situation necessitates an improvement in the instructional process sufficient to insure both that the student will assimilate significantly more knowledge, skills, and habits, and that he will do so more rapidly than he does at present.

The struggle to increase labor productivity, the struggle for time, is being waged in all areas of life. This struggle has begun in the area of education as well. Improving the quality of education and training and decreasing learning time (where this is possible and expedient) are problems of enormous significance. The scientific and technical progress of all countries depends to a significant degree on the quality and duration of this education and training. It is for this reason that making instruction and learning efficient at all levels—elementary school, secondary school, technical school, and university, as well as in the area of industrial education—is such an important scientific and practical problem.

One of the prerequisites for efficiency in the instructional process is the extensive elaboration of the theory of learning and instruction. There are grounds for assuming that significant success in this field may be achieved only by radically restructuring instructional research, and in particular, by introducing into educational psychology the concepts and methods of modern logic, mathematics, cybernetics, and associated sciences.

The possibility of applying cybernetics to instructional phenomena derives from the fact that education (in the sense of formal instruction, *Ed.*) and upbringing may be considered as a type of regulation and control, namely control of the formation and development of cognitive processes and personality characteristics.* Cognitive processes are in principle as controllable as physical, chemical, biological, and other processes. Although there exists definite specificity here, the problem lies in discovering the principles underlying this control, and, on the basis of this knowledge, mastering the processes in question. The elaboration of the theory and techniques of such control is, in our view, one of the most important tasks confronting the science of educational psychology (i.e., learning and instruction, *Ed.*). If this is so, however, then educational psychology has a cybernetic aspect and should, on the one hand, be founded on cybernetics, and, on the other hand, enter into that complex of sciences which contribute to the development of cybernetics itself. The fact that instruction is a form of control permits us to consider the principles of instructional control as a special case of more general control principles.

Of course, the theory of learning and instruction is not equivalent to and cannot be reduced to cybernetics. The sphere of application of cybernetics to educational psychology as well as to other sciences is limited. Education has its specific goals, its

*Considerable contribution to the development of the cybernetic approach to learning and teaching was made in England, first of all, by G. Pask and B.N. Lewis (see, e.g., Pask, 1960a, 1960b; Pask and Lewis, 1962); in the U.S.A. by L. Stolurow (e.g., Stolurow, 1961); and in West Germany by H. Frank (e.g., Frank, 1965), although Frank approached learning and instruction chiefly from an information theoretical point of view, which is only one of the aspects of the broader cybernetic approach viewed as the science of regulation and control. The development of the cybernetic approach to education began at approximately the same time independently in Western countries and in the USSR and has proceeded in parallel but, unfortunately, with very little mutual influence.

specific features and laws, and to study it from the point of view of cybernetics alone would be wrong. Cybernetic analysis in no way implies "destruction" of all that humanistic educational theory and practice have achieved thus far.

We believe that analysis of the instructional process from the point of view of control principles and the requirements which a "good control system" must fulfill would expose some significant shortcomings in instructional theory and practice and could to some degree indicate how these shortcomings might be eliminated. In particular, an analysis of this sort would permit the formulation of some requirements of instructional programming, which is a very important factor in the implementation of this process.[1]

Instructional programming should not be confined to programming of the material which is to be taught. It must unquestionably include as well programming of the processes by means of which this material is to be learned, that is, of the capabilities which must be developed in the student in the course of the instructional process and programming of the instructional activity itself, that is, of the means by which these capabilities are to be developed.

The first type of programming mentioned above is equivalent to specification of instructional content and of the sequence in which this material is to be presented to the student; this type of programming is always represented in instructional programs. The second type of programming is equivalent to specifying the outcomes of instruction, for example, of the system of operations the student must learn in order to successfully solve a given problem, perform a given activity, etc. This type of program controls the student's *functioning* by specifying the procedures which he should be able to execute and which must be developed in him; the development of these processes constitutes, from the teacher's point of view, the instructional objective. Finally, the third type of programming is equivalent to specifying the instructional method to be used, i.e., of the procedures which the teacher should carry out in order to achieve these objectives. The discussion below will be concerned with instructional programming of the latter two types.

1.   **Programming Learning Activity:**
     Objectives and Modeling

In instruction, as in other forms of control exercised by human beings, the controlling activity is directed toward the achievement of a particular objective, i.e., toward the solution of a particular problem. The purpose of instruction is to develop in the student psychic (covert, *Ed.*) and behavioral (overt, *Ed.*) processes with the prescribed characteristics.[2] The processes and their characteristics which are to be achieved through the instruction constitute what one will term the objectives of instruction.

One of the major shortcomings of instructional programs is the fact that their objectives are often formulated in an extremely general and indefinite way, with the result that they cannot fulfill their basic function: the direction and regulation of instructional activity.

As a rule, they amount to a mere enumeration of the material being studied. If the material in question consists of skills which are to be developed during the instructional process, then these skills are usually merely named, without reference to their *composition* or *structure*.

We encounter an analogous situation in many psycho-educational textbooks and manuals. Thus, for example, in one handbook we read: "the student must be taught alertness, intuition, the ability to orient himself to the material, and the ability to grasp connections between facts" (Nemytov, 1947).

These are, of course, legitimate objectives. But is it really possible to develop these qualities, not knowing their make-up, the "elements" of which they are composed, or what happens inside a person's head when he displays "intuition," "alertness," or rapid orientation? It is precisely these questions which are not answered, as a rule, in textbooks and manuals. The teacher is asked to shape processes about which he or she is given no information and the substance of which is unknown to him (her). It is clear that this sort of description of educational objectives gives the teacher very little to work with and cannot significantly influence instructional activity. It is almost impossible to control the formation of these processes consciously and purposefully by proceeding from objectives which have been formulated in this way. It is not surprising that the development of specific capabilities usually occurs haphazardly as an uncontrolled and poorly regulated process. Haphazardness in the formation of specific capabilities, skills, and habits, in particular, very often results in their improper development. In turn, this leads to mistakes, inability to solve problems, and learning difficulties.

From the above, it is clear that the first condition for structuring (organizing, *Ed.*) instruction as a "good control process" is correct programming of its intended results, that is, a precise, detailed, structural specification of the capabilities which are the objectives of the educational process. But to do this it is necessary to analyze the processes which are to be formed, for instance, the process of intellectual activity, into their elementary components (the "bricks" of which they are composed) and to determine their structure. These components may be either specific images and concepts or discrete intellectual operations.

How are we to specify the structure of the processes which are to be given to the teacher as instructional objectives? How can we establish the components which constitute the process which is to be taught to the student, and the interrelationships between these components? It can be done by the same method used in other sciences, and especially cybernetics: the construction of models.

Let us assume that a particular skill, for example, the ability to prove that a given object is a member of a given class of objects, is to be taught. In order to properly map out a program of instruction, it is first necessary to determine the components of this skill; and to do this, it is necessary to analyze the "proving process" into elementary operations and to determine their structure. On the basis of formal considerations, observations, and, when necessary, experiments, an hypothesis is formed as to what proving membership of an object in a particular class means, i.e., the sequence of operations which must be followed in order to carry out the proof is determined. The discovery of these operations and their structure constitutes the construction of a model of the process in question.[3]

A model, once constructed, must be tested. If the process in question has been analyzed into operations which are simple enough for computer processing, then the model may be tested in this way, although experiments on humans may be performed as well. If the subject is able successfully to complete the proof by performing the given sequence of operations, then the model is properly constructed. If carrying out the given operations does not lead to successful completion of the proof, then the model is wrong (or incomplete) and must be revised. A correct model of a thought process should appear precisely as that program of thinking activity which the learner should assimilate, which must be made the basis of the instructional program and which is to be furnished to the teacher as a precisely defined objective.

But designing and teaching students the programs of learning and thinking activity is only one of the tasks facing educational processes. Instruction cannot and should not be equated solely to teaching students programs of activities given from outside. One of the most important tasks is to teach students to discover and design programs of efficient activity independently, i.e., to develop in them the ability of *self-programming*.

To design a program independently, however, it is necessary to know how to do this, i.e., to possess a program for designing a program, or the program of the second order. There may and must exist programs also of still higher orders which represent, each, programs of higher and higher self-organization and self-control.

From what has been said, it follows that programming of students' activity does not mean equipping them only with ready-made programs and teaching them to follow these programs (to act according to these programs). It includes, as one of the most important parts, teaching them programs of self-programming and self-control, which presupposes the design of hierarchies of programs and the mastery of these hierarchies by students.

It should be noted that the notion of "program" should not be identified with the notion of a *hard* (rigorous, strict, rigid) program, i.e., an algorithmic program which completely determines the course of action. Side-by-side with algorithmic programs there may exist also programs of other, non-algorithmic types, knowledge of which is usually necessary to be able independently to design programs of the algorithmic type, or, in other words, to effect self-programming.*

A number of questions arise in regard to the design of a model of cognitive processes. The first of these is the question of how detailed the analysis of complex processes should be. It was stated above that complex processes must be analyzed into elementary components. (We will speak henceforth of operations.) But the concept of an elementary operation is not absolute; it is, rather, a relative concept. The same operation may be elementary for one system but non-elementary for another, depending on the complexity and structure of the system. It may be said that the elementarity of operations is always relative to the system of which these operations are the constituents.

The above comments on the relativity of the concept of elementary operations do not apply only to the comparison of systems such as human beings and computers. It is quite clear that many operations which are elementary for an adult are non-elementary for a child. The process of teaching a human being is characterized by the fact that, in learning, he develops his capabilities so that operations which are non-elementary on one level of development become elementary on a different level.

It is for this reason that the question of what, for a given system or developmental level of a system, constitutes an elementary operation should, ultimately, be answered experimentally. With regard to the instructional process, this means that, for correct structural specification of objectives during instructional programming, it is necessary to analyze the developmental level of the student, that is, to discover what he can and cannot do, and to determine which operations are elementary on his level of development. This analysis determines the "level of detail" which must be achieved in breaking up complex processes into elementary operations.

Of the various models which must be constructed in order to

*The problem of non-algorithmic processes and non-algorithmic programs will be discussed in more detail below and in subsequent chapters. (*Editor.*)

form the basis of instructional programs, some of the most important are algorithmic models of cognitive functioning.

Turning to the practical aspects of instruction, we see that one of its most serious shortcomings at the present time is the fact that students, in many cases, either are not taught algorithms (and/or algorithmic procedures) at all or are taught inefficient ones. As a result, knowledges, skills, and habits which students should quickly and effectively master are learned slowly and painfully, and often poorly as well.

Experience in constructing grammatical algorithms and teaching them to students has shown that they are highly effective (Landa, 1961b).

Analysis of the logical structure of the problems which are to be solved by means of these algorithms plays an important role in their design. Very little attention has been paid to this problem in education. As a result of this neglect, textbooks often contain material which is inadequately presented, which hampers perception and learning of the material, and which often causes errors in its application.

An important factor in the elucidation and description of the logical structure of instructional material could be the utilization of the means and notation of mathematical logic. Although this notation would permit precise and economical expression of the basic ways in which phenomena and their properties arc associated (joined, *Ed.*), as well as precise specification of their structure by means of specific formulae, it is being used only sparingly in education at the present time. Yet greater use of such notation is necessary, since it would introduce rigor into the analysis of instructional phenomena by revealing and precisely describing relations which had previously remained obscure.

In constructing algorithms for use in the educational process, it is very important to take into account psychological as well as logical factors. Algorithms must be constructed in such a way that they are learned and applied in accordance with the psychological laws which govern the formation and flow of cognitive processes.

Algorithms should be optimal in regard to the number of

operations involved. The application of mathematical techniques, in particular those of information theory, to the analysis of instructional material makes possible the construction of problem-solving algorithms which are optimal in this regard, thereby making possible the mathematical evaluation of certain aspects of proposed instructional programs.

Together with algorithms, the formation of procedures which are non-algorithmic in nature should occupy an important place in the instructional process. Students should be able to solve problems for which an algorithm does not exist, or has not been discovered, or is unknown to them. Moreover, there are a number of problems for which algorithms may be constructed, but which cannot be solved efficiently by means of these algorithms. It is, for instance, possible to construct algorithms for the proof of geometric theorems, but such algorithms would require that the student systematically consider all the characteristics of the geometric figures in question and derive all possible implications from them. Experience and experiments show, however, that people do not generally solve problems by deriving all possible implications from the initial data. How, then, do they proceed?

The most characteristic feature of problem solution in instances in which one is not guided by an algorithm is, evidently, the utilization of "the most probable paths." Proceeding according to an algorithm excludes the necessity of choice. The algorithm precisely specifies the operation to be performed in any given situation. If one does not know an algorithm by means of which the problem may be solved, then one is often able to choose among several paths leading to the solution. In some cases the difficulty consists in determining the set of paths themselves among which one could try to choose this or that path (this is characteristic of genuine heuristic problems), but this question will be considered in more detail below (Chapter Six).

How does one make a specific choice among various ways of solving a problem, between one or another "path"? One makes this choice, obviously, by means of a probabilistic evaluation of both the circumstances of the problem and the means available for its solution.

One of the most important tasks facing psychology and education at the present time is the study of cognitive mechanisms which are probabilistic in nature. There is reason to suppose that many creative processes (intuition, guessing, and others) are based on probabilistic mechanisms and can be understood and rigorously explained on the basis of a probabilistic conception of thought.[4]

In particular, it seems to us that a probabilistic analysis of cognitive activity would permit the development of some objective criteria for evaluating the degree of difficulty of a given problem from a definite point of view. Clearly, one of the most important factors which makes a problem difficult (though not the only one) is the fact that the path which must be followed in order to solve it may be an improbable one.

Proper instructional programming and structural specification of instructional objectives require construction of models not only of algorithmic processes, but of stochastic (probabilistic) processes as well. Instruction can be effective only if the teacher knows the mechanisms of both the algorithmic and the creative processes which he must develop in the student. The structure of these processes should be specified in the program in sufficient detail, and the processes should be analyzed into discrete operations which are sufficiently elementary, to ensure the program's effectiveness; where possible, estimates of the probabilities associated with them should be given as well.

In discussing processes which are to be formed in the student as a result of instruction, we have considered them up to this point only from a structural point of view. The programming of instructional objectives, however, should include specification not only of the structure of these processes, but delineation of other of their properties as well. Thus, for example, knowledge should be stable, generalized, and systematized, while cognitive operations should be conscious, or automatic, etc.

The properties of the processes which are to be developed in the student at one or another stage of his education should be indicated in the programs. The basic task here, and at the same time the basic difficulty, is not the indication of these properties (they are usually specified in educational manuals), but finding, in the first place, methods for establishing them, and in the second place, ways of measuring them accurately. Educational literature is full of claims to the effect that some methods spur the student to greater activity or lead to greater awareness than others, etc. However, these claims are usually of a purely intuitive character, since the authors do not indicate any means for measuring "activity" and "awareness."

Academician G.S. Landsberg[5] has written: "Any concept introduced in physics takes on concrete significance only when it is associated with a particular method of observation and measurement, without which this concept can find no application whatsoever in the investigation of actual physical phenomena."

This principle is important not only for physics but for other sciences as well, and psychology and education in particular. It is quite clear that concepts such as activity, awareness, generalization, etc. (to say nothing of level of activity, level of awareness, and level of generalization), take on concrete significance only when they are associated with specific methods of observation and measurement, that is, if there exist methods for discerning these properties and evaluating them quantitatively.[6] Educational psychology cannot be transformed into an exact science, until precise scientific methods of diagnosis and measurement of cognitive processes are developed. Without these techniques, exact methods for both influencing these processes and rigorously evaluating the effects of this influence are impossible. How, in fact, can one prove that awareness and activity have increased or decreased as a result of the application of given instructional methods if there are no means of discerning these processes and no means for quantitatively evaluating them?

2. Programming Instructional Activity: Optimizing the Educational Process

In the previous section we discussed means for specifying the instructional objectives of and some of the problems associated with modeling and programming of the student's cognitive activity during the learning process. However, a precise structural specification of instructional objectives and modeling the learning activity leading to them is only one of the conditions which must be fulfilled in order to implement the instructional process. In order to teach something, it is not enough to know *what* must be developed in the student; it is necessary to know *how* this is to be accomplished. This is the problem of how instruction itself is to be programmed.

For the instructor, teaching is nothing other than the solution of a series of problems. He has at each moment a specific objective (to impart some piece of knowledge, to develop some cognitive process in the student, etc.) and a set of specific techniques for achieving this objective, and is faced with particular conditions in which he must operate (a given level of knowledge or development on the part of the student, etc.). A typical problem facing the instructor is that of deciding which of the available techniques he should employ in order to achieve a given objective under given conditions.

One of the shortcomings of contemporary education is the fact that the instructional process is seldom considered to be the solution of a particular kind of problem.

If educational practice is the solution of practical instructional problems, then educational theory, i.e., the science of education, must of necessity include the study of general methods for solving these problems (i.e., to develop means for instructional decision-making). These methods should permit the instructor to find optimal ways of teaching, with the objective of enabling the student to assimilate knowledge, skills, and habits as efficiently as possible, as well as developing his cognitive capacities. Of course, the above does not constitute an exhaustive description of theory's tasks in the field of education (instructional content, organization of public education, and a number of other problems are likewise of concern), but it accentuates important questions with which educational theory should deal and to which it is paying insufficient attention at the present time. The elaboration and development of methods for optimal instructional decision-making is a part, or aspect, of a broader educational problem, i.e., the problem of the optimization of education as a whole. The latter problem should be considered as one of the important tasks and, at the same time, subjects of educational theory.

The question arises as to how this characteristic correlates with the existing definition of educational psychology as the science of the objective laws of education and upbringing. It is our view that there is no contradiction between them.

Indeed, in order to be able to control phenomena and processes of whatever sort, it is necessary to know the laws which govern them. The theory of the control of any process is, in essence, the theory of ways of utilizing objective laws in order to achieve specific, practical objectives. The study of the laws governing processes and phenomena is valuable not only for its own sake, but also so that these processes and phenomena may be controlled. It is clear, therefore, that, together with the discovery and formulation of the laws governing the processes themselves (the theory of these processes), it is necessary to construct a theory of the utilization of these laws for the attainment of practical objectives (an applied theory of the phenomena in question). Since the same laws may be used with varying degrees of effectiveness, the question arises as to how optimal means for utilizing these laws to control the processes in question are to be developed.

Instructional laws are nothing but functions of a particular sort expressing the dependence of the development of given thought processes on given instructional procedures under given conditions. These functions may, of course, be expressed symbolically, and thus can be modeled.

There are two stages in the investigation of instructional laws (as well as the laws of other sciences): first, the functional dependence of the formation of the process or effect in question must be determined (qualitative analysis), and then the precise nature and degree of this dependence must be ascertained (quantitative analysis).

A very important function which educational psychology must perform is that of formulating research in such a way as to elucidate and describe precisely the *logical structure* of the conditions which insure certain effects when specific instructional procedures are applied. This formulation may be expressed in the notation of formal logic (propositional logic and predicate logic).

In formulating psycho-educational laws, it is possible to indicate only a number of *basic* factors influencing the production of a given effect in a number of *typical* instructional situations. Psycho-educational phenomena are extremely complex, and so in discussing psycho-educational laws it is impossible to exhaustively describe the conditions and situations which may be encountered in practice. It is possible to consider only the most frequently encountered combinations of conditions.

Very often the application of a particular instructional procedure to the same initial characteristics (i.e., capabilities of a student, *Ed.*) yields, as follows from what has been said above, different results at different times. This occurs either because of the presence of other, unknown initial characteristics which influence the effects of the procedure in question, or because of the presence of random factors which could not be foreseen and taken into account in each individual case. It is quite obvious that, when a single instructional procedure gives rise, in different situations, to different results to which probabilities may be assigned, the psycho-educational laws in question are of the nature of stochastic laws and should be formulated as such.

Psycho-educational laws of the stochastic type may be described using either the notation of probabilistic logic or in the form of a matrix, although in the latter case the matrix elements will not be single but multiple effects, together with a designation of their distribution probabilities.

It is generally recognized that one and the same given effect may often be achieved by means of several different instructional procedures. An important aspect of the instructional process, however, is the fact that these procedures may differ in their effectiveness. One operation, for example, achieves the desired result faster or yields a more stable knowledge than another, etc. It is often the case that instructional procedures are more effective in one respect than in another.

A precise appraisal of the functional properties of instructional procedures requires the development of quantitative means of evaluating their effectiveness in achieving a given result. These techniques should permit evaluation of effectiveness both as a function of individual parameters and as a function of all relevant parameters simultaneously, and thereby serve the important task of allowing the teacher to *select the best from among many possible procedures.*

In solving instructional problems, it is often necessary to take into account not one but many conditions, some of which may interact with one another in a rather complex manner. In this case the selection of an instructional procedure or procedures should be considered as the solution of a complex optimization problem.

Since, in solving instructional problems, it is sometimes necessary to operate, on the one hand, under conditions in which information is incomplete (the instructor cannot know all the conditions essential to the solution of the problem) and since, on the other hand, the psycho-educational laws on which this solution must be based may be stochastic in nature, the expediency of applying a given instructional procedure may be evaluated only to a certain level of probability. Obviously, solutions in most cases can be only probabilistic, and the task confronting science is to develop methods which will permit selection of the best procedures on the basis of an evaluation of their probable effectiveness.

Many instructional problems consist of specifying an optimal program of procedures to be followed, and the methods used in other sciences for the solution of analogous problems may naturally be applied in instruction as well. It may be assumed that the mathematical description of discrete factors will make possible the construction of mathematical models of instructional problems, which may then be tested with the aid of electronic computers, so that optimal programs may be selected. Experiments of this sort would doubtless be extremely interesting. In the future, when instructional laws have been precisely formulated and described, and when effective methods for solving instructional problems have been developed, it will be possible to use computers to determine the instructional techniques which are most effective under various conditions. The instructor, by feeding into the computer information regarding the conditions and objectives of instruction, will be able to determine the best procedures for the circumstances in question.

However, the development of suitable methods for solving instructional problems has implications not only for the programming of computers, which, we have no doubt, will be used in instruction for solution of optimization problems, but also for proper organization of student training in schools of education and for raising the level of teachers' qualifications.

Students graduating from schools of education in most cases prove to be inadequately prepared for practical teaching, inasmuch as they do not know the methods for solving the instructional problems which arise in practice. As a rule, they are not taught these methods. In a situation in which one must make a decision or find non-trivial ways of influencing one's students, the young teacher is often at a loss, since it is not known how to proceed in order to find such ways, and how to reflect and reason for that. He or she has some knowledge of psycho-educational principles, but has not been taught to think instructionally. The problem of developing the *ability to think instructionally* is primarily the problem of teaching methods for the solution of instructional problems.

It is now quite clear that the path to instructional skill may be considerably shortened. But, in order to accomplish this, it will be necessary to investigate seriously the psychology and logic of instructional thinking, to develop methods for solving instructional problems, and, on this basis, to restructure the current system of teacher training.

Many instructional problems, like problems in other fields, may be solved by means of specific algorithms. An important problem in instruction is the discovery and formulation of algorithms for solving instructional problems. This applies both to the design and development of algorithms governing instructional thinking (where this is possible), and to the design and development of algorithms governing instructional activity itself, i.e., to the development of systems of instructional procedures which lead to the attainment of specific objectives.

As well as teaching teachers the instructional algorithms underlying many types of developed, practical instructional technology, it is also necessary to teach them to discover and/or design instructional algorithms independently. This is a specific process which requires specific procedures and methods. If the instructional algorithm for the solution of some type of instructional problem may be seen as a program of instructional activity for a teacher (and, more broadly, for each instructional agent), then teaching *how* to discover and design such programs may be regarded as teaching teachers programs of a higher order.

We have noted above the programs of students' activity of different orders which emerge as programs of different degrees of self-programming and self-control. The same is true not only of learners' but also of teachers' activity. Teachers must be taught not only to follow and apply programs of instructional activity deriving from instructional science, but also to follow programs when needed *for their own activity*, i.e., to effect *self-programming* on the basis of programs of a higher order.

The establishment of *types* of instructional problems and the development of general algorithms applicable to each type are indispensable to a science of instruction. Inasmuch as many instructional problems may be solved in more than one way, it becomes important to be able to evaluate different algorithms for their solution and to devise and choose optimal algorithms. These algorithms should be described precisely, and formulated and included both in psycho-educational textbooks and in specific instructional procedures.

One of the prerequisites for solving the problem of increasing educational effectiveness is the development of methods for designing optimal instructional algorithms which will permit us to make precise and unambiguous recommendations for instructional practice.

3.   Organization of the Instructional Process:
     Feedback in Instruction

Explicit programming of learning processes and knowledge of optimal algorithms governing instructional activity constitute only

two of the prerequisites for effective instruction. Another necessary condition is a good practical organization of instructional
procedure, i.e., the creation of those conditions which will permit
the fullest possible control of the student's cognitive and other
psychological processes. (For the sake of specificity we shall speak
below of cognitive processes, though all that will be said relates as
well to other psychological processes to be developed in the course
of instruction.)

The concept of comprehensive control is very important. It
denotes a formulation of instructional procedure in which the
cognitive processes of the student are formed in a direction which
is precisely specified by an instructional program, in which
the teacher has the means to influence these processes, i.e., to
regulate and control them, and in which haphazardness in the
development of these processes is excluded. Total control of the
student's internal processes is impossible, but adequate, i.e.,
sufficiently complete control for practical purposes, is unquestionably possible, and the development of methods for achieving this
control is the task facing instructional science.[7]

Psychological analysis of the knowledge, skills, and habits of
students shows that currently haphazardness in the formation of
cognitive processes is extremely great. The teacher very often has
no inkling of the degree to which the knowledge and skills
which he attempts to transmit are distorted in the minds of his
students. One of the main causes of this distortion is the teacher's
ignorance of the elements out of which complex processes are
composed, and the fact that he does not "build up" the complex
from the simple, or the whole from its parts.

The most important prerequisite for comprehensive control
of cognitive activity is the ability to influence complex processes
by influencing their components, i.e., by forming cognitive (and,
in particular, conceptual) processes element by element and
operation by operation, uniting them gradually in internally
related complexes which, as complexes, acquire new qualities and
properties and cannot be later reduced to properties of their single
elements as for a simple arithmetic sum of elements.

Today the teacher does not always face a task of this sort.

Moreover, he does not have available to him the means which would enable him to form cognitive processes in this way. In explaining new material or conducting training exercises, he cannot be certain that all his students are performing precisely those operations which are needed, or are performing them properly, i.e., that they are *combining* these operations *into the required system*. He cannot always evoke a needed correct operation by means of a precisely calculated action, correct a defective operation, or interdict an unnecessary or incorrect one. It is this lack of control which gives rise to the haphazardness in the formation of cognitive processes which we encounter consistently in instruction.

It is clear, then, that we need to find ways of molding cognitive processes by combining separate operations, and we need to organize instruction in a way which will guarantee that every student will, at the end, as a result of operation-by-operation formation, unfailingly and reliably acquire all necessary systems of knowledge and procedure.[8]

However, it is impossible successfully to develop cognitive processes on the basis of discrete operations without developing the means of controlling these operations while the processes in question are occurring, in particular, while algorithmic processes are being "compiled" in the student's mind.

In order that the teacher note and correct in time deviations from the normal flow of a cognitive process, he must continually receive information concerning what is taking place in the student's consciousness while the student is absorbing knowledge, solving problems, or executing a given procedure. Without this information, no "adequately" complete control of the processes taking place in the student's consciousness is possible. In other words, in order that comprehensive control of thinking activity be possible during the instructional process, it must be a process with good feedback.

The principal shortcoming of instruction at present is the fact that it is a process with poor feedback. The teacher often does not know, while he is teaching, how the information imparted to the student is processed in the student's consciousness and whether the necessary procedures are being carried out during this processing.[9] Not knowing this, he is unable to regulate his actions so that they conform to the actual course of the student's assimilation of the material. As a result, instructional procedures often prove inadequate in the situation in which they are applied. Thus, control proceeds to a significant degree blindly, and often fails to achieve its intended objective.

Substantial increases in instructional effectiveness and comprehensive control of cognitive processes are possible only if means are found for shaping and directing these processes on the basis of discrete cognitive operations, and if this shaping and directing is performed while these processes are actually occurring.

At this point, however, a new problem arises. Increasing the quantity of information flowing from the student to the teacher while the teacher is attempting to control the student's cognitive operations will make it impossible for the teacher to process this information. Calculation shows that even a small increase in information flow results in the teacher's being unable to receive and evaluate it, since the quantity of information rapidly exceeds his capabilities in this respect, to say nothing of the enormous number of reactions which are required of him in response to information from the student. According to the American psychologist D. Porter (1958), in order for the instructional process to be successful, each student should receive approximately 150 reinforcements per 20 minutes of classroom instruction in his native language. In a class of 30 students, the average number of reinforcements (reactions) required from the teacher in a 20-minute period is 4,500. This is equivalent to 225 reinforcements per minute, which is clearly impossible. It would seem, therefore, that an unbridgeable gap exists between what is required of the teacher and what he is capable of doing.

How is this discrepancy to be resolved? It can be resolved by introducing modern technological aids into the instructional process, in particular, cybernetic teaching devices (teaching machines).

Instruction in the proper sense of the word (as distinguished from *self-instruction*) occurs only when a two-way process takes place, in which actions on the part of the student evoke reciprocal actions on the part of the teacher, which, in their turn, change the student's actions, such that a continually interactive process occurs between student and teacher. In this process, the teacher's actions regulate the student's actions, and direct them toward a specific objective in accordance with a specific program (of which there may be no overt awareness).

In contrast to other technological aids to instruction (radio, television, films, etc.), the only devices which may be termed teaching machines are those which perform the teacher's most important function: to exert a "countereffect" on the student, to control his actions and cognitive processes by adaptively reacting to them in a specific way. The efficiency of a given type of teaching machine depends directly on how fully and how well it performs this function.

There is reason to assume, and some data available confirm this, that adaptive teaching with the aid of cybernetic devices will significantly intensify the student's learning activity, increase the relative significance of independent work, individualize education by taking into account each student's personal characteristics, and improve the quality of the knowledge, skills, and habits assimilated by the student, while simultaneously decreasing the time required for this assimilation.

The application of cybernetic teaching devices does not displace the teacher from the instructional and learning process. It only alters his functions. He is freed from tasks which are unproductive and which often do not require high qualifications—tasks which at present sap much of his time and energy, leaving him few opportunities for the close and detailed work with the student which is so important for the development of his individuality, abilities, and talents. The teacher will remain the most important component of the educational process. Moreover, his role will expand significantly. He will have to solve more complex procedural problems; have a deeper understanding of educational psychology and the psychology of his students; be able to analyze the causes of learning difficulties on the part of individual students, and to shift teaching strategies as a function of the situation and the task at hand; etc. All of this will require changes in the organization of teacher training, and will increase teacher qualification requirements.

The utilization of cybernetics and cybernetic technology in instruction, however, should not be limited to the construction and use of teaching machines. It also creates extensive possibilities for the development of the theory and methods of psycho-educational research. The introduction into psycho-educational science of the ideas and methods of mathematics, mathematical logic, information theory, game theory, and other exact sciences will make possible new forms of psycho-educational research and will permit the construction of a theory of instruction which will create the conditions necessary for a sharp increase in instructional effectiveness and efficiency.

Notes

1. "Instructional programming" should not be confused with "programming" in applied mathematics, which denotes giving an algorithm a form suitable for computer processing. "Instructional programming" should also not be confused with "programmed instruction." Programmed instruction is a special form of the implementation of an instructional program, namely, by means of special devices—programmed text books and teaching machines. But one can program not only the functioning of a teaching device but also the efforts of a teacher as well as the efforts of a learner (in the latter case it is a question of equipping the learner with an unambiguous prescription of how to proceed independently). Thus, instructional programming cannot be reduced only to programming for teaching by means of special devices (automated teaching). In this connection, it must be noted that the term "programmed instruction" in the sense of "automated instruction" is not adequate. The denotative meaning of this term refers to *any* instruction along a precise prescription of how to proceed in the process of teaching and/or learning, irrespective of the fact of who is the

instructional agent: a living teacher or a special device. But historically it has happened that the generic term "programmed instruction," i.e., instruction along a definite program, began to designate a particular case of programmed instruction, namely instruction in which the instructional program is implemented by means of programmed books and/or teaching machines.

2.   The intention, which is lost in translation, is to say that the cognitive process—the system of operations—is one for solving some (class of) problems or accomplishing some (class of) tasks. (*Editor.*)

3.   To prove that a given object belongs to a given category, for example, that a given geometrical figure is a parallelogram, one must:

      (1) call to mind the characteristics or attributes (elsewhere called "indicative features," *Ed.*) of the category as reflected in the mathematical conception of a parallelogram, i.e., what a parallelogram is in general;

      (2) determine the structure of these characteristics, i.e., the logical connectives joining them;

      (3) compare the characteristics of the category with the characteristics of the object under consideration, i.e., determine whether or not the given geometrical figure has all or at least one of the characteristics—depending on the kind of logical connectives—of a parallelogram; and

      (4) draw a conclusion, positive or negative, as to the belonging of the object to the category "parallelogram."

4.   Algorithmic processes may also be treated as a special type of probabilistic (or, stochastic, *Ed.*) process, namely one in which the probability associated with a particular "path" is equal to one.

5.   A member of the Academy of Sciences of the USSR. The title "Academician" implies that its bearer enjoys a distinguished reputation as a scientist. (*Editor.*)

6.   With regard to observation, both direct and indirect observation must be considered.

7.   Comprehensive control presupposes the discovery and development of the individual characteristics of each student. Moreover, it does not imply depriving the student of his independence. *Independence, and self-control too, must be encouraged* and this is one of the most important tasks of education. But the process of encouraging the independence and of developing the ability for self-control is also a process of control. It is control of the formation of self-control. The more completely we control the development of independence and self-control in the student, the sooner he will learn to control himself. It may be said that one of the purposes of comprehensive control of cognitive processes during the educational process is to relinquish this control as soon as possible, once the student's capacity for self-control has developed. The concept of comprehensive control is important not only for psychology and education, but for other sciences as well. There are different degrees of "comprehensiveness" of control. One of the most important problems in many sciences is the discovery of techniques whereby the processes which these sciences study may be subjected to more and more comprehensive control.

8.   Reliability is a problem which arises not only in engineering, but in education as well, although in the latter case it has certain distinguishing characteristics.

9.   The basic sources of information regarding the student's assimilation of knowledge, skills, and habits are questioning and various other verification procedures. But the teacher is very often unable to question each of the 30 or 40 students in his class. With regard to verification procedures, the teacher is concerned for the most part with the results of the student's cognitive activity (whether or not he solved the problem or made a mistake), and does not have the opportunity to examine the activity itself (e.g., to determine which operations the student used to solve the problem) and to control the sequence and character of the student's

cognitive operations—even though the most important factor in instruction is the formation of these processes. As we know, the fact that a particular cognitive process may, on a given occasion, yield a correct result does not in any way prove that the process itself is correct.

Chapter Two

Instructional Effectiveness and Efficiency

This chapter will be concerned with the effectiveness and efficiency of instruction.

The discrepancy between what students are *able* to learn by attending school for a given period of time and what they *should* learn is continually increasing. One of the ways in which this discrepancy manifests itself is the fact that students are overworked.

There are at least two ways of eliminating (or narrowing) this discrepancy, which do not exclude each other, or more precisely, which should supplement each other. The first is to modify the content and structure of instructional programs (curricula). The second is to introduce certain factors into instructional methods so as to increase the efficiency of the instructional process.

In this chapter, we will discuss, for the most part, the second approach.

The problem of increasing efficiency is common to all areas of human activity, whether practical or theoretical. The field of education is no exception, as noted in the first chapter. We must find ways of improving the efficiency of the instructional process which will permit the student to assimilate more knowledge per unit of time and to develop his skills, habits, and capabilities more fully.

Why, in formulating this problem, do we turn to cybernetics?

We do this because cybernetics, which is now finding application in the most diverse scientific and professional fields, enables us to achieve a sharp increase in efficiency. It offers approaches and methods which permit improvements in the efficiency of human activity in the most diverse areas.

Cybernetics is, according to one of the widespread definitions, the science of control. Control processes are to be found everywhere: the operator controls his machine, the brain controls the muscles, the thermostat controls the temperature of the refrigerator, etc. Control permeates all human activities, since organized systems cannot function without it.

Until recently, different types of control were studied by different sciences, which were often partially or wholly independent of one another. During the 1940's, however, the question arose as to whether or not the various forms of control had common elements. These common elements were found to exist. The discovery of general features in the most diverse forms of control has the same significance as the discovery of any other general laws, or principles.

The importance of such principles is generally recognized. They are important primarily because they permit us to predict specific phenomena without performing experiments in each instance.

Thus, for example, if someone were to attempt to build a device which is to produce more energy than it consumes, it could be said *a priori* that this attempt would be unsuccessful, because it would contradict the law of the conservation of energy. The importance of general laws is also that they permit us to transfer knowledge from one field to another without having to perform experiments, thereby allowing us to conserve energy and resources. General oscillation theory, for example, analyzes within a single framework the behavior of mechanical, electrical, optical, and even biological systems. The fact that vibrating objects differ in nature does not prevent them from vibrating in accordance with the same laws. Knowledge of these laws permits the substitution of inexpensive experiments involving current oscillations in simple electrical circuits for expensive ones involving, for example, the vibration of an aircraft wing.

Cybernetics has established general control principles which apply equally well to electro-mechanical, biological, and human phenomena.

Cybernetics indicates that the general pattern shown in Figure 2.1 underlies all control processes.

Figure 2.1

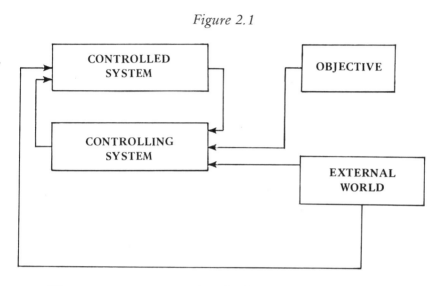

There are two systems involved in any control process: the controlling system and the system which is controlled. For example, a machine operator is a controlling system, while the machine which he operates is the system which he controls. The controlling system always seeks to achieve a goal. Let us take as a simple example the manufacture of some product which is to have the following characteristic as it comes out of the apparatus: it should be at a temperature between 110 degrees and 130 degrees. Control is effected by feeding signals—information—into the controlled system. Let us suppose that these signals can be generated by turning a knob on a control panel to the right or left from a neutral position. In order for control to be possible, the controlling system must operate in accordance with a well-defined control program. Possibly one appropriate control program might be the following: if the temperature of the product falls lower than 110 degrees, it is raised by turning the knob to the left; if the temperature exceeds 130 degrees, then it is lowered by turning the knob to the right. The external world influences both the controlling and the controlled systems. The influence of the external world on the controlled system might specifically take the form of continual fluctuations in the temperature of the oven in the apparatus, which would naturally lead to fluctuations in the temperature of the product as well. In order to correct in time deviations from the norm (from the objective) the operator must constantly receive information regarding the state of the controlled system. The information which the controlled system sends to the controlling system is termed "feedback," while the commands which flow from the controlling system to the controlled one are termed "feedforward." Both feedforward and feedback are necessary if the control process is to be successful.

We have cited an example of control which in reality applies to one specific type of control, that is to *regulation*. Regulation is directed to maintaining some state (one or multi-dimensional) of the controlled system within some given limits. But control does not uniformly reduce to regulation. It may be directed to *transformation* of a state as well (this type of control will be considered later, in Chapter Ten). Thus, control is a more general concept than regulation: each regulation is control but not each control is regulation. But for our purpose in this context the type of control itself is not essential. The subsequent reasoning would not have changed considerably if we had taken an example in which the controlling system should have transformed the state of the controlled system, for instance, to raise the temperature each hour in 10 degrees until 200 degrees is reached.

The relations expressed in Figure 2.1 are characteristic of all forms of control, "regulative" or "transformative."

How does the above relate to instruction?

It can be shown that the instructional process is nothing other than a particular type of control, and that the same relationships exist in it as exist in other control processes.

The controlling system in the processes of learning and instruction is the teacher, and the controlled system is the student. The teacher has a particular objective and effects control of the student by feeding him specific information. The teacher's task is to evoke from the student, by means of this information, that activity and behavior which will lead to the formation of the capabilities corresponding to a given objective. This influence on the student is exercised in accordance with a specific program. In addition, various external circumstances (the external world) exert a continuous influence both on the teacher and on the student. In order for the teacher successfully to control the formation in the student of the required capabilities, he must continually receive information regarding the characteristics of his actions and their results (as to how well, for example, the student understood an explanation or learned a method for solving problems). In other words, constant feedback is required. If even one of the components of the control process fails to function properly, control becomes inadequate or impossible.

Since instruction is simply a special type of control process, it is to be hoped that application of the methods of cybernetics to educational phenomena will lead to useful results in this area.

However, control in the area of education and development possesses an important characteristic which should be noted. This characteristic is the fact that the object which is being controlled during the instructional process (the child) is simultaneously *a subject* capable of acting on its own initiative, of learning, of accepting or rejecting the teacher's objectives, and of developing its own objectives, etc. The learner is not only a controlled, but also a self-controlled system with a high capacity for self-organization. This fact does not invalidate the general control laws formulated by cybernetics, since the capacity for self-control must also be taught and its development regulated.

The basic task facing cybernetics is the development of methods for optimizing control processes, i.e., for calculating the procedure by means of which an objective may be achieved with minimum expenditure of time and energy. A basic feature of cybernetics is that it solves this problem by means of exact quantitative methods based on mathematics and logic.

In everyday life, we constantly solve control problems without resorting to the use of exact and rigorous calculations. If the problem is simple, intuition and normal common sense are all that are required to solve it. If the problem is a complex one, however, it is generally difficult to solve it on the basis of intuition and common sense. And, even if we somehow manage to solve such a problem in this way, our solution often proves to be less than optimal.

Let us consider a simple example. Let us suppose that we are to compose a schedule of lessons for a school in which there are two teachers. This is a simple problem which may be solved without performing complex calculations. But now let us suppose that we must work out a schedule for a school in which there are not two, but 50 teachers. In this case, working out a suitable schedule on the basis of common sense alone, without performing any calculations, would be difficult and perhaps impossible, since this situation involves an enormous number of factors and requirements which are often mutually contradictory. The schedule must be convenient, it must observe the proper alternation of subject-matters, make optimal use of the teaching staff and the available classroom space, etc. Working out a schedule in such circumstances requires quantitative methods for analyzing and evaluating all relevant factors, as well as precise techniques for calculating optimal solutions on the basis of these factors. Such methods have been developed. Now, thanks to them, optimal schedules may be compiled by computers as well as by people.

The importance of quantitative methods consists, thus, in the fact that, by permitting us to analyze the situation in which we must operate, they make it possible for us to determine the best possible strategy, i.e., the most efficient means for achieving our objective. Without such analysis, it is often difficult or impossible to make sound decisions, since decisions in such circumstances must always be, to one degree or another, haphazard.

One other simple example illustrates the role of quantitative analysis of situational factors.

Let us consider the hypothetical case of a person who gets sick and is told that he must have an operation. He wants to know whether or not the operation is dangerous, and is told that it is more often successful than unsuccessful. This information, needless to say, does not satisfy him. He wants to know to what extent the operation is more frequently successful than unsuccessful. If

95 percent of such operations are successful, he will probably be satisfied; if, on the other hand, only 55 percent are successful, then he will no doubt have second thoughts. The words "more frequently," without any indication of degree, provide very little basis for making a decision. A decision made without a quantitative evaluation of possible outcomes can prove correct only by accident.

The development of any science proceeds through several stages: the stage of qualitative analysis of the phenomena which it studies, the stage of quantitative analysis of these phenomena, and finally the stage of structural analysis.

Educational psychology, as a result of historical factors relating to the enormous complexity of its subject-matter, has thus far utilized primarily the methods of qualitative analysis. It now faces the task of developing methods of quantitative and structural analysis.

Cybernetics, like educational psychology, is concerned with complex systems and so is developing methods for solving the problems associated with such systems. The more complex a system is, the more factors must be taken into consideration in order to control it, and the more important become methods of quantitative and structural analysis of conditions and problems (situations), as well as possible approaches to the solution of these problems.

Instructional problems are, of course, usually multifactorial. In order to select the appropriate instructional procedure, it is necessary to take into account the nature of the material being taught, the level of the student's knowledge, his level of development, age, interests, etc.

At the present time, we often solve this problem empirically, on the basis of experience, if not simply on the basis of common sense. This is unavoidable, since we do not as yet have precise methods for reviewing, measuring, evaluating, and correlating the various factors involved.

Can such methods be developed? There is reason to believe that this is, in principle, possible. Cybernetics has been used to develop such methods in economics, medicine, and other sciences.

Problems in medicine, for example, are, like those in educational psychology, multifactorial.[1] Like psycho-educational problems, medical problems were long solved imprecisely and unrigorously on the basis of intuition and experience. Now, however, methods for solving many of these problems have been developed, and these methods are so rigorous and precise that the problems in question can often be solved by a computer. In fact, a diagnostic computer often performs better than an experienced physician. The problem of optimizing control has always faced instruction, although it has never before been posed in this form. This new stage in the development of educational psychology is characterized by the fact that instructional problems will be solved in new ways, on the basis of modern mathematics, mathematical logic, and cybernetics.

The following example illustrates the significance of mathematical methods in instruction.

Let us suppose that we are to teach students in a technical school or in a factory to locate defects in some machinery. Let us suppose, further, that it is known that, if and when this machinery breaks down, there are only three possible causes of the trouble: a malfunction in unit A, a malfunction in unit B, or a malfunction in unit C.

We know that equipment breakdown leads to enormous production losses. It is important, therefore, to teach mechanics to locate equipment malfunctions as quickly as possible. But, in order to teach this ability, we must know the optimum search strategy, that is, we must possess a method which will permit us to determine the optimal sequence in which the units should be checked. Today this question is usually not even posed, and students are not specifically taught an optimal method for locating malfunctions. Yet such methods are possible and have, in fact, already been developed. Let us suppose that, from frequent observation of the functioning of our hypothetical machine, we have determined that six out of 10 breakdowns occur as a result of malfunctions in unit A (yielding a probability of 0.6 that the malfunction is in unit A), that three of every 10 breakdowns are due to malfunctions in unit B (yielding a probability of 0.3), and that one breakdown out of every 10 is due to malfunctions in unit C (yielding a probability of malfunctions in unit C of 0.1). It is now clear which unit should be checked first: unit A. It is in unit A that we have the greatest chance of finding the malfunction. If it turns out that the malfunction is not in unit A, we should check unit B next. Unit C should be checked last.

We are able in this way to arrive at an optimal strategy for locating malfunctions. This strategy is a good one, however, only if the time required to check each unit is the same. It could be, however, that although unit A breaks down more frequently than unit B, the time required to check it for malfunctions is greater. Which unit, then, should be checked first? It is difficult to solve this problem on the basis of common sense. The solution requires precise calculation, which in turn requires consideration of the ratios of the probability of malfunction in each unit to the time required to locate it. There is no need to demonstrate the importance of knowledge of such methods of calculation for every teacher of industrial education and every foreman training workers on the job.

We have examined the underlying structure of control and have seen that it determines the conditions, or requirements, which a control process must fulfill if it is to operate effectively. These requirements are as follows:

(1) a precisely defined objective;
(2) an effective and precisely specified program of control;
(3) good feedback, i.e., consideration of changes taking place in the controlled system; and
(4) adaptive influences on the controlled system according to a decision based on consideration of the relation between the objectives and the present state of the controlled system.

We are now in a position to understand some important causes of the ineffectiveness of modern education. We do this by analyzing the instructional process from the point of view of the requirements of a good control system.

We stated above that precise and concrete specification of the objective (e.g., that the temperature in an oven is to be maintained between 110 degrees and 130 degrees) is extremely important in achieving good control.

Let us consider how objectives are often specified in the instructional process. For example, one can often encounter statements in educational texts and manuals that the teacher must develop in his or her students the qualities of *active involvement* and *conscious knowledge*. But what is *active involvement* and *conscious knowledge*, and how are these qualities to be observed and measured?

The concepts of *active involvement* and *conscious knowledge* are empirical and intuitive, and as such are extremely imprecise. No precise means either for observing or for measuring them are usually proposed by the authors who appeal to teachers to develop these properties in students. Statements to the effect that method A evokes greater *active involvement* on the part of the student than method B are, therefore, correspondingly imprecise. Yet it is clearly possible to find some sort of means for measuring and assessing this property. Research in this direction would no doubt be more useful than the numerous efforts in which this phenomenon is much discussed but in which no approaches to its measurement and assessment are proposed.

No concept can be precise and effectively applied in practice if there are not associated with it specific procedures for observing, measuring, and evaluating the phenomena corresponding to it.

If we examine instructional concepts from this point of view, we see that the overwhelming majority of them do not fulfill this condition.

The development of procedures for observing and measuring instructional phenomena is an extremely difficult undertaking, and such procedures will hardly be developed in the immediate future. A beginning, however, has been made. This is an extremely important problem, and its significance should be fully recognized.

Thus, the first reason for the ineffectiveness of education lies in the fact that educational and instructional objectives are often imprecisely formulated, in that those parameters which must be known if the student's cognitive and other processes are to be effectively controlled are usually not indicated.

The second reason for ineffective control of the student's cognitive activity during the instructional process is the fact that the control program is often not concretely specified. Above we cited an example of a well-defined program: if the temperature of a product is less than 110 degrees, the knob should be turned to the right, and if it is greater than 130 degrees, it should be turned to the left. A well-defined control program always indicates precisely not only the objective of the controlling activity, but also the conditions within which this activity must proceed, as well as the nature of the activity under each condition.

Returning to the area of education, we see that here the programming of control is often extremely imprecise. For example, we read: "the teacher should strive to cause the student to assimilate the material well"; "the teacher should elicit a high level of active involvement on the part of the student"; etc. What does "strive" mean? What does "elicit" mean? What specific actions under what conditions are necessary in order to achieve these goals? These are the things which usually are not indicated. Yet instructional activity being, as we now recognize, a form of control, may be analyzed into discrete actions (operations) just like any other activity, and a precise program governing these actions may be written.

Poor programming of instructional activity is one of the reasons for the fact that different teachers under similar conditions teach the same subject in different ways. They proceed according to different programs.

This situation, is, it seems to us, irrational. If 30 teachers shape the same process in students with similar characteristics and in similar conditions in 25 different ways, then it is not probable that all of these approaches are equally optimal.

Of course, one may say that there do not exist optimal instructional procedures (programs) as such, since for different teachers different procedures are optimal depending on their background, personality, skills, knowledge, etc. This is true if we view the problem in regard to teachers. But teaching procedures are directed toward students, and aimed at control of their activities. That is why the problem of optimization should be viewed from the point of view of students. Some teaching procedure which works best for the teacher (where the teacher is most skillful) may not be best for some students.

Speaking of optimal programs for students in conditions when the instructional agent is a teacher who instructs simultaneously dozens of students, it must be taken into consideration that we speak here only of statistical rather than individually oriented optimization. Statistical optimization means that some program is more efficient than all other ones (on the basis of accepted criteria) only on the average. But some program optimal on the average may not be optimal for each individual student. The final aim of optimization of instructional programs consists, therefore, in overcoming statistical optimization and the creation of conditions for teaching which will be optimal for each individual student. But individually oriented optimization presupposes individualized instruction, which cannot be translated into reality in conditions of standard, traditional instruction, but which can be implemented by means of programmed or automatized instruction.

The problem of evaluating alternative control programs and selecting the best from among them is one which many different sciences now face. This problem should be formulated in education as well. We must strive not to achieve a situation in which each teacher develops, by dint of his individual creativity, his own ways of conducting the instructional process, but rather to develop educational programs which are optimal under specific conditions at any given stage of the development of science, and to put these programs into universal practice. The teacher's creativity should be directed toward improving the existing programs, adjusting them to new specific conditions, and to finding instructional decisions in circumstances where programs do not exist or cannot be designed because of the uniqueness of some situations, and not toward discovering independently that which science has already discovered.

We stated above that the third prerequisite of good control is the presence of constant and operative feedback from the controlled system to the controlling one, i.e., that the controlling system should continuously receive information as to the state of the controlled system. This means, in pedagogical terms, that the teacher should not only communicate knowledge to the student and form different skills, habits, capacities, and so on, but that he should receive an unbroken flow of information from the student regarding his assimilation of this knowledge and his formation of desired abilities and capacities.

One of the reasons for the inadequate effectiveness of instruction is the fact, stated by many authors, that it is now organized in such a way that feedback is poor.

What, in fact, are the teacher's sources of feedback? Questioning of the student is his primary source, followed by various testing and verification procedures.

As far as questioning is concerned, it is impossible for the teacher to question all of his students often enough. Feedback from this source is extremely time-consuming.

With regard to testing and verification procedures, they yield more information than does questioning, but this information is of less value. Why is this the case? In checking test papers, the teacher is able to observe only the results of the student's cognitive activity: whether he got the problem right or made a mistake. But the cognitive process itself which leads to a mistake is, in many instances, not discoverable. The major task in instruction, however, is to influence these processes so as to influence their results. But it is precisely this information about the student's cognitive processes which the teacher often lacks.

The following example will illustrate what is meant by the above. Research performed by my colleague at the Psychological Institute, S.F. Zhuikov, has established the following: correct determination of the ending in the word "svirel,"* as in the sentence "Pastushok igral na svireli,"** requires that 11 associations or operations be made. Let us suppose that a student has written this word incorrectly: "na svirele." What can we say

*Nouns in Russian take case endings. (*Translator.*)

**"The shepherd played the pipe."

regarding this mistake? We can say only that the student made a mistake; we can say nothing about *why* he made this mistake. The fact of the mistake itself says nothing about whatever it was that did not "click" in his head. If we assume that the mistake was caused by the student's failure to perform an operation or by his incorrect performance of an operation (although he could fail to perform or could perform incorrectly two or more operations), then we are immediately faced with 11 possible causes of the mistake.

It is common knowledge that "backward" students in our schools receive considerable supplementary attention. Yet it often happens that several months of supplementary work with a student fails to yield any progress—he continues to lag behind his classmates. As a rule, this lack of progress is caused by the fact that the teacher does not know why the student is a slow learner, i.e., what it is that goes wrong when he tries to assimilate material or solve problems. The teacher often does not know the set of operations which must be carried out in order to solve a given problem, or knows them imperfectly. He may, for example, assume that five operations must be carried out in order to determine the ending of the word in the previous example, although the actual number is, in fact, 11. And if the teacher thinks that the student does not know operation number two and therefore directs his efforts to teaching this operation, and in fact it is operation number nine, the existence of which the teacher does not suspect, which the student is unable to perform, then the student may receive years of supplementary instruction and still make mistakes.

Thus, one of the causes of ineffectiveness in instruction (in supplementary instruction for slow learners in particular) is the fact that we "heal without diagnosis." We give the student information without receiving the necessary feedback from him. Testing yields information about the results of his cognitive activity, but often yields no information about the actual processes, the mechanisms of thought, involved in this activity. This is one of the major reasons for the fact that control is inadequate in the instructional process.

The significance of operative feedback from the student to the teacher goes beyond the fact that it enables the teacher to continually alter his actions as a function of the student's assimilation of knowledge, skills, and habits (i.e., to direct the learning process while at the same time adapting to it); feedback also is a necessary condition for reinforcing the student's performance. If the student is to assimilate knowledge, skills, and habits correctly and with maximum speed, it is necessary that he know the results of his actions (whether or not he performed the required operation, whether or not he performed it correctly, etc.). This appraisal should originate with the teacher, although it can also be carried out by means of a programmed textbook or a teaching machine.[2] But if the teacher, programmed textbook, or teaching machine is to evaluate (reinforce) the student's actions, there must be available from the student a constant flow of information regarding these actions. At present, the teacher does not receive this uninterrupted feedback from each student. The student, in his turn, does not receive sufficient reinforcement from the teacher.

We have indicated several of the present defects in instructional control which give rise to the ineffectiveness of modern instruction. The factors which we have thus far indicated are, of course, not the only ones responsible for this ineffectiveness; we will devote special attention below to another important factor, the absence of individualization in education. Some of these shortcomings have been long recognized, while others have only recently been clearly perceived.[3] Recognition of these defects has led, in many countries, to a search for instructional methods which will permit their elimination. "Programmed instruction" is one of these methods.

The basic principles of programmed instruction are as follows:

(1) availability of a precise objective and a precise instructional program on how to achieve it;

(2) realization of the instructional program by means of automatic or semi-automatic devices;

(3) analysis of instructional material into elements (steps)

and putting at the end of each step a question (problem) which requires an active answer on the basis of which one can judge the character of assimilation of the material;

(4) operative feedback to the instructional agent, and, if needed, to the learner (i.e., immediate reinforcement of the student's responses); and

(5) adaptation of teaching influences to the characteristics of assimilation and other learner traits, i.e., individualization of instruction (at least in regard to the student's pace).

The question arises as to whether these principles are new. The answer is that they are not. We all know that it is better for the student to be active rather than passive, that testing and reinforcement must be as frequent as possible, that the individual characteristics of each student must be taken into account, etc. But the group character of instruction and its present organization, in most schools, preclude the realization of these principles. Thus, it is physically impossible for the teacher to supply immediate reinforcement of the actions of each student; the teacher is likewise unable to individualize instruction: it is difficult in a group situation to present material in small steps. The significance of programmed instruction lies in the fact that it makes possible the implementation of these principles and provides a framework within which special educational materials, audio-visual aids, and new forms of educational organization may be developed.

It is evident that programmed instruction is an attempt to organize instruction in the form of a system with good feedback. Since the instructional material is divided into units, there exists the possibility of utilizing special devices—programmed textbooks or machines (teaching machines are discussed in greater detail below)—in order to present the material to the student. Teaching machines are capable not only of presenting information to the student, but also of controlling his assimilation of this information.

In spite of the virtues of this method of instruction, it has, in the form in which it has been developed by a number of authors in various countries, a number of shortcomings. I will indicate here only a few of them:*

1. Many didactic and methodological problems (such as selection of instructional content, procedures for introducing this material, exercises, etc.) are solved, as in the past, by empirical means. In other words, the instructional content and methods which are programmed often have not been demonstrated as optimal.

Of course, it is possible to program conventional content and conventional procedures of instruction so that the instructional program is made to simulate the ordinary methods of instruction, which are often imperfect and inefficient. It is clear, however, that if the conventional instruction controls the formation of students' cognitive processes poorly, programming of such instruction will not substantially improve overall efficiency of the instructional process. The overall efficiency of programmed instruction depends on the content and instructional procedures to be programmed and also on the methods of their programming. If one of these components is imperfect, the final result also will be imperfect. Programmed instruction, as one organization of the interaction between the student and the instructional agent, does not possess its own absolute efficiency irrespective of the content and instructional procedures being programmed. Rather, the efficiency of programmed instruction as a type of interaction is *relative* and depends on the content and procedures being programmed. One and the same method of programming may perform differently (i.e., may increase the efficiency to different degrees) depending on what is programmed (what is expressed in programmed form). Programming of one kind of content and instructional procedure may increase the efficiency of instruction to a greater degree than programming of some other kind of content and procedure. The relative weight of the contribution of one and the same way of programming to overall efficiency is different, because the relative

*Some others have been repeatedly emphasized to psychological and educational literature and are well known.

augmentation is different. Perhaps this explains the great diversity in results of the experiments directed at the evaluation of the efficiency of programmed instruction compared with that of conventional instruction. Some researchers have demonstrated the advantages of programmed instruction, while others that there are no essential differences; there were even some who demonstrated the advantages of conventional, non-programmed instruction. From what has been said, it follows that the view that programmed instruction or its specific forms have their own, inner, absolute, and independent degrees of efficiency which can be attained and simply added to the efficiency of conventional instruction is not justified. That is why one of the important means for increasing the efficiency of programmed instruction involves an improvement in the organization of the content and instructional procedures which are to become the basis of the instructional program. Clearly, the relative efficiency of programmed instruction, or of its specific types, depends not only on the content and instructional procedures being programmed but on some other factors (particularly, on the learner's personality characteristics*), but this is a special topic of discussion.

2. There is no doubt that, for many didactic problems, analysis of instructional material into elements (units) is extremely useful. This principle, however, cannot be universalized. In many instances, the student must be acquainted with a general pattern of phenomena and processes. And, what is especially important, he must learn to analyze independently the whole into its parts and to discover how these components interact with one another.

In order for the student to acquire this ability, it is necessary to present him with material in a form not broken into constituent elements, and particularly to teach him methods of how to analyze the material into elements independently.

The tendency to universalize some other principles of programmed instruction also seems wrong. This applies, especially,

---

*A summary of findings on this issue obtained by various authors appears in *Perspectives in Individualized Learning*, Robert A. Weisgerber (*Ed.*), F.E. Peacock Publishers, Inc., Itasca, Illinois, 1971, pp. 54-57.

to the principle of error-free learning. Undoubtedly, there are cases when errors in the assimilation of knowledge and habits and patterns are harmful (for instance, when one learns the pronunciation of a foreign language, listening to wrong pronunciation patterns is harmful). But there are cases when acquisition of correct knowledge or habits proceeds more successfully through comparison of correct and incorrect patterns and their differentiation—which is the basis for active inhibition of present or future incorrect patterns. (This is important, for instance, when some everyday physical notion contradicts or does not fully coincide with the corresponding scientific physical concept to be learned; when the semantic field of a word in a native tongue does not fully conform to the semantic field of a corresponding word in a foreign language; and so on.) Thus, presentation to the student of correct as well as incorrect patterns with their subsequent juxtaposition may be the most effective way to assimilate many correct patterns.

It is important in instruction not only to prevent students' mistakes but also to actually teach them to learn from mistakes. The ability to learn from mistakes is one of the most important human abilities, and it is impossible to develop this ability in students when all efforts in instruction are directed toward preventing and excluding mistakes.

One more principle which often tends to be universalized is that of immediate reinforcement of students' responses. Clearly, in many cases immediate reinforcement is not available, or even impossible. For instance, in the solution of any multi-step problem which involves trial-and-error, immediate reinforcement of each trial is impossible. Reinforcement may appear here only at the end of a long series of actions and can be related only retrospectively to actions performed. The necessity to act, in a situation of uncertainty as to the correctness of each action at the moment of performance, is a common one in human activity, and it is very important to develop in students the ability to act in such situations. (The latter includes, for example, such abilities or sub-abilities as that of fixing and holding in short-term memory sequences of actions carried out, in order afterwards to be able to compare each sequence with the results obtained; the ability to search for and find a wrong action in the sequence, if the final result was wrong; the ability to reconstruct the sequence of actions which have led to a wrong result; etc.) In order to develop these abilities in students, they should be trained in them. But if students are getting used to act only in situations when each of their actions is immediately reinforced, then it is impossible to shape in them these abilities and to teach them the general ability to act in situations involving uncertainty.

We have tried to show the negative aspects of universalization and absolutization of certain principles of programmed instruction. Since every absolute leads to one-sidedness, some important aspects of a problem, of an object of influence, etc., may remain unconsidered and uncontrollable.

In order that programmed instruction might be adequate to a greater variety of instructional objectives and be able to solve a greater scope of educational tasks and do this more effectively, its principles should be freed from unjustified one-sidedness, limitations, and absolutes. They should be more general and flexible and not establish new educational dogmas in place of old ones.

3. One of the major shortcomings of many programs is the fact that they do not teach the student, or teach him inadequately, such things as methods of independent thought and the ability to investigate and analyze problems creatively. The main goal of many programmed textbooks is simply to give the student specific knowledge or to enable him to answer specific questions, i.e., to elaborate in him ready-made reactions to definite situations. This is done by forming direct associations in the student's mind between a question and an answer, i.e., a stimulus and a response. It is known that in a great number of problems there exist no direct connection(s) between what is given in the problem and its answer and that in many cases it is impossible to establish direct associations between them. For instance, one and the same stimulus may require different reactions depending on the task which is before a man. One and the same problem may have not a single but various correct and equivalent solutions. It also happens that one and the same problem has different correct (but not

necessarily equivalent in some respects) solutions. One solution may be preferable for one person possibly from some one point of view and another for another person or from another point of view.

Although there are many situations (they are usually relatively simple) where it is possible and necessary to establish direct associations between stimulus and response, these situations should be not universalized and absolutized. The other kind of situations—more difficult from an educational point of view and particularly for the highest form of creative human activity in problem-solving—are those where such direct association cannot be established, since there do not exist direct unique and unequivocal connections between the stimulus and the response. This is why the major task in teaching students to solve such problems consists not in teaching them answers to given problems but, rather, in teaching *methods* of *how to arrive independently* at the answer, i.e., in teaching thinking in the proper sense of the word. Such thinking includes not only reproduction and application of established associations but also their recombinations and reconstructions as well as establishing new associations which were not and could not be foreseen and established (created) beforehand. The restructuring of associations and the establishment of new ones occur as a result of the solver's own active efforts (including trial-and-error and search efforts) with objects and their images in mind. These actions involve singling out new properties of objects and new relations between them which become manifest in new images and associations and in the restructuring of the existing ones.

Thus, one of the most important tasks in instruction, including programmed instruction, is not simply establishing associations between stimulus and response and their consolidation by means of repetition and applications to solving problems, but teaching students the methods of *how to arrive independently* at these responses (answers, solutions to a problem), i.e., teaching them the techniques of real thinking. The establishment of associations and their sequences and structures should be included as a component in appropriate instructional activity of a teaching agent which is the necessary but not sufficient condition for the development of students' thinking abilities. But how to think, to reason, in order to deduce the answer, i.e., to find the answer independently—these procedures are often not explicitly taught in many widely used programmed textbooks. In many cases, instruction is structured in such a way that it does not develop the ability to think. This shortcoming has been pointed out, incidentally, by many American educators. A great advantage of some Soviet research in this field is the fact that a number of Soviet investigators have devoted a great deal of attention to studying the mechanisms of cognitive activity which operate during the assimilation of knowledge and the solution of problems. It is now becoming more and more evident that high effectiveness may be achieved only by instructional procedures in which the student is explicitly taught *procedures of thought*, including procedures of productive, heuristic thought. And one of the important tasks of programmed instruction is that it should simulate (imitate, model) the method of teaching the procedures for thinking. This method, of course, depends on the character of the procedure to be taught. In particular, one of the efficient methods for teaching productive thinking processes is a discovery or heuristic approach. One may sometimes come across a viewpoint that programmed instruction precludes the discovery approach and represents something which is incompatible with it. There is some justification for this view in the present state of programmed instruction, but it is not justified in principle.

One of the aims of research in the field of programmed instruction is the development of techniques for simulating and programming any efficient method of instruction including the discovery method. It is not easy to program the discovery method and any attempt faces some substantial difficulties. However, there are no obstacles which cannot, in principle, be overcome, at least in the future. The error of some critics of programmed instruction does not reside in their emphasis on the distinction between programmed instruction (in its current most widespread forms) and discovery teaching but, rather, in the fact that they regard the current features of programmed instruction as inherent and unique to the technique, and, hence, view the current distinctions between programmed instruction and discovery teaching as absolute and insuperable. The more constructive approach is to try to find ways of programming the discovery method in order to make programmed instruction, when needed, really discovery instruction. Such instruction will be programmed discovery instruction, having the advantages of both.

It should be noted that the discovery method applied in group instruction functions as such only for a small number of the most active students. Observation shows that it is only these students who respond to the problem questions posed by the teacher and try to find solutions to them independently. The others wait until the active students have given an answer, and thus respond only to the completed answer itself. For these passive students, the discovery method does not involve any discovery. Since the teacher has to deal with some dozens of students simultaneously, it is inevitable that he or she has no means to induce each student to think independently nor even to check how each individual student reacts to a problem question put to the group and whether he does or does not try to answer it independently. It seems reasonable to think that programming the discovery method and its implementation through programmed instruction is the only way to ensure a genuine discovery for *each* student.

Efficient teaching of the ability to think presupposes a knowledge of the inner structure of corresponding thought processes. This is a particular manifestation of a general principle of efficient control. The better one knows the structure and laws of controllable processes, the better one can control them. One of the merits of cybernetics lies in the fact that it has developed methods of controlling phenomena whose inner structure and laws are not known, i.e., represent a "black box." This, however, does not invalidate the principle that the more "transparent" is the "box," the more efficient can be the control of its processes. This fully applies to thought processes to be shaped.

The basic technique used at present in psychology and cybernetics to study cognitive activity is to analyze cognitive processes into discrete, elementary operations and units of knowledge, and to represent each cognitive process as a specific combination of operations for analyzing and transforming knowledge about something. The essentials of this method may be easily grasped by analyzing a physical rather than a cognitive activity. (This analytic and descriptive method, incidentally, has long been known.) Let us suppose that we wish to teach someone how to start an automobile. In order to solve this problem, we must know precisely what "starting an automobile" means, i.e., we must know the components (operations) of which this activity is composed and the objects at which they should be directed. When we have discovered these operations and have determined their sequence, we can describe the process precisely as a specific combination of operations. At this point we may proceed to instruct the student.

The activity which we are considering is a very simple one. It consists of only a few operations, which are performed under relatively stable conditions. Cybernetics is now developing methods for describing activities which consist of thousands of operations, which take place under complex and changing conditions. Methods have been developed which permit these activities to be represented entirely as symbolic formulae similar to those of mathematics or chemistry. Let us consider the example of a railroad dispatcher's function, which consists of receiving and dispatching trains and in directing shunting operations.[4]

The dispatcher's activity may be analyzed into the following basic operations:

    A.   Dispatching trains
    B.   Receiving trains
    C.   Delay of dispatch
    D.   Delay of reception
    E.   Coupling and decoupling of trains
    F.   Directing inquiries to the next station regarding train departures
    G.   Shunting procedures

The sequence of operations which the dispatcher performs in any given situation depends on the presence or absence of certain conditions (so-called logical conditions). Thus, for example, if a train is approaching on a free track, the dispatcher receives it (i.e., he performs action B); if it is approaching on a track which is being used, he checks to see whether or not there is a track available for shunting and, if so, orders the decoupling and subsequent recoupling of the train (i.e., he performs operation E); if there is no track available, he delays reception of the train (i.e., he performs operation D); etc.

In the same way in which we denoted the dispatcher's activities by means of letters of the alphabet, we use letters to denote the conditions on which these activities depend:

p—availability of free track for reception

q—correspondence between an approaching train and a free track

z—availability of a free block-zone for dispatch

s—availability of a free track for shunting

ω—the logical untruth condition.

The dispatcher's activity may now be described exhaustively by means of the following formula:

$$\overset{7}{\downarrow} F \overset{5}{\downarrow} p \overset{1}{\uparrow} q \overset{2}{\uparrow} B \omega \overset{4}{\uparrow} \overset{2}{\downarrow} s \overset{3}{\uparrow} E G \omega \overset{4}{\uparrow} \overset{1,2}{\downarrow} D \omega \overset{5}{\uparrow} \overset{4}{\downarrow} z \overset{6}{\uparrow} A \omega \overset{7}{\uparrow} \overset{6}{\downarrow} C \omega \overset{4}{\uparrow}.$$

The formula is read from left to right beginning with the first letter. If the appropriate logical condition is present, the arrow pointing upward from the right of the letter is ignored and the action denoted by the subsequent letter is performed; if the appropriate logical condition is *not* present, then the action denoted by the letter to the right of the correspondingly numbered downward pointing arrow is performed.

It is clear that this formula shows *all of the actions required under all possible conditions*, and, therefore, constitutes a precise description of the dispatcher's activities.

This description is possible only because the activities in question have been analyzed into a finite aggregate of components, i.e., elementary operations, and the conditions under which they are applied (the logical conditions).[5]

In this way, any specific act on the dispatcher's part may be represented by a combination of these components.

The method which we have been using to analyze and describe physical activity can and should be used to analyze and describe some kinds of cognitive activity. This is not easy to do, since cognitive operations, unlike physical ones, cannot be directly observed and so are often difficult to establish. This explains why we are often unable to describe how we think when we solve a problem, that is, to determine which operations we perform. Many complex cognitive processes seem to us to be simple, "one-act" events (we simply "understand," "figure it out," etc.), while, in fact, they are often extremely complex and consist of a large number of operations. It is difficult to shape an intellectual process if we have never brought the corresponding operations to light and therefore do not know them. When such a process has been analyzed into its constituent operations and the structure of these operations has been discovered, however, it can be taught much more quickly and easily.

In the fields of psychology and education there is a need to analyze the cognitive processes into their elementary operations and for the elucidation and precise description of their interconnections (structure). In cases in which cognitive processes are algorithmic in nature, their algorithmic description should be given. A different kind of description may be used to describe processes which are creative in nature.

An algorithm for solving the problem of classifying simple sentences in the Russian language is presented below. The algorithm consists of a specification of the operations which must be performed on a sentence in order to classify it.[6]

This algorithm is a general method for solving the problem of categorizing a Russian simple sentence. Algorithms should not be just handed to the student in their final form during the instructional process. The student must be taught to discover them independently. The teaching of independent construction of algorithms is of enormous significance for the development in the student of a number of aspects of creative thought. Experience in teaching students to devise and apply algorithms has shown that this procedure is highly effective.

Algorithm

In order to classify a simple sentence, the following questions must be answered:

1. Does the sentence have a subject?

yes	no

2. Does it have a predicate?

2. Is the predicate expressed by a verb in the first or second persons?

yes	no	yes	no

Conclusion: definite-personal

Conclusion: elliptical

Conclusion: definite-personal

3. Is the predicate expressed by a verb in the third person plural (or by a verb in the past tense plural)?

yes	no

Conclusion: indefinite-personal

Conclusion: impersonal

We stated above that instruction is a particular type of control process, specifically, control of the cognitive activity of the student. Clearly, the more comprehensive this control is (including the control directed at developing of mechanisms of self-control in students and, thus, gradually negating itself) the more effective the instructional process will be. At present, the development of many processes in the student's consciousness occurs haphazardly and outside the teacher's control. As a result, these processes (for example, skills and habits) often develop with defects in their structure. Defective skills and habits give rise, in their turn, to learning difficulties and chronic failure. All of this could be avoided if the teacher could control the student's performance of all cognitive operations, and correct every incorrect operation immediately. More accurate and complete control of the student's cognitive processes can be achieved by discovering methods and organizational forms which will permit the formation and control of intellectual processes on the basis of their constituent operations. The importance of this problem is illustrated by the following example. In experiments in teaching grammatical algorithms, we discovered that some of the students, in spite of a good knowledge of the operations necessary for the solution of a given grammatical problem, made significant numbers of mistakes when tested on their ability to solve these problems. This was unexpected. The students had been explicitly taught how to think in solving grammatical problems, i.e., which operations to perform and in what sequence. The cause of these difficulties, however, proved to be simple. The teacher had used every means to induce his students to perform the required operations, but those students who had had difficulty or who were simply lazy had not performed them. The teacher, however, was not even aware of this fact. He did not possess the means for controlling the students' performance of the operations in question; he had no operative feedback. It is for this reason that these students, though instructed by the teacher, did not learn. We were able to solve this problem by introducing specially prepared manuals which we called "exercise-books for independent study." They were constructed in such a way that the student had to record in them the results of the performance of each operation. In using these workbooks, each student, whether he wished to or not, was forced to work actively, performing all the required operations; the information contained in the workbook, meanwhile, enabled the teacher to control the student's assimilation of the operations in question. The development of special workbooks for independent work is one of the means for controlling the student's cognitive processes more effectively. However, such workbooks do have their disadvantages. One disadvantage is the impossibility of obtaining direct control of the operations being performed by the student while he performs them (as is possible with a teaching machine). A second disadvantage is that the teacher has the additional task of checking the workbooks (the work required in checking these workbooks is greater than that required in correcting the normal type of homework exercise). A third disadvantage of this method is that recording the results of each operation in the workbook is time-consuming. Teaching machines can eliminate these disadvantages, preserving all advantages of operation-by-operation regulation and control.

We have touched on only a few of the problems associated with the utilization of the ideas and methods of cybernetics in instruction. Even this short survey shows, however, that the continued successful development of instructional technology depends to a significant degree on the extent to which mathematical, logical, and cybernetic methods are introduced into it.

One of the most important tasks facing instructional science is the creation of such a psycho-didactic theory of the instructional process, which uses and includes cybernetic and logico-mathematical approaches and methods. The synthesis of psycho-didactic and cybernetic methods would raise instruction to a new, significantly higher level of effectiveness.

Notes

1. In order to diagnose only one type of heart disease, a minimum of 90 symptoms and 56 correlations among these symptoms must be taken into account.
2. The student himself is able to appraise his actions if answers relating to the results of individual actions are included in textbooks and assignment books. However, comparison of answers with those indicated in the textbook has the disadvantage that the student who does not want to think is able to look up the answer without the required cognitive effort.

3.   As we have seen, analysis of the instructional process from the point of view of control principles, i.e., cybernetic analysis, is especially useful in revealing these shortcomings.
4.   See V.N. Pushkin, "The Psychology of Supervision of Railroad Transport," *Problems of Psychology*, 1959, No. 3.
5.   A description of this sort is called algorithmic, since the process being described is algorithmic, i.e., it is performed in accordance with instructions—with an algorithm—which precisely specifies the actions to be taken under any possible set of conditions.
6.   The considerations from which we proceeded in writing this algorithm are described in greater detail in the author's article on "The Teaching of Methods of Efficient Thought and the Problem of Algorithms," *Problems of Psychology*, 1961, No. 1. See also L.N. Landa, *Algorithmization in Learning and Instruction*, Englewood Cliffs, New Jersey: Educational Technology Publications, 1974.

Chapter Three

"He Couldn't Figure It Out
Because He Couldn't Figure It Out"

The principal of a school in which I once worked used to assign the tenth graders, on the last day of school, a theme on the topic "Ten Years in School." He asked the students to describe all the impressions, both good and bad, which they had accumulated in their 10 years of school experience.

These were interesting compositions. One of them was particularly noteworthy because of the ideas expressed in it regarding teaching methods. I was particularly struck by the following passage: "The years which I have spent in school give me much to think about. I cannot complain about the knowledge which I acquired. I learned quite a bit. But I would like to say one thing: we were taught a lot of things which can be found in any reference book, but we were not taught to reason. Sometimes I try to reason, but I don't get anywhere . . . ."

It is probably the case that learning to think is more difficult than assimilating knowledge. But the most important point in this regard, I believe, is that we still do not really know what "knowing how to think" means, and, unfortunately, do not usually devote much attention to this question.

I recall a conversation with a young teacher of mathematics. She was distributing graded tests to her class: Abramov—B, Vershinin—A, Zaitsev—D.

Zaitsev's grade caught my interest. He was a bright and diligent boy, but he just could not master geometry. Actually, he always received good grades for oral recitation, he knew all the theorems, axioms, and definitions, but he just could not solve written problems.

After the lesson, I went up to the teacher and asked her:
—"Irina Sergeevna, what happened with Zaitsev this time?"
—"He couldn't solve the problem again."
—"What was the trouble?"
—"He doesn't know how to think. He didn't figure out that the chord should be considered as the side of an inscribed angle."
—"Why couldn't he figure it out?"
She looked at me as though I did not really understand what I was saying:
—"What do you mean 'why couldn't he figure it out'? He couldn't figure it out because he couldn't figure it out, that's why."

I do not know whether my question was a good one, but the answer clearly indicated that, for Irina Sergeevna (i.e., the teacher, *Ed.*), the problem ended where it really should have begun. To say that Zaitsev missed the problem because he "doesn't know how to think" or because "he couldn't figure it out" or "didn't think" is, essentially, to say nothing at all. The entire problem is, what does it mean to say that "he doesn't know how to think," etc.? What doesn't "click" in a person's head when he fails to figure out a problem, and what must be done in order to develop this ability in him?

The "secret of thought" is one of the most profound secrets of nature. Philosophers, psychologists, logicians, linguists, and mathematicians have tried and are still trying to understand it. Now, armed with the latest scientific tools, cyberneticists have taken on this problem.

Cognitive processes are difficult to study because they are, on the one hand, hidden from external observation, and, on the other hand, often unconscious. Try asking a person how a given thought came into his head. He probably will not be able to tell you very much about how this happened: the thought came, that's all! But even someone who describes in more-or-less detailed fashion the flow of his thinking is usually conscious of only a small portion of what is going on in his head. Moreover, a person's attention is usually directed not toward *how* he is thinking, but toward *what* he is thinking about, that is, toward the object of thought rather than its flow.

Nevertheless, in spite of these difficulties, scientist have succeeded in fathoming the structure of thought.

1.   What Is Thought?

We read in textbooks of psychology that thought is the process of generalized and indirect or mediated cognition of reality.

The meaning of "generalized cognition" is clear enough. When one *studies*, for example, a triangle, one recognizes the properties not only of a specific triangle, but of triangles in general.

"Indirect cognition" denotes cognition of one object (or its properties) through the instrumentality of other objects. For example, you walk down the street and see smoke coming from a chimney. You immediately come to the conclusion that a fireplace in the house is lit. You learn of one phenomenon—a fire in the fireplace—through the instrumentality of another phenomenon—smoke. The well-known aphorism "there's no smoke without fire" in fact reflects the essence of thought as indirect cognition of reality.

How is it possible to come to conclusions concerning some phenomena by observing other phenomena? The objective connections between phenomena (if there's smoke, there's fire) are reflected in the brain in the form of knowledge. In living, working, and studying, we accumulate an enormous quantity of knowledge, which is to say that a large number of associations (relations, *Ed.*) are formed in the brain.

Knowledge, however, is not thought. It is only the prerequisite for thought. It is possible, for example, to know all the theorems of geometry and still not be able to solve geometrical problems. It is possible to know grammatical rules and still make mistakes in writing, etc. It is not accidental that we often hear: "He learned everything, he knows all the material, but he just can't think." And, in fact, knowing something and being able to think are not identical, although the process of thinking is impossible without knowledge.

By studying how people think while solving problems, it is possible to establish that "thinking" actually consists of the performance of specific cognitive operations.

We all know quite well what practical or physical operations are; as when someone, for example, picks up an object and moves it from one place to another. But what is a cognitive operation? This occurs when someone does exactly the same thing, but with psychological images of the object, i.e., "in his head."

Cognitive operations develop on the basis of physical operations. But, once formed, cognitive operations usually precede their physical counterparts. Someone who works by "using his head" thinks about what he is going to do before he actually does it. If the result of the operations carried out in his head is satisfactory, he proceeds to carry them out physically. If the result is unsatisfactory, he performs different cognitive operations, and continues in this way until he intellectually achieves the desired result.

People are able to perform cognitive operations not only on the visual images of objects, but also on abstract concepts derived from them. Thus, a person can not only "mentally" transpose some particular triangle lying before him onto a plane surface, he can also discover its general properties, compare them, draw specific conclusions, etc.

The difference between "knowing" and "thinking" is now clear. Knowing is having concepts and ideas of objects, phenomena, and the relations among them. Thinking is being able to operate with those conceptions and ideas.

We note in this regard that knowledge may be not only about objects and phenomena, but also about operations themselves.

A person may not only know what an automobile is, he also may know how to drive one. Knowledge of operations plays a particularly important role in thinking. But knowledge of operations and the ability to perform them are two different things. A beginning swimmer knows *what to do* in order to swim, but he is still unable to swim. A student may know that he should mentally rotate the object in front of him by 90 degrees and may still be unable to do it.

Observation of the thought processes of school children who are unable to solve problems or who do so poorly has shown that their being "unable to think" is, in particular, a result of the fact that they often do not know what to do with the conditions of a problem in order to solve it, i.e., they do not know the cognitive operations which must be performed on the given information.

This situation is due to the fact that they are usually not taught these operations and the knowledge(s) about them specifically. The more able students "discover" the operations on their own (often as a result of trial-and-error), while the less able ones do not succeed in doing this. But even students who independently discover these operations and become good problem-solvers spend more time solving problems than they would if they had been specifically taught the required operations.

2.   Students Must Be Taught to Think

It is now clear how this is to be done. The process of assimilating knowledge and solving problems must be analyzed into discrete operations, and these operations must be taught specifically to the students.

I performed an experiment involving these procedures two full decades ago. Students who, in two to two-and-a-half years of studying geometry, had not learned to solve geometrical problems well and who, according to teachers' evaluations, "reasoned poorly," showed a sharp improvement in their "ability to think" after a short period of specific instruction in the performance of cognitive operations. They not only solved most of the problems which they had long been unable to solve, but also they began to reason in a different manner.

At this point the question arose as to whether Russian (i.e., grammar, *Ed.*), for example, could be taught in the same way. Research had shown that the cause of difficulty in solving "grammatical problems" was the same as in the case of geometrical problems: the students often did not know the necessary operations. The only difference was that, in this case, the operations involved words and sentences rather than geometric figures and concepts.

For example, a typical "grammatical problem" is whether or not to place a comma before the word "and" in the sentence: "I don't feel well, and I intend to go and see a doctor." In order to solve this problem one must analyze the sentence into discrete elements, examine these elements for specific features, etc. But to do this, one must know which elements to look for, which operations to apply, and in what sequence they should be performed.

Analysis of grammatical phenomena and rules as well as grammatical thought processes has permitted us to isolate these operations. For many grammatical problems we have been able to write instructions (algorithmic prescriptions) which specify the sequence of operations which should be performed on a word or sentence in order to determine how to write it.

It should be noted that, although some grammatical algorithms are taught in school (without being called algorithms), many of them are implicit, are not complete, not general, and until recently very little attention was paid to developing them.

Teaching certain specially devised algorithms had a marked effect on the students' performance. Using the algorithms, they made approximately five to seven times fewer mistakes.

It may be assumed that algorithmization would permit us to teach many subjects significantly better and faster, although it should be emphasized that instruction cannot and should not be reduced solely to the teaching of algorithms.

3.   The Teacher and Feedback

We have seen that cognitive processes "consist" of specific elements: images and concepts as well as cognitive operations which are directed at the transformation of images and concepts. These are, as it were, the bricks of thought. But if this is so, is it not possible to "construct" intellectual processes using these operations in the same way that builders use bricks to construct a house?

Clearly, this can be done. The first step is to determine which bricks are required for a given "house" and how they are to be put together. An algorithm is an analysis of a cognitive process into discrete operations—"bricks"—and a specification of at what they should be directed and how they should be "organized."

Let us imagine that we have designed an algorithm for solving a particular type of problem, for example, recognizing a given type of sentence, and we wish to teach it to our students. In order to learn this algorithm, it is not enough for the students to memorize the operations to be performed; they also must learn how to use them. This requires training.

Let us suppose that this training has begun. Thirty students are doing an assignment. But how, precisely, are they going about it? Are they carrying out the required operations? Are their thought processes proceeding in the proper manner? Are they thinking at all? Are not some of them simply trying to guess the answer? The teacher neither knows the answers to these questions, nor has any way of finding them. When he has collected the students' papers and gone over them, he can only judge the results of the cognitive activity of each student (whether or not he solved the problem or made a mistake); he does not know *how* the student thought while he was attempting to solve the problem, that is, which processes led to this result. Any mistake which the student may have made could have had many different causes. If the psychological reason for a mistake is unknown, it is difficult to correct it. The teacher is in a position in which he must heal without the benefit of diagnosis.

But this is not all. Let us assume for a moment that knowledge of the results of cognitive activity, of a mistake, for example, would permit us to determine and deal with the operations causing this mistake. Would this permit full control of the formation of the students' cognitive processes? It turns out that it would not.

In a classroom situation, the teacher has no opportunity to correct faulty operations as they are being performed by the student. If a student does something incorrectly today, the teacher is able to inform or tell him of his mistake tomorrow at the soonest—after correcting the student's written work. Thus, exercises may not be beneficial, and they may do even a certain amount of harm, since within this time incorrect operations may consolidate themselves and lead to the development of incorrect associations by the student which should later be broken and reformed.

Instruction is, as we see, insufficiently effective. The basic reason for this ineffectiveness, in cybernetic terms, is the fact that operational feedback is absent from the learning process. When the teacher provides his students with information (for example, instructions on how to think in order to solve a given type of problem), he does not immediately receive reciprocal information from the students with regard to their thought processes as they actually occur while the students are attempting to solve a problem. Without this information, the teacher cannot routinely regulate and correct these cognitive processes. Under these conditions, the formation of the processes in question is to a considerable degree haphazard, and, therefore, often defective. This is one of the causes of the difficulties which we constantly encounter both in secondary schools and institutions of higher education.

Good control of cognitive processes is achievable only if means are found for forming and controlling them on the basis of their constituent operations.

How is this problem to be solved? One answer lies in the use of cybernetic teaching devices—teaching machines.*

4.   Teaching Machines

Let us suppose that we wish to teach an algorithm for recognizing some type of sentence. Each sentence is written on a card, and a number of holes are punched in the card. The card is fed into a device which "reads" the perforations, after which the machine "knows" the characteristics of the sentence and, therefore, which operations should be performed by the student in order to determine its structural classification.

Let us suppose, further, that the following sentence is written on the card: *(They) took the damaged radio to the repair shop,*

---

*The first Soviet teaching machine, "Repetitor-1," was built by the author in collaboration with S.P. Khlebnikov, an engineer. (*Editor.*)

*and the next day (they) repaired it.** (Each word in the sentence is numbered.) The problem is to determine whether a comma is to be placed before the word "and." To do this, the student must first determine the structural classification of the sentence, i.e., whether it is simple or complex. If it is a complex sentence, then a comma should be inserted. If it is a simple sentence with coordinate clauses, then the comma is not required.

There are three rows of switches on the panel of the machine, each of which may be in one of two positions: "yes" or "no." The first row designates the first operation of the algorithm—determining the main clauses of the sentence. There are *no subjects* in this sentence, but there are predicates consisting of the words "took" and "repaired." In order to tell the machine that these words are predicates, the student flips the appropriate switches (the switches are numbered so as to correspond to the numbered words in the sentence).

Let us assume, however, that the student thinks that the word "radio" is the subject and flips the switch corresponding to this word. As soon as he does this, a red light flashes, indicating that a mistake has been made, and a counter is set to record this fact.

After the principal part of the sentence has been identified, the next step is to determine whether or not the sentence possesses the characteristics defining its type. These characteristics are written above the middle row of switches.

We look to see whether or not the predicates are in the third person plural. We flip the switch above which this characteristic is written to the "yes" position. There is one operation left to perform: to determine whether or not the actions expressed in the two predicates were performed by the same persons. No, the radio was taken to the repair shop by its owners, but was repaired by people in the shop. We flip the last switch to the "no" position. If

---

*A subjectless sentence with the verb in the third person plural (Russian verbs are declined according to person and number) is a common impersonal construction in Russian, corresponding to the use of the passive in English: "they" took the radio = the radio was taken. (*Translator.*)

at any point the student should make a mistake, thinking, for example, that the actions described in the two predicates were carried out by the same people, and therefore flipped the last switch to the "yes" position, then the error signal would flash again, and the error counter would record another mistake.

The analysis of this sentence is now finished. All that remains is to answer the final question. The two possible answers ("complex" or "simple") are written over the third and final row of switches. If the student answers incorrectly that the sentence is a simple one, the error signal will flash once again and the error will be recorded. If he answers correctly, a green light will flash and a correct answer will be registered. The machine treats everyone in the same way, exposing lack of knowledge, carelessness, or inattention in all students equally.

We have considered the example of machine-aided teaching of Russian grammar. But other subjects may be taught in the same way. Doing this requires only that we develop the necessary algorithms. This form of instruction not only indicates *that* a student is making mistakes, but also reveals *why*—the sources of the mistakes. Appropriate remedial action can be taken based on this data.

Chapter Four

Some Problems in the
Algorithmization of Instruction

To teach thinking effectively presupposes knowledge of internal mechanisms which underlie problem-solving ability, i.e., knowledge of their constituent elements and the ways they are linked, function, and interact. This problem is one of the most difficult in psychology. Various attempts to describe the structure of cognitive processes have been made—the Gestalt concept, the concepts of analysis and synthesis, various forms of association-istic approaches, etc. Even now psychologists often explain the same facts in different ways, and these different explanations often seem to be equally true or at least appear not to contradict one another. Without discussing the reasons for a "multiplicity of non-contradictory explanations" in psychology, we will indicate one of the means by which this difficulty may be overcome. Let us turn to the example of a student who in the process of solving a geometric problem failed to "figure out" that the chord AB is simultaneously the side of inscribed triangles ABE and ABC, while looking at the diagram shown in Figure 4.1. The student's failure to solve this particular sub-problem may be explained, and usually is explained, by saying that the student "was unable to analyze the diagram," "didn't see," "did not figure out," that he "couldn't relate" segment AB to other segments, AE, BE, BC and AC, etc. All of these explanations are true, to one degree or another. Which, then, is to be preferred, or, if none of them is satisfactory, how may we arrive at another explanation?

The principle by which we should be guided in answering this question is, in our view, as follows. The most fruitful explanations

Figure 4.1

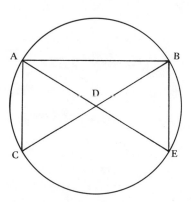

in educational psychology are those which permit us to separate out those elements of a psychological mechanism and their interconnections which may be influenced and controlled with a view toward transforming them during the instructional process. If one explains the stopping of a damaged automobile by saying that the motor is not functioning properly, one is giving a perfectly correct explanation, but one which is not very useful, since it does not indicate any means for eliminating the malfunction. Any explanation of a phenomenon must be associated ultimately with the solution of the constructive problem of controlling this phenomenon, i.e., of influencing and transforming it.

An explanation must create the necessary prerequisites for this transformation. The property of an explanation to suggest specific ways of constructively influencing, transforming, and controlling that which serves as explanation we shall call "constructiveness of explanation."

If the criterion (or at least one of the most important criteria) for a fruitful explanation is the possibility of solving the constructive problem of transformation (albeit in the future) on the basis of this explanation, then it becomes clear why the explanations adduced above are unsatisfactory. Being unconstructive, they fail to make clear what must be done concretely in order to teach the student to solve problems of a particular sort.[1]

Automatized and non-conscious processes (and the processes of, for example, guesswork, insight, and so on, are usually not conscious) are in many cases a later phase of the development of voluntary and conscious processes. They may be obtained as result of these (such) processes in the process of instruction, understanding what "didn't click" in the student's head when he failed to solve a definite problem requires that we determine what *should have* "clicked"—or, more to the point, what the student should have done in order to arrive at the correct solution. But this requires that we isolate elementary cognitive operations which are sufficient to lead to the solution when performed. These cognitive operations must, moreover, be controllable—subject to both external and internal (self-) regulation.

The operations involved in problems of the type we have been considering are, it appears, the following: (1) conceptual isolation of a given element (chord AB)*; (2) systematic relation of this element to other elements in a particular system (a clock hand, for example); or (3) evaluation of the resulting figures on the basis of comparison with images of known figures or with the characteristics of known figures.

Let us apply these operations to the diagram shown in Figure 4.1. The first relation is to the arc AB. Segment AB is a chord relative to this arc. The second relation is to segment AC. Relative to this segment, AB is the side of the inscribed angle BAC. Segment CB begins at point C. Segment AB is, relative to segments AC and CB, the side of the triangle BAC (this is the third relation). The fourth relation is with the segment AD. In relation to this segment, AB is the side of the angle BAD. Segment DB begins at point D. In relation to AD and DB, segment AB is the side of the triangle BAD (this is the fifth relation). Segment DE also begins at point D. In relation to AE, segment AB is the side of the inscribed angle BAE (this is the sixth relation). Segment EB originates at point E. In relation to AE and EB, segment AB is the side of the triangle BAE (this is the seventh relation). In relation to segments

---

*Conceptual isolation of elements, like other cognitive operations, is a concrete (real, practicable, *Trans.*) transformation of forms and concepts.

AC, CD, DE, and EB, segment AB is the side of the polygon ACDEB (the eighth relation).

It is clear that, in carrying out all of the above (covert, *Ed.*) cognitive operations, it is impossible not to stumble over ("see," "figure out") the fact that AB is the side of the inscribed triangles ABE and ABC. Obviously, a student who fails to see this has not performed the above operations, although it is precisely this system of cognitive operations which underlies diagram-reading and geometric insight of this sort. Clearly, a person who is good at reading diagrams, who knows how to "surmise" regarding the properties of geometric figures, carries out the above operations, rapidly and, usually, unconsciously. This is why it seems to him (and to others) that he *saw* the relevant properties of the figures at once, and simultaneously had the insight.

Our idea of the system of operations we have been discussing may be considered as a model of the process which underlies the type of geometric insight involved in the above example. But how can we verify the correctness of the model?

This may be done by compiling, on the basis of the component operations, instructions which specify what to do and how to proceed in order to see the required relationships (figures) in the diagram. If performance of the operations in accordance with the instructions leads to perception of the required relation in the diagram, in other words, to the solution of the problem, then the model has been properly designed; otherwise, it has not. The character of the operations and their system determines also the character of the exercises which should be required of the student in order to teach him the required operations.

An experiment which we performed two decades ago involved teaching students the ability to read a diagram (the type of geometric problem-solving we have been considering) and showed that our model of the corresponding process was correct. By training students to perform the operations specified in the instructions, it was possible to teach them in a relatively short time to read a geometric diagram and, therefore, to solve problems of this sort.[2]

We have discussed only one example of the approach used in

the research we carried out, which was devoted to teaching students some quite general cognitive techniques for solving problems (namely, problems involving geometric proof). Analysis of the process whereby poor students solve problems has shown that they do not know and/or have not fully mastered all of the operations which must be performed in order to arrive at a solution. They may know theorems, rules, and axioms, i.e., the properties of geometric objects,[3] but do not know what to do with them, i.e., the operations which must be performed in order to achieve the desired result. Knowledge of the first sort (knowledge of objects and their properties) is often properly taught in school, while knowledge of the second sort (cognitive operations, methods of reasoning) are often poorly taught. This is due to the fact that people are not aware of many of the cognitive operations which must be performed in order to solve a given type of problem. Not only students, but teachers as well, are unaware of them. They are in many cases even unknown to science. People who master (and are able) to solve problems well discover these operations often through a process of trial-and-error, of "adaptation"[4] to objects, and precisely for this reason are not conscious of them and are thus unable to transmit them to others.

This situation may be represented in the following general way. Let us assume that the solution of some class of problems requires the performance of 20 operations: $a_1, a_2, a_3, \ldots, a_{20}$. The majority of students, as our experiment showed, do not know all of these operations, but only some of them. This explains why students can solve some problems, but not others. If a problem requires the application of operations which the student knows, he is able to solve it, and otherwise not.[5]

Usually, there are not one but many ways to prove many geometric propositions (for example, the proposition regarding the equality of two segments), such that some methods are appropriate in some instances and other methods in other instances. The variety of these methods is due to the fact that geometric figures and the relations between them or their elements may have various attributes, different subsets of which may form different sufficient conditions for proving one and the same statement, and, therefore, be bases for different methods of proof. (In our example there are various attributes which are sufficient conditions for the equality of two or more segments: two segments are equal if they are corresponding sides of equal triangles, or if they are both equal to some third segment, or if they cover equal arcs of a circumference, i.e., are equal chords, etc.) In order to solve problems successfully, one must know the specific operation required to proceed from one sufficient attribute to another, if the preceding one did not fit. Our experiment showed that this is one of the operations which many students do not know well and often do not know at all. If the first few attributes which they attempted to use did not lead to success, they fell into a rut and did not know what to do next. Yet the operation which should be tried in a given "rut situation" is that of reproducing other known sufficient attributes of the figure in question (or of the attributes of the relations between them or its elements) with the subsequent attempt to use these attributes. If this operation, too, fails to solve the problem, the operation to be applied is one involving systematic correlation of these elements with other elements and subsequent "reconception" of the figure.[6]

The basic research problem referred to above consists of determining the operations composing the process of thinking about a problem involving geometric proof (or, what is the same thing, the process of searching for a proof) and in deriving from the established system of operations a model of the process which could serve to prescribe what to do and how to proceed (i.e., which operations to perform with geometric objects and how to relate basic knowledge to them) in order to solve the problem.[7] These prescriptive directions must refer to elementary operations. Therefore, they will be applicable not just to one problem, but to many. Hence it may be termed a technique of reasoning which is sufficiently general to enable the user to prove most geometric propositions.*

We note that different types of problems require the ability

---

*At least, geometric propositions of the type encountered in secondary schools.

to perform different cognitive operations. This situation is analogous to what takes place with physical operations during various forms of physical activity: driving a car requires knowledge of one kind of operation, working a lathe requires knowledge of others. Very often in psychology and logic the characterization of cognitive activity is limited to indications of operations such as analysis, synthesis, generalization, discrimination, and a few others. This characterization is correct, but not sufficient. The specific operations in which analysis and synthesis appear are extremely diverse (there are hundreds, if not thousands, of them), and it is possible to know some analytical operations and not to know others. The task facing psychology, especially educational psychology, requires it not to be limited by simple characterizations of cognitive activity such as that involving analysis and synthesis, but rather to discover the specific cognitive actions (operations) in which analysis and synthesis manifest themselves and which are required for the solution of a given class of problems.

Our study was designed in the following manner.[8] In a preliminary experiment performed before beginning instruction, students were given a set of 20 problems, half of which were of low and half of average and somewhat more-than-average difficulty. After having determined which problems the students solved and which they were unable to solve (even the best students solved not more than 45 percent of the problems of average and more-than-average difficulty, while mediocre and poor students solved a significantly smaller percentage), the experiment in teaching operations—via instructions that specified what to do in order to prove a proposition—was carried out. In other words, instruction in a general method for proving geometric propositions was presented. This instruction involved problems different from those given in the preliminary diagnostic experiment. After the students had mastered all the required operations and their interrelations, i.e., the general method of reasoning (proceeding), they were again given those problems which they had been unable to solve during the preliminary experiment. The result was that the overwhelming majority of these problems were solved. The fact that students were able to solve problems other than those used during instruction supports the assumption that they had in fact learned a method of reasoning which was sufficiently general to be applicable to an entire class of problems.

The question arose as to whether this method for proving geometric propositions was applicable to other, non-mathematical problems. In other words, the question was whether there exist methods applicable to widely differing subject-matters (for example, mathematics and grammar, grammar and chemistry, chemistry and biology), and whether they would be transferable from one area to another. If such methods existed, or could be developed, they would have enormous significance in instructional practice. They would make possible the teaching of mathematics in such a way as to make the learning of grammar easier, and vice versa. It is easy to imagine how this would facilitate the instructional process as a whole and increase its efficiency.

In order to answer this question, we chose a subject which, at first glance, would seem rather far removed from mathematics, i.e., grammar. Analysis of the difficulties which students encounter in learning their native Russian language (we will henceforth consider mainly native language grammar and, in particular, its syntax), and of the mistakes they make in writing, shows that the situation here is in many ways analogous to that prevailing in the study of mathematics, namely that students often have a good knowledge of theory, definitions, and rules, but are unable to solve grammatical problems.[9] Deeper analysis of this situation shows that the reason for this in native language learning is the same as in the learning of mathematics. Although they may have a good knowledge of theory—definitions and rules—students do not know what to do (which cognitive operations to perform) with the objects encountered in grammatical phenomena (words, sentences, etc.), in order to find the solution to the problem.

It is clear that elimination of this shortcoming requires that the same procedure be carried out as in the experiment involving geometric material:

(1) discover the cognitive operations involved in the process

of solving grammatical problems of a given class as well as their organization (i.e., the operative procedure);

(2) determine, on the basis of these operations, how to proceed in order to solve problems correctly (i.e., design a model of the corresponding process);

(3) write appropriate instructions for directing the student's actions during the problem-solving process (i.e., formulate techniques for solving this class of problems); and

(4) structure the teaching of the operations and their system (techniques) on the basis of these instructions.

In writing these instructions, we began with the assumption that instructions for solving grammatical problems can be algorithmic in nature, i.e., that algorithms for solving grammatical problems may be devised.[10] After such instructions had been compiled for a given class of grammatical problems, it proved to be the case that they were, in fact, algorithmic in nature, and were, in essence, algorithms.

In mathematics, algorithms are defined as instructions for the performance, in a particular order, of some system of elementary operations for solving all the problems of a given class. Algorithms have the characteristics of specificity, generality, and resultivity. (These terms are explained in some detail in Chapter Five.)

The simplest example of an algorithm would be the rules for dividing two numbers. Let us assume that we are to divide two natural numbers (for example, 243/3). The algorithm prescribing how to proceed is well-known:

1. isolate the first digit of the dividend

2. check to see whether it is divisible by the divisor

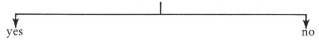

yes   no

3. divide it   3. isolate the next digit

4. write the result, etc.   4. check to see whether the number formed by the first two digits is divisible by the divisor, etc.

There was a time when such algorithms were unknown, and only the most intelligent people could divide two moderately large numbers. After these algorithms were discovered they were eventually taught to children so that today students in primary school are able to divide large numbers. This example shows clearly the importance of algorithms in teaching, in particular the degree to which they lower age barriers in education and raise the efficacy of instruction in general.

A characteristic of the above arithmetic algorithm and others of the same type is the fact that they are directed toward the transformation of particular objects. Before application of the division algorithm, there were two numbers, 243 and 3, to be divided, while after its application these numbers were transformed into another number, 81, which is the quotient resulting from the division of the first number by the second.

Turning to grammatical rules, we see that each of them may be considered as some transformation algorithm reduced to one operation. For example, let us consider the following somewhat simplified rule: "If a sentence is compound and its component main clauses are connected by the conjunction "and," then place a comma before the 'and.' "*

Application of this rule to a sentence possessing the characteristics indicated in the left part of the rule results in its transformation. To begin with, it was a sentence without a comma. After application of the rule a comma is present. Therefore, the sentence became transformed.

The question is why students who know such algorithms well nevertheless make mistakes and, in many cases, are unable for years to learn how to write grammatically. Why is knowledge of these algorithms insufficient?

The essence of the problem is easily seen from the following example. Let us consider a schematic sentence of the form $- - - - -$ and $- - - - -$, where the dashes represent words. Let us assume, further, that we must determine whether or not to insert a comma before the conjunction "and." The rule states (in

*This is a deliberately simplified rule of Russian grammar.

its simplified form) that, if the conjunction "and" is located in a compound sentence and connects two main clauses, then a comma is to be inserted before the conjunction; if the conjunction is located in a simple sentence or clause and connects two homogeneous parts, then the comma is not inserted. We may write the given rules in an even simpler form as follows:

If sentence is complex → insert comma

If sentence (with homogeneous parts) is simple → do not insert comma

Let us designate the expression "compound sentence" by α, the expression "simple sentence" (containing homogeneous parts) by the letter β, "insert comma" by the letter A, and "do not insert comma" by an A with a bar over it: $\overline{A}$ (the bar indicating negation of the expression).* The above simplified rules may then be written:

$$\alpha \rightarrow A$$
$$\beta \rightarrow \overline{A}$$

Let us imagine now that the student has encountered (or is required to write) a sentence x in which there is a single conjunction "and." Is he to insert a comma or not? He refers to the rules, and they inform him: if the sentence is compound (α), then insert a comma (A); if it is simple (β), then do not insert a comma ($\overline{A}$). That is, the rules indicate how to proceed (how to transform the sentence) if the sentence type is known (simple or compound), but it is precisely this which is not immediately evident to the student. Consequently, before applying any rules (procedure A or $\overline{A}$), he must determine (recognize) the class to which the sentence belongs: α or β. The rules say nothing about this, however; they assume that the sentence type is obvious or that the student knows how to determine it. But it is often not obvious, and the student often cannot determine it. He knows what operations to perform on the sentence after its type has been

---

*We will also designate the actual act of inserting or not inserting a comma by A and $\overline{A}$, respectively.

determined, but does not know what operations to perform in order to determine the type.

This introduces the topic of identification algorithms.

The basic difference between identification algorithms and transformation algorithms is the fact that the purpose of the latter is to change objects, while the purpose of the former is to place them in a particular class (in order to determine the applicability of the rules of specific transformation algorithms and to effect the actual transformations in question on the basis of these rules). Moreover, transformation algorithms always include identification operations, although identification algorithms may or may not include transformation operations (or algorithms).[11] We will henceforth confine ourselves to the consideration of "pure" identification processes, i.e., ones which contain no transformation operations.

The essence of any identification process* involves a search for particular attributes (indicative features) of the object in question; and, on the basis of the presence or absence of these attributes, a conclusion is drawn regarding the object's membership in a particular class. But this process requires knowledge of the attributes which define particular classes of objects. These attributes are usually given by definitions and other theoretical propositions (rules, theorems, etc.).

Analysis of such statements shows that, in the first place, they may all be expressed in the form "if . . ., then . . . ." For example: "Verbs are words which indicate actions or states and which answer the question 'what is being done' " (Barkhydarov and Kryuchkov, 1965). In the "if . . ., then . . ." form, this definition will appear as follows: "If a word denotes an action or a state and answers the question 'what is being done,' then this word is called a verb." Our study showed that it is extremely important for the development of the student's ability to think to teach him

*We are here not considering identification at the *perceptual* level, but only at the *conceptual* level.

to express any theoretical proposition in the "if . . ., then . . ." form.*

Analysis of such propositions shows, in the second place, that the attributes indicated in formal propositions are always joined in a particular way. We have already indicated linkage by means of the logical connective "if . . ., then . . . ." Other logical connectives which join attributes are "and" and "or."

An example of a linkage using the logical connective "and" would be the following: "If any parts of a sentence answer the same question (attribute *a*) *and* refer to the same part (attribute *b*), then these parts are termed homogeneous (H)."

An example of linkage using the logical connective "or" would be: "If the shape of a solid body (attribute *c*) *or* its volume (attribute *d*) changes, then such change is termed a deformation (D)."

Let us write both these definitions in the language of symbolic logic. In order to do this, we will designate the logical connective "if . . ., then . . ." by the symbol ⇒, the connective "and" by the symbol &, and the connective "or" by the symbol V. The possession by an object *x* of an attribute *m* we write as *m*(*x*).

The above definitions may then be written:

$$a\,(x)\,\&\,b\,(x) \underset{\text{Df}}{\Leftrightarrow} \text{H}\,(x)$$

$$c\,(y)\,\text{V}\,d\,(y) \underset{\text{Df}}{\Leftrightarrow} \text{D}\,(y)$$

where *x* represents "parts of a sentence," and *y* "change." The two-headed arrows indicate that a linkage of the "if . . ., then . . ." type operates in both directions (i.e., "if, and only if, . . ." *Ed*.). The letters "Df" stand for the words "by definition."

If the expression "any parts of the sentence answer the same question," which we wrote as *a* (*x*) is regarded as a unit and represented by the letter *a*, and if the expression which

---

*The precise reason for this will become clear below. We will henceforth transform all formal propositions into the "if . . ., then . . ." form.

we wrote as b (x) is represented by the letter b, etc., then these definitions may be written in an even simpler form:

$$a \,\&\, b \underset{\text{Df}}{\Leftrightarrow} H$$

$$c \lor d \underset{\text{Df}}{\Leftrightarrow} D$$

We will term the joining of attributes by a given logical connective the logical structure of those attributes. Thus, attributes joined by the connective "and" (i.e., conjunctively) constitute a conjunctive structure, while attributes joined by the connective "or" (i.e., disjunctively) constitute a disjunctive structure.

These considerations are important because identification of objects depends on the way their attributes are associated, that is, on their logical structure.

If the relevant attributes are joined by the "and" connective (i.e., conjunctively), then, in order to determine whether a given object x is a member of a given class K, one must:

1. Check whether or not it has the first attribute.[12] If it does not, cease further checking and draw a negative conclusion.

2. If it does, then check whether or not it has the second attribute.

If it does not, then cease checking and draw a negative conclusion.

If it does, then

.

.

.

$n.$ Check whether or not it has the nth attribute. If it does not, then draw a negative conclusion. If it does, then draw a positive conclusion.

Let us apply the above method to two sentences: "*Young athletes and experienced masters were sitting in the room.*" "*Young and experienced athletes were sitting in the room.*" We must determine whether the words "young" and "experienced" are homogeneous parts. In the former sentence, these words have the first attribute characteristic of homogeneous parts, but not the second. They are thus not homogeneous parts. In the latter sentence, these words have both the first and the second attributes (i.e., all the attributes characteristic of homogeneous parts) and are, therefore, homogeneous parts.

If the attributes in question are joined by the connective "or" (disjunctively), then, in order to determine whether or not a given object y is a member of a given class L, one must:

1. Check whether or not it has the first attribute. If so, cease checking and draw a positive conclusion.
If not, then

2. Check whether or not it has the second attribute. If so, cease inspection and draw a positive conclusion.
If not, then

.
.
.

n. Check whether or not it has the nth attribute. If so, draw a positive conclusion.
If not, then draw a negative conclusion.

We will leave to the reader the application of this method to specific examples.

It is easy to see how these two methods differ. This difference may be expressed as follows. Let us assume that we have two formal statements or propositions, in one of which the attributes are conjunctively joined and in the other of which they are disjunctively joined:

$$a, \& a_2 \& a_3 \& \ldots \& a_n \Leftrightarrow K$$
$$b_1 \vee b_2 \vee b_3 \vee \ldots \vee b_n \Leftrightarrow L$$

Let us assume that we apply these statements to a set of objects and that, if a given attribute is present in the object in question, we write a plus-sign above the corresponding symbol, and if this attribute is absent, a minus. In the first instance, a plus in the right side of the definition may be written only when there are plusses over all the symbols in the left side. In the second definition, a plus may be written in the right side when there is a plus over at least one symbol. The reverse is also true: in the first instance a minus in the right side appears if even just one minus appears in the left side. In the second case, a minus in the right side appears only when minuses are written over all the symbols in the left side. For example:

$$\overset{+}{a_1} \,\&\, \overset{-}{a_2} \,\&\, a_3 \,\&\, \ldots a_n \Leftrightarrow K \qquad \overset{-}{b_1} \,v\, \overset{-}{b_2} \,v\, \overset{+}{b_3} \,v \ldots v\, b_n \Leftrightarrow \boldsymbol{L}$$

$$\overset{+}{a_1} \,\&\, \overset{+}{a_2} \,\&\, \overset{+}{a_3} \,\&\, \ldots \overset{+}{a_n} \Leftrightarrow \boldsymbol{K} \qquad \overset{-}{b_1} \,v\, \overset{-}{b_2} \,v\, \overset{-}{b_3} \,v \ldots v\, \overset{-}{b_n} \Leftrightarrow \boldsymbol{L}$$

These procedures for identifying phenomena are quite general and do not depend on the specific content of the attributes of the phenomena in question, nor on the subject area to which these phenomena belong.

We have examined instances in which attributes are joined either conjunctively or disjunctively. Very often, however, attributes are joined conjunctively-disjunctively and disjunctively-conjunctively. An example of this type of joining would be the definition of a verb introduced above: "If a word designates an action (attribute *e*) or a state (attribute *f*) AND answers the question 'what is being done' (attribute *g*), then this word is called a verb (V)."

This may be written symbolically as:

$$(e \lor f) \,\&\, g \underset{\text{Df}}{\Leftrightarrow} V$$

The above procedures applicable to purely conjunctive and purely disjunctive attribute structures imply the procedures appropriate in instances involving conjunctive-disjunctive and disjunctive-conjunctive structures as well.

Analysis of mistakes made by students in solving many mathematical as well as grammatical problems (it may be assumed, clearly, that this applies equally to problems in other areas) has shown that these errors are often caused by the fact that students:

a. do not understand what an attribute is, why they are necessary, and what should be done with them during learning of the material and during the solution of problems;

b. know nothing of the possible ways in which attributes may be joined and are unaware of the logical connectives joining them; and

c. do not know methods of operating with objects as a function of a given type of joining (linkage) between attributes (i.e., their logical structure).

We will cite only one example. Students in elementary school and even later grades very often make the following mistake. Let us assume that they are required to determine what part of speech a word such as "whiteness" might be. They often answer that it is an adjective. Why? Because it denotes an attribute which an object may possess.

Here is a definition of the adjective written in the "if . . ., then . . ." form. "If a word denotes an attribute (attribute *a*) of an object AND answers the question *which*? (attribute *b*) or the question *whose*? (attribute *c*), then this word is termed an adjective (A)."

In symbolic form this would be:

$$a \ \& \ (b \lor c) \underset{Df}{\Leftrightarrow} A$$

The students' mistake is caused by the fact that they check the word in question for attribute *a* only, although this attribute is followed by a conjunction sign (i.e., the connective "and"), which means that, for the word to be an adjective, attributes *b* or *c* also must be present. But the students' fail to check the word for these attributes and so draw a positive conclusion on the basis of the presence of attribute *a* alone. It is immediately clear from this example that the source of error lies in the students' lack of awareness of the logical structure of the attributes which define the adjective and in lack of correspondence between their method of proceeding and this logical structure.

We stated above that algorithms are instructions for carrying out, in a particular order, some system of operations for solving all problems of a particular class. In transformation algorithms, the importance of the order in which the operations are performed is often quite obvious. Thus, for example, changing the order of operations in the division algorithm will prevent the numbers from dividing properly, or will result in error. This does not mean that there is only one possible order of operations in all transformation algorithms. Transformation problems may often be solved using various orders of operations. This means, however, that there exist various algorithms for solving the same problem. The number of algorithms for solving a given transformation problem—whether there is one or many—must be determined for each individual case. Identification algorithms are another matter. If the number of attributes which must be verified in an object during its recognition is more than one, then there is always more than one algorithm by which it may be identified. This is due to the following circumstance. Let us assume that we have some formal proposition, for example the rule a & b & $c \rightarrow$ A. The logical connective "and" (as well as the logical connective "or") possesses the property of commutativity.[13] This means that it does not matter whether the object is checked for attribute a first, then b, then c, or c, then b, then a, etc. It is clear that for three attributes the number of possible orders is equal to the number of permutations of three objects, i.e., $P_3 = 3 \times 2 \times 1 = 6$. For n attributes the number of possible verification sequences is equal, therefore, to P_n. We may, then, say that there are six algorithms corresponding to the formal proposition (formula) a & b & $c \rightarrow$ A (each sequence of operations being one algorithm) or, equivalently, that six algorithms are contained latently, as it were, in the formula. We note in this connection that the formula itself is not an algorithm, since it itself does not prescribe how to proceed (it is only a formal proposition establishing a dependence between a, b, c, and A), but various algorithms correspond to it, in that it may serve as a basis for them.*

*For example, instruction No. 1: "First check attribute a; if it is present, check attribute b"; etc. Instruction No. 2: "First check attribute b; if it is present, then check attribute a"; etc.

Is it necessary to devise and teach algorithms if formulae exist? Is it not sufficient to teach students to go from formulae to algorithms? In fact, the basic task facing education in this regard is to teach students to discover independently the logical structure of theoretical propositions (and, where necessary, to design these statements independently) and to move independently from a theoretical proposition to one of the possible algorithms corresponding to it. But to which one?

At this point, it turns out that, although it makes no difference logically which of the algorithms corresponding to a given formal proposition is used to carry out the identification process—they all lead to the same result—it makes a great deal of difference psychologically. "Psychologically" speaking, we have in mind here that aspect of cognitive activity which is associated with the efficiency of the methods of thinking which are being applied. The following simple example will clarify what is meant.

Let us assume that we must find a book which is located either in location a, or in location b, or in location c (for example, in a bookcase, on a shelf, or on a writing table).* Symbolically the situation may be represented as follows: the book is located in a V b V c. Logically it makes no difference how we find the book, or in what sequence we check the different possible locations. If the book is located in one of the three places, we have found what we are looking for. But from the point of view of the efficiency of search, the sequence in which the locations are checked is extremely important. It is clear that, for example, if the probability of finding the book in location a is greater than that of finding it in location b, and the probability of finding it in location b is greater than that of finding it in location c, then the optimal search strategy (checking of locations) will be the following: check a first, then b, then c. If the probability of finding the book in location a is denoted by p (a), and similarly with the other two locations, and the instruction "check the locations in the sequence a, b, c" is denoted by the symbol T (a, b, c), then the optimal search strategy (the optimal algorithm) may be written:

*In a more general form this situation was considered in Landa (1974).

$$p\ (a) \geqslant p\ (b) \geqslant p\ (c) \rightarrow T\ (a,\ b,\ c).^{14}$$

However, this formula is correct only for the case in which the times required to check each location are the same. Thus, although it seldom happens that the probability of finding a book in a large bookcase is greater than that of finding it on a small shelf, the search time in the former case is significantly greater, and so it is far from obvious that the search should begin with the bookcase. The formula indicating the optimal search strategy for this case is:

$$\frac{p\ (a)}{t\ (a)} \geqslant \frac{p\ (b)}{t\ (b)} \geqslant \frac{p(c)}{t\ (c)} \rightarrow T\ (a,\ b,\ c)$$

where $t\ (a)$ is the time required to check location a, $t\ (b)$ is the time required to check location b, etc.

It is easy to see that this example is fully analogous to the identification process. In this process, also, we check something (search), namely particular attributes of the object in question. These attributes may be encountered with varying probabilities, and the search for (checking of) various attributes may require different amounts of time. From this it is clear that although logically (with regard to achieving a final result) all algorithms corresponding to some theoretical statement (formula) are equivalent, they are not equivalent from the point of view of efficiency. It is for this reason that it is insufficient to teach students theoretical propositions and ways to go from theoretical propositions to a possible algorithm; they must be taught the most efficient algorithms and methods for designing them independently. Calculations show that working with inefficient algorithms results, in the case of repeated solution of problems of the same type, in the necessity of performing thousands and tens of thousands of superfluous operations. This hampers and slows the learning process in any particular problem solution, and sharply lowers the productivity of the learning process as a whole.[15]

The situation changes when the process of *consecutive*

checking of attributes of an object is being gradually transformed into a process of a *simultaneous* (or parallell) singling out of its relevant attributes during its cognizing or recognizing.* It is a very important stage in the formation of a student's cognitive abilities which result in the development of the ability to identify objects (phenomena) instantaneously, at the first glance.

The transition from a consecutive to a simultaneous process (or, the transformation of a consecutive process into a simultaneous one) changes its character and its underlying regulatory mechanism. Since it proceeds now not in a "step-by-step" manner but in an "at once" manner, it would not be justified to call it algorithmic in the proper sense of the word. We shall call it "post-algorithmic simultaneous process" or "overlearned algorithmic."

The essential difference between these two processes in their psychological regulation consists, as we can suppose, in the following.

Actions taken in accordance with an algorithm (guided by a prescription) are carried out at the first stages of their assimilation through "self-commands" or "self-instructions." Proceeding according to the instructions of an algorithm, an individual says to himself (gives himself self-instructions) what is to be done at each step of the corresponding activity. Gradually, direct associations are established between the actions and the objects toward which they are directed, on the one hand, and between the actions themselves, on the other hand. After these associations have been established, the actions can be elicited not by self-instructions, i.e., by signals of the second signal system, but directly by the objects themselves and/or other actions. The necessity for special self-instructions disappears, and they are gradually extinguished.

Formation of direct associations between actions and objects means formation of associations between primary and secondary images of objects, on the one hand, and images of actions, on the

---

*It would be more accurate to say "simultaneous" or "nearly simultaneous," but we for brevity will sometimes say below "simultaneous," having in mind both cases.

other hand. The image of an object which appears in the mind as a result of its perception or is elicited by other images or signals from the second signal system brings about images of certain actions which may lead to the goal facing the individual. The latter images entail, in turn, performing real actions. But since each object is "made-up" of definite components and is a substratum of definite attributes which are structurally associated with each other, the corresponding image of the object is, in turn, "made up" of associations between images of these components and the object's attributes (we will speak below only of attributes). It represents a constellation of associations.

Each system or constellation of associations has as its material physiological substratum a system (or a constellation or a mosaic) of nervous excitations. According to Anokhin's conception (1962), when a system of consecutive stimuli repeatedly affects an organism, the initial stimulus arouses a chain of heightened precursory (anticipating) excitations in the brain which correspond to stimuli which were previously associated with the eliciting one. These increased excitations prepare the brain for the perception of forthcoming expected stimuli. These expectations are not necessarily psychological; often, they are, so to say, expectations of the nervous system—"nervous expectations"—of which the conscious mind is not aware. One may suppose that precisely this mosaic of precursory increased excitations which are probabilistic in nature creates the brain's readiness for a simultaneous perception of sets of an object's relevant attributes and which enables instantaneous identification. But why does the brain single out and select exactly the relevant attributes when simultaneous identification has been formed on the basis of previously consecutive identification guided by an algorithm?

Earlier, at the first stage of proceeding according to an algorithm, there was no mosaic of required increased excitations in the brain which would correspond to relevant attributes of an object to be identified. In order to isolate this or that relevant attribute of an object in the process of its perception and identification, a special self-instruction to examine this attribute had to be given by the individual to himself (each self-instruction was determined by a corresponding instruction of the algorithm). This self-instruction created a psychological set for singling-out a specific attribute of the object which expressed itself physiologically in the development within the brain of a corresponding increased precursory excitation (in reality it is, of course, a whole system of excited "points"). The latter created a readiness for singling out the required relevant attribute, and facilitated its isolation and perception. The next self-instruction created the set for singling out the next relevant attribute, which was involved with the development of one more precursory increased excitation, etc. Thus, the whole system (set) of precursory increased excitations arises, which creates preparedness for directed and easier isolation and perception of a system of relevant attributes. Now it is sufficient to perceive only one attribute of the object or merely to imagine the possibility of encountering the object or to intend to check whether some object belongs or does not belong to a definite class, and the system of precursory increased excitations is evoked and the brain becomes ready to isolate and perceive all relevant attributes. After a mosaic of increased excitations has been established, it becomes possible to perceive and identify a number of attributes simultaneously, or nearly simultaneously, on the one hand, and without self-instructions, on the other hand.* The conscious, deliberate, and consecutive algorithmic process of perception and identification is being transformed into a non-conscious (more accurately, post-conscious),** involuntary and simultaneous (or nearly simultaneous) post-algorithmic process.

*There are some reasons for thinking that the transition from a consecutive to a simultaneous (or nearly simultaneous) process (or: turning of a consecutive process into a simultaneous one) proceeds not by leaps but gradually in the sense that at some stages of transition some attributes are already being isolated simultaneously while others are still being isolated consecutively in accordance with self-instructions.

**It is important to distinguish between two kinds of non-conscious processes: those which have never been conscious (initially non-conscious or pre-conscious) and those which became non-conscious as a result of a

As a rule, the transformation from one type of process (algorithmic) to another (simultaneous post-algorithmic) proceeds by itself (spontaneously) in the course of repeatedly acting according to an algorithm. Observations show, however, that, with some students, some difficulties and delays can occur in this transformation. Some students are sometimes not sure that they have learned algorithmic instructions and their corresponding operations sufficiently well and, therefore, address themselves to the explicitly given algorithmic instructions (for instance, written on the blackboard, in the notebook, etc.) or to memorized self-instructions for a much longer period of time than is needed. Others are afraid of making a mistake if they cease to consult the explicit algorithm or to recall self-instructions, or if they cease to check consciously each action and its results, comparing them with the instructions of the algorithm (in the latter case, they reproduce instructions *after* the corresponding action has been performed, and instructions appear here as a means of self-checking). Thus, these students hold on to an initial mode of conscious and consecutive actions even though they are able to give it up and to begin to act "automatically" and simultaneously. All this artificiality hampers the transition from the first to the second type of regulation and control of identification processes.

There exist some other reasons which may hamper the transition from one stage or type of process to the other. That is why it is in some cases important to control and direct the process of transition from one type to another, for which some techniques (procedures, methods) were developed. The description of these

---

transformation of previously conscious processes into non-conscious ones (secondary non-conscious or post-conscious). The transformation consists, as we have already mentioned, in a gradual extinction of regulation and control over these processes through self-instructions. Self-instructions gradually cease to be recalled and to guide the progress of the cognitive operations. They begin to be elicited "automatically" by the goal, i.e., images of the objects to be obtained by forthcoming transformation, by the objects perceived and by other actions. One may suppose that transition from the first type of regulation and control of actions to the latter type represent precisely that which is often called "automatization."

techniques is a task of its own. Here we intend only to show that processes which are currently non-conscious and simultaneous may have been originally conscious, consecutive, and algorithmic. Moreover, our experience suggests that the most effective way to shape them perfectly, i.e., without defects in composition and structure, is to shape them *gradually*, operation-by-operation, since only in this way can their formation be controlled and not be haphazard.

We have tried to show above that the conscious, consecutive isolation of objects' attributes in the course of acting according to an algorithm creates a set of precursory, increased excitations in the brain. These excitations are the basis, on the one hand, for "nervous expectations" of forthcoming stimuli and for their instantaneous (simultaneous) perception and identification, on the other hand. But expectations may arise not only on the "nervous level" but on the psychological level as well. The process of consecutive isolation of objects' attributes which are therefore perceived may result, and often does result, in the formation of psychological associations between them (chains of associations). This creates the ability while perceiving one or several attributes of an object to anticipate the availability in the object or the appearance in it of some other attributes which were linked earlier with this (or these) one (ones). Since the linkage between attributes is often of a probabilistic nature, the prognosis is usually also probabilistic.

What has just been said may seem to contradict what had been said earlier as to simultaneous perception of sets of attributes and simultaneous, or nearly simultaneous, identification of objects. In reality there is no contradiction, since there exist cases when, because of physical conditions, it is impossible to perceive *all* attributes simultaneously. There exist also situations when even the access to some attributes, whose consideration is necessary for a sufficiently founded conclusion is for various reasons impossible or difficult. In another situation one may perceive the whole set of attributes from which one may draw deterministic conclusions as to the category to which the object belongs (this complex set being sufficient for such a conclusion) but isolate only a part of this set and draw a probabilistic conclusion. We shall not here discuss the psychological reasons for this phenomenon and note only that they may be different, e.g., lack of time, high probability of availability of some specific attributes when some others are available (consideration of all attributes here is in many cases not economical), and some others. What is important for us here is the fact that chains of probabilistic associations condition perception so that only one or a small number of *insufficient* attributes of an object may immediately elicit the imaging of some other probable attributes of the probable category to which this object belongs.* (The "middle chain" of the process drops from consciousness, and there is awareness only of the beginning and final stages of the process.)

This is precisely what takes place in some types of intuition and insight. An example which may serve is that of the common and well-known situation of first meeting a person with whom one has been previously unacquainted and, after instantaneous perception of some external attributes, coming to a conclusion that he is a kind person or he is wicked, or he is artful, and so on. One did not and could not perceive these psychological traits, because they are for the most part not observable. One could also not perceive those acts of behavior in which these traits are displayed and which are sufficient for such a conclusion. One could only perceive some of such external features of another person which were, in the observer's past experience, associated

---

*All this is true not only of the anticipation (prognosis, expectation) of the availability or appearance of some attributes in an object provided some others have been perceived, but also of the anticipation of certain (specific) objects (things, phenomena, etc.) when other objects previously associated with this have been encountered. In other words, all that has been said in regard to perception and prognosis of attributes within one object is true of perception and prognosis of objects themselves and even their systems. Identified in the latter case are not single objects (on the basis of their attributes which appear as indicative or distinctive features), but systems of objects (situations) or systems of objects' systems (complex events). The distinguishing, indicative features which appear here are not attributes of particular objects but the objects themselves and/or their subsystems.

with this or that behavioral trait and whose perception evokes a probabilistic conclusion. To the question: why do you think that this man is kind or wicked, etc., often follows this answer: "I feel it *intuitively*."

Obviously, such "intuitive feeling" is simply the assignment of the perceived person to a definite class, i.e., his identification, on the basis of insufficient attributes, due only to the systems of probabilistic associations which were established earlier. Since any conclusion(s) on the basis of insufficient attributes is merely probabilistic, intuitive conclusions of such kind are also merely of a probabilistic character and may prove to be wrong.

We have indicated above in regard to intuition that one is not always aware of the "middle chain" of the process but is aware of the starting and final points. There may and do exist also varieties of intuition in which one is not aware of the starting point of the process. In one case the observer does not know which attributes were the basis for his conclusion. In other cases he is not even aware of the act of perception itself of the object, which is the bearer of appropriate attributes. His intuitive conclusions emerge here in the form of unfounded presentiments, expectations, estimations, etc.

Chains of associations are being formed in people in the course of everyday life and routine activity and, thus, create the prerequisite conditions for intuition to arise spontaneously and to develop haphazardly. This spontaneously formed intuition may be more or less rich, more or less correct, and this expresses itself in the fact that one person "intuitively feels" something at times when another does not "feel." One person may "feel" (foresee, prognose, guess, etc.) correctly more often than the other, because he assesses the degree of probability of correctness of his prognosis more precisely than the other.

What has this to do with the problem of teaching algorithms?

The qualities of intuition just mentioned depend on which attributes of the object a person isolated or singled-out in the process of perception, and how he structured them. They depend on the relevance of each of these attributes and their different combinations. They depend further on the person's subjective, probabilistic estimation of the object's belonging to some category, provided he isolated the appropriate attribute or their appropriate structure.

The latter abilities mentioned depend, in turn, on which attributes of an object someone has encountered in his preceding experience and with which probabilities; were these attributes relevant or not, and, if relevant, which was the degree of their relevancy; how often did specific combinations of these attributes prove to constitute the basis for correct conclusions as to the object's belonging to a definite category and how often did they lead to erroneous conclusions; did the person in question manage to correctly grasp the logical and probabilistic structure of attributes or not; and so on.

In everyday life all this is a result of a great many random and haphazard factors, which helps to explain why the quality and development of intuition in various people is so diverse.

Teaching algorithms may make these factors (or at least most of them) controllable to a considerable degree, thereby creating conditions for purposeful and conscious formation in students of abilities underlying our type of intuition. Indeed, teaching algorithms may form in students the ability to isolate attributes in objects and to take into account those attributes and their structures which are relevant for correct conclusions. Knowing the appropriate algorithm enables them to encounter with them that frequency which will shape the most appropriate probabilistic estimates, and so on.

In ordinary life the abilities underlying intuition are usually not the result of any previous consecutive and conscious processes. However, when formed on the basis of algorithms, they can be shaped through a transition from conscious consecutive to post-conscious, simultaneous (instantaneous) processes. But in contrast to simultaneous post-algorithmic processes, which are deterministic (these processes were discussed some pages above when the definition of post-algorithmic processes was introduced), the latter are probabilistic.

A simple example may demonstrate how the transition from consecutive algorithmic to simultaneous post-algorithmic (both processes are deterministic), and then to simultaneous probabilistic processes, are brought about.

Let us assume that some object x belongs to some class A, if it has attributes a, b, and c.

$$a\,(x)\ \&\ b\,(x)\ \&\ c\,(x) \rightarrow A\,(x).$$

On the basis of this formal proposition, it is easy, if needed, to design an algorithm which will indicate which attributes of any specific object x one must examine and in which sequence in order to determine whether it does or does not belong to class A. (There can exist a total of $3 \cdot 2 \cdot 1 = 6$ possible identification algorithms depending on the sequence in which attributes are examined.)

When one examines the attributes in the object consecutively, one executes a consecutive algorithmic process.

When one arrives at the ability to perceive all the attributes in the object simultaneously, one has progressed to a simultaneous post-algorithmic process, i.e., the consecutive algorithmic process has turned into a simultaneous post-algorithmic process.

Both processes are deterministic in the sense that the person in question examines *all* of the indicated attributes (indicative features) in the object and draws a univocal conclusion, depending on which attributes are present or absent in some specific object x. Thus, for instance, if some object x has attributes a, b, and c, one may draw a conclusion that it belongs to class A with complete confidence. If at least one of the attributes is absent, then one draws a conclusion that it does not belong to class A, also with complete confidence. In connection with what has just been said, a simultaneous, post-algorithmic process of this type may be called also a simultaneous, deterministic, post-algorithmic process.

Let us assume, however, that someone acting in just such a way for some time observed that when attributes a and b are present in the object, as a rule (but not always!) attribute c is also present. In the language of science this means that the probability of attribute c under conditions characterized by the presence of a and b (i.e., a conditional probability) is rather high.

Having encountered such a regularity of co-occurrence, the person consciously or unconsciously began, while engaged in the process of recognizing, to save time and effort by examining for the presence in the object not of three but only two of three indicative features (attributes) a and b.

It is clear that the presence in an object of only two attributes does not permit one to draw the univocal, i.e., deterministic, conclusion that object x belongs to class A. In some cases, namely, when a and b are combined with $\bar{c}$, object x belongs to the class A. But if the probability of $\bar{c}$ under conditions of a and b is low—say, pab $(\bar{c})$ = 0.02 which is equivalent to pab (c) = 0.98, then the probability of erroneously relating object x to class A on the basis of checking only *two* attributes is also low (in our example there would normally be only two errors in each series of a hundred identifications). In any case, however, the conclusion as to the belonging of some object x to class A on the basis of examining an incomplete set of attributes is of a probabilistic nature.

Thus, the process in question is probabilistic and simultaneous (both attributes are checked simultaneously). It is also post-algorithmic, since it was formed on the basis of preceding actions carried out according to an algorithmic prescription, and represents some transformation of a simultaneous post-algorithmic deterministic process. As distinct from a simultaneous post-algorithmic deterministic process, the latter may be called a simultaneous post-algorithmic probabilistic process.

Returning now to the examination of the mechanisms in some types of intuition, we can say now that one of the mechanisms is a simultaneous post-algorithmic probabilistic process.

The difference between intuitions formed on an algorithmic basis and those formed spontaneously lies not only in the fact that the first is post-algorithmic while the second is not, but also in the character of awareness: the first is post-conscious while the second is sub-conscious. We shall not repeat here what was said earlier about possible differences in the degree of "richness" and the correctness of intuition.

We have just noted the difference between a simultaneous deterministic post-algorithmic process and a simultaneous probabilistic post-algorithmic process in regard to the character of their results. The result of the former represents a deterministic (absolute, univocal, reliable) conclusion as to the belonging of an object to a definite category. It presupposes and requires the isolation and taking into account of the complete set of the relevant object's attributes, i.e., their sufficient set. The result of the latter represents a probabilistic conclusion based on the isolation and consideration of an incomplete set of relevant attributes, i.e., their insufficient set. In order to increase the probability of the correct conclusions in the presence of insufficient attributes, it is important to previously create experiences for the students (when it is possible) in drawing conclusions on the basis of sufficient attributes. It is exactly this experience which is successfully created during teaching in accordance with an algorithm. All this explains why development of algorithmic processes is the first stage in the development of future intuition. Algorithmization may be one of the ways for purposeful and controllable shaping of "efficient intuition."

What has been said is true, one may think, not only of the controllable development of this type of intuition but, also, for the development of similar processes. For example, if a student is taught to apply different algorithms to one and the same object leading to its inclusion, at different times, into different classes (categories), then this develops in the student the ability to isolate different subsets of attributes in one and the same object. The transition from consecutive algorithmic (via different algorithms) to simultaneous post-algorithmic processes leads to the development in the student of the ability to grasp various subsets of an object's attributes instantaneously (or nearly instantaneously) and to include it instantaneously or in rapid succession in different categories. One may believe that precisely this ability underlies the capability of "regarding the objects from different points of view," of "seeing relations," of "being able to approach the objects differently," of "reconceptualizing them," and the like. Though, at the first glance and phenomenologically, these processes have nothing to do with algorithmic ones and are antithetical to them, they may—if formed in an appropriate way—become, through development and subsequent transformation, algorithmic processes.

The design of efficient identification algorithms is a relatively simple task when the algorithm is to be designed on the basis of one proposition in which attributes are joined by the connectives "and" or "or." The situation is significantly more complicated when an identification algorithm is to be derived from several propositions. In this case, the most efficient sequence in which attributes should be examined is often not at all obvious, and design of an algorithm is a rather complex task. Much more complex is the task (of designing an algorithm) when the propositions themselves have not been formulated, or have been formulated incompletely or defectively. Here the design of the algorithm must be preceded by a theoretical analysis of corresponding phenomena, establishing their attributes and the relationships between them, determining the attributes which may serve as necessary and/or sufficient indicative features for identification, and, therefrom, stating definitions, theorems, and other formal propositions.

It is easy to imagine the difficult situation in which the student finds himself when a large number of far from simple rules are "piled" on top of him. How is he to proceed in a given specific situation? Which rules should he apply? Which attributes of the object should be examined and in what sequence? Rules alone do not give the answers to any of these questions. The answers can be given only by an algorithm. But such an algorithm does not derive directly and automatically from the rules themselves (although it is compiled on the basis of them). It cannot be found in textbooks, and it is usually not taught to the teacher, either. (Is it any surprise, then, for example, that so many grammatical topics are so difficult for students to learn and that, even after finishing school, they make such a great many grammatical errors? Yet, writing an identification algorithm in many cases permits the solution of a complex grammatical problem in three to five operations at most.)

Experience in teaching algorithms has shown the high efficacy of such instruction. It would be wrong to suppose, of course, that it is necessary to present algorithms in completed form. Correctly structured teaching of algorithms presupposes that students will learn to discover them and the general methods for devising them independently. These skills are of great importance in the development of the students' ability to think creatively. Properly conducted teaching of algorithms also develops such qualities of thinking as organization, systematicity, precision, and thoroughness.

In this chapter, we have examined only an insignificant proportion of the issues relating to the problem of the algorithmization of instruction. In particular, we have not even touched on questions concerning the place of algorithms in a general instructional system, the relation between algorithmic and non-algorithmic processes in thinking (in particular, we did not compare methods for solving geometric problems, which have a significant non-algorithmic, i.e., heuristic, component, with algorithmic techniques for solving grammatical problems), the structure of non-algorithmic processes and the importance of explicitly teaching them to students, methods for teaching algorithmic processes, algorithms governing the activity of the teacher as well as that of the student, the relation of the problem of algorithmization to the problem of programmed instruction, and others. Answers to some of these questions may be found in subsequent chapters.

Notes

1. This is relevant to the preceding example as well. The statement that the student "was unable to relate segment AB to segments AC, BE, CB, and AE" does not imply any means of teaching the student to solve the problem. In this example, the student may be taught to correlate the segments in question, but doing this will not help him solve other, similar problems, since other problems may require him to correlate other segments.

2. This experiment is briefly discussed in Landa (1959). Problems of reading diagrams are touched upon also in Kabanova-Meller (1962) and Zykova (1955).

3. Poor students, of course, often have a weak grasp of these things as well. But we will not discuss this aspect of the problem at this time. For purposes of the experiment, we tested our subjects' knowledge of all relevant geometric information, and filled in any gaps in this knowledge where these were found to occur.

4. A.N. Leontiev's term (1947).

5. The degree of the student's mastery of each operation (in particular, the degree of its generalization, or the degree to which he can generalize it) is also a significant factor, but this is another question, and we will not deal with it in this chapter. We will concentrate our attention, for the most part, on the composition and structure of the operations required for the solution of particular classes of problems and on their systematic interrelationships.

6. It is sometimes expedient to apply the second operation before the first.

7. This sort of problem was posed, for example, by G. Polya (1942). Polya's prescriptions, however, are in many cases so imprecise and non-specific (for example, "examine the unknowns," "formulate the problem in a different way," "derive something useful from the givens") that they cannot be used to direct the flow of cognitive operations. We have set ourselves the problem of analyzing the process of searching for proof into operations which are elementary enough for the task at hand and of writing instructions based on these operations. An analogous problem in the area of writing programs to prove theorems by computer is described by Newell, Shaw, and Simon (1959, 1960). However, our effort and that of these authors were carried out independently of each other, and the American authors published their first results after our project was completed in 1955 and defended as a Ph.D. dissertation.

8. The methodology and results of the experiment are described

in greater detail in Landa (1959). See also Chapter Eight of this book.

9. A typical problem would be having to decide whether to write the letter "e" or "i" in a given word (the corresponding sounds are often indistinguishable in Russian, *Trans.*), or whether or not to insert a comma at a particular point in a sentence.

10. We note that the instructions which we compiled for proving geometric propositions were, to a significant degree, heuristic in nature. In this chapter, however, we will not be concerned with the distinction between algorithmic and heuristic instruction, since this aspect of the question has been discussed elsewhere (Landa, 1966, 1974). See also Chapter Six of this book.

11. An example of identification by means of transformation would be operations for transforming some device (dismantling it, for example) in order to ascertain (recognize) the reason for its malfunctioning.

12. Some numeration of attributes is assumed. Such numeration is normally arbitrary.

13. This property is well-known in mathematics. Thus, for example, if we are to add the two numbers 8 and 5, then it is of no consequence whether we add 5 to 8 or 8 to 5 (i.e., $5 + 8 = 8 + 5$). The order of the operations makes no difference.

14. In this and analogous formulae we will use the non-rigorous inequality. This is done for purposes of generality, in order to include cases in which quantities related by $\geq$ (or $\leq$) are equal.

15. Lack of space prevents us from describing here methods for calculating efficient algorithms of cognitive activity; instead, we refer the reader to our book, *Algorithmization in Learning and Instruction* (1974). This book goes into much of the subject-matter of this chapter in greater detail.

Chapter Five

The Relation Between Heuristic
and Algorithmic Processes

The potential of various educational techniques and organizational forms is determined primarily by the material which is to be taught, and by the characteristics of the processes which are to be influenced and controlled through instructional procedures. It is obvious that different types of processes require different means for their formation and regulation. This applies, first of all, to algorithmic and heuristic processes. In order to be able to determine the potential of some instructional method in this respect, it is necessary to consider the characteristics of creative (heuristic) processes relative to those of non-creative (non-heuristic) processes.

In spite of the fact that much material has been published on the subject of heuristics and heuristic programming, the concepts and terms of heuristics and heuristic processes are not entirely unambiguous and are interpreted differently by different authors.

Thus, some authors (e.g., Feigenbaum and Feldman, 1963) understand heuristics as rules which are capable of directing heuristic activity,* and others (e.g., Newell, Shaw, and Simon, 1957) as specific sorts of processes.** Still others (e.g., Miller,

---

*Feigenbaum and Feldman state: "A heuristic (heuristic rule, heuristic method) is a rule of thumb, strategy, trick, simplification, or any other kind of device which drastically limits search for a solution in a large problem space" (p. 6).

**Newell, Shaw, and Simon state: "A process that may solve a given problem, but offers no guarantees of doing so, is called a *heuristic* for that problem" (p. 114 in Feigenbaum and Feldman, 1963, where the paper of these authors is reprinted). And: "We will use heuristics as a noun synonymous with heuristic process" (*Ibid.*).

Galanter, and Pribram, 1960) utilize this term in both senses, depending on the context. It should be noted that the terminology in this area is very diversified and not always sufficiently differentiated. Thus, on only one page (p. 183), Miller, Galanter, and Pribram utilize such terms as "heuristic devices," "heuristic methods," "heuristic rules of thumb," "heuristic schemes," "heuristic tricks," and "heuristic suggestions." On other pages they speak also of "heuristic plans," "heuristics," and "heuristic principles." Other authors speak of "heuristic procedures" (e.g, Gelernter, 1959), or of "heuristic connections" (Minsky, 1961), and so on.

To our view, it is advisable to understand heuristics as specific rules of instructions governing actions and not as the actions themselves or any processes influencing the solution of a problem involving creativity. The basic problem in heuristic programming consists precisely of the writing of programs which are capable of evoking and directing heuristic processes, and this requires that a sharp distinction be made between heuristic rules and heuristic activity (or processes). Of course, the heuristic process, like any other cognitive process, can proceed in a non-rule-governed way, but it can be modeled and controlled only on the basis of rules.

Henceforth, as some other authors do, we will understand heuristics as meaning rules of heuristic activity, or as instructions on how to perform this activity.

The relation between heuristic and algorithmic processes and methods (rules) is also not uniformly defined identically in current work on heuristics. Some authors (e.g., Tonge, 1963) simply state that the relation between them is often vague, while others—the majority (e.g., Feigenbaum and Feldman, 1963; Gelernter and Rochester, 1958; Miller, Galanter, and Pribram, 1960)—consider the distinction between them to lie in the fact that algorithms *guarantee* a solution to a problem, while heuristic methods do not, although they often permit reaching a solution with less expenditure of time and resources.

This characterization of the relation between heuristic programs and algorithms is quite true but not sufficient. It emphasizes their distinction from the point of view of final results of processes which are governed by them (this is, so to say, the characteristics of external behavior), but leaves unclear the distinction in inner relationships between instructions, of which both algorithms and heuristic programs are made up, and their governed processes. This is why a question arises as to what constitutes the "creative factor" in heuristic programs, and why it should be considered that they model (simulate, imitate) creative thinking and may therefore be termed heuristic.

In order to examine these questions, we will consider one of the well-known heuristic programs, the "General Problem Solver" (GPS) elaborated by Newell, Shaw, and Simon (1959, 1960, and 1961). This program initially was written for the purpose of proving logic theorems, but the main ideas of the program may be applied to programs for the solution of other problems which are to some extent analogous (proving geometrical theorems, transforming trigonometric expressions, playing chess, etc.). Effective non-search algorithms cannot be written to solve these problems. The only type of algorithm which can solve these problems is the trial-and-error algorithm (i.e., search, *Ed.*). However, the number of variants which must be searched through and tested in order to arrive at a solution is often so large that the exhaustive search procedure is impossible in practice. This leads to the problem of reducing the number of searches which must be performed, or of reducing the size of the field from which variants may be selected. This reduction is achieved through the use of what program authors call heuristics (heuristic rules, methods, procedures, processes, etc.).

The following are examples of rules of this sort: Begin not with what is given but with what is to be proved; break up the goal into subgoals; find the difference between that which is to be proved and that which is given (a special table of differences* is introduced for this purpose); transform that which is to be proved (the subgoals) in such a way as to reduce these differences; etc.

In order to answer the question posed above as to whether

*Between initial conditions and desired outcomes. (*Editor.*)

this program and similar ones constitute a simulation model of creative thinking and may therefore be termed heuristic, the question must be formulated in another form: Are these programs algorithms? If they are not, then how do they differ from algorithms?

The basic properties of algorithms, as they are formulated in the classical (mathematical) theory of algorithms (see, e.g., Markov, 1954; Trakhtenbrot, 1957), are specificity, generality, and resultivity.

Specificity indicates the fact that all actions of the user of an algorithm (a person or a machine) are unambiguously determined by instructions (rules), and that these instructions are identically (or uniformly) understandable and understood by all users, since they are addressed to sufficiently elementary operations to be performed in the same way by all users of the algorithm; having started from the same initial conditions and proceeding in accordance with the instructions, all users will arrive at a single, identical result.

Generality means applicability of an algorithm to an entire (often infinite) set of problems belonging to a particular class, rather than to a single problem, or, in other words, that any objects from some class of objects, and not just certain particular ones, may constitute the initial data of a problem (for example, numbers, logical expressions, etc.).

Resultivity indicates that the algorithm is always directed toward achieving the sought-after result, which the user, once he (or it) possesses the appropriate initial data, always achieves. We note, however, that resultivity does not mean that the goal is achieved with *any* type of initial data. The initial data may be deficient such that the algorithm may terminate without result or continue indefinitely without arriving at the desired result.

From this characterization it is clear that resultivity is only one of the properties of algorithms (and, in addition, not absolute), and that one of the most important properties is the unambiguous and complete determination of actions performed by a problem-solving system (man or machine) on the part of the instructions of which algorithmic prescriptions are made up. By the way, precisely this property provides the high "guarantee" of correct solutions by the solving systems, when all problem-solving systems, acting in accordance with a valid algorithm, arrive at one and the same identical solution. Of course, the "guarantee" in the latter sense is different from that in the sense of the resultivity of which there is a question in heuristic programming. We want only to emphasize that algorithms do provide a "guarantee" in both senses.

If we examine so-called heuristic programs from the point of view of these properties of algorithms, it is clear that they do not differ from algorithms in two basic properties stipulating the character of relationships between instructions and their implementing operations (processes) and, thus, the type of regulation and control over operations on the part of instructions. Heuristic programs display both specificity and generality (the programs in question rigorously and fully determine the solution process, evoking from different users identical actions and leading, with the same initial data, to the same transformations; moreover, like algorithms, they can utilize as initial data any objects from a given class). The only difference between them and algorithms is in regard to resultivity, or, more precisely, the degree of resultivity. The resultivity of algorithms is significantly greater than that of the programs in question, but this difference, though significant in practice, is nevertheless only quantitative in nature.

Let us attempt to understand the nature of this difference. In order to do this, we will consider the problems in logical or geometric proof which are typically discussed in publications dealing with heuristic programming.

In any problem involving proof, there is an initial object (the given information) and a final object (that which is to be proved). The problem consists of establishing a connection between them. This connection is established by applying to the initial object(s) definitions, axioms, and theorems (for example, "if a, then b;" "if b, then c" etc.), which are termed "rules" in the works in question and which permit the gradual transition from or transformation, on the basis of specific rules of logical deduction, of the initial object until the final object is obtained.[1] If the system of rules is complete, then all possible paths by which any theorem may be proved may be represented by means of a tree graph, such as for example:

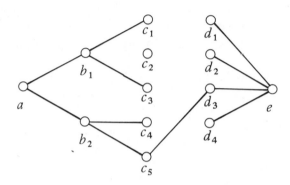

where a is the initial object, and e the final object. Not all paths necessarily lead from the initial object to the final; sometimes only a few or one do so, and it is unknown beforehand which ones do.[2] In the graph shown above, path $a\ b_2\ c_5\ d_3\ e$ leads from the initial to the final object, and the solution is achieved by applying the following system of rules: $a \to b_2$, $b_2 \to c_5$, $c_5 \to d_3$, and $d_3 \to e$.

If the system of rules is complete, then testing all possible paths (according to an exhaustive search algorithm) will lead to the solution of the problem. If a given program does not invariably lead to the desired proof, then this can occur only because not all of the paths have been tested, i.e., because the system of rules applied is not complete.

Let us assume, for example, that there are 20 ways of proving the equality of two segments, and these ways constitute a complete system. They are based on the application of 20 rules (definitions, axioms, and theorems) which establish 20 different *sufficient* conditions for the equality of segments (two segments are equal if they are corresponding sides of equal segments; two segments are equal if they are corresponding sides of equal triangles; if they are diagonals of a rectangle; if they are chords of a circle subtending equal arcs; etc.). Each path segment of the tree diagram describing the 20 possible ways of proving the equality of two segments should correspond to one of the sufficient conditions of equality.

Let us suppose now that some problem-solving system (a person or a machine), while solving a specific problem, was unable to prove the equality of two segments (which are, in fact, equal, *Ed.*) This could be due to a failure on the part of the system to test for the presence of one of the previously defined conditions (i.e., to move along one of the existing paths which must lead to the goal). If the system had tested for all conditions (corresponding to all possible paths on the tree diagram), then the required proof would have been obtained.

This example supports what was said above to the effect that failure to arrive at a proof (or, as heuristic programmers say, the absence of a guarantee of proof) can occur only as a result of the incompleteness of the rule system which is being applied, or was applied in this or that specific case. This results in a situation in which some problems are solved (those for which a complete set of rules is included in the system and, correspondingly, the paths leading from the initial conditions to the goal are included in the set of paths tested in the course of solving the problem) and others are not (those for which the incomplete set of rules is included in the system or paths leading from the initial conditions to the goal were not tested). In other words, an incomplete rule system causes the program not to function successfully for some of the objects to which it is applicable,[3] which results in a limitation on the algorithmic property of resultivity.[4]

This explains, first, why so-called heuristic programs do not guarantee a solution, and second, why, when a solution is achieved, it is achieved with a smaller expenditure of time and resources (the number of paths tested is reduced).

Inasmuch as so-called heuristic programs differ from algorithms only in that they operate on the basis of an incomplete system of rules, they may be considered to be simply "incomplete" algorithms.[5] If this is so, then to term such programs heuristic is correct only in the sense that they include some evaluations of paths or rules (say, geometric), which is preferable to testing all possible paths (rules). It is incorrect in terms of the mode of regulation and control over solution process(es) on the part of the instructions of which the program is made up and which evoke and determine corresponding operations (processes). These "heuristic" instructions determine the corresponding operations as unambiguously and completely as do algorithmic instructions, and in this regard differ from them in no way. If so-called heuristic programs do not differ from algorithms in terms of the mode of their regulation and control over corresponding processes (operations), these processes likewise do not differ in this respect from algorithms and, in this sense, can not be termed heuristics. They are "incomplete" algorithmic processes.

It follows from the fact that so-called heuristic programs are essentially algorithms (although "incomplete" ones) that the concept of heuristics, in the sense in which it is used in heuristic programming theory, does not characterize creative processes from one very essential aspect and is not related to creativity, in terms of the mechanisms of its regulation and control. Moreover, heuristic programs and the processes on which they are based do not imitate one of the most characteristic aspects of creative activity expressed, as we will discuss in more detail below, in an incomplete determination of heuristic processes on the part of the corresponding instructions. Stated differently, the concept of heuristics in heuristic programming reflects only one aspect of creativity and has, as a whole, a different meaning than that which is usually assigned to it and which relates it to creativity, seen not only from a resultive but also—and in the first place—from a procedural point of view. Neither machines nor humans, operating in accordance with such a heuristic program, display any creativity or implement any creative process, since each action they perform is, as pointed out, completely and univocally determined by a prescription (in exactly the same way in which their actions are determined when they solve problems in accordance with "ordinary" algorithms). The fact that heuristic programs are "incomplete" algorithms in no way influences the character of the actual problem-solving process, its nature, or its regulation, and lends it not a particle of creativity. In discussing the fact that so-called heuristic programs do not model (or, more accurately, imitate) creative processes, we are referring to the modeling (imitating) of the processes themselves rather than the results of these processes. Heuristic programs may achieve (and, in fact, do achieve) the same results that a human being does, but they do it in a different way (e.g., a plane achieves the same results that a bird achieves, but by means which are different from those employed by the bird; the plane does not imitate the process of bird flight). The means by which heuristic programs achieve results (solve problems of a particular class) are algorithmic means, while a human being often (but by no means always) solves these problems by non-algorithmic, creative means. This is why one may say that so-called heuristic programs we are speaking of represent *algorithmic* models of heuristic processes and are not fully adequate, i.e., *heuristic* models, if it is justified to use such a term. The fact that there exist and will always exist problems for the solution of which an algorithm does not exist or has not yet been developed demonstrates that the algorithmic way of modeling heuristic processes has definite limitations and may not be considered as the sole one. Another matter is that current machines operate only on the basis of deterministic algorithms or algorithms which include the operation of random or probabilistic choice. They are sometimes termed stochastic and probabilistic algorithms, respectively (on probabilistic algorithms, see, i.e., Glushkov, 1962). It should be noted, however, that these ones are not algorithms in the strict, "classical" sense of the word, since the concept of the (classical) algorithm excludes all random or probabilistic operations and presupposes that systems, carrying out algorithmic process, act deterministically and, with identical input data, arrive at an identical output of results. But it would not be justified to adjust theory and terminology of the problem being treated to the limited potential of contemporary machines. Quite to the contrary, the theory should show directions and stimulate the development of desired machines themselves. The fact is: inasmuch as there exist and will exist problems for which there do not exist or have not been developed algorithms, we have to solve them by means of non-algorithmic methods. If such problems are to be solved by machines, it is necessary, firstly, to develop heuristic models of heuristic processes and, secondly, to work on developing machines which will be capable of functioning not only in accordance with algorithmic but also heuristic models. In this case, machine programs and their implementing machine processes will genuinely and completely imitate the creative thinking by which a human being solves creative problems without using algorithms. An algorithmic model of a heuristic process turns a creative problem into an algorithmic one, i.e., into a problem of another type, and any problem-solving system (man or machine) which is governed by such an algorithmic model (i.e., by a heuristic program in the sense of heuristic programming) treats this creative problem as algorithmic and performs algorithmic rather than creative processes. Creativity is destroyed and disappears. It is quite another matter that, from a practical point of view, an algorithmic model of the creative process and an algorithmic treatment of a (previously) creative problem (especially by means of a computer) may, as compared with "natural" creative treatment, in some or even many cases have certain advantages (for instance, lead to the solution more rapidly, enable one to examine more alternatives and select more efficient ones, etc.). However, we are concerned now not with the problem of comparing practical effectiveness of different types of modeling creative processes and approaches to creative problems but only with the comparison of different types of modeling and their possibly precise comparative characterization(s) from the procedural rather than from only the resultive point of view.

The fallacy which has developed in heuristic programming to the effect that heuristic programs and the processes on which they are based constitute simulation (imitating) models of creative processes as processes has influenced the way these processes are conceived of and characterized in this field. This situation is encouraged to a significant degree by the character of the problems and the way in which the problems to be solved by heuristic programming are formulated. The process by which these problems are solved serves as a prototype and model for conceptions as to the nature of the creative process.

The specific features and formulation of these problems—we shall call them "proof-problems" in heuristic programming—are characterized by the following features:

1. The initial object (the given information) and the final object (that which is to be shown to be derivable from the initial object) are presented.

2. A complete list of the means (rules) which may be used in solving the problem, i.e., the *complete* field of known means, is presented.[6]

3. The path leading from the initial to the final object is unknown, and there is no algorithm by which it may be discovered beforehand. Moving from the given information to that which must be proved may be accomplished only by testing (i.e., searching down, *Ed.*) various paths. The only algorithm which may be written and which will with sufficient reliability lead to the solution of the problem is a trial-and-error or complete search algorithm.

4. The complete set of possible solution paths, i.e., the complete proof-tree diagram in accordance with which the search for a solution must be carried out, is known or may be devised in principle.

5. The testing of alternate means for solving the problem may be performed by *choosing* paths from the given list (field) of possible paths.

6. The number of possible paths is usually so great that it is often practically impossible to find a solution by testing all paths, i.e., by means of a complete search algorithm (an algorithm of exhaustive sorting). That is why special procedures (devices) are sought after and utilized which are based on certain evaluations of paths from the point of view of their ability to lead to a solution more rapidly and economically but with less of a guarantee. Determining and isolating more promising (prospective) paths, these procedures are able to reduce the number of paths tested. Precisely these procedures are called heuristic (heuristic rules, methods, etc.).

Thus, the problems considered in heuristic programming are problems whose solution consists of the *choice* of alternate *approaches* from a *finite* and *predetermined* field of possibilities and the testing of these approaches. The solution of such problems is sometimes represented as analogous to a search in a maze, and that is why a model of these problems is viewed as a "maze model of a problem" (e.g., Feigenbaum and Feldman, 1963).

The view that thinking is a choice process is widely held in cybernetics (e.g., Ashby, 1962) and in heuristic programming theory (e.g., Feigenbaum and Feldman, 1963). Thus, answering the question of what a problem is, Feigenbaum and Feldman state: "A problem exists for a problem-solver when he is faced with the task of choosing one of a set of alternatives placed before him by a problem environment" (p. 4). If the solution of problems for which the solver (human being or machine) is given a set (list) of possible means for solving the problem is taken as a model of the thinking process, then indeed problem-solving may be carried out through choice, and the task of finding a more economical and efficient way of solving problems then becomes that of reducing the field from which alternative means may be chosen as much as possible (the number of paths to be examined) and of the associated testing of these alternatives.

But are these features characteristic of every problem-solving and thus of cognitive processes in general? Clearly not. This is because problems exist for which the solver does not possess a predetermined field of choice—a complete list of means from which to choose, or the knowledge of how to apply these means, or even an idea of the type (sort) of means which might be tested. These are problems for which the field of possible paths to a solution is undefined (in general or for this specific person), i.e., problems with an *undefined* field of choice. They cannot be solved by simply *choosing* some path to a solution from a given set of possible paths (whether with the help of heuristics which suggest more promising paths or with any other help), since the solver does not know this set of paths beforehand. Feigenbaum and Feldman proceed, as we have seen, from the fact that a set of alternatives is placed before a problem-solver by the problem environment. In reality, this is not always the case, and the most characteristic feature of problems with an undefined field of search is that the set of alternatives is not placed before a problem-solver and must be determined independently.

In other words, if it is assumed that, with regard to problems of the sort considered in heuristic programming theory, the solver has available a complete set of possible paths (approaches, alternatives) before beginning to work on the problem, and that he is to choose one or several of these paths for testing, then in solving problems with an undefined field of choice the solver does not have available (in front of him or in his mind) this complete set of possible paths (and often does not know what they might be or how to go about discovering what they might be) and so has nothing from which to choose. Before choosing, he must determine these possible paths (alternatives), i.e., to create or generate a field of paths in order to be able to choose within it, and this constitutes the most difficult stage in the cognitive process involved in solving problems of this sort. Pushkin's (1965) cogent observation is worth quoting in this regard, to the effect that, in solving problems a person strives not to lessen the number of alternatives, but to increase the number.

Thus, conception of problem-solving as a process of choice (with subsequent testing and selection) cannot be regarded as universal.* Problem-solving by choosing is only a special case of cognitive processes and does not represent a general feature (characteristic) of these processes. Neither is Pushkin's characterization of thinking universal. In solving some problems, a person strives to *increase* the number of alternatives which may lead to a

---

*Compare doubts as to the correctness of this conception and the criticism of it by Miller, Galanter, and Pribram (1960). They write: "The concept of a set of alternative hypotheses that might be the solution of the problem is a very useful one, since it enables us to reduce many problems to a similar form—how to search most efficiently through a large set of possibilities. Sometimes the analogy can get a bit strained—it is difficult to think of writing a book as a process of selecting one out of all the possible ways 100,000 words could be strung together" (p. 163). And in another place: "It would be quite wrong to believe that all problems are given in a well-defined form and that thinking consists merely of searching through a set of alternatives for one that will work" (pp. 172-173).

solution, but in solving others he strives to *reduce* them. This issue cannot be resolved in an abstract way (the representatives of the heuristic programming approach have stipulated as absolute one type of cognitive process, while Pushkin has similarly stipulated another type). Cognitive processes should be viewed in correlation with those types of problems which they can be used to solve, i.e., as a function of the specific requirements on thought imposed by these problems. These processes differ in different circumstances, and specific types of cognitive process must be isolated through the analysis of various problem types. This question will be discussed in greater detail below.

The following is an illustration of the principle that thought cannot be reduced to choosing from a previously given set of alternatives (or, more precisely, that not all thought is choosing from a given set of alternatives), and that the maze model of a problem is only one of many models, and which reflects only one type of problem.

The problem called by Dunker (1926) the "Mark Twain Problem" and used by him in his experiments is well-known. One day Huckleberry Finn left his island in order to find out how things were in his home town. In order to disguise himself, he dressed as a girl. He entered the first cabin he came to. A woman was inside. He made her suspicious by his reaction to being addressed by a girl's name and his inability to thread a needle. Dunker posed the following problem to a group of subjects: "Put yourselves in this woman's place. She wants to find out whether she is dealing with a boy or a girl. What should she do?"

It is a feature of this and many other problems (in comparison with those discussed above) that the field in which a solution is to be sought is not known (given) beforehand, and neither is the actual set of possible solutions from which one or several might be *chosen* for testing. This field and this set of possible solutions must be supplied from memory and experience. The important point is that it is not present beforehand—it must be *found*. Dunker's experiments showed that subjects discovered two fields in which possible solutions to the problem might be discovered (in the experiment in question these fields were actions which possess the property of achieving the desired goal, namely finding out whether the child is a boy or a girl). The actions, directed at the child, included in these two fields are: (1) actions which could put him (her) in typical circumstances in which the two sexes behave differently; and (2) actions which could put him (her) in unusual circumstances in which preliminary preparation is of no use and in which boyish behavior (the woman suspected that she was dealing with a boy) would be evoked.

Determining (or finding) the fields in which a solution may be sought, however, is not sufficient; it is necessary to find in these fields specific actions which possess each, or at least one, of the indicated characteristics. These actions likewise are not supplied beforehand in the form of a set of alternatives; they must, as was indicated above, be discovered. (In Dunker's experiments the subjects arrived at the following solutions: let a mouse go in the room in order to see whether the "girl" would scream; introduce "her" to another girl and observe "her" reaction; etc.)

The difficulties posed by this problem and others of the same sort are difficulties not of *choosing* but rather of *searching*, on the one hand, for fields in which the objects which can serve as solutions to the problem may be found (in the example just cited, these fields were comprised of actions possessing the indicated characteristics), and, on the other hand, for the objects themselves (concrete actions with these characteristics).

In this regard, three distinct problem types can be distinguished: (1) problems in which the basic difficulty is finding (determining, defining) the field in which to search for a solution; (2) problems in which the basic difficulty is finding the solution in an already known or easily determined field of possible solutions; and (3) problems in which both of these difficulties are present.

The specific difficulties posed by many creative problems are due to the fact that the problem suggests that the solution be sought in one field, when in fact it is to be found in a different one. The following well-known problem is of this sort. "Using six matches, make four triangles with sides of equal length, each side being equal to the length of one match." In this case, the situation suggests that the solution be sought in the field of two-dimensional figures, when in fact it lies in the field of three-dimensional figures. The difficulty posed by this problem consists precisely in the necessity of moving from one field (planar solutions) to another (three-dimensional solutions).

It is particularly clear from this example that difficulties in creative thinking often lie, as Pushkin has noted, not in limiting the field of choice and the number of alternatives chosen and tested, but in crossing the boundaries of one field into a new field, one not given beforehand and not suggested by the problem, but in which are to be found objects from which a solution may be selected.

We note that, although the process of solving geometric, logical, and other problems in so-called heuristic programming is represented as one of choosing (since all alternatives are given beforehand), when human beings actually solve such problems their solution is not always based entirely on such a process; it often is accomplished by means of searching (which always is either based on analysis or includes analysis). This is due to the fact that human beings, in approaching a problem, do not consider all of the possible alternatives in order then to choose from among them. Choice processes alternate with search processes, and a solution is achieved as a result both of successful choices and successful "finds."

In this regard, it is necessary to make a clear distinction between heuristics which aim at limiting the field of choice and facilitating the choosing of one or several alternatives from the given (possible) ones and heuristics which aim at widening some field of choice, e.g., moving out of it into another field, and facilitate the finding of a solution in this new field.

Before moving to a more detailed examination of different types of problems in their relationship to the types of thinking processes, we now examine in more detail the types and characteristics of search fields and the relationships between choice and search processes.

A search process presupposes that a searching system (man or machine) has definite criteria as to what it intends to find, i.e., which requirements should satisfy an object to be found, which are its properties, functions, relations with other objects, etc. These criteria may be specified more or less precisely.

It follows from what has been said above that a search process may proceed in a predetermined or in an uncertain field. Under predetermined field we shall include any set of objects about which a solver (searcher) knows or believes that the object sought after resides within it.

The fact that the solver knows where, i.e., in which set of objects, a sought after object may reside, practically means that he can address himself to this set in subsequently extracting its elements and checking for their appropriateness to criteria which they should satisfy.

All of the facts and considerations introduced above indicate that the cognitive processes which constitute problem-solving depend to a significant degree on the problem being solved, and are determined by the demands which flow from this problem. Let us summarize the basic problem types as a function of basic features of the cognitive processes occurring during the problem-solving activity.

The predetermined field of objects may exist in the form of real objects (e.g., a set of books in the bookcase where a needed book must be found) or in the form of ideal objects, i.e., internal images or concepts of real objects. The first field emerges as a field of perception, the second as a field of imagination, i.e., field of secondary images and concepts.*

Both real and ideal sets of objects may appear before a solver as actual or as potential fields. In the first case, all objects of a set are in front of the solver's eyes (external or internal) and he can easily extract (isolate) individual objects for detailed examination and testing as to whether they fit available criteria. In the second

---

*The field of images involves not only images of outer objects but also images of someone else's or one's own actions. A characteristic feature of many problems is that they require searching not only for some real objects or images or concepts but for an action or a course of action. To solve such a problem means to find appropriate actions, operations, or their system, i.e., some procedure.

case, when the field is potential, objects to be examined are not (or not all) before the solver's external or internal eyes, and in order to be examined and checked they should be referred to when they are real, or reproduced in the mind when they are ideal. Examples are: consecutive addressing of books in the bookcase for finding the needed one; consecutive reproducing in the mind of images of members of some team to find an appropriate one for some job; consecutive reproducing in the mind of concepts of the sufficient indicative features (critical attributes, *Ed.*) of some geometric object in order to find appropriate ones (in given conditions) or to prove a given statement; consecutive reproducing in the mind of images or concepts of some actions to find those appropriate for the solution of a given problem.

It should be noted that specific characteristics of the processes of operating with fields and their belonging objects depends, to a great degree, also on whether the set of objects is finite or infinite and how large the set is if it is finite. The success in search and, hence, in the solution of a problem depends, in turn, on whether the set (external or internal) within which one is seeking is complete or incomplete. Incompleteness, for example, in the solver's mind of a system of images or concepts may not enable him to find the appropriate (sought after) object and to solve the problem. The success of search and solution depends, thus, both on the objective features of predetermined fields (sets) of objects within which one searches and on the subjective, psychological design of the fields and their characteristics. This includes the composition of their constituent images and concepts, the degree of their completeness, and the remoteness (or closeness) in terms of the number of segments in the path linking them, i.e., characteristics of their structures and some others.

An undefined field of search, as opposed to a certain or predetermined field, exists when the solver does not know where the sought after object resides or may reside; he does not know where to seek in order to try to find the sought after object.

The notion of an undefined or uncertain field should not be confused with the notion of an unknown field. In the case of an unknown field, the seeker is not familiar with those objects among which the object sought after resides or may reside. He has never had any images or concepts of the objects in his head. In the process of search they may be discovered only as a result of encountering them in the process of direct contact. In the case of an uncertain field of search, the solver has known the set of objects where the needed object may reside, and their images and/or concepts have been in his mind in a clear or, usually, in a vague or general form. Yet, having a task to find an object with required properties, he does not know that he should refer to this specific set and seek within it. This set as an object of search does not "come to his mind," it usually does not emerge specifically.

The simplest example is the experience when one has lost somewhere something and wants to find it, but one cannot recall where it might have been left so as to come back to that location and begin seeking. No set of circumstances comes to mind, no idea, no image. The seeker does not know where to refer himself for seeking, though images of all circumstances where he was during the day and where he could have left the thing are in his mind in non-specific form. In such a case, he usually tries various statagems so as to reconstruct how he had spent the day (where he had been, whom he had visited, etc.). The re-creation of corresponding images leads to specification of some set (field) of objects (in our case, circumstances) where it is possible to begin searching. In this way, one turns an undefined field into a defined one.* Now it has become possible to begin the search in a defined field, in which the search is characterized by the following features or operations:

1. There is before the external or internal eyes a set of objects to which one will refer, for one is able to reproduce consecutively a set of objects, i.e., to consecutively put them before his eyes for subsequent analysis.

2. One isolates one of the objects.

---

*This does not mean that the defined field comprises all objects (circumstances) where the thing sought after may reside. The defined field may be incomplete and it may become necessary later to create a new, more comprehensive field, or even another field.

3. One checks it for conformance to accepted criteria.

4. If the object conforms, one selects it and terminates the search.*

5. If the object does not conform, one rejects it and moves on to the next object for examination.

This cycle of operations is repeated until an object with required properties is found.

Now we shall discuss the relationship between choice and search processes.

Here and below we will speak of choice only as a psychological process. This should be emphasized, since there exists also choice as a physiological process, i.e., choice on a physiological level. Specific features of choice as a psychological process are that (1) it involves external operations with outer objects in terms of their internal, subjective reflection in the form of images and/or concepts, or (2) it involves internal operations with inner, ideal objects, i.e., with images and/or concepts of outer objects. Choice on the physiological level (in the nervous system) may, however, have nothing to do with operations on internal images or concepts or on their prototypes in objective reality. Not all nervous processes become internalized and acquire features of subjective internal reflection. The term "choice" is often applied in two senses. Let us begin with the first one.

It is natural to accept that one can choose something in the psychological sense of the word only when one has before him some set of objects from which this can be chosen. In other words, the choice process may take place only when there exists, firstly, a real or ideal field of objects, and secondly, when this field is actually there.

It is easy to notice that choice (in this sense of the word) is a

---

*We are here describing a very simplified model, since, in some cases, after an object which satisfies the criteria has been found it is not selected but is only remembered for possible subsequent selection. Other objects are being sought. And when there are some more objects found which conform, they are compared in order to select from them the object which conforms to a greater degree (if this is a case where there exist different degrees of conformance).

component of a search process in a predetermined field and simply represents the isolation of an object from among a number of given ones for subsequent testing (examination) and decision-making as to its conformance to given criteria. In this meaning of the word, choice represents operations Nos. 2 and 3 in the list of operations cited above. In this sense, the search process in some field represents a series of choosing acts with subsequent testing of each of them for their conformance to accepted criteria.

In another sense of the word, choice means "selection" (as in the expression "he made a choice") and represents operation No. 4 in the list above.

For us, here, only the first sense of the word "choice" is of importance (i.e., the first notion of choice) and, speaking of choice, we will have in mind mainly the first of its underlying actions.

A question arises whether the notions "field of search" and "field of choice" are interchangeable when we speak of predetermined fields in the general case. This question must be answered negatively, since some specific field of choice (it is always, as was mentioned above, an actual field) may constitute only a part of the field of search (the latter is not necessarily an actual field, it may be potential, i.e., let us remember its elements or parts may be reproduced consecutively). A field of search often involves a number of fields of choice and represents a set of their sets. From this it follows, however, that in some cases these fields may coincide with one another (this often takes place when the field of search is not large), and it makes no difference whether one speaks of a field of search or of a field of choice. In this case, these notions are interchangeable.

We have considered the case of search in some field performed on the basis of choice or rather a series of choices with subsequent testing of the objects chosen and, finally, selection of the appropriate one (or ones). But a search process can be carried out also on the basis of consecutively addressing objects when no actual field of choice is available. One variety of this case is the search in the field of real objects: here, a searcher consecutively (but not necessarily systematically and exhaustively) refers to real objects one by one, object by object, testing each for accepted criteria. The other variety is the search in the field of ideal objects when a person consecutively recalls images or concepts of real objects or actions for their subsequent testing and selection.

It hardly would be justified to assert that this type of search in a predetermined field is also carried out on the basis of choice, since, as we have already said, there is no actual field of objects (real or ideal) from which it is possible to choose. An actual field for choice is *created* at each step of the process when one moves from one sub-set of objects to another one. But this moving from one sub-set to another does not represent, by itself, a choice process. Choice begins *after* each sub-set of objects proves to be before one's eyes.

And, indeed, in the case of real objects to be tested, they are not chosen here, they appear before a person as a result of consecutive contacts of his eyes with certain members of the set of objects. When, for instance, a person consecutively searches for a definite book in the bookcase, he moves his eyes from one book to another and he does not know at each given moment which book will appear before his eyes the next moment. Which specific object appears before him for subsequent examination is not a result of his choice, but the result of what the external world presents him in consequence of his contacts with it.

The analogous situation takes place on the level of imagery. Consecutive calling up of some ideal objects for subsequent testing is not a choice. Usually, a person does not know which will be the next image or concept from a predetermined field (set) which the brain will present to him for examination. If some process of choice were to take place, this could occur only on the physiological and not on the psychological level.

Thus, we have considered two types of search in the predetermined field: search based on choices (it could be termed search via choice) and search based on a consecutive referring to or addressing and contacts with objects (in the case of real objects) or consecutive recall of their images or concepts (in case of ideal objects). The latter could be termed search via consecutive contacts (in the case of real objects) and search via consecutive recall (in the case of ideal objects), respectively.

Now we move on to consideration of search in an undefined or uncertain field.

It is clear, first of all, that if search in a predetermined field may be carried out via choice and represents a series of choices with subsequent checking of objects chosen (the first type of search), then the search in an undefined field may not be based principally on choice, since there is no predetermined actual field (set) of objects from which something may be chosen. Search in an undefined field represents a quite specific process of roving aimed at coming across some real or ideal object which might have desired (necessary) properties or which could, by a mechanism of association, arouse some ideas as to other objects which, in turn, could possess desired properties. Such a chain can be rather long. This roving process may be more or less directed or absolutely undirected,* depending on whether a solver has some preliminary information (and what kind of information) as to, roughly, where (i.e., in which field, area) it might be advisable (promising) to try to make some probes. In the case of search in an undefined field of real objects, roving actions are directed toward stumbling upon real objects. In the case of search in an undefined field of ideal objects, they are directed toward stumbling upon some appropriate images of concepts which serve to recall these ideal objects for subsequent choice and testing (if several objects were actualized) or only for testing (if only one object was recalled).

What is the difference between recall of images or concepts in the case of search in a predetermined field, as distinct from recall of images or concepts in the case of search in an undefined field?

In the first case, the task, i.e., knowledge of the properties which the object to be found should have, evokes (at once or consecutively) a number of images or concepts whose prototypes have the required properties. In the second case, there is no such arousal. Nothing may come to mind when the task has appeared. It is natural to suggest that the first type of process may be possible only because a chain of direct or indirect associations between the knowledge (an image or concept) or properties

---

*In this latter case it represents a process of random roving or walking.

stipulated by the task, on the one hand, and images or concepts of objects which bear these properties, on the other hand, has been established in someone's past experience. In the second case, there are no such associations, though there may be in the person's head both images (or concepts) of properties stipulated by the task and images (or concepts) of objects bearing these properties. However, they have not been associated in past experience and therefore cannot be recalled through any mechanism of association.

It follows that notions of predetermined and undefined fields of search are derivable, since what will be a specific field for someone is determined by the composition and structure of associations established previously (in his past experience). There is no other way to identify which is a specific field for this specific individual other than to trace how his search process proceeds, i.e., whether appropriate images or concepts come into his mind associatively or non-associatively.* If they come associatively, one can conclude that the given field of search is predetermined for this specific individual; if they do not come to mind associatively and he utilizes some special cognitive devices for the recall of certain images or concepts, then this field is undefined. Thus, determination of the character of the field is obtained as a conclusion to an experiment or observation and is not known beforehand.**

From all that has been said above, it is also clear that notions of predetermined and undefined fields are relative, since, as has been just mentioned, the character of a field depends on the

*There do exist some experimental devices with which the internal search process, in particular, the flow of associations, may be externalized and, thus, made accessible for indirect observations.

**Of course, when one knows rather well the history the cognitive development of an individual (types of problems which he encountered in his life, the ways in which he was taught how to solve them, etc.), one can predict beforehand with rather high probability which will be which field for him: predetermined or undefined. However, it should be stressed that such predictions can be only probabilistic and in some cases of not very high probability, since many details in the cognitive development of an individual usually remain outside the bounds of observation and control.

composition and structure of the psychological processes of each individual person, which are specific to him. One and the same field may be predetermined for one person and undefined for another, if the composition and structure of their associations are different.

The fact that someone can recall an image or concept, i.e., find in his memory some appropriate object, which has not been associatively linked with what it satisfies (the latter may emerge as a requirement of a problem to be solved, as some stipulated criterion, etc.), demonstrates two important points. First, that recall can occur not only on an associative basis by means of direct associative reviving, and, second, that the associative structure of man's knowledge does not predetermine completely and fatally the direction and flow of his thinking processes and, thus, his intellectual (cognitive, *Ed.*) potential. He is able not only to utilize his associations but also to overstep the limits imposed by them, to break out of them, and to establish new ones.* The agents which enable him to do this are operations. By means of internal operations it is possible to actively change the images and concepts being retained in his memory, on the one hand, and to reconstruct linkages between them, on the other hand. By means of external operations, it is possible to get into direct touch with the outer world, isolating its objects (in some cases quite new for a person), breaking them down into elements, reconstructing them, bringing them into new relations, and so on.** All this generates new

---

*Precisely these abilities are most characteristic of creative thinking.

**Of course, operations (more precisely: their images) are also connected associatively with images and concepts of outer objects as well as with each other, as has been already mentioned. But generalization of images of operations enables one to transfer them and to apply them to new real and ideal objects, thus obtaining new information. Of highest importance is, one might suppose, the capability incorporated in humans and animals for spontaneous activity, which manifests itself in the ability to apply actions to objects (real or ideal) which were previously never associated with them (an example is the orientation activity of humans and animals). Application of actions to new objects or their images or concepts, when the process of application is not being directed by already established associations between images of objects and that of actions, leads to obtaining new information from the outer and inner world, and this extends psychological experience.

information (new images and concepts) which "flows into the head" and may perform the following functions: the images and concepts may happen to be the very missing ones which are being sought after in the process of searching, they may evoke the previously retained images or concepts which are being sought after but could not be found so far, since they had not been recalled; they may evoke those images or concepts which, in turn, may recall the images or concepts sought after; they may change the composition and structure of already available images and concepts and their associations, breaking up existing associations and creating new ones; and so on.

It should be noted that in the process of seeking a solution to a difficult problem, external (with real objects) and internal (with ideal objects) operations constantly alternate, which ensures the appearance in one's mind of new images and concepts or recall of available ones, or reconstruction of their connections from, both, inside and outside. It is this which creates the possibility for a person to exceed the bounds and go out of the limits imposed by available associations and not to be a slave of the structure of one's own experience. What has been said explains how one may, using his experience and proceeding from it, overcome it, at the same time, recalling those images or concepts and, thus, find those ideal objects in an undefined field of search which were not associatively linked with actually present stimuli (in particular, stimuli coming from conditions and situations of the problem) and which cannot be recalled through the associative mechanism.

Let us consider in some more detail how internal and external search actions alternate, while seeking a solution to a problem in an undefined field.

First of all, an experienced problem-solver usually tries to find an appropriate object (image or concept) via recall from inside, carrying out search in the "inner sphere" by means of internal operations. It is a special point of discussion—particularly important for the development of corresponding instructional techniques—which are those operations or cognitive devices by means of which one is able to recall images or concepts in an undefined field, i.e., without being able to evoke them through association. Let us suppose, however, that the problem-solver does not manage this. Then, he usually tries to recall from outside some images or concepts, among which the appropriate one might reside. To do so he begins to perform actions directed toward outer objects which, frequently according to some vague suppositions, might have some relation to those which are being sought after (in some cases, when there are not even vague suppositions, the area toward which actions are directed is quite random). The purpose of referring to outer objects is that they might recall from outside some images or concepts among which might occur the ones which are sought after or some which might, in turn, recall some objects which are sought after, or which might provide a cue as to the field in which appropriate objects might reside. The aim is to hit upon such objects which might be either the sought-after ones or might recall, in turn, sought-after objects or some idea of the field where they could be sought.

After the image or concept has been recalled from outside, one begins to operate with it as with objects of a predetermined field, testing it for their fitness and carrying out on it other operations from among those mentioned above. When a sought-after object is found, the problem is solved (assuming there is no desire to find a better solution, i.e., another object which is more appropriate according to some criteria). When the sought-after object is not found, there may be different ways of operating further. One of these ways is the following.

Recall of some images or concepts from outside has often a far greater influence on the subsequent course of thought processes than the bringing before one's eyes of specific images or concepts. Recall of some specific images or concepts often brings with itself recall of the idea of a field to which these specific ideal objects belong or, stating it otherwise, recall of the category which embraces these objects. This has the following impact on the subsequent flow of the search process. The (logical) extension of the field is usually broader than that of specific objects recalled, i.e., it comprises a greater number of objects. After the idea of a field has arisen, and if objects recalled first are unsuitable, the possibility is open to begin searching within this field by consecutively recalling other objects belonging to it and operating with them as in the case of search in a predetermined field via consecutive recall (i.e., via the second type of search in a predetermined field). Acting in such a way within the field of recall, one usually strives to "squeeze out" as much as possible from it, hoping that, perhaps, some other objects from this field might turn out to be appropriate.

But sometimes the process proceeds in another way. Negative results of testing for conformance of some objects extracted from the field which was recalled may cause the feeling of a lack of any prospect, or even of hopelessness, to continue search in this field. If search in this field has not recalled an idea of some other field where it might be expedient to begin a new cycle of search, and again "nothing comes to mind," then a problem-solver refers anew to the outer world in the hope of hitting upon other objects and fields which could prove to be appropriate, or might, if not appropriate in their turn, recall other, now appropriate objects or ideas of appropriate fields. This process of moving on from search in the "inner sphere" to search in the outer world and conversely may continue for a long time, up to the moment of finding an object (solution) sought after, or up to giving up on trials to find a solution.

It is worth emphasizing the distinction between searching (as well as finding) for an object in an undefined field and searching (and finding) for a field of objects, or—what is the same—for a field of search, when search for a field of search is undertaken in an undefined field.

We have noted above that coming across some objects of the outer world recalls often not only their corresponding images or concepts but simultaneously the idea of a field to which they belong. It is clear that these things are not identical. The image of a specific object is its "picture in the mind," while the idea of a field to which it belongs is its categorization, i.e., relating it to a definite class. The latter presupposes carrying out, with the image recalled, some specific operations characteristic of any process of identification and, first of all, isolating in the image some of the attributes of a prototype object which enable one to relate it to a definite category. From this, as well as from our experiments and the experiments of other authors which have been analyzed from the point of view of the problem with which we are concerned now, it follows that:

1. One and the same image recalling different attributes of corresponding object may be singled out and, thus, this object may be related to different classes (categories); from the point of view which interests us here, this means that recall of one and the same image may recall ideas of different fields to which the prototype object belongs and where it is possible to begin to search.

2. Not all people in whom some image is recalled relate it to some category and, thus, arrive at an idea of a field where subsequent search can be begun. Stumbling upon some object (appropriate or inappropriate) does not always give rise to the appearance of an idea of a field where, if the object stumbled upon is not suitable, one could begin the search process, trying to find another object which, perhaps, might fit.

3. Not all people in whom some image was actually recalled relate the corresponding object to *different* categories. This means that in some persons the image recalled evokes ideas of *various* fields to which one may turn for subsequent search, while in others only *one* field suggests itself. Individual differences among people in this respect are very great (ranging from the inability to arrive at an idea of even one field to the ability of arriving at ideas of many fields). The ability to extract maximum information from one and the same object by relating it to different categories enables one to arrive at ideas of many different possible fields for subsequent possible search. This ability is one of the most important characteristics of creative thinking; and—what is most important—the operations underlying this ability can be taught. Precisely this ability leads to the generation of a still greater number of fields for subsequent possible search and, thus, to an increasing probability of finding the solution (and possibly various solutions). This creates, at the same time, the prerequisites for stumbling upon such fields from which quite unexpected and highly original solutions may be extracted.

4. The distinction between processes of searching for (and finding) an *object* and searching for (and finding) a *field* of objects creates the prerequisites for the genesis of different approaches to a creative problem whose solution presupposes a search in an undefined field. Some problem-solvers are oriented chiefly to searching for specific objects which could satisfy the requirements posed by the task and, thus, fit, while others are oriented toward searching for fields, i.e., to the relating of objects recalled to various categories for subsequent search in corresponding fields. For the former, finding an object is a final aim, while for the latter it is first of all a means for identifying fields where, after the greatest possible number of fields will have been identified, search for an object will be begun. This difference in approaches creates not only different potentials in ability to find a solution to a problem which presupposes search in an undefined field, and to find more original solutions, but also creates quite different styles of creative cognitive activity or creative thinking.

It is well known that one and the same object may be related to different categories, which differ from each other not only in the specificity of their content (when different categories reflect, each, *different* aspects of an object), but also in the degree of their generality when different categories reflect *one and the same* aspect of an object but do this differently from the point of view of generality.* The possibility to reflect the same aspects of things or relations with each to different degrees of generality is the basis for the well known problem of hierarchical composition of categories. Since relating an object to some category in the process of search leads, in our context, to recall of an idea of a field in which one can begin search processes, the problem of the hierarchical composition of categories emerges, in our context, as a problem of the hierarchical composition of the structure of

---

*A simple example easily clarifies this. For instance, one and the same person may be, at the same time, a father, a brother, a husband, a clerk, a passenger, etc., depending on which of his attributes are used as the basis for categorization. But this specific person may be related to various categories differing in the degree of their generality: a father, a human parent, a creature contributing to posterity, etc.

search fields. Fields may be more or less comprehensive. It is evident that both kinds of effectiveness of a search, i.e., the degree of probability of success and the specific features of the searching process itself, depend largely not only on how many categories (and, thus, fields) to which some specific object recalled will be related, but also on how broad each of the recalled fields will be. There may be cases when a solution (i.e., the sought-after object) is not found, not because the field recalled was inappropriate but because it was too narrow. On the other hand, there may be cases when the field recalled and used for search was so broad that the solver was unable to examine and test even a minor part of the objects belonging to this field and, thus, to hit upon a suitable object. Unfortunately, there do not exist and may not exist any general rules regarding the breadth of a field in which one should carry out a search. That is why the ability (which also can be taught and must be taught) to progress from narrower to broader fields and vice versa is of great importance. The most disappointing circumstance in connection with failures in finding a solution while searching in an undefined field is that when one cannot find an appropriate object with the required properties, it is usually not known where the cause lies. It is not clear whether one is searching in a narrow field or in a broad one or not in an appropriate field at all. There may be no general rules to determine which is the cause for some specific case of failure. The task of determining the cause in these circumstances is algorithmically unsolvable.

We have cited above a number of abilities on the development of which depends, to a considerable degree, the success of search in an undefined field (the probability of success). The role of chance in such a search also is clear. We have already mentioned that recall of an appropriate image, concept, or idea of a field usually depends on hitting upon an appropriate real or ideal object which is able to bring about such a recall. But such hitting upon is, to a considerable degree, a matter of chance, especially if one searches in a very broad field of objects or a broad field of fields. Development of science and technology has demonstrated many instances of such "lucky stumblings" which led to scientific discoveries or technical inventions. It is evident, at the same time, that higher probability of "lucky stumbling" depends on the higher degree of development of search(ing) operations and underlying search(ing) abilities characterized above.* On the other hand, stumbling upon an appropriate object may lead to a scientific discovery or a technological invention only under such conditions as a psychological preparedness (readiness) to notice and isolate the objects which have sought-after properties or are linked with appropriate objects. This preparedness represents a heightened selective sensitivity and, thus, the tuning of the brain to noticing, isolating, and perceiving sought-after properties in all objects coming into the external or internal field of view. This then leads to a greater and easier selective noticing and isolating of objects which bear these properties. The increased selective sensitivity is associated with a set (attitude) to search and may become very stable and even sub-conscious (more precisely: post-conscious). This becomes apparent not only in the process of purposeful (deliberate), active search, but also when such purposeful search is not possible and the individual is busy with other things. The increased selective sensitivity may remain even during sleep, which explains scientific discoveries and technological inventions made in this state. Due to the stable, unconscious, selective, increased sensitivity to specific properties (or relations) the sleeper may notice and isolate (extract) those appropriate images or concepts which happen to appear accidentally among the great number of images and concepts spontaneously arising during sleep.

The increased selective sensitivity of the brain to certain properties as a result of an ongoing search task or of a previously directed search activity permits one to explain the role of accident in scientific and other creative discoveries in a broader context than merely that of one's sleep.

---

*For instance, the ability to extract in an object a greater number of different attributes may lead to recall of a greater number of fields and, thus, increase the probability of coming across the appropriate object. The probability is higher when intensity of the operations is higher, when they are more flexible in the sense that one more easily switches over from performing one kind of operations (or within one field) to performing another kind of operations or within another field, etc.

Every genuine creative discovery is accidental in the sense that it is a result of a lucky stumbling upon an appropriate object, but it is not accidental in the sense that both the stumbling upon and the extracting of information from the objects stumbled upon are results of active-directed, purposeful-conscious, or directed post-conscious search actions. Stumbling upon some object which provides the solution to a problem may be to a greater or lesser degree accidental,* but *noticing* and *isolating* a suitable object is in no way accidental. It is conditional upon a psychological set for noticing and isolating objects with certain properties and on the underlying increased selective sensitivity which ensures such a noticing and isolating even on the sub(post)-conscious and non-deliberate level after it has become stable.

All of the facts and considerations introduced above indicate that the cognitive processes which constitute problem-solving depend to a significant degree on the problem being solved, and are determined by the demands which flow from this problem. Let us summarize the basic problem types as a function of basic features of the cognitive processes occurring during problem-solving activity.

The first problem type: These are problems for which there exists one or more previously known series of transformations from the initial to the final object. A complete set of properties and states of the object to be transformed is known. A complete list of actions (rules, operators) is known, the application of which leads to the transformation of the object from one state to another. The states and actions (operators) which must be used in order to arrive at the final state are known. For these problems, it is possible to construct an algorithm which will systematically, step-by-step, lead to the goal (solution) without the need of trials, choices, and search.

The second type: These are problems for which a series of transformations from the initial object to the final is unknown, but for which, as with problems of the first type, a complete set of

---

*Although this is usually not completely accidental, since searching activity increases the probability of coming across a sought-after object.

important properties and states of the object which may be transformed is known, as well as a complete list of actions (operators) the application of which will cause a transformation of the object from one state to another. It is unknown, however (as distinct from the previous problem type), which specific state of all possible known states should be utilized in any particular case (specific problem) and which operator of all possible operators applicable to each specific state should be applied in order to reach the required final state. The distinction between the first and the second problem types may be stated otherwise. If in the first case one knows what *should* be done in order to arrive at a solution, in the second case one knows only what *may* be done. The rules of transformation utilized in the first case are of a prescriptive nature, while the rules utilized in the second case are of a permissive nature. They do not *prescribe* which transformation should be performed at each step of the solution process; they only *permit* one to make definite transformations. Precisely what should be done is unknown. This is why the system of transformation of rules represents in the first case an algorithm, while in the second case it amounts to a calculus. If the calculus does not determine what should be done, in order to reach a solution, and this is unknown with the second type of problems, the only way to find a solution is to try to utilize, at each step, some of the known properties of the given objects and some of the applicable rules of their transformation. Thus, these problems may be solved only by trial-and-error procedures. It is possible to introduce an order into the trials by means of specifying their sequence, the operations which should be performed on the result of each trial, etc. This means that the trial-and-error process may be algorithmized. It is another problem whether algorithmization of trial-and-error processes while solving problems of the second type is always expedient (for more detail, see Landa, 1974). For us, it is of importance only to stress here that the only algorithms which may be written to solve them are trial-and-error algorithms. A reduction in the number of trials may be accomplished only by decreasing the "completeness" of the algorithm, i.e., by the means employed in so-called heuristic programming. These are problems with a well-defined field of search.

The third type: These are problems for which a series of transformations from the initial object to the final (or individual steps in this series) are not known and for which the solver does not know either the set of properties and states of the objects which are to be utilized to arrive at the solution of the problem or the set of required actions (operators), although he knows them in the sense that their images or concepts are available to his memory, or for which some combination of these conditions is present. These problems are not solvable by algorithms, trial (search, *Ed.*) algorithms included, because it is unknown which kind of properties and states of objects must be referred to and utilized or which kind of operators must be applied from among that great number of properties and operators which are, in principle, known to a person. In the second problem type, kinds of properties and operators as well as sets of their constituent elements were known. It is unknown only which specific elements of each of the sets must be utilized to arrive at the solution. In this case (the third problem type), not only are specific elements of each of the sets unknown but also the kind of sets themselves. This does not mean that it is impossible to write search algorithms for problems of this type. But as distinct from search algorithms for the problems of the second type, these algorithms must be, first of all, algorithms for searching fields (i.e., sets of objects, etc., *Ed.*) rather than searching specific objects within predetermined fields, which is the case with the problems of the second type. Only after an algorithm for searching fields has determined some field where it is expedient to attempt a search for a specific object, which may lead to a solution, an algorithm for searching objects within a pre-determined field may come into play. It is another question whether people, while solving problems of the third type, as well as problems of the second type, are guided by algorithms and proceed algorithmically. Usually they do not, and this is not because of the fact that such algorithms have not yet been compiled. Even if they had been compiled, they would be, in many cases, so bulky and vast, that it would be impossible practically to apply them. Even computers will not be able (at least in the near future) to implement such algorithms, and a problem will arise as to the ways of (i.e., heuristics in the sense of heuristic programming) how to reduce the number of searches in order to hit upon an appropriate field more rapidly than in the case when search of fields would be carried out on the basis of a complete sorting of fields.

From what has been said, it is clear that problems of the third type cannot be solved by choosing, since they have an undefined field of choice (alternatives from which to choose are not given and are unknown before the problem-solving process begins, although they may be stored in memory). These problems with undefined fields of choice may be solved only by means of a search process. The difficulty posed by these problems consists not in knowing which alternative to choose and test, but in determining the field in which a solution is to be found and in making the transition into this field. However, since all of the knowledge which is necessary for solving problems of this type is potentially available (in memory), they may be solved by applying such knowledge, that is, by means of (intuitive, *Ed.*) processes which are generally described as "guessing," "insight," etc.

The fourth type: Problems of this type differ from those of the third type in that the solver does not have stored in memory the knowledge required for their solution, and therefore cannot solve them by simply applying knowledge (by "guessing" or manifesting "insight"). This knowledge must be discovered by an active process of cognition, yielding new information.

Thus, in some cases it may be necessary to discover (in the sense of scientific discovery) a property of some object which was so far unknown; in other cases, to discover a principally new course of action(s) or a new procedure—it may be necessary to discover a new relation, a new law or rule, etc.

Let us summarize the general and distinctive characteristics of all the problem types considered above in the following table, where we will include under "object" everything to which some action may be applied and which may be operated on (a thing, its property, its state, etc.); see Table 5.1.

It is obvious that classification of problems may be far more detailed, even if we proceed from characteristics of

Table 5.1

	The first problem type	The second problem type	The third problem type	The fourth problem type
The field of objects to be operated on as well as the field of operators (or transformation rules) are defined	+	+	—	—
Complete set of objects and complete set of operators (or transformation rules) within corresponding defined fields (or after a field has been determined) is known	+	+	+	—
It is known which object should be chosen for operation on it and which operator (rule) must be applied to each object at each step of the solution process	+	—	—	—

problems we used, but such a classification is not our task here.[7]

We have suggested a classification of problems from the point of view of requirements which a problem puts before the thinking process. Some problems demand that one kind of process be performed in order that these problems be solved, while other problems demand that other kinds of processes be performed. It is clear that the belonging of some specific problem to some specific type or other is not its absolute characteristic; it is not an absolute characteristic of the problem. This is a relative characteristic, since, psychologically, the requirement(s) posed by a problem is always some specific *relation* between the condition of a problem and its composition—the content as well as the structure of the psychological processes by means of which the problem must be solved. But composition, content, and structure of psychological processes are different in different persons. That is why one and the same problem (more precisely: problem formulation) may appear as a problem, for example, of the second type for one person but as a problem of the third or even the fourth type for another person.

Solvers differ in their psychological thesauri.* One's "psychological thesaurus" is defined as the stock of images, concepts, and actions which determine the flow of thinking processes in some specific individual while he solves problems.

The peculiarities of the flow of the thinking process while solving a problem are affected not only by the requirement(s) coming from the problem but also by the peculiarities of the methods by means of which this problem may be solved and which the solver knows and applies. That is why it is of interest to examine not only the classification of problems from the point of view of demands which a problem poses to the thinking process, thus influencing its course, but also the classification of methods

---

*For instance, there may be such problems (or problems formulated in such a way) that all who solve them will not have the information needed for their solution as a problem of the first or second type (even if it is possible to build an effective algorithm for their solution), and they will be forced to solve it as a problem of the third or, even, fourth type.

of thinking which influence, from another direction, the flow of the thinking process.

One may aproach the classification of methods of thinking, like other phenomena, from different points of view. One of the most important is how a method regulates and controls the course of a thinking process and how it determines the character of its results. The mode of regulation and control of thinking processes on the part of a method may be characterized by means of a number of parameters, one of which is the following.

As we have mentioned in foregoing chapters, operative knowledge of a method is simply the knowledge of some prescription as to the operations which must be carried out to arrive at a solution of some problem or of problems belonging to some class.* A prescription indicating the proper course of actions may be considered as a model or pattern or program of processes to be performed. By means of external prescriptions, one may regulate thinking activity of an individual from outside. However, after the method has been acquired (assimilated), he becomes able to control his own thinking processes independently, from inside, by means or internal or self-instructions. Knowing what one should do in order to arrive at a solution of a problem of any particular type, the individual gives himself specific self-instructions which evoke corresponding operations leading to the solution. Later on, these self-instructions may be extinguished and the operations may start to be elicited directly by the conditions of the problem and other operations. Explicit instructions and self-instructions become implicit, they come to be incorporated into the structure of operations themselves, disappearing as independent entities, i.e., as independently and separately acting phenomena. Elicitation of operations by the conditions of a problem and by other operations rather than by self-instructions

---

*"Knowledge of a method," as was mentioned above, must not be confused with the "mastery of a method," which means the ability to perform adequately the system of general operations leading to a solution of the problem. Mastery of a method may develop from the knowledge of a corresponding prescription. But it may arise and exist also without knowledge of a prescription.

change the type of regulation of the flow of the thinking process. However, the progress-pattern of regulation of the thinking process usually does not disappear completely. It becomes a potential and reserve ability, reserved for use as an emergency mechanism of regulation and control. When the process of solution proceeds smoothly through direct elicitation of operations by the problem conditions or other operations, the solver usually does not refer to his knowledge of courses of actions (i.e., to the knowledge of the prescription or method), and does not recall instructions nor formulate self-instructions. When this type of regulation begins not to "work," and operations cease to be elicited directly by the conditions of the problem and other operations (this becomes apparent as not knowing what to do next, as finding oneself at an impasse, and the like), then the solver usually reverts to the first type of regulation, or more precisely in this context, to self-regulation. He begins to recall what one should do in order to arrive at the solution and again begins to act on the basis of self-instructions. Of course, such a mode of self-regulation is possible only if the problem-solver has been taught previously and explicitly methods of thinking (or discovered them independently) and knows the corresponding (appropriate) instructions. The solvers who were not taught general methods of approach to problems of particular types, or did not discover them independently, find themselves in a difficult situation, and are often not able to get out of the impasse.

Thus, acting upon the basis of prescriptions is not only a means for the formation of proper structures of thinking processes and a means of their self-regulation at the first stage(s) of acquisition of corresponding thinking processes, but also a means for their self-regulation and self-control, after they have been acquired and formed, when another way of regulation fails to "work."

We have considered different types of regulation and control of thinking processes through prescriptions from the point of view of whether some prescription (either external, or in the form of internal self-instructions) guides corresponding thinking processes explicitly or implicitly. With respect to the latter, let us remember the case where they are not recalled and are, as it were, incorporated within the structure of the operations themselves, which are elicited not by instructions or self-instructions but directly by the conditions of the problem and other operations).

Another very important dimension of analysis and characterization of prescriptions is how some method specifies the character of the results of the solution of problems when the solution process is implemented according to some specific prescription.

What are the characteristics of the results of solutions which may underlie classification of prescriptions from this point of view?

We suggest the following ones:

(1) whether all people acting according to a prescription solve a specific problem;*
(2) whether all solve it correctly; or
(3) whether all solve it identically, i.e., arrive at the same solution.

On the basis of this set of parameters or attributes or indicative features, we may describe different prescriptions by a single procedure and, thus, quite precisely define each type of procedure in terms of accepted parameters. The possibility of such a description stems from the idea that different prescriptions (methods) may be distinguished from each other (in the stated sense) according to which values are in each of their parameters. If some specific prescription possesses some set of values, then it belongs to one type of prescription, if it possesses another set of values, it belongs to another type of prescription. There are only four possible combinations of values of given parameters, which determine four types of prescriptions. We shall call these prescriptions algorithmic, semi-algorithmic, semi-heuristic, and heuristic. Since each type of prescription determines, to a great extent, the

---

*Under "all people," we mean, naturally, not all mankind but some large or small group of persons which have an approximately equal background with respect to their abilities, knowledge, and skills (for instance, students of one and the same grade).

characteristics of thinking processes carried out on the basis of this prescription, algorithmic, semi-algorithmic, semi-heuristic, and heuristic can be termed not only prescriptions but their corresponding processes as well.

Algorithmic Prescriptions (Methods) and Their Corresponding Algorithmic Processes. One can cite prescriptions on how to divide one number by another, or how to find the common denominator of two numbers. Such prescriptions completely and unambiguously specify the procedure. This accounts for the fact that (1) all people following the prescription solve corresponding problems, (2) all solve them correctly, and (3) all solve them identically.

This can be expressed in the following kind of table:

	Algorithmic Prescriptions
all people solve	+
all solve correctly	+
all solve identically	+

Semi-Algorithmic Prescriptions (Methods) and Their Corresponding Processes. As an example of this kind of prescription, we can give the prescription for how to express in general form the regularity of the type: $(3 + 4)^2 = 3^2 + 2 \cdot 3 \cdot 4 + 4^2$. The prescription may include such instructions as: (1) take some alphabet; (2) pick out of the alphabet some letter to designate the first item; (3) pick out some letter to designate the second item; (4) designate both items by the letters which were selected; and (5) write down the arithmetic expression in symbolic form.

Prescriptions of such a kind no longer specify the problem-solver's actions completely but leave him some degree of freedom. In our example this relates to the freedom both of choice of alphabet and choice of letters within the alphabet. As a result one person may express the formula as $(a + b)^2 = a^2 + 2\,ab + b^2$, another as $(x + y)^2 = x^2 + 2\,xy + y^2$, the third as $(a + \beta)^2 = a^2 + 2\,a\beta + \beta^2$, and so on.

This type of prescription specifies the following characteristics of the solution process: (1) all people acting by a prescription solve corresponding problems; (2) all solve them correctly; and (3) not all solve them identically.

Let us make a supplement to our table:

	Algorithmic Prescriptions	Semi-Algorithmic Prescriptions
all people solve	+	+
all solve correctly	+	+
all solve identically	+	—

Semi-Heuristic Prescriptions (Methods) and Their Corresponding Semi-Heuristic Processes. As an example we might consider a prescription on ways of editing a text including, for instance, an instruction: "When in two neighboring sentences the same words are repeated and this produces an impression of monotony, then replace one of them by its synonym. If no synonym comes to mind, consult a dictionary of synonyms."

Such a prescription, as compared with previous ones, specifies to a lower degree the process of solving a problem. Since the above mentioned instruction permits the problem-solver to consult a dictionary, all the solvers will solve a problem. But since the acceptance and assessment of some word as a synonym or not a synonym is usually subjective and depends on a specific individual experience of a person, which is not identical with other persons' experience and may be incorrect, it may be that not all of them solve the problem correctly. A correct solution is not guaranteed even using a dictionary of synonyms. Not all words given in dictionaries as synonyms may be always replaced by each other, since they may be only partial synonyms. Hence errors are possible even when using dictionaries. If all the solvers do not solve a problem correctly, there is even less chance that they will solve it identically. Thus, this type of prescription specifies the following characteristics of the solving process: (1) all people acting according to such a prescription solve corresponding problems; (2) not all of them solve the problem correctly; and (3) not all of them solve it identically.

Let us establish our table:

	Algorithmic Prescriptions	Semi-Algorithmic Prescriptions	Semi-Heuristic Prescriptions
all people solve	+	+	+
all solve correctly	+	+	−
all solve identically	+	−	−

While in the preceding case the field of choice of objects within a field as well as a field of choice of fields was identical for different people, not only objectively but also subjectively (all of them knew the same letters of an alphabet and the same alphabet), here the field becomes subjectively non-identical. The vocabulary of different people is different; in addition, as was already mentioned, the assessment of certain words as being synonyms or non-synonyms also may be diverse depending on different subjective experiences. Precisely because of this fact, different people acting according to one and the same prescription may solve a problem not only non-identically but, as contrasted to the preceding case, also non-correctly. This makes it clear why semi-heuristic prescriptions specify a person's activity still less than semi-algorithmic ones.

Heuristic Prescriptions (Methods) and Heuristic Processes. As an example, one can point out a prescription which contains instructions of a type such as: (1) examine the object (i.e., problem, *Ed.*) from various vantage points; (2) recall a similar problem; (3) try to apply some other method if the previous one was not successful; and so on.

Such instructions specify the process of solving a problem to a still lower degree than semi-heuristic ones and do not guarantee the solution of a problem.

The problem-solver may not know precisely from which

vantage point one should examine the object and therefore he will not manage to examine it from the necessary one; he may fail to recall the similar problem; he may not know another method or it may not come to his mind, and so on. Hence this type of prescription determines the following characteristics of solution processes: (1) not all people solve a problem; (2) not all of them solve it correctly; and (3) not all of them solve it identically.

Let us establish our table:

	Algorithm. Prescrip.	Semi-Algorithm. Prescrip.	Semi-Heurist. Prescrip.	Heuristic Prescription
all people solve	+	+	+	—
all solve correctly	+	+	—	—
all solve identically	+	—	—	—

The still lower degree of specification of the solution process by heuristic prescriptions as compared with semi-heuristic ones is accounted for by the fact that the search field here is not only non-identical for different people but also indefinite. It is for this reason that they may not know where to look for a solution and may not find it.

Clear differentiation of different types of prescriptions (methods) and their corresponding thinking processes is an important condition for purposeful control over them and for the formulation of appropriate instructional rules.

We have considered how by means of a set of properties which characterize the results of a solution (of problems of some type) one may uniformly, by a single procedure, describe and unambiguously define different types of prescriptions (methods). Comparison of prescriptions from the point of view of accepted criteria shows that the basic distinction between them lies in how they specify the results of a solution of some problems. Each subsequent type of prescription specifies the results less and less (to a lower degree).

Having examined how different types of prescriptions specify the *results* of solutions to problems, it is natural to turn to a consideration of how they specify the *process* of solution itself, i.e., those procedures of thought which lead to specific results and stipulate them. This question may be stated also as the question of the psychological consequences of decreasing the "specification force" of the prescriptions of each subsequent type or, in other words, of how each subsequent type of prescription changes (and increases) the demands on the thinking processes which are carried out on the basis of this prescription.*

To answer this, let us examine the demands on thinking processes posed by each type of prescription. First, however, let us consider some characteristics of instructions, of which prescriptions are made up.

All instructions may be divided into two large groups:

1.   Instructions which indicate only actions to be performed.

2.   Instructions which indicate also objects (or content areas) toward which some action should be directed.

Examples of the first are instructions (commands) such as: "Go on," "Get up," "Hurry up," and the like. Examples of instructions of the second type are: "Give me a book," "Consider these triangles," "Think over this question," etc.

Often, an instruction consists only of one verb, but it belongs to the second type, since the context or the situation specifies the character of those objects toward which the action should be directed. For example, when a teacher says to a student in quite definite circumstances: "Think it over," the both of them know what should be thought over (the question which was put, a problem which the student failed to solve, etc.).

Below, we will be concerned mainly with instructions of the second type, which are more often found in prescriptions utilized in the instructional process.

---

*When considering above different types of problems, we examined demands on thought processes which arose from the specific features of problems; now we will examine demands on thought processes which flow from the specific features of prescriptions (methods) when a problem solver utilizes them in the process of solution and is guided by them.

Thus, instructions with which we will be concerned consist of at least two components: indications as to the character of the action to be performed and indications as to the object or object areas toward which action should be directed. Let us call these components the "operational component" of the instruction and the "content component" of the instruction. Both the first and the second may specify the solver's operations differently—each, with different degrees of specificity.

Thus, the operational component of an instruction may address itself to either elementary or non-elementary actions and, hence, specify each of them in different ways. We proceed from the understanding that elementary action is such that the solver knows how to perform it and performs it uniformly in various cases when he needs to or is required to perform it (for more detail about elementarity of operations, see Landa, 1974). In a group of people (for example, students of one and the same grade), some action (operation) may be considered as elementary when all of them perform it uniformly in response to an instruction or self-instruction. Obviously, the notion of elementarity of an action (and, respectively, instructions referring to actions) is relative, since one and the same instruction may evoke one and the same uniform action in one group of people (say, in the students of whom we spoke) and different actions in another group (say, in students of another grade). The instruction being elementary for the first group may not be elementary for the second one.

We should distinguish between elementarity of the operational component of an instruction and elementarity of the content component of an instruction, which may not coincide with each other. Some instruction may be elementary with respect to one component (say, the operational one) since it unambiguously indicates the character of the operation to be performed, and not elementary in respect to another component (content component), since it ambiguously indicates objects on which the action (operation) is to be performed.

This explains why an instruction elementary in its operational component and non-elementary in its content component may lead to different results when performed by different people even when they belong to one and the same group. Some may apply the action to one set of objects (content), while the others, to another. Thus, for instance, the instruction "Give me something to eat" is elementary in its operational component and not elementary in its content component. The indication "give" is unambiguous, and everybody who will realize it will perform the action "giving" and not, for instance, "taking" or "breaking down," and will perform this action in an identical way (uniformly). "Something to eat" is, on the contrary, ambiguous, since it is not specified precisely what (from what is, for instance, available at home, or in the refrigerator) should be given. This is why the identical action "giving" will or may be applied, by various solvers, to different objects and will or may lead to non-identical results. Some people will choose and give one particular food, others another.

In this example the content component of the instruction was ambiguous as to the specific objects (content) to which the action pointed out had to be applied, but the *field* of objects was quite well defined (specified by the situation). It is easy to give examples where ambiguity in the content component refers to the field of objects as well, i.e., does not only not specify the particular objects to be operated upon, but also does not specify the field in which they may reside. In the latter case, the solver is not only not instructed as to the specific objects from some predetermined field to which his actions are to be applied, but where (which field) he is to look in order to find the objects to which the actions can or should be applied.

We have given above an example in which the operational component of the instruction ("give") was elementary, but the content component ("something to eat") was not elementary. The instruction "Think over what is given in this problem" is an opposite example. The content area is indicated quite unambiguously (this is the "given" of the problem) but the operation(s) to be performed with these givens is indicated highly ambiguously. "Thinking over" may be done by means of a great number of different operations. What operations are to be utilized are not specified in the instruction. That is why different solvers, while performing this instruction, may use different operations. And although these operations will be applied to one and the same content (objects), the result of these operations will be (or may be) different, because the identical objects will or may be transformed in different ways.

There are a great number of examples where both components of an instruction are ambiguous and the instruction contains uncertainty as to both the operational and the content components of the action. "Think over which properties of the given object may be used to solve a problem" is an example of such an instruction.

Thus, we have shown that instructions in prescriptions may, from the point of view in question, differ from each other in the character of specifying the operational component of an action, on the one hand, and the content component of an action, on the other hand. These may be regarded as the parameters of prescriptions which are involved in their characterization from the point of view of how they specify (and, hence, regulate and control) corresponding operations while solving a problem.

Specification of both the operational and the content (objects) components may be complete or incomplete. They (i.e., completeness or incompleteness) may be viewed as values which each of the parameters mentioned assumes.

Incomplete specification may, in turn, be of different degrees. The degree of incompleteness of a specification essentially influences the character of the solution process and determines, to a great extent, the difficulty of solving a problem: the less specified is the process of solving, the more difficult is the problem. The lower degree of specification demands a greater degree of independent activity (i.e., independently determined activity by the problem-solver, *Ed.*) of which we will speak below. It may be said also that the less is the degree of specification of a solution process by a corresponding prescription, the higher is the degree of "heuristicity" of the problem. In this book, however, we will not deal with different degrees of incompleteness of specifications, limiting ourselves to consideration of two values of completeness: complete or incomplete. The extreme point in incomplete specification is reached when some instruction does not specify one of the action components (content or operational) at all. Either the field of objects to be operated upon,* or only the objects within the field which (the field) may not be specified, by an instruction or by the content or due to lack of predetermination by the situation. Both, fields and objects within them, may only be poorly specified.

Summing up what has been said regarding the character and the degree of specification of actions (both, their operational and content components) by a prescription, we may formulate this classification: an action may be specified completely or incompletely, and, when incomplete, it may be specified incompletely either with respect to specific objects within the field which is specified, or it may be predetermined in some other way, or it may be incomplete with respect to the field itself.

This may be expressed in the form of a tree-diagram:

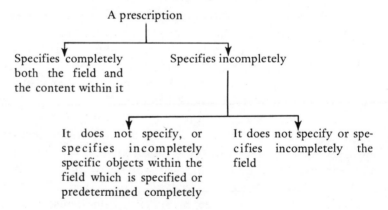

---

*Such objects may be not only things of the outer world or their reflections in the mind (i.e., real or ideal "things") but operations as well, since, while solving problems, it is often necessary to find not appropriate objects-things but appropriate objects-actions. Actions may be searched for, may be broken down, combined, etc., i.e., they may be objects of other actions which are performed according to a prescription. In this sense objects-actions do not differ, in principle, from objects-things which may also be searched for, broken down, combined, etc.

Let us consider separately how diverse values of specification become apparent with respect to the operational component of an instruction and with respect to the content component of an instruction.

The operational component of an instruction may unambiguously specify:

(1)   neither the specific operations (actions) to be performed, nor the field (set) of operations from which required operations might be extracted (indication as to what is to be done is so ambiguous here that the problem-solver may not know how to begin to proceed), nor what sort of specific operations are to be utilized or even might be utilized; the indication does not elicit any idea as to where (to what kind of operation, to what field of operations) one is to turn in order to find some appropriate operation;

(2)   the specific field of operations but not the specific operations within the field (here, specific operations within the field must be chosen or sought independently); or

(3)   the specific operations within the specific field (here, there is no need for choosing or for searching for operations, since they are unambiguously indicated by the instruction which addresses, in this case, elementary operations*).

In a similar way, the content component of an instruction may unambiguously specify:

(1)   neither the specific objects to be operated upon (sought after etc.), nor the field of objects;

(2)   the specific field of objects, but not specific objects within the field; or

---

*Elementarity here applies only to the operational component of the operation and may not apply to the content (object) component. This means that some instruction may unambiguously indicate the character of a uniform operation (for example "give") and ambiguously, to some degree of uncertainty, indicate the objects or fields of objects toward which the elementary operation is to be directed (for example, "something to eat").

(3)   the specific objects within the specific field.

As we have already mentioned, one and the same instruction may completely specify, say, the operational component of an operation and not completely specify the content component, or conversely. From the just cited types of specification of each component, it is clear that there exist nine possible combinations: the first type of specification of the operational component may combine with each of three types of specification of the content component; the second type of specification of the operational component may also combine with three types of specification of the content component; the same is true of the third type of specification of the operational component.

If we designate the three types of specification of the operational component by the letters A, B, and C, respectively, and the three types of specification of the content component by the letters X, Y, and Z, respectively, the following combinations are possible:

$$AX, AY, AZ; BX, BY, BZ; CX, CY, CZ.*$$

Types of specification may be seen as characteristic features of different types of prescription(s) by means of which the latter may be described and defined (from the point of view in question). Let us state these definitions.

$$CZ \underset{Df}{\Leftrightarrow} \text{Algorithmic Prescription}$$

$$AY \lor BX \lor BY \underset{Df}{\Leftrightarrow} \text{Semi-Algorithmic Prescription}$$

$$AZ \lor BZ \lor CX \lor CY \lor CZ \Leftrightarrow \text{Heuristic Prescription}**$$

From what has been said it is obvious that algorithmic prescriptions are characterized by complete specification of, both,

---

*AX, AY and others represent the more complete notation: A & X, A & Y, etc.

**Attributes of semi-heuristic prescriptions will be discussed below.

operational and content components of instructions (prescriptions); in semi-algorithmic prescriptions either the operational component or the content component or both components specify the field of objects, (i.e., the field is predetermined, possibly by context, etc.), but do not specify the particular objects within the field. For heuristic prescriptions it is sufficient that at least one of the components does not specify a field, whether the field of operations or the field of objects to be operated upon (operations which are objects of other operations included). Naturally, both fields may not be specified as well. In this case the "heuristicity" of a prescription is, one might say, double.

All this may be expressed in the form of the following table (Table 5.2).

Table 5.2

	Algorithmic Prescriptions	Semi-Algorithmic Prescriptions	Heuristic Prescriptions
Both fields are specified or predetermined	+	+	−
Objects to be separated within the (predetermined) field are specified	+	−	−

Until now we have not considered characteristics of semi-heuristic prescriptions (methods) with respect to the aspects in question, since this implies utilization of one more characteristic. This derives from the fact that instructions entering prescriptions may explicitly or implicitly address themselves to actions which involve univocal and unambiguous assessments or evaluations of objects to be operated on.

Let us explain in more detail.

Each instruction involves not merely operational and content components. It implies that there exists in a person to whom it is addressed the ability to assess the fields and objects toward which the action is directed and which it transforms (this is true of real as well as of ideal objects).* For example, the instruction "Give me a book, please" involves an explicit indication as to the character of the operation to be performed ("give" and not, say, "take") and as to the object toward which the action should be directed ("give a book" and not, say, "a note-book"). However, it is implicitly assumed that the addressed person is able to discern a book from a note-book, i.e., that he has some criteria according to which he distinguishes one object from some other one. The instruction cited is such that all normal people who know what the book is have identical criteria for the book and, therefore, perform this instruction identically.

But this is not always the case. Let us change the cited instruction to: "Give me some interesting book (from among those which are in the bookcase)." The word "a book" is unambiguous, but the indication "an *interesting* book" is not unambiguous, since criteria for "interesting" are different in different people. One will choose and hand over one book, the other, another book. The latter instruction quite unambiguously specifies the operational component of the action as well as the field of objects among which the required object can be found, but it contains uncertainty with respect to the evaluative component of the action, since it does not specify what "interesting" means.

One of the objective reasons for non-identical assessment of a great number of objects and phenomena lies not only in the absence in some specific prescription for the specification of criteria for assessment, but also in the fact that often these criteria, if they were indicated, are difficult or perhaps even impossible to make absolutely unambiguous. This is associated with the absence, in many cases, of clear boundaries between definite notions or, more accurately, between attributes by means

---

*In terms of actions, it can be said that each action involves operational, content (objects), and evaluative aspects.

of which we try to separate one set (or sub-set) of objects from another one. This fact has lead to the invention of the concept of "fuzzy sets" (see, e.g., Zadeh, 1965). This concept and its corresponding theory are aimed at the description of such sets and operations on them.

Comparison of instructions such as "give me a book" (from among those which are in the bookcase) and "give me an interesting book" (from the same set) shows that if in the first case instruction imposes no limitation as to the sub-field or initial field of objects (one may select *any* book from the given set), then in the second case there is an indication regarding the sub-field of the objects among which something should be chosen (not any, but an *interesting* book). However, this indication limiting the initial set of objects is ambiguous and admits of the possibility that different people may refer to different sub-fields, since they may have different ideas as to what is interesting.

It should also be noted that the performance of the second instruction, i.e., the solution of the second task, is more difficult than that of the first one, and this is so because it demands from the addressed individual some additional and independent activity. This is the necessity to specify independently the ambiguous criteria and to apply them to the given situation. In some cases such specification represents no difficulty for the person (when he, for example, knows quite well what, from his point of view, is "interesting" about a book), in other cases, specification of criteria may be a rather difficult task, which presupposes the carrying out of a number of varied, special operations.

We have spoken above of two sorts of fields which may or may not be completely specified by a prescription or conditions of the problems and which demand some independent searching or specification. These were the field of operations (more accurately of operational components of actions) and the field of the content (objects) component of operations. Now we can add one more field, namely the field of criteria for evaluation or assessment of, both, the operational and the content components.

A good (more frequently successful) problem-solver differs from the less successful one not only in that he is able to find an appropriate field of objects (alternatives), but also in that he possesses or may find better criteria for comparative assessments of these alternatives from the point of view of their promise for utilization in solving some specific problem. The ability to find a better assessment of alternatives makes possible the selection of more promising alternatives for subsequent testing, and may lead to a solution with a higher probability. What has been said applies not only to criteria for assessments of individual alternatives, but also to assessment of the promise of the fields themselves, as when a solver comes across not one single but several possible fields.

It should be mentioned that ambiguity of the criteria for the assessment of objects, which leads to the necessity for a problem-solver to utilize his own subjective criteria, may refer not only to sub-fields of objects within some predetermined and univocally specified fields but also to these initial fields. Thus, for instance, a direction to "recall some analogous problem" may elicit (evoke, recall) in two persons, quite identical sets of problems (in this sense, such a direction specifies the field of search or choice for each of the solvers), but these elicited fields may be diverse. The reason for the difference lies in the fact that, firstly, the set of problems previously solved by these solvers may be different (their experience in this respect may be different) and, secondly, the criteria of what is "analogous" may also be different.

Let us call instructions (prescriptions) which contain uncertainty or ambiguity as to the criteria of assessment of fields (or sub-fields) and which demand independent utilization of some subjective criteria—*semi-heuristic instructions*. This type of instruction specifies fields of search or choice for each individual solver, but these fields may be different in different solvers—which leads to the fact that different solvers may solve one and the same problem not only differently but even incorrectly if their subjective criteria are incorrect.*

Now we can suppplement the previous table in this chapter and introduce into it characteristics of semi-heuristic

---

*We have already cited above the example in which a subjective assessment of a word as a synonym to the given word may be incorrect.

processes. The table will now read as follows (see Table 5.3).

On the basis of the attributes pointed out in this table, it would be easy to give the same precise definition for semi-heuristic prescriptions which were given for other types of prescription.

Table 5.3

	Algorithm. Prescrip.	Semi-Algorithm. Prescrip.	Semi-Heuristic Prescrip.	Heuristic Prescrip.
Both fields are specified or predetermined	+	+	+	−
Fields elicited are identical in different solvers	+	+	−	−
Objects to be operated on within the (predetermined) field are specified	+	−	−	−

Let us represent this table in the form of a tree-diagram (see the following page), where the characteristics of the specification of fields will be the input and objects within the fields and types of prescriptions the output:

Analysis of demands on thinking processes which flow from different types of problems as well as from different types of prescriptions (methods) show that each subsequent type determines the course of the thinking process less and less and, correspondingly, places greater and greater demands on the independent thinking of a problem-solver. Thus, if algorithmic prescriptions (methods) completely determine the course of thinking processes and do not demand, therefore, independent search and even choice, semi-algorithmic prescriptions determine the thinking process less completely. Specifying the field of

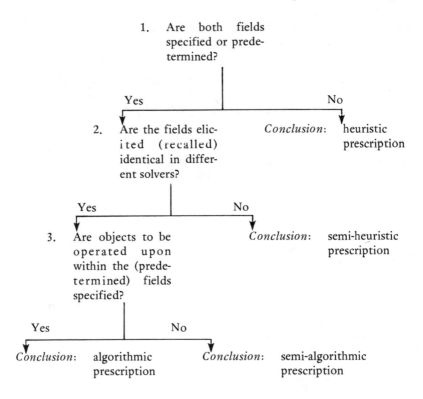

1. Are both fields specified or predetermined?

Yes — 2. Are the fields elicited (recalled) identical in different solvers?

No — *Conclusion*: heuristic prescription

Yes — 3. Are objects to be operated upon within the (predetermined) fields specified?

No — *Conclusion*: semi-heuristic prescription

Yes — *Conclusion*: algorithmic prescription

No — *Conclusion*: semi-algorithmic prescription

choice, they do not specify the objects to be chosen, and this must be done independently. Semi-heuristic prescriptions determine the thinking processes still less. They demand not only an independent choosing of an object within a given (predetermined) field, but also independent specification of criteria for the assessment of objects and fields. If the first three types of prescriptions (methods) do not demand independent determination (specification) of a field of choice or search, the fourth type adds this demand and, thus, increases the degree of required independency still more.

All this brings us to the question of the criteria for creativity in problem-solving.

Though we do not claim to be able to define the criteria in full, we can indicate some features of creativity which we regard as important. We begin with the generally accepted assumption that algorithmic processes (i.e., processes based on some set of algorithmic instructions) are not creative in nature. However, if complete determination of the actions of the problem-solver is characteristic of algorithmic processes, then, clearly, creativity is present only when the solver's actions are not determined or are incompletely determined by such instructions (Landa, 1974). In other words, a problem is creative if there does not exist or the solver does not know an algorithm for its solution and must search for a solution in a field in regard to which it is not known beforehand which of its elements should be utilized to arrive at a solution; in some cases the fields to be utilized are also unknown, although in principle relevant knowledge—including knowledge regarding actions—may be stored in the problem-solver's memory.

These ideas may be expressed in a somewhat different way. A problem is creative if there does not exist or the solver does not know an algorithm for solving it and the knowledge and actions required for its solution are not directly, associatively recalled (elicited) when the conditions of the problem are perceived. This point is quite important, since, if in perceiving a problem the solver associatively (automatically), through past experience, arrives at a solution or a set of possible alternatives from which he need only select and test a few, then it would be better to say that, in this case, the solver knows how to solve the problem than to say that he discovers (guesses, through insight, arrives at) its solution. Thus, the creative process occurs in those situations in which solution is not directly determined either by instructions or by past experience, and this means that it cannot be achieved on the basis of direct associative recall of knowledge and actions (methods for solving the problem). Of course, a creative problem may be solved only on the basis of experience, but creative processes are characterized by the fact that in them experience must be retrieved, that a specific non-algorithmic search through experience (i.e., knowledge stored in memory) must take place, as a result of which experience yields objects (images, concepts, actions) which would not have been recalled in and of themselves (automatically, associatively).

But the lack of knowledge of an algorithm is a necessary but not a sufficient feature of a creative process. All creative processes are non-algorithmic, but not all non-algorithmic processes are creative if we proceed from the usual intuitive conception of a creative process. Thus, a process of expressing in general form the regularity of the type $(3 + 4)^2 = 3^2 + 2 \cdot 3 \cdot 4 + 4^2$ is a non-algorithmic process, but it can hardly be called creative. The same is true of the process of finding a synonym to a word. Above, we have termed these processes and their corresponding prescriptions semi-algorithmic and semi-heuristic, respectively.

Between the two poles of algorithmic and creative processes there is, thus, a number of conceptual processes which might be termed independent non-creative processes. They differ from algorithmic processes in that they are not determined, or not completely determined, by instructions, and involve independent choice or search, and from creative processes in that the choice and search are made in a predetermined field. Characteristics (at least a great number of them) of choice and also of search processes and their result are determined, to a great degree, by the composition and structure of associations established (formed) in the past experience of the problem-solver, although a definite role is played by the spontaneous activity of the psychological search system, which generates random recall of images, concepts, and actions.

From what has been said, it is clear that all creative processes are independent (in that they are not determined or not completely determined by instructions), but not all independent processes are creative (since they do not always involve searching in an undefined field). From this point of view, all cognitive processes may be divided into non-independent (algorithmic) and independent (non-algorithmic) processes, and independent processes may be divided in turn into independent non-creative and independent creative processes.*

---

*In speaking of algorithmic processes as non-independent, we mean by non-independency only that aspect of these processes which manifests itself

Both independent non-creative and independent creative processes may vary in the degree to which they are independent and in the amount of difficulty entailed in performing them. For example, a small number of properties of some object is easier to recall and isolate independently than a large number, frequently encountered properties are easier to recall and isolate than infrequently encountered ones, "overt" properties are easier to isolate than latent ones, etc. It is clearly possible in principle to isolate the factors which determine the degree to which thinking is independent and to which a given process is creative. These factors at the same time determine the difficulty of a given cognitive process. These factors could serve as the basis for criteria for the evaluation of the degree of difficulty of various types of problems (both, independent creative and independent non-creative).

Let us now consider the problem of heuristics in greater detail and from a new point of view.

We stated above that the heuristics embodied in so-called heuristic programs are equivalent to a set of rules which completely determine the actions performed in the course of solving a problem and which in no way differ in this regard from the rules (instructions) contained in ordinary algorithms. These heuristics, therefore, cannot serve as a source of creative processes and cannot evoke or control them, since they exclude any independent activity by their implementing system. They are, therefore, not truly heuristic in nature. Clearly, only rules which do not completely determine cognitive activity and which contain in themselves some indeterminacy with regard to the way in which instructions are carried out are truly heuristic, i.e., in evoking and directing the creative process. A true heuristic presupposes

---

in the absence of the necessity to compile independently a *program* of corresponding operations. The program is given either by an unambiguous prescription or embodied in the system of established associations which are being consecutively recalled (and are, as it were, unfolding themselves) in the process of activity. But algorithmic processes are quite independent in the sense that *implementation* of the program is carried out by the solver himself, which demands the independent performance of a series of operations.

independence in the system to which it is addressed, amounting to a capacity for independent activity and self-organization in the carrying out of indeterminate instructions. As soon as an instruction ceases to be indeterminate and begins to determine completely the actions involved in solving a problem, it becomes algorithmic, and the necessity for independence and self-organization disappears. It follows that creativity is impossible without independence and self-organization, and that creativity is creative because it does not occur in accordance with rigorous instructions which completely and unambiguously determine action, but rather on the basis of self-organization. As soon as an algorithm which completely determines the problem-solving process is written for a creative process, the latter ceases to be creative. Computer models of creative processes should be based, therefore, not on the algorithmization of particular problems (as in so-called heuristic programming), but on the creation of self-organizing systems which possess an independent internal activity which is not fully determined by external instructions that have been stored in the computer (or created by it). But this requires that models be constructed of those processes (imaging of the outside world, associations, internally active, and, probably, even spontaneous and random actions) which underlie the human ability to show independence and self-organization, or performance of operations which are not prescribed by any external or internal (learned) or independently developed algorithm, i.e., which are not algorithmically determined.

What is the function of true heuristics in thinking? It is to facilitate in a specific way the recall and organization of knowledge and operations which can be of use in finding a solution to a problem, and also to direct and regulate the search process which is an indispensable part of all creative thought. Heuristic prescriptions, as soon as they are learned or independently discovered, serve as a means of self-organization and self-regulation. They, being controlling systems of the highest levels, permit the problem-solver to evoke (recall) consciously and deliberately the knowledge and operations which may be of use in finding a solution to a problem (but do not guarantee that it will be found). Heuristic rules are simply rules which enable the problem-solver to lead himself to the solution to a problem.

It is easy to find examples of what has been said. Let us take the following well-known heuristic procedure (see, for example, Polya, 1942). "If you are unable to solve a problem, try to remember some similar or related problem the solution to which you know." This procedure does not indicate either the field of search (a similar problem might be one from another field of knowledge, for example, from another subject of study) or the precise attributes which are to be utilized in looking for a similar or related problem. It is, therefore, quite unspecific. But it elicits a search for similar problems (without it this search might never begin) and to some degree directs this search (similar or related problems are sought while dissimilar or nonrelated ones are rejected, even if the solver has no precise criteria of similarity and relatedness, and experiences hesitations in some cases). To the extent that it leads to a solution to a problem, this procedure serves as a means by which the problem-solver may guide himself to a solution.

We note that heuristic rules are not all unspecific (and, therefore, "indeterminate") to the same degree. The more general a heuristic instruction, the less it determines the actions of the problem-solver and the more independent and creative thinking it requires of him. On the other hand, the less general a heuristic instruction is (the closer it approximates an algorithmic instruction) the less independent and creative thought it requires for its execution.

In applying a heuristic rule, a problem-solver does not wait for something to "come into his head" of its own accord. In acting in accordance with heuristic rules, he helps to create the conditions (external and internal) which facilitate things "coming into his head." Success in solving problems, in the final analysis, depends, therefore, not on heuristic procedures (by themselves they do not yield a solution to a problem), but on the knowledge and operations which are recalled by these instructions and the functioning which they direct and regulate.

However, for knowledge and operations to function in such a

way as to give rise to the creative process, it is necessary that this knowledge and these operations possess certain specific properties (for example, generality, ease of recall and transformation, etc.) and that they be organized in a particular way (for example, systematized according to specific principles). The development of such properties and organization is clearly a most important problem in instruction and one which must be solved in a systematic way.

We have argued that the most important functions of heuristic rules (instructions) in guiding the thinking process are, first, to recall (elicit) the specific knowledge and operations which "make up" the creative process, and second, to regulate this process by directing the search and guiding the problem-solver to a solution.

Are the functions of heuristic prescriptions (methods) limited to those mentioned? Clearly not. Heuristic methods can also perform the important function of forming the knowledge and operations necessary in creative processes, of serving as the means for organizing them and lending them specific properties.

Notes

1. For the sake of brevity, we will also refer to them as rules, although this is not quite correct. Definitions, axioms, and theorems are primarily specific formal statements about properties of objects and relations among objects, from which particular rules are derived and to which these rules correspond.

2. The essence of this sort of problem resides in the fact that it is impossible to write an algorithm which will recognize beforehand the path or paths which lead to a solution of the problem.

3. This situation was emphasized by our associate M.M. Sholomii in one of his seminar reports at the Institute of General and Educational Psychology in Moscow.

4. The relevant property is resultivity rather than generality,

because the initial data of the problem may be objects of various sorts, and deficiencies in the program (deadlock situations, for example) can arise at the level of transformation of initial data.

5. We emphasize that this expression is used conditionally. In the precise sense of the term, incomplete algorithms cannot exist. Any system of algorithmic rules (including the rules on which so-called heuristic programs are based) is complete in itself. The term "incomplete" is intended to indicate only that there could be more rules in some systems of rules.

6. This list may be incomplete in the sense of not containing all of the information it might contain (e.g., all of the known attributes of some geometrical forms which could be used in the problem-solving process), but it is complete in the sense that the user is given all of the means from which to choose in solving the problem.

7. We emphasize again that the typology introduced above describes not only problems per se, but the relation between the conditions of a problem and the means which are available for its solution. It is impossible, therefore, to tell simply from a description of the conditions of a problem the type to which it belongs. If one knows an algorithm for solving a problem, it is a problem of the first type, but if one does not know such an algorithm, it is a problem of the second, third, or fourth type.

Chapter Six

The Programmed Teaching of Algorithmic and Heuristic Processes

The discussion in Chapter Five of the role of creative (heuristic) processes and of heuristic procedures in influencing these processes implies the following instructional problems in this area:

1. Heuristic processes and the mechanisms of self-organization which underlie them (these mechanisms are implicit* in the properties and structure of the appropriate knowledge and operations) must be formed (i.e., created, developed, *Ed*.) in the student.

2. The student must be taught heuristic rules (procedures) and their systematic interrelations, which involves:

   (a) acquainting him with these procedures, their characteristics, structure, and functions;

   (b) organizing his assimilation of the procedures, i.e., ensuring that the rules, which initially appear to the student as external (given from outside), become internalized, i.e., become the student's "own" rules; and

   (c) teaching him to use the procedures, i.e., the ability consciously and deliberately to recall them, to apply them, to be guided by them, and thus to use them as a means of self-organization and self-regulation.

3. The student must be taught to discover (find, formulate) heuristic rules independently.

Efficient and practical ways of achieving these goals will have

*Literally, "guaranteed." (*Translator*.)

171

to be based, however, on the scientific investigation and resolution of a number of questions, among them the following:

(1) the discovery of the structure, properties, and mechanisms* of the knowledge and operations which underlie heuristic processes and give rise to their self-organization;

(2) the specification of a general system of heuristic rules, as well as partial systems of particular significance in the solution of certain classes of problems;

(3) the development of effective methods of teaching heuristic rules and processes, in particular, exercises for shaping specific heuristic processes and promoting the assimilation of specific heuristic rules and systems of rules;

(4) the discovery of the psychological mechanisms by means of which the transition from heuristic rules to heuristic processes (activity) is effected, i.e., the mechanisms by means of which cognitive actions are regulated on the basis of given, learned, or independently discovered heuristic rules; understanding of such mechanisms would serve as a basis for the elaboration of appropriate methods for developing similar self-regulation mechanisms in the students; and

(5) the discovery of the psychological mechanisms by means of which human beings independently discover and formulate heuristic rules and the elaboration of a methodology for teaching the ability to discover heuristic procedures independently.

The majority of these problems have not been solved as yet or have been solved only to a minimal degree, and so it is more appropriate to speak of the formulation of the problems of instruction in this area than of how they are to be solved, especially as regards the possible usefulness of programmed instruction for this purpose (see Correll, 1965, for a more detailed discussion of this topic).

The problem of teaching algorithmic procedures and methods

---

*Undoubtedly, the term *mechanism* as used here and later must be interpreted to mean the organized system of associations and operations constituting the actual, underlying psychological and/or neurophysiological process(es). (*Editor.*)

and, correspondingly, of shaping algorithmic processes poses considerably less difficulty. The resources of programmed instruction are adequate for teaching these procedures and are already being used for this purpose (see, e.g., Belopol'skaya, 1963; Gentilhomme, 1964; Kelbert, 1963, 1964; Landa, 1966; Landa and Khlebnikov, 1963; Landa, Orlova, and Granik, 1965). Inasmuch as this problem has been discussed in detail in the literature, we will not discuss it further here. We note only that an algorithm for solving a given class of problems permits the program writer to analyze the process of solving a problem into elementary operations (steps) and to form these operations in a step-by-step manner. However, programmed instruction offers great possibilities not only for the step-by-step (operation-by-operation) molding of cognitive processes, but also for the step-by-step (operation-by-operation) control of these processes. Such control is especially important in the generation of algorithmic processes.

The most difficult aspect of the teaching of heuristic processes is that of the internal mechanisms of heuristic activity which make possible independence and self-organization in the process of searching for the solution to a problem. It may be assumed that this independence and self-organization is based primarily on the following "elements":

(1) specific motivation as an internal source of cognitive activity and self-organization;

(2) specific properties and organization of knowledge;

(3) specific properties and organization of cognitive and physical actions (operations); and

(4) certain typological properties of neuropsychological activity in general.

The first three of these elements must be formed in the student during the instructional process.

With regard to motivation, the stronger the demand for cognitive effort, the wider is the body of recallable knowledge and operations which can be involved in cognitive activity, and the easier is this recall. The intensity ("strength," speed, etc.) with which operations are performed is likewise higher. The development of positive motivation depends, for the most part, on the instructional techniques used, as well as on general training and education, in particular, on the frequency with which cognitive tasks are given to the student during instruction and the degree to which the problem-solving and discovery approach is used; it depends, too, on the extent to which the problems presented to the student are within his problem-solving capabilities and the methods with which he has been provided for solving them. The extent to which instruction is interesting and encourages active cognitive effort is of great importance. In short, the development of positive motives for study and cognitive striving is influenced by everything which facilitates the development of cognitive interests and habits of cognitive effort. Educational theory and practice have evolved methods for motivating the student, and most of these methods are applicable in programmed instruction.

With regard to the specific properties and organization of knowledge, inasmuch as heuristic (creative) activity is always a search in some field (often not determined beforehand), the success of this activity always depends on the organization of knowledge in the field (or fields) in which the search is to be carried out. The better this knowledge is organized, the easier it is to find the desired object.

Of particularly great importance is the systematization of knowledge in accordance with various principles—its inclusion in various relational systems. For example, in geometry, knowledge should be systematized not only in accordance with the units into which the geometry course is divided, the properties of the figures studied in each division—knowledge regarding the properties of triangles, quadrangles, circles, etc.—but also in accordance with the sufficient conditions (attributes, indicative features) of various relationships which may exist between the elements which make up the various geometrical figures studied in different lessons— knowledge of the sufficient conditions for the equality of segments, angles, etc., or for the parallelness of segments, etc. The more diverse the principles of the systematization of knowledge and the greater the number of systems into which a given element of knowledge enters, the more firmly established are the prerequisites for successful discovery of the knowledge necessary for solving creative problems.[1] This does not mean that the need for searching will eventually be eliminated. As long as a problem is a creative one for a particular individual, he will have to carry out a search for knowledge in accordance with the principle by which it was not systematized for him. A many-sided systematization of knowledge (inter-subject connections are especially important for the problem-solver in this regard) increases the probability that the required knowledge will be found. In the process of systematizing knowledge according to different principles, the student acquires the ability to examine phenomena from various points of view, to see them in various connections, to "rethink" and "resystematize" them.

There are objects which are studied in different subjects, for instance, in physics and in biology, but from different points of view. It is desirable that when one comes across the object, there should occur a recall of knowledge which was studied under various subject-topics. But in order for such transfer to take place, it is necessary that associations (connections) between knowledge acquired in different topical areas be established.

The search for the knowledge required to solve a problem is facilitated not only by its good organization (for example, multifaceted systematization), but also by some of its properties, such as generality, disposition to rapid recall, and several others which have been discussed above and whose significance has been noted in the literature (therefore, we will not discuss them further here).

The question arises as to whether it is possible to use the resources of programmed instruction to organize in appropriate ways the student's knowledge (for example, to systematize his knowledge in accordance with various principles, to include it in various associative structures), and to lend this knowledge various properties (generality, disposition to actualization, etc.). This question may be answered in the affirmative. If this can be done using normal textbooks and workbooks, then it can also be done using programmed textbooks (or teaching machine programs). No special organization of instruction is required for this purpose, and programmed textbooks and machine programs impose no constraints on the process.

The above discussion regarding organization of knowledge and the presence of certain properties as conditions for the implementation of heuristic processes applies equally to cognitive actions (operations).

Different types of heuristic activity require the performance of different search processes through the performance of various cognitive actions (operations) and systems of such actions. Such operations would be, for example, the isolation and abstraction of certain properties of objects, the transition from one category of property to another, comparison of objects for the purpose of establishing general similarities and differences, the systematic inspection of objects in order to discover the presence or absence of specific properties, the systematic search (in one or several fields) for objects with certain properties, the examination of objects from various points of view, the inclusion of them in various systems of associations and relations, the transition from one field of search to another, the testing of alternate possibilities, etc. Many of these operations (and perhaps all of them) are not specific to creative thought, but under some conditions their performance gives rise to the creative act. The scientific analysis of various types of creative problems makes possible, in many cases, the discovery of the operations which must be performed in order to solve these problems, which in turn allows these operations to be taught and developed.

The larger the arsenal (repertoire) of operations a person possesses, and the more available these operations are for him (i.e., the easier they are to recall), the more varied are the operations he is able to perform in the absence of instructions or in accordance with instructions which incompletely determine the actions in question, and, consequently, the greater is his capacity for independence and self-organization.

There are also some properties of operations which are important in the performance of the active searching activity which is the basis of the heuristic process, such as flexibility, mobility, ease of recall and restructuring, and several others.

Finally, the self-organization and flow (and also the formation) of heuristic processes is obviously and significantly influenced by certain typological properties of higher nervous activity, properties which are currently being studied intensively by physiologists and psychologists (see, e.g., Leites, 1960; Nebylitsyn, 1966; Teplov, 1961).

The question arises again as to whether it is possible to use programmed instruction to develop in the student the operations—their properties and their organization—which are required for the implementation of heuristic processes.

We note first of all in this regard that programmed texts and machine-administered programs show no less promise in this area than standard texts and workbooks. Everything that can be done using standard texts and workbooks can be done using programmed texts and machine-administered programs. Programmed texts are no worse in this regard than standard ones. But are they better? Do they offer a wider range of possibilities for developing heuristic processes than standard texts and workbooks?

In order to answer this question, we must examine the characteristics of the problems which may be used to form the cognitive operations—their properties and their organization— which underlie heuristic processes. Many of these operations are developed in the process of working through the exercises which are standard in the teaching of various subjects. But creative skills and abilities are developed as a result of solving creative problems, the distinguishing feature of which is that they require trials and error in the course of searching activities (often in fields which have not been defined) which are not determined or are incompletely determined by instructions. (This is the reason for the fact that one problem-solver may test possible solutions from one area, while another solver tests possibilities from another area.)

In order to control the flow and development of creative search processes in accordance with the principles of programmed instruction, i.e., in a step-by-step manner through feedback, it is necessary first to determine an efficient step size for controlling such processes, and second, to predict the student's actions at each step so as to be able to respond to and reinforce their results appropriately (positively or negatively).

Let us consider each of these requirements separately.

To begin with, there is some doubt as to whether it is possible at all to develop creative search processes in a step-by-step manner. After all, it was stated above that heuristic (creative) processes imply independence and self-organization, which properties in turn imply non-determination or incomplete determination of actions by instructions. There is no contradiction here, however. The step-by-step development and control of these processes does not necessarily imply operation-by-operation development and control. Furthermore, programmed instruction in general does not prescribe any formal criteria of step size (at least not at present).[2]

The step-wise aspect of programmed instruction (when it is correctly understood, which is not always the case, since much work on this topic is aimed at finding formal criteria of step size) reduces to the idea that the cycles of information exchange between teacher and student should be smaller than in standard instruction, but how much smaller and just how small they should be is undefined in the basic (Skinnerian, *Ed.*) theory of programmed instruction. The problem consists (or, at any rate, should consist) of the writing of textbooks and machine programs which will be able to guarantee the breaking up (i.e., formal, logical decomposition, *Ed.*) of the instructional process into steps, without placing restrictions of any sort on step size. Step size clearly should be a function of the teaching situation (content, level of preparation of the student, the student's abilities, etc.); programmed instruction should provide whatever step size is required in any given situation. If step size may be different in different situations, then the idea of step-by-step instruction in no way contradicts the aim of developing independence and self-organization in the student. It is always possible to choose that step size which is optimal for the development of these processes and properties. What this step size should be for the development of creative processes is a special problem which goes beyond the issues under consideration at this particular point.

We note that step size should probably be greater in the teaching of creative processes than in the teaching of algorithmic processes, for which operation-by-operation instruction and control is possible and desirable. But in the development of creative processes, step size generally should be, clearly, smaller than in standard instruction in which only the correctness (or incorrectness) of students' solutions to the problems given them, i.e., the final result of their cognitive activity, and not its various stages, is controlled.

Let us now consider the second requirement. Since one of the most characteristic features of programmed instruction is that it requires information from the student at each step of the instructional process and responds to this information in a particular way (for example, by positively reinforcing the student's responses and actions, correcting them if they are wrong, etc.), it is necessary that the possible responses and actions on the part of the student be predicted. But can this be done in the teaching of heuristic processes, considering that in solving creative problems the student must search and test in fields which are unknown to him?

This question is extremely complex and has not as yet been fully resolved. At the moment it is possible to say only that, in many instances, possible student responses can be predicted. The programmer, knowing the solution to a creative problem (and he does know the solution!) and knowing from observation and experiment the possible lines along which a solution typically is sought, is able to form an idea of how the student will go about looking for a solution, and this permits him to specify at least fundamental program responses to the student's actions. But a creative problem remains a creative problem, and there may be cases in which the student's actions are not foreseen. Such cases may be dealt with in the same way they are dealt with in programmed texts and machine programs: "If your answer (or action) does not correspond with one of the specified ones, turn to such-and-such a page of the text" (or the instruction may even refer the student to the teacher). How to respond to such unpredicted responses or actions is a problem of instructional methodology and strategy, and is as much a problem in non-programmed, standard instruction as in programmed instruction. The means used to solve this problem in "good" standard instruction should serve as models for the solution of the same problem in the writing of programmed texts and machine-aided instruction programs.

Difficulties arise in the development of specific techniques for controlling the development and flow of heuristic processes in teaching programs. Thus, for example, the technique of filling in blanks, in the form in which it is often used in linear programs, is poorly suited to the teaching of heuristic processes, since it excludes or almost excludes searching. The student, as a rule, knows exactly or almost exactly what should go in the blank—the word, group of words, number, or whatever. This program framework in effect leads him to the correct answer, and this reduces the need for creative thinking by eliminating the need for searching for this correct answer.

There are difficulties also with multiple-choice responses. With this method, of course, the student is given a set of alternatives from which he is to choose one as a solution. In other words, he is given a predefined field of choice. But creative problems, as was indicated above, do not involve predefined fields of choice from which the problem-solver is to choose and test possible solutions to the problem. Therefore, as soon as the problem-solver is given a set of alternatives, the problem in question ceases to be creative, because that which makes it creative—an undefined field of choice—has been excluded. The student is not required to search for a solution, and this search is the essence of the creative process. Instead, he is faced with the simpler task of choosing from a given field of alternatives.

Does this mean that the multiple-choice method is of no use in the teaching of heuristic processes? No, provided that the student is not given a set of alternatives *until* he has carried out an independent search for a solution.

This requirement is also extremely important in the teaching of non-heuristic, non-creative processes by means of programmed instruction. However, in the teaching of heuristic, creative processes it assumes exceptional and decisive significance. Knowing of alternative possibilities for solving a problem *before* beginning to solve it, or during the process of looking for a solution, reduces the need for that process which the problem was intended to stimulate in the first place and which develops only as a result of being stimulated. We will not discuss here the methods by which the probability of the student's having a preliminary "peeping" knowledge of alternatives is reduced or eliminated, since this problem is a basic one in programmed instruction and a number of techniques for solving it have been developed.

Serious problems arise in connection with the use in programmed instruction of various cues, prompts, hints, etc.

It should be stated that the functions of these elements should vary, generally speaking, as a function of the goals of instruction (the goals of instruction in general and of each stage of the process in particular). Thus, if the goal of instruction is to develop certain direct (literally, "one-link," *Trans.*) associations in the student's mind, to evoke and reinforce a set of correct responses to a set of specific stimuli (as is often the case in programs of the Skinnerian type), then cues, hints, prompts, etc., are useful. They do, indeed, lead the student to the correct response, minimize the probability of error, and reinforce this response.

But instruction is not and cannot be reduced to the evocation and reinforcement of correct responses to specific stimuli, to the development of simple (one-link, *Trans.*) or even complex (multi-link, *Trans.*) associations. One of the most important goals of instruction is to enable the student to determine the conditions for any action independently, to know when to respond in a particular way (and not simply to respond mechanically to "prepared" stimulus conditions), to select from a number of possible conditions and actions those which are suitable (appropriate) from the point of view of goals available, and to carry out a search process with the goal of finding these conditions and actions, if they cannot be found in some predefined set of alternatives. Cues and prompts of the usual sort may exert a negative effect when they are used for this purpose in instruction.

Let us suppose that the student is to solve a creative problem and must, in order to do this, make use of a hidden, non-obvious property p located in field A. Let us assume further that this problem is one which induces the problem-solver to look for a solution in a completely different field, field B. The student chooses and tests all possible properties from field B without, of course, finding a solution. Then he is told (as students often are told during instruction of the standard variety) to direct his attention to the property or field of properties which must be used in order to arrive at a solution. Of course, he now arrives at a solution immediately, but only because the most difficult step in the solution of the problem, the one requiring creativity, has been performed for him. The purpose of presenting him with the problem was to induce him to seek and find a solution independently (in this case, the required property or field of properties). The hint which he was given made it unnecessary for him to seek and find a solution, i.e., it rendered the problem purposeless. Such a hint will undoubtly lead the student to the solution of this specific problem, but it will not teach him what is to be done (what operations should be performed) in order to be able to transcend similar impasses independently. The principal goal of teaching consists, in this respect, not of bringing about a series of specific solutions to specific problems, but of shaping general methods of actions which will make possible the independent searching for a solution to the most widely different problems and the independent finding of ways out of impasse situations. Errors in teaching occur frequently, in both standard and programmed instruction, when improper hints eliminate or diminish difficulties instead of equipping students with operations (procedures, methods) for overcoming them independently.

How can the student be taught to seek and find the way out of difficult situations more effectively, to succeed more often in finding solutions in spite of obstacles in his path? Only by teaching him effective heuristic procedures which point out operations that help him to find the way out of difficult situations *independently*, as well as the ability to select independently the particular heuristic procedure which will be most useful in seeking a solution to a particular problem.

A student should be equipped with a set of hierarchically organized heuristic procedures (rules) and be taught to know in which situations which heuristic procedures (or which set of heuristic rules) may be helpful in order to be able to refer to corresponding rules. He must be taught also to move from one heuristic to another when a heuristic which has been tested did not lead to the solution.

He should be taught to carry out a search not only among objects which are indicated in the text of a problem or are connected with them or may be obtained from them by means of their transformation, etc., and related knowledge (for example, within corresponding definitions, theorems, rules of transformation of these objects, etc.), but among the heuristic rules as well. Knowledge of heuristic rules is a special field of knowledge, and the process of searching within this field for a suitable procedure does not differ in principle from that of seeking a suitable theorem in the field (or set) of theorems. The distinction lies in the results of the search. A heuristic rule which has been found as a result of a search process represents knowledge of a higher order than knowledge of some specific theorem.

If knowledge is viewed as a specific psychological controlling system (and, really, knowledge directs man's actions and, thus, controls the process of his activity), then it is natural to assume that different knowledge represents different controlling systems, and that knowledge of different orders represent controlling systems of different orders. The distinction between psychological controlling systems of different orders lies not only in how this or that knowledge controls certain processes but, first of all, in *which* processes it controls. Thus, knowledge of a theorem (or any other formal proposition or rule of action) controls operations directed at the search for and isolation (i.e., identification, *Ed.*) of objects indicated in the theorem (objects to which the theorem is applicable) with subsequent transformation of these objects according to the mode of transformation shown in the rule or in the subsequent transformation

from these objects to other ones.* Knowledge of some heuristic
procedure controls actions directed at the search for and isolation
not of objects indicated in the theorem but of theorems
themselves within the field of theorems that are known, with
subsequent assessment of each theorem extracted for its fitness
and then its application, if it fits. It is clear that knowledge of how
to operate with theorems themselves rather than with their objects
is of a higher order than knowledge of how to operate with objects
indicated in any specific theorem. This might be called a
meta-knowledge.**

It should be noted that operations on theorems, in particular,
those directed at searching for a suitable theorem, do not exclude
and even presuppose operations on geometrical objects. But
operations on an object aimed at *finding* a suitable theorem are of
quite another nature than operations on objects aimed at an
application of a theorem. Application of a theorem presupposes
that the theorem to be applied is already known in the sense that
it is already identified (isolated), recalled, indicated from outside,
etc. This theorem unambiguously indicates which specific
attributes of an object should be isolated and what should be done
with them. Quite another situation is the case when there is a task
of *finding* a suitable theorem. The theorem which may fit the
problem situation is unknown beforehand and, thus, cannot
indicate which attributes of the object should be isolated,
transformed, etc. It follows that it is unknown beforehand which
attributes of the object should be looked for, isolated, and
transformed. A number of exploratory actions should be applied
to the object here in order to establish which attributes are present
in it. These attributes will determine which theorems are applicable to this object. The process of determination proceeds in such
a way that isolation of sets of attributes in the object during the

*For brevity, we shall speak only of transformations.

**Compare in Miller, Galanter, and Pribram, 1960: "In the more complex
kinds of problem-solving, therefore, we must have some way to generate
alternative Plans and to operate on them, test them, evaluate them. These
[are, L.L.] meta-Plans—Plans for forming other Plans. . ." (p. 169).

process of its investigation recalls the theorems (or other formal propositions) which have these indicated attributes to the left, e.g., of an implicational operator. Thus, for instance, if attributes *a, b, c* were discovered in some object *x*, these attributes may recall a theorem $a(x)$ & $b(x)$ & $c(x) \rightarrow A(x)$, which contains directions regarding these attributes on its left side. What has been said shows why the mode of operation on an object with the aim of *finding* some applicable theorem differs substantially from the mode of operation on the object aimed at *application* of a theorem which has been already found or indicated from outside.

In the next to the last paragraph we spoke of knowledge concerning operations on objects indicated in theorems, as well as of knowledge, and namely heuristic rules, concerning operations on theorems themselves (meta-knowledge).

There may, however, exist and does exist knowledge of how to operate with heuristic rules themselves, directed at search, isolation, and application within them. This knowledge and its corresponding controlling system is of a still higher order than the preceding one, and represents a meta-knowledge on the preceding meta-knowledge, i.e., meta-meta-knowledge or meta-knowledge of the second order.

The widespread shortcoming of current instruction (both standard and programmed) lies in the fact that students are mainly taught knowledge as to how to operate with specific (say, geometric) objects on the basis of corresponding formal propositions (this is knowledge of the first order), but are often not taught how to operate with these formal propositions themselves (how to search for them, compare them, test them, select them from among them the most appropriate ones, etc.). In other words, they are not taught corresponding heuristic rules or knowledge of the second order. This is why they often do not know how to get out of an impasse when none of the theorems which were recalled fit, and it is necessary to find another one which has not come to mind.

If the students are not usually or not often taught the rules of how to operate with rules such as theorems,* then even more so they are not taught how to operate with the heuristic rules themselves, i.e., they are not provided with the knowledge of how to operate with rules of operating with rules.

The role of knowing rules of different orders may be illustrated as follows.

Let us assume that, while solving some creative geometric problem, no suitable theorem has come to the problem-solver's mind and he found himself at an impasse. The only way to possibly find a suitable theorem is to utilize some heuristic which will direct and control the search for a theorem.** Let us assume then that the solver knows some heuristic rule of how to proceed in such a situation (i.e., he has corresponding knowledge of the second order) and tried to make use of it in searching for a suitable theorem.

However, the heuristic rule used did not fit and did not enable the problem-solver to find a suitable theorem. The only way out is to try to find another heuristic, i.e., to go on from the heuristic recalled to another one. But this requires the transition from the level of operation *with theorems* of some heuristic to the level of operation *with heuristics themselves*.

*Theorems, as well as other formal propositions (definitions, for example), may be regarded, and are regarded by some authors, in particular those working in heuristic programming, as rules in some broad sense. And this is in a sense justified, since formal propositions indicate the mode of transformation or the mode of transition from objects indicated on the left (antecedent) side of the formal statement formulated in the "if . . ., then" form to objects indicated on its right (consequent) side. In the proper, i.e., narrow, sense, rules, as distinct from other formal propositions, are only propositions which indicate, on their right side, an action, i.e., one which determines the transformation of objects rather than the transition from one object to another. However, in this part of our discussion we will refer to rules in the broad sense of the word.

**On a similar issue, Miller, Galanter, and Pribram (1960) write: "Searches are generally conducted according to some kind of Plan, usually a heuristic Plan. So we must have a heuristic Plan for generating a proof Plan for transforming a mathematical Plan for performing certain computations" (p. 179).

What is the proper procedure? We have already mentioned that there may exist and do exist rules of operation with heuristic rules which indicate what is to be done when some heuristic rule does not fit, how to search for another one, to which other heuristic it may be advisable to go on, etc. If the number of heuristic rules to be operated on is limited in any particular case, then operation with heuristic rules may even be algorithmized, and the rule of how to operate with heuristic rules may be formulated as an algorithm. In the more general case, it may be impossible or inexpedient to compile and utilize an algorithm for searching for heuristic procedures, and the rule of how to operate with heuristic rules will be of a heuristic nature. These heuristics (heuristic rules) of how to operate with heuristic rules will be heuristics of the second order and, in terms of knowledge, knowledge of the third order. The system of heuristic rules (instructions) of the second order may be regarded as a heuristic method of the second order, which indicates operations (a system of operations) as to what should be done on the heuristic rules or, if the latter are systematized, on the heuristic methods of the first order.

Let us return to our problem-solver who did not manage to find a suitable theorem via a heuristic rule of the first order which he tried to use. Now it is necessary to go on to another heuristic rule and to try to make use of it. For this purpose, the problem-solver must utilize heuristic rules of the second order. If the problem-solver knows these heuristic rules of the second order, and is able to apply them, he will be able to search for some suitable heuristic rule of the first order from among those which he knows. If he manages to find such a heuristic of the first order, it may help him to find a suitable theorem and to solve the problem. If the problem-solver does not know a heuristic rule of the second order, he may be unable to find a suitable heuristic of the first order which might lead to finding a suitable theorem, and, thus, will not solve the problem.

We have just said: "he *may* be unable to find a suitable heuristic of the first order" and not "he *will* be unable to find a suitable heuristic of the first order." This is because the transition from one heuristic to another may occur not solely on the basis of heuristic rules of the higher order which control the deliberate process of transition from heuristic to heuristic within the field of heuristic rules of the lower order, but also the transition from heuristic to heuristic may occur through an association mechanism when associations between them have been established earlier in one's experience. We note, however, that one of the effective ways of forming these associations is purposeful, deliberate, and controllable transition from heuristic to heuristic on the basis of heuristic rules of the higher order.

Let us assume that our problem-solver did not know heuristic rules of the second order and was unable to pass on to another heuristic of the first order by an association mechanism. He will find himself in an impasse of the second order.

What this means can be explained as follows.

Let us call "impasse of the first order" when a problem-solver is not able to find a suitable theorem on the basis of some heuristic of the first order. (The reason may lie in the fact that this heuristic was unsuitable.) Then it is natural to call an "impasse of the second order" a situation in which he is unable to find a suitable heuristic. If he were able to find a way out of the second impasse, and find an appropriate heuristic, this heuristic might help him to find a suitable theorem and, thus, to find his way out of the impasse of the first order.

We have spoken above of the fact that in order for search processes to proceed successfully within some field, it is necessary for the corresponding objects to be systematized in a particular way (associations between objects must be many-sided, multi-faceted, hierarchically organized, etc.). The same is true of the field of heuristic rules in which a search is to be carried out, when some heuristic that had been employed did not lead to the solution. The search within the field of heuristic rules may be more successful and the probability of finding a suitable heuristic is higher, when the heuristic rules themselves are well systematized (in the sense mentioned) and, in particular, well organized hierarchically.* The basis for such hierarchical systematization

---

*On the hierarchical organization of Plans in the sense of Plan used by the authors, see also Miller, Galanter, and Pribram (1960).

(organization) of heuristic rules resides generally in the different degrees of generality of different heuristic rules.

However, proper systematization of heuristic rules of the first order is only a necessary, but not a sufficient, condition for successful operation upon them. A second necessary condition is the deliberate teaching to students of methods of how to operate upon them, i.e., explicit teaching of heuristic rules of operations on heuristic rules (heuristic rules of the second order). Without such prior teaching, an individual may be able to utilize some heuristic when it is spontaneously recalled or suggested from outside as a cue, but not be able to search for and find a suitable heuristic independently. He will also not be able to go on purposefully and deliberately from one heuristic to another, when the preceding one proved to be unsuitable or did not lead to a success.

In a more general form, it must be said that it is necessary to teach students to carry out a search on *each* level by using rules of a corresponding order, as well as to teach them to go from one level to another. The necessity for deliberately teaching how to search on each individual level is explained by the fact that the ability to search successfully on one level is usually not transferred automatically to search on another level. A student may be successful in searching, say, for theorems and be quite unable to search for heuristic rules. This is especially true of the ability to make use of heuristic rules of different orders. A student may be successful in utilizing heuristic rules of the first order and be unable to utilize heuristic rules of the second order. This is so because heuristic rules of different orders involve operations directed at different content objects. The operations themselves are also not identical. Thus, heuristic rules of different orders are diverse and quite specific, which requires that they be taught separately and deliberately.

If the function of teaching heuristic methods of each specific order consists of the formation in students of corresponding psychological controlling systems of a corresponding order, then teaching the ability to proceed from methods of one order to methods of another order consists of the formation of the ability to "switch on," when needed, the controlling systems of corresponding orders. This applies both to "switching on" systems of a higher order when a system of a lower order has not "worked," and to "switching on" systems of a lower order when a system of a higher order has determined the direction of search and the search itself may be carried out now by the system of a lower order. Only the ability to proceed independently from methods of one order to methods of another order creates the ability to break impasses of different orders independently, and represents the mechanism of self-organization and self-control of which we spoke above.

Now we can return, on a new level, to a consideration of the question of prompts and cues which we began to discuss above.

Many of the prompts and cues which we have earlier considered and which are given to the student in the course of both standard and programmed instruction are in a sense heuristic in nature. It is entirely a question of how to apply these heuristic devices in teaching—of how to make use of them. Standard use of these techniques is inadequate, because (1) they appear to the student as being provided from outside, and (2) they are preselected and handed to him in final form (i.e., those heuristic procedures which are required to solve the problem at hand are selected from all possible relevant procedures and handed to the student).

From what has been said, it is clear why this is undesirable. This is so, because the fundamental difficulty in the solution of creative problems with the aid of heuristic procedures is that, first, the problem-solver must independently select the appropriate procedure from the set of all known procedures, and, second, he must give himself the appropriate heuristic cue. It is precisely these important steps which are usually taken for him and which he does not learn to take for himself, when he is handed preselected and prepared heuristic procedures,[3] i.e., like those which the student should assimilate and perform using internal means of self-control.[4] For this purpose, the student, if we summarize what was said above, must be taught: (1) the individual heuristic procedures; (2) the organization (literally, "system,"

Trans.) of these procedures on each level and their corresponding systematization; (3) the organization (literally "system," *Trans.*) of connections among procedures of different orders and their corresponding placement into a hierarchy; (4) the ability to search, in case of difficulty, for the appropriate procedure within one level, which includes, in particular, the ability to go from procedure to procedure, if the current one proves not to be useful in finding a solution, to test each procedure and to select suitable one(s); (5) the ability to go from procedures of one order to procedures of another order in both directions; and (6) the ability to perform operations, i.e., to carry out the processes, which each procedure specifies.

Since heuristic procedures are rules of a particular sort (rules for seeking the solution to a problem, rules for thinking), and programmed instruction is effective in teaching rules, the methods of programmed instruction, in principle, impose no restrictions on the teaching of these procedures[5] and, in many cases, of their corresponding processes.

To summarize, the teaching of not only algorithmic but also heuristic processes is an important problem in the field of programmed instruction. We have tried to show that programmed instruction may be used not only to teach elementary skills and habits, but also to develop rather complex heuristic processes. The development of these processes unquestionably requires a specific approach to the programming of instructional material, and of students' activity for its acquisition and processing, especially as regards the selection and presentation to the student of creative problems, as well as the control of the assimilation of this material and the solution of these problems. The detailed study of such an approach is a problem for future research.

Notes

1.   A number of authors have treated the question of the systematization of knowledge in accordance with various principles and the teaching of multifaceted associative

systems (see, e.g., Kabanova-Meller, 1962; Samarin, 1962; Shenshev, 1960).

2. Attempts to find such formal criteria have not succeeded as yet and it is improbable that they ever will succeed. The problem of finding such criteria is apparently not well-formulated.

3. On the basis of heuristic procedures provided to students from outside, they may be taught only to *make use* of these procedures—to *apply* them (which is, in itself, of great significance at some stages of instruction). But this makes it impossible to teach students independently to *search for* them and *select* them, which is the prerequisite for the application of heuristic procedures when there is a question of an independent solution to problems.

4. An experiment in the use of instruction as applied to the solution of geometric problems is described in Chapter Eight of this volume.

5. Since the problem of teaching the ability to discover and formulate heuristic rules independently has been little investigated as regards standard educational procedures, it would be inappropriate to discuss in this chapter the use of programmed instruction for this purpose.

Chapter Seven

Algorithmization and Heuristics in Foreign Language Teaching

1. **Algorithms and Algorithmic Processes**

Very often in the study of both their native language and foreign languages, students have a good grasp of grammatical rules but nevertheless make mistakes in speaking and writing. Psychological studies have shown that knowledge of rules in itself often does not guarantee the ability to use language correctly (to write grammatically, for example) precisely because students do not know the algorithms governing their application.

As we have already said, the concept of an algorithm should be distinguished from that of an algorithmic process. If an algorithm (algorithmic prescription) is a system of commands (instructions) specifying the actions or operations which must be performed in order to solve a given problem, then an algorithmic process is the actual system constituted by these operations. Moreover, it is possible to know an instruction and yet be unable to act in accordance with it, and vice versa. In addition, one may, in many instances, even be unaware of the operations one performs in solving a problem successfully. This phenomenon is especially common in verbal behavior.

For example, a person who speaks German will say: "Ich *kenne* ihn"—"I know him," but "Ich *weiss* dass er kommt"—"I know that he is coming" or "Ich *weiss* es"—"I know it." If asked why he uses the verb "kennen" in one case and the verb "wissen" in another, he may not be able to answer. He may not know which semantic and syntactic factors (attributes) he considers in choosing one verb or the other, although he must isolate these factors by means of specific operations before he selects the appropriate verb. But being unaware of these operations, still he cannot fail to perform them.* In the opposite case, he would be unable to choose the required verb and would make a mistake.

An important conclusion follows: processes which occur instantaneously and unconsciously on the basis of intuition (those involving linguistic intuition in particular) often occur in accordance with specific rules. Shevaryov (1959) isolated a specific type of processes, more precisely associations, which occur in accordance with specific rules while the rules themselves are not recalled. He called these associations "conforming-to-rules associations"). They may even have an algorithmic or algorithmoid character. This means that underlying them there are operations (or, more precisely, systems of operations) which, although unconscious, are always performed and which often may be algorithmically described (i.e., specific algorithms corresponding to them may be written). The idea that some verbal acts have no operations underlying them is an illusion resulting from the fact that the operations involved are often performed unconsciously, and neither the teacher nor the learner may be aware of them.

We have just introduced the term "algorithmoid" process as distinct from "algorithmic" process. The difference is as follows. Since an algorithm is a sequence of instructions, it is more appropriate to designate with the term "algorithmic" these processes which occur sequentially (consecutively) or one after the other. Processes which occur simultaneously, or nearly simultaneously, or partially simultaneously, we shall now call "algorithmoid."

Algorithmoid processes may be formed in two ways: (1) as a result of the development of an algorithmic process when the

*So long as there is no specific awareness of semantic and syntactical operations and the rules that govern them, the individual is bound to perform in accordance with these long-established and "unconscious" patterns. To exercise "conscious" control and make deliberate choices/changes he would have to have some awareness of the system of operations and how it can be altered. In the vernacular: "You've got to know what you're doing" to accomplish it.

consecutive process has been transformed into a simultaneous or nearly simultaneous or instantaneous process; in this case, the process is simultaneous, deterministic, post-algorithmic, as discussed in the preceding chapter; or (2) as simultaneous (nearly simultaneous or partially simultaneous) from the very beginning; in this case it is already initially haphazardly algorithmoid.

Algorithmic processes as well as algorithmoid processes may be conscious or unconscious, i.e., the individual may or may not be able to express them in a verbal form. (A person is or is not able to tell which actions he is performing or was performing when he is—or was—solving some problem; he is or is not able to give an account of the actions being performed or which were performed.) In turn, conscious processes as well as the unconscious ones may be formed on the basis of algorithms or on the basis of a teacher's example—through imitation, or haphazardly by means of "adjusting" to a situation. We show a taxonomy of according-to-rules processes in Figure 7.1a and 7.1b.

The question may arise: how can it come about that algorithmic or algorithmoid unconscious processes of which a person is not aware are formed on the basis of algorithms which are always conscious? Or vice versa, how can it be that algorithmic or algorithmoid processes formed on the basis of a conscious algorithm become unconscious? The answer is that they may be the results of *automatization*. The process, at first conscious, ceases to be conscious as it automatizes itself. Consciousness passes (transforms) into unconsciousness. Here we have to consider secondary unconsciousness. This must be distinguished from primary unconsciousness, which often takes place in the case of initially haphazardly algorithmoid processes when they have never been in one's awareness earlier.

Although, as has been said above, according-to-rules processes proceed without one's first recalling an algorithm (algorithmic prescription) and, therefore, not on the basis of self-instructions, algorithms may represent them, i.e., they may be algorithmically described. However, if in the case of the algorithmic process only one single algorithm may represent it, in the case of an algorithmoid process these may be a set of algorithms. This is

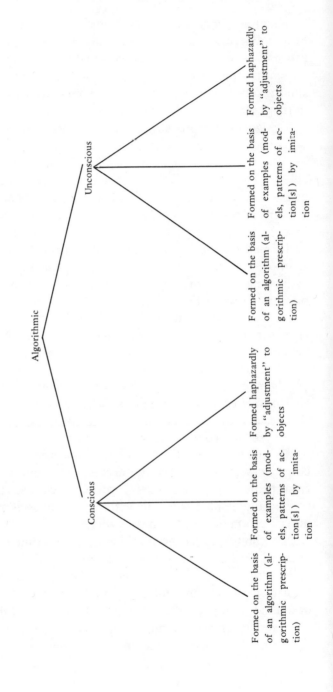

Figure 7.1a

According-to-Rules Processes

Figure 7.1b

According-to-Rules Processes

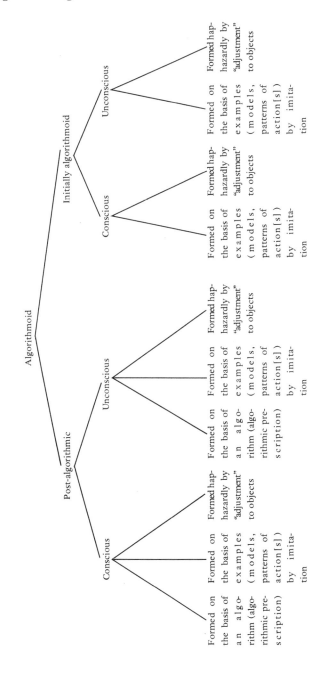

explained by the fact that in order to express an algorithm or algorithms in accordance with an algorithmoid process, the latter must be first unfolded, i.e., transformed, from a simultaneous into a consecutive form. But there are usually a variety of ways for such an unfolding. This means that there exists not one single sequence (order), but a set of different sequences (orders) of operations into which one and the same process may be unfolded. That is why a number and not one single algorithm may be made to conform with an algorithmoid process as distinct from an algorithmic process.

Linguistic intuition, the ability to perceive and act instantaneously, is presently recognized by many authors as being not the initial point in the development of habits and skills, but rather the final result of a developmental process.

If specific operations underlie verbal habits, and these operations often are algorithmic or algorithmoid in nature, then they should be discovered by the teacher or communicated to him, and described algorithmically. Knowledge of the appropriate algorithms can enable him to develop verbal performance in the student in a conscious and deliberate manner.

2. Verbal Activity as Problem-Solving

It was stated above that algorithms are always directed toward the solution of specific problems. A problem is a situation in which something is given and something is to be obtained. Problem-solving consists of the transformation of that which is given to that which is to be obtained.

In order to increase the effectiveness of language teaching and, specifically, to apply algorithms for this purpose, it is extremely important to regard verbal activity from a particular point of view, namely as the solution of a series of problems.

In all verbal acts there is, in fact, something which is given and something which is to be obtained, and the verbal act itself is the transformation of the given to that which is to be obtained, and the design of a specific solution.

Thus, in perceiving speech (listening or reading), one proceeds from certain verbal phenomena (words with particular morphological attributes, and phrases and sentences with particular syntactic attributes), in order to obtain (find, extract) the meaning which is hidden in them. The process of perceiving and understanding speech, therefore, represents a transition from that which is explicitly given (language forms) to that which is to be obtained (meaning). The meaning which is found is the solution to the problem of perceiving and understanding speech.

Speech production is, in essence, the process of solving the converse problem. In this case, the givens are thoughts (meaning) which must be transmitted, and the problem is to obtain (find, utilize) the linguistic forms which are capable of expressing and transmitting these thoughts.

The thesis that verbal behavior is a process of solving a series of problems may give rise to objections. It is widely assumed that problems are solved on the basis of logical reasoning; anatomized speech acts, however, are not performed on the basis of logical reasoning and should not be so performed. However, the idea that problem-solving always occurs on the basis of logical reasoning seems to be incorrect.

If we take problem-solving to be the transformation of something given to something which is to be obtained, regardless of the means by which this transformation is accomplished (it would seem to be unnecessary to include more than this within the general phenomenological concept of problem-solving), then it is clear that problems may be solved not only on the basis of logical reasoning, but also on the basis of a direct (associative) transition from what is given to what is to be obtained (i.e., a person sees a table and says: "a table"; he wishes to communicate the fact that he is leaving, and thus says: "I am leaving"; etc.). There can be no doubt that, in this sense, verbal activity is fully congruent with the concept of problem-solving, and may be considered as the process of solving a series of problems.

In language teaching, it is well to keep in mind that there are various types of problems and various ways of solving these problems.

It is interesting that these various ways of solving problems usually co-exist in the mind. Thus, while solving some problems automatically, without thinking about the kind of solution, one may think about how to solve other problems (for example, how best to express something). It may be noted parenthetically that this fact refutes the widely held notion that knowledge of a language (either one's own or a foreign language) is purely automatic or habitual in nature. Language teaching, including the teaching of foreign languages, cannot therefore be directed only toward the development of habits; the problems which the language teacher must solve are considerably more diverse than that.

The diversity of the problems which one must solve during the process of verbal communication engenders the diversity of the processes by means of which one can solve these problems. It should also be said that, in the process of teaching language and developing verbal skills and habits, different ways of solving problems may appear, in many instances, as different stages in the formation of verbal skills and habits. Problems which are solved automatically at the higher stages of the formation of verbal skills and habits may be solved at lower stages by means of choice, search, and even, in some cases, reasoning. Since there is no way to insert fully developed speech habits into a person's head, it is necessary in many cases to pass through various stages of problem-solving during the teaching process.

The problems which must be solved during verbal activity are communicational in nature, and, therefore, emerge as verbal-communicational and communicational-verbal problems. They are communicational because each verbal act performed during the process of verbal production (each phrase or sentence) is intended to transmit some amount of information. The process is reversed in the case of verbal perception and comprehension: one is given (or assigned) certain verbal phenomena which must be analyzed in order to discover and extract the information contained in them. The problems which are solved in the process of producing speech are thus communicational-verbal problems, while those which are solved in the process of perceiving and understanding speech are verbal-communicational problems.

The concept of an elementary *communication unit,* of which

we will make use in the following discussion, is very important, and warrants a detailed description. It is used here to denote the minimum information which can be transmitted during the verbal act.

For example, when a person says: "I met him on the street," he transmits the following communication units:

(1) *I* did the meeting, and not anyone else;
(2) I *met* him, and did not see, embrace, or strike him;
(3) I *met*, but not *meet* or *shall meet*;
(4) I met *him*, not her, you, them, etc.; and
(5) I met him *on the street*, and not at the theater, on a train, etc.

Of course, the sentence as a whole also represents a communication, but it is a complex one, i.e., it consists of a combination of elementary communication units; but, in using this concept below, we will be referring, for the most part, to the elementary units of information of which complex units are composed. It is clear that transmission of communication units becomes necessary whenever the addressee does not know something or there is the possibility of uncertainty in comprehension.

3. Analysis and Transformation Operations in
    the Solution of Communicational-Verbal and
    Verbal-Communicational Problems

The solution of any problem consists of two sorts of processes: (1) analysis (cognition) of that which is given;* this process is based on specific operations for isolating the properties (attributes) of the object under analysis; and (2) transformation of that which is given into that which is to be obtained, or transition from the first to the latter; this process is carried out by means of special transformation or transition operations.

These two processes (analysis and transformation) are easily illustrated by means of a simple arithmetic example.

---

*The notion of "analysis" is applied here in a broad sense; analysis in this sense may include specific analytic as well as different specific synthetic operations.

Let us consider the following problem:

$$\frac{100 \div (2 + 3)^2}{(4 + 6)(2 + 3)} = \quad ?$$

In order to solve this problem, it is necessary, first, to isolate the characteristics of the given (mathematical) objects, to see (notice, isolate, direct one's attention to) the fact that, for example, there is a numerator and a denominator, that there is a division sign after the number 100, that the digits 2 and 3 in the numerator are in parentheses, etc. Then the given expression must be transformed in accordance with particular rules, in order to arrive at the answer.

Failure to perform any of the analytic operations, i.e., failure to isolate (see, notice) even a component of this complex object (for example, the parentheses, division sign, addition sign, etc.) immediately results in a mistake. On the other hand, failure to perform a transformation (for example, failing to add, raise to a power, or divide) or accomplishing the transformation not according to the rules (e.g., first dividing the number 100 in the numerator by the sum [2 + 3], and then squaring the result), would likewise give an incorrect result.

An analogous process takes place during the solution of communicational-verbal and verbal-communicational problems. We will consider here only problems of the second category.

Let us assume that a person is to read and understand the German sentence: "Er teilte mir etwas mit." If he were to fail to perform any of the required analysis operations, for example, if he did not isolate (notice) the word "mit" at the end of the sentence, or did not relate "mit" to the verb "teilte," or did not notice the "e" at the end of the word "teilte" (i.e., if he perceived "teilte" as "teilt"), or if he failed to effect, in accordance with specific rules, the transition from the given verbal phenomena to the meaning expressed by them, he would immediately have made a mistake or several mistakes. Thus, instead of correctly understanding the sentence as meaning "He informed me of something" ("mitteilen" means "to inform of"), he would think that someone had uttered the absurd statement "He divided me something" ("teilen" by itself means "to divide"), or that the statement was in the present tense instead of the past: "He informs me of something" ("teilte . . . mit" is past tense, while "teilt . . . mit" is present tense).

It is often stated nowadays that students must be taught to comprehend spoken and written communications directly and immediately rather than by means of analysis. This distinction is meaningless, since it is impossible to comprehend something, directly or otherwise, without perceiving (seeing, isolating) the elements of grammatical (or, more generally, verbal) form by means of which thoughts are transmitted (e.g., without perceiving the prefix "mit-" in the above German sentence, relating it to the verb "teilte," noticing the ending "-e" in this word, etc.); yet *this perception of elements constitutes analysis*, and it is carried out by means of specific operations.

We have noted the distinction between analytic and transformation operations, and have illustrated their significance in solving a verbal-communicational problem. The same distinction exists with regard to the solution of communicational-verbal problems, except that, in this case, analytic operations are directed toward analysis (isolation, consideration) not of verbal phenomena, as in the case of the perception of foreign speech, but of communication units which must be transmitted actively through speech or writing; the transformation operations are directed not toward the transition from linguistic forms to the communication units carried by them, but toward the transformation of communication units which the speaker or writer wishes to transmit to linguistic forms which are capable of transmitting them.[1]

From what has been said above concerning the role of analysis (isolation, detection) of the elements of verbal form in speech perception and comprehension, and analysis of communication units in speech production, as well as the role of operations for making the transition from language form to communication units, and vice versa, it is possible to draw some conclusions about the fundamental causes of the mistakes which students make in studying and using a foreign language:

(1)   they do not know what to isolate (consider); or
(2)   they do not know how to isolate it; or
(3)   they fail to isolate all of the factors that must be isolated; or
(4)   they do not know the rules for going from what is given (isolated) to what is required.

4.   **Difficulties in the Solution of Communicational-Verbal and Verbal-Communicational Problems**

Let us examine two such difficulties.

The first is the necessity of taking into consideration (isolating) a large number of formal grammatical and semantic factors, as well as the rules governing the transformation of what is given in the problem to what is to be obtained.

The following are mistakes committed by (native, Russian speaking, *Ed.*) students while trying to solve the problem of understanding and translating the English sentence: "He is like a child."

Student A: He likes the child.
Student B: He likes children.
Student C: He likes his child.
Student D: He likes the child.
Student E: The child likes him.

What factors did these students fail to isolate in perceiving this sentence, and what analytic operations did they fail to perform?

Student A failed to consider (1) the presence of the word "is," (2) the absence of the ending "-s" on the word "like," and (3) the presence of the indefinite and not the definite article before the word "child." As a result, he perceived and understood the sentence as if it had been: "He likes the child."

Student B failed to take into account (1) and (2) above as well as (3), the fact that the word appearing in the sentence is "child" and not "children." He perceived and understood the sentence as if it were: "He likes children." The other students failed to consider a number of other factors.

We see that comprehension of even a simple sentence such as this one requires consideration of quite a number of factors (attributes of verbal form and different meanings which words may have). If the students had isolated and considered the required attributes, they would have understood the sentence correctly. In more complex sentences, there are dozens and sometimes hundreds of cues which must be taken into account. Yet it is sufficient to fail to isolate even one factor, for a mistake in comprehension to arise. (In many instances failure to isolate individual factors is compensated by semantic cues which permit guessing of the meaning without perceiving all the attributes of linguistic form. This decreases in no way the importance of teaching students to consider all relevant components and peculiarities of linguistic form as well as the ability to move from the components and peculiarities to the information which they carry.)

When we speak of considering various factors in the process of perceiving and producing speech, we certainly do not mean to imply that this process occurs deliberately or consciously (at least at the higher stages of habit development), i.e., by means of specific self-instruction which the individual gives to himself: don't forget to consider this factor, don't forget to consider that factor, etc. It occurs automatically, the speaker as listener being unaware of the fundamental operations which he is performing, and moreover without his carrying out any discursive-logical reasoning whatever. We wish only to emphasize that the process of considering factors cannot fail to occur (consciously or unconsciously), and that the number of factors to be considered is often enormous.

Consideration of those factors specific to foreign languages presents special difficulties. Let us examine some of these difficulties in somewhat greater detail.

Consideration of Factors Specific to a Foreign Language (Elements of Verbal Form in Speech Perception and Communication Units in Speech Production) as Opposed to Native Language Factors
In foreign speech perception these difficulties result from the fact that it is necessary for one to consider (notice, pay attention

to, orient oneself to) elements of verbal form which differ from those of one's native language (there always exist, of course, elements common to both, but we are not concerned with these at the moment). Thus, many of the difficulties associated with understanding a foreign language are due to these factors. For example, Russian students often do not pay attention to articles (since there are none in Russian) and to word order (in Russian, word order is freer), although both articles and word order, in many instances, carry important semantic information.

Difficulties associated with consideration of factors not present in one's native language are especially apparent in the process of speech production. One must, first, consider all of the specific communication units which are to be transmitted (many errors in verbal production are due to failure to consider *all* of them), and, second, find and apply appropriate means for transmitting them which are specific to the language in question.

One of the greatest difficulties in speaking, and therefore in teaching, a foreign language is the fact that often the student's native language and the foreign language he is learning require that not fully coinciding sets of elementary communication units about a given event be sent, and they often utilize different means of transmitting this information.

Let us consider these factors separately.

When an English-speaking person wishes to state that someone is working on his book, he must convey the information that *he* (and not she, we, you, etc.) is doing the work, that he is *working* on the book (and not, say, reviewing it), that he *is* *working* (not worked or will work) on the book, etc. All of these communication units are expressed in the sentence: "He is working on his book."

A Russian-speaking person, in stating this same fact must express all of these items of information except one. A Russian-speaker does not have to communicate (and reflect this information in the grammatical form of the verb) whether the person in question is working on his book in general or at that particular moment. In the first case he would use the present indefinite tense, while in the second case he would use the present continuous tense.

What has been said does not mean that it is not possible in Russian to express or emphasize, when needed, that someone is working (not works) on the book. But since, in any case, this distinction is not obligatory in Russian, and therefore, not fixed in the formal syntactical construction, it is expressed by other means, namely, lexically. The Russian-speaker who wishes to communicate (emphasize) that "He is *working* on the book" would add the word *now*, or *presently*, etc.

Differences between languages consist primarily of different requirements as to the communication units which must be transmitted when communicating in these languages. Examples such as that given above are well-known and may be multiplied at will (see, for example, Belyaev, 1964, 1965; Revzin and Rosenzweig, 1964; Retsker, 1950; Shenshev, 1960). Science long ago established the fact that different languages conceptually segment reality in different ways. According to the hypothesis of linguistic relativity, which is in Russian linguistic literature usually referred to as the Sapir-Whorf hypothesis (see, e.g., Sapir, 1931, Whorf, 1956; and in relation to language teaching, e.g., Carroll, 1963), this leads to the fact that people perceive reality differently depending on the categories which are specific to their language. Though this dependence was established in a number of studies, the connection between verbal categories and perception is not always direct and strict. If, for example, the segmentation of colors in some language is not highly fractionated, this does not mean that people do not discern hues which are not reflected in language categories. Important also is the fact, emphasized particularly by Vygotsky (1956), that the content of categories changes in the process of historical development as well as in individual development, which is one more argument against rigid conditioning of perception by a language category.

For us, here, it is essential, however, to note quite other aspects of the fact that languages, at each given level of historical development, differently segment reality, namely: differences in segmenting reality give rise to different requirements on the communication units which often must be expressed in these languages, when speaking of the same events, and therefore to different requirements on speakers of these languages. In teaching, however, it is the consequences of the basic differences in the ways that languages segment reality, i.e., the different requirements for communication units to be transmitted, that are of primary importance. These requirements may be formulated in the form of specific rules or, as we will see, in the form of algorithms. In the example cited above, such a rule might be formulated as follows. "In speaking about an action in English, check whether this action occurs in general or only at a given moment, and on this basis choose the appropriate grammatical form (the indefinite or the continuous tense)." It is clear that requirements of this sort are, as Shenshev (1960) emphasized, requirements primarily on thinking and not on speech. In order to communicate information about an action, the English-speaking person must *think* about something that the Russian-speaker does not have to think about, i.e., he must perform a different cognitive activity.

The specific requirements which a foreign language imposes on its speakers give rise in turn to important requirements on the content and methods of foreign language instruction. Obviously, before it is possible to teach the student how to express a given unit of information in a foreign language, he must be taught which units of information to communicate, i.e., the requirements which the foreign language imposes with regard to information to be communicated, as well as the ability to meet these requirements.

The teaching of this ability constitutes that important part of teaching students to think in a foreign language which a number of authors regard as essential (see, e.g., Anan'ev, 1957; Belyaev, 1964, 1965; Retsker, 1950; Shenshev, 1960), although none of them has precisely formulated the concept of thinking in a foreign language in terms of requirements on information to be transmitted which a speaker of this language must fulfill, i.e., on the level of algorithmic instructions which can be written for the purpose of teaching a foreign language and which may be specifically and particularly taught.

The basic difficulty in learning a foreign language is perhaps not so much in mastering ways of transmitting various sorts of communication units as in assimilating the requirements which the language in question imposes on the communication units to be transmitted in each specific situation and becoming accustomed to fulfilling these requirements in each act of communication, i.e., to get accustomed to take into consideration all specifics (foreign language communication units) to be conveyed. In other words, the initial and perhaps major difficulty is, as has been emphasized in the literature, learning to think in the conceptual categories of the people whose language is being studied.

These considerations indicate that defects in "thinking in a foreign language" give rise to two basic possible psychological causes of mistakes in verbal production*:

(1) students may fail to consider *any* of the specific requirements on communication units to be transmitted, communicating only that information which their native language requires to be transmitted; and

(2) students may fail to consider *all* of the specific requirements on communication units to be transmitted in the foreign language.

Knowledge of a foreign language presupposes, also, knowledge of the specific means by which communication units are expressed in that language. The psychological difficulty involved in learning these means results from the fact that students, acting from habit, often attempt to transfer into the foreign language not only the communication units transmitted in their native language, but also the means of expressing these communication units (including those which are specific to the foreign language), which they use in their native language (for example, word order, grammatical constructions, intonation, etc.). Both of these habits must be overcome in the course of learning a foreign language.

Before discussing the question of how to teach students to consider all of the specific communication units which must be transmitted in each individual situation when speaking a foreign

---

*The general psychological causes of mistakes, without regard to the specific requirements imposed by a foreign language on thinking (information), were indicated above. Here the sources of mistakes associated with this factor are described.

language and the role which algorithms can play in this regard, we will consider the possible role of patterns in foreign language teaching.

5.   Patterns in Foreign Language Teaching

It is generally recognized that linguistic patterns (in particular, the use of substitution drills and other procedures) play an important part in the teaching of linguistic skills and habits. Learning these models helps the student to develop the ability to construct sentences correctly without thinking about it, which is of great importance in learning to speak a language well.

However, one may believe that this skill by itself is not sufficient. It is possible, for example, to have a thorough mastery of English sentence patterns of the type "He works" and "He is working" and still answer the question "What is he doing now (at this moment)?" by saying "He works" instead of "He is working."

In order to choose (use) the correct patterns, one must consider the specific communication units which the language in question requires to be transmitted. There may be a large number of such communication units, and taking proper account of them constitutes a separate and not always simple task. But it is precisely the solution of this task, the ability to analyze and properly utilize information, which knowledge of patterns alone cannot provide.

Knowledge of patterns, then, is a necessary but not a sufficient condition for being able to speak a foreign language.[2] In order to choose, combine, and use patterns correctly, it is necessary to be able to analyze the communication units which are to be transmitted and to go on from this analysis to a synthesis of those patterns which are capable of expressing them. Patterns are only bricks from which the "speech house" is built, not the house itself, and teaching (individual) patterns is equivalent to teaching the making of bricks (which is absolutely necessary), but is not the same as teaching how to build houses, i.e., which bricks to use (since foreign languages are constructed of different sorts of bricks), when to use them, and how to put them together.

Can algorithms be of use in solving this latter problem, to

which as yet a satisfactory solution has not been found? In other words, is it possible to design algorithms which will teach the student *what* to pay attention to and *how* to proceed in the process of perceiving and producing speech, which will teach him to consider *everything* which must be considered and to *go on* from these factors (in verbal perception, these factors are elements of linguistic form; while in verbal production, they are communication units) to the information (meaning) and linguistic form (phrases and sentences) corresponding to them? This question may be answered in the affirmative. Moreover, it may be said that the use of algorithms for these purposes can significantly increase the effectiveness of language instruction.

Because algorithms which can be used in the reception process for verbal communications (perception and comprehension) are different from those which should be used in the verbal-production process, these two types of algorithm should be discussed separately. We will term those of the first type perception algorithms, and those of the second type production algorithms.[3]

6. Perception Algorithms

Perception algorithms may be divided into two broad groups: algorithms for analyzing (recognizing) grammatical phenomena and algorithms for determining the meaning of grammatical (syntactical and lexical) phenomena (comprehension algorithms). An example will help to clarify these distinctions.

Let us consider the German sentence "Dem Lehrer gab der Schüler das Buch." One of the ways of understanding this sentence is first to isolate (recognize) the syntactic functions of the words of which it is composed, specifically, to determine which word is the subject, and which are complements (the subject of this sentence is "der Schüler," while "dem Lehrer" and "das Buch" are complements). Then the grammatical meaning of the subject and complements must be considered; specifically, it must be noted that, in a sentence with a transitive verb in the active voice, the subject represents the agent which is performing the action denoted by the verb, while the complement indicates the object toward which the action is directed. This information permits correct comprehension of the sentence: "The pupil gave the book to the teacher." Failure to identify the subject (or the other components of the sentence) or failure to consider their grammatical function, immediately results in a mistaken comprehension: "The teacher gave the pupil the book." Such errors are frequently encountered in language teaching.

Unambiguous and general instructions on how to solve the first of these problems, namely recognition of the class (type) to which the grammatical phenomena in question belong, would constitute an algorithm for recognizing grammatical phenomena (grammatical recognition algorithm). Unambiguous and general instructions on how to solve the second problem—determining the meaning of grammatical phenomena—would constitute an algorithm for determining the meaning of grammatical phenomena (a grammatical comprehension algorithm).*

In the above example, recognizing the subject is easy. It is sufficient to look at the articles modifying the nouns ("dem" in front of the first noun is the marker of an oblique case, and so indicates that this noun is not the subject; "der" modifying a noun of the masculine gender indicates that this noun is the subject of the sentence or clause). In other situations it is not so easy to recognize the subject, since several articles (including the article "der") are homonymic and so do not unambiguously indicate the case of the noun they modify (e.g., the articles "die" and "das"

---

*We call this algorithm "grammatical comprehension algorithm" and not simply "comprehension algorithm," since it conditions (stipulates) comprehension only on that part of meaning (i.e., only those communication units) which is conveyed by grammatical forms. These are grammatical forms of words (morphological forms) and forms of their connections (syntactical forms or syntactical constructions). To comprehend a sentence as a whole, it is necessary to recognize also the semantic meaning of words (perhaps via a semantic comprehension algorithm) and to bring (combine, synthesize) all meanings together. In a real verbal perception, all these processes often proceed in parallel, or nearly simultaneously, or in rapid succession; very often they interact. The recognition of the semantic meaning of the word may influence, for example, the recognition of its morphological and syntactical functions and vice versa.

can be both the nominative and the accusative). If these articles occur in the first and third positions in a sentence, it is impossible to determine from them alone which of the words accompanying these articles is the subject and which the complement. How is the subject to be recognized in this case? What operations must be performed on the sentence in order to accomplish recognition?

Many of the mistakes which students make in understanding and translating sentences are due to the fact that they often are unable to locate the subject, because they do not know what to do to the sentence in order to find it, i.e., they do not know which elements to isolate and correlate and how to go about doing this.

A set of general instructions describing what to do with any sentence in order to find its subject would constitute an algorithm for identifying the subject. Such algorithms for German have been written, for example, by A.R. Belopol'skaya, who is one of the pioneers in the development and application of morphological and syntactic analysis algorithms in the field of German language teaching (see Belopol'skaya, 1963; Belopol'skaya and Krylova, 1964; Belopol'skaya and Landa, 1963).

Since we are unable to present this algorithm here, we refer the reader to Belopol'skaya and Landa (1963). Examples of algorithms for recognizing grammatical phenomena may be found also in several other methodological works on foreign language instruction (e.g., Eiger and Hochlerner, 1964; Krupatkin, 1965; Gunther, 1965; Bung, 1967; Edwards, 1967; Malir, 1967).

Specific grammatical objects (words, phrases, sentences, etc.) constitute the input to any grammatical identification algorithm, and information regarding the class to which the grammatical object belongs (e.g., whether a given word is a noun or a verb, the subject of a sentence or a complement, whether a given segment of a sentence is construction *a, b, c, d,* or *e,* etc.) is the output. An identification algorithm indicates the name of the class to which an object belongs by checking for the presence of certain attributes in the object; in other words, it assigns the object to a specific class.

In order to understand a sentence, it is not enough to recognize the grammatical phenomena contained in it (for example, the type of construction involved), and it is also not enough to recognize the grammatical meaning of these phenomena, i.e., the information which they convey. As pointed out above, the semantic meanings of individual words must also be recognized (determined). This process, too, may be carried out on the basis of specific rules, which, in this case, indicate the correspondence between a foreign word and its semantic meanings (it is on the basis of rules of this sort that single-language dictionaries are compiled; in bilingual dictionaries, these rules appear in another form). In some instances, the recognition of the semantic meaning of a word is accomplished easily, on the basis of a single rule and by means of a single operation. In other instances, such recognition is a complex task requiring a number of operations (and often a long series of operations).

These operations as well may often be described in algorithmic form. It may be noted parenthetically that many of the mistakes which students make (and sometimes even translators, especially when translating scientific or technical material) in understanding and translating certain words are caused by the fact that they do not know which operations to perform on the word and the sentence (or, often, the series of sentences) in which it occurs in order to understand the meaning of the word correctly. In other words, they do not know the relevant algorithmic process, to say nothing of the relevant algorithm.[4] The problem of designing algorithms for recognizing the semantic meanings of words is very important and interesting, but discussion of this subject would be out of place here.

Let us bring together and put in order what has been said of perception (recognition) algorithms.

One may divide these algorithms into two large classes: grammatical and comprehension algorithms.

Grammatical algorithms, in turn, may be divided into morphological and syntactical algorithms, and comprehension algorithms into algorithms for comprehension of grammatical meaning (of morphological phenomena and syntactical constructions) and of semantic meaning.

The function of grammatical algorithms is to relate a

grammatical phenomenon (a word or word-combination) to some grammatical class (morphological or syntactical). The function of comprehension algorithms is to relate a grammatical class to its grammatical meaning, i.e., to a set of communication units which it expresses, or to relate a grammatical phenomenon (a word or word-combination) directly to a set of corresponding grammatical and semantic meanings (communication units).

The structure of perception algorithms may be represented in the following diagram:

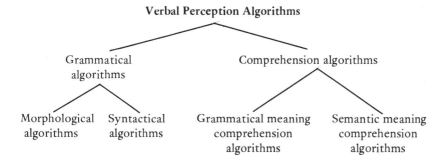

Verbal Perception Algorithms

Grammatical algorithms   Comprehension algorithms

Morphological algorithms   Syntactical algorithms   Grammatical meaning comprehension algorithms   Semantic meaning comprehension algorithms

There are two ways of developing in a student the ability to recognize grammatical meaning or grammatical phenomena.

The first way is to teach the student initially to recognize (via an algorithm for recognizing grammatical phenomena) the grammatical function of a particular grammatical phenomenon by relating it to a particular grammatical category (class), assigning to it the name of this category (for example, that a given word is the subject), and then to teach him to go on (transit) from this category to the meaning which it bears (for example, that the subject of a sentence conveys a specific set of grammatical communication units) on the basis of rules (algorithms) for establishing the meaning of grammatical categories.

The second way is to reduce these two processes (and their corresponding algorithms), namely, the process of proceeding from the attributes of a grammatical phenomenon to the name of the class to which it belongs, and then from the name of the class to the meaning which this class has, to one process and to teach the student by means of a single process to proceed directly from the attributes (or, more precisely, the complex of attributes) of a grammatical phenomenon to the meaning (communication units) which it carries. The input of a "reduced" algorithm of this sort is a grammatical phenomenon, and the output is the meaning of this phenomenon (the information which it carries) without the intermediate stage of naming (and, therefore, recognizing and becoming aware of) the grammatical category to which the phenomenon belongs.

Thus, for example, a person using this algorithm to understand the sentence "Dem Lehrer gab der Schüler das Buch" would isolate the article "dem," but would not say to himself "this is an indicator of the dative case, and so 'dem Lehrer' is not the subject." He would immediately go on to the meaning (both grammatical and semantic) of the word associated with this article: something was given *to him* (in this case, the teacher), as opposed to his giving something to someone else.

The first of these ways of teaching is based on creating an awareness of the grammatical categories to which the phenomena studied by the student belong. This method requires inclusion of knowledge of grammatical concepts in the process of perceiving, analyzing, and understanding speech.

The second method involves teaching without including a knowledge of grammatical concepts in the process of perceiving, analyzing, and understanding speech and without creating awareness of the grammatical categories to which linguistic phenomena belong. This method is based on direct transition from the attributes of grammatical phenomena to the meaning of these phenomena (the information which they carry).[5]

Obviously, both approaches must be utilized to one degree or another in different cases, since each of them has its advantages as well as its shortcomings. Moreover, one and the same characteristic of the method may appear as an advantage in one respect and as a shortcoming in another. Thus, the advantage of teaching the student to proceed directly from attributes of some grammatical phenomenon to the meaning they bear without becoming aware of the corresppnding grammatical category, lies, in particular, in the fact that there will be no need later to inhibit and to overcome the operation of grammatical categorization of verbal phenomena to be comprehended. Such categorization is not necessary for "natural" comprehension. In another respect, however, namely, the cultivation of the student's conscious approach to the language, his language culture, and language thinking, the same advantage appears as a shortcoming, since it does not develop these qualities.

The use of one of the method mentioned above depends, firstly, on the aims to be achieved in teaching a foreign language and, secondly, on the individual peculiarities of learners. Thus, some types of learners assimilate verbal skills and habits better when they are grammatically aware of language phenomena with which they deal. For other learners, grammatical categorization of language phenomena learned is unnecessary. Moreover, such categorization may hamper their progress in language learning.

As to the dependence of choice of a method on the specific aims of teaching foreign language, it might be said that the second method may, on the average, have more advantages than short-comings when the aim amounts to giving the student a practical command of a language; and more shortcomings than advantages when the aim is broader. Thus, one may think that becoming aware of grammatical phenomena may be desirable, or even necessary, when the aim of foreign language teaching is not purely pragmatic (i.e., only the practical command of a language) but instructive and educative as well. The latter broader aim pre-supposes the development in a student of a conscious approach to the language and the formation of linguistic thinking. There the student must not only be able to practically react in a correct way to some grammatical phenomena, but also to understand the underlying grammatical laws and rules and to be able to become aware of these phenomena—of their formalisms—when necessary.

But, in any case, the operation of relating grammatical phenomena to corresponding grammatical classes and, thus, grammatical categorization, must be only a stage (and, perhaps, one of the means) in arriving at corresponding skills and habits. This stage must be passed as rapidly as possible.

The difference between the two mentioned instructional approaches in regard to a practical command of a language lies not in the final product of instruction—the direct connection between language phenomena and their corresponding meanings—but in the paths which lead to this product. In the first case, the direct connection is a final result of the formation of indirect connections which are mediated by the awareness of the grammatical categories to which the grammatical phenomena belong. In the second case, direct connection is the object of initial and direct cultivation.

Does the significance of the second method in foreign language teaching imply that algorithms are unnecessary? Of course not. In utilizing this approach, after all, it is still necessary to teach the student to isolate specific grammatical (morphological and syntactical) phenomena and their attributes and to go from the isolated complexes of attributes to their grammatical and semantic meanings (the information which they carry). It is simply that, in the second approach, the two algorithms (one for recognizing grammatical phenomena and one for recognizing the grammatical meaning of these phenomena) merge, as was stated above, into one "reduced" algorithm such that the intermediate stage—awareness and naming of the class (category) of grammatical phenomena to which a given phenomenon belongs—falls away. The teaching of algorithmic processes with the aid of algorithms of this sort should develop in the student the ability to perceive and understand speech directly, without discursive thinking.

It should be noted that it would be wrong to think that perception algorithms are *algorithms of translation* from a foreign language into the native tongue, that these algorithms control the process of translation and, when taught, teach languages through translation.

As we already stated, these algorithms—which include or do not include intermediate grammatical categorization—govern the transition from the grammatical and syntactical phenomena of a foreign language to the meaning (communication units) they carry. The process of translation presupposes, however, the subsequent transition from this meaning (communication units) to the grammatical and syntactical phenomena of the native language which are capable of transmitting this meaning. But the latter transition is not governed (not controlled) by the perception algorithms. That is why they do not teach translation; they model the process of natural comprehension of verbal messages* when a person, perceiving text in a foreign language, arrives at its meaning (i.e., comprehends it) without subsequent transition to his native language, i.e., without translation into the native language. He elicits communication units (i.e., comprehends) directly from the text in the foreign language and not from an equivalent text in this native language which is its translation. Rather he does so from this original text itself.

What has been said makes clear why people may understand (comprehend) the text in a foreign language well and yet may not be able to translate it easily or adequately. They are able to make the transition from grammatical and syntactical forms of a foreign language to the meaning they carry and are not able to make the transition from this meaning to the grammatical and syntactical forms of their native language. This is a special process and a special type of activity, which must be specially taught.

For this purpose, special algorithms can be designed whose input will be meaning (communication units) elicited from language phenomena of a foreign language and whose output will be language phenomena of a native language which is capable of transmitting this meaning.

From what has been said, it is clear that to teach one to *comprehend* a language and to teach one to *translate* from a language are different instructional tasks deriving from different psychological processes, though the second task includes the first one as a component or sub-task.

---

*This applies to algorithms of direct transition from the very beginning of their assimilation, and to algorithms of indirect transition (transition through intermediate grammatical categorization) at the final stages of their assimilation.

7. Production Algorithms

Basic work on the application of algorithms in instruction has proceeded heretofore along the lines of developing algorithms for analyzing (recognizing) grammatical phenomena, i.e., perception algorithms.

Is it possible to design algorithms which will teach speaking (or writing), i.e., verbal *production* algorithms? The answer to this question, is yes. It is possible and indeed necessary to devise such algorithms and to use them to teach language.

If perception algorithms (we will be referring henceforth to "reduced" algorithms) are directed toward going from the attributes of grammatical and lexical phenomena to the information which they carry, then production algorithms solve the opposite problem: they are directed toward going from the information which must be transmitted to the linguistic phenomena which are capable of transmitting them. Thus, if perception algorithms first analyze (isolate and consider) the attributes of information-bearing linguistic phenomena and then specify this information, then production algorithms first analyze (isolate and consider) information which must be transmitted by means of specific linguistic phenomena, and then specify these same phenomena. Correspondingly, if the goal of teaching perception algorithms is to cause students to pay attention to all of the attributes of relevant linguistic phenomena, especially those specific to the language in question, and to move from them to the communication units which they carry, then the goal of teaching production algorithms is to cause students to pay attention to all relevant communication units, especially units which are specific to the language in question, and to choose words and construct sentences in accordance with the requirements of this language.

Let us consider an example of a production algorithm, namely one designed to teach the ability to express correctly in English the meaning (information) contained in the Russian word "pozhaluysta." Using this algorithm, students learn to differentiate and consider the required information, and quickly, consciously, and deliberately acquire the habit of correct usage of different English words and expressions which in different cases correspond to one and the same Russian word "pozhaluysta." This process can be successfully automatized.

An Algorithm for Expressing the Russian Word "Pozhaluysta" in English

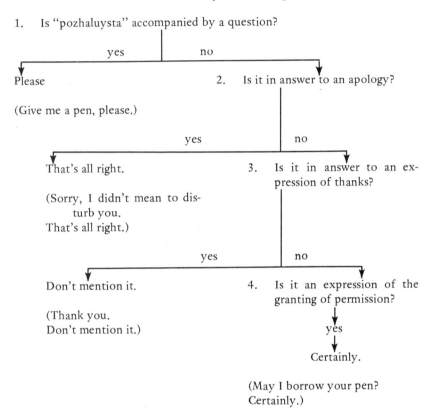

1. Is "pozhaluysta" accompanied by a question?

    yes | no

    Please   2. Is it in answer to an apology?

    (Give me a pen, please.)

    yes | no

    That's all right.   3. Is it in answer to an expression of thanks?

    (Sorry, I didn't mean to disturb you.
    That's all right.)

    yes | no

    Don't mention it.   4. Is it an expression of the granting of permission?

    (Thank you.   yes
    Don't mention it.)
                                          Certainly.

                                   (May I borrow your pen?
                                   Certainly.)

It should be noted that this algorithm is not the only one possible, since the order of operations does not play any role here. A number of other algorithms with other orders of operation are equivalent to this algorithm.

Such a situation, however, is not common. In many cases, the order of operations plays a substantial role and a change of order will not lead to the solution of a problem, or will lead to an incorrect solution.

We note that an instructional method of this sort is not in any way incompatible with the situational method; these techniques can, and, clearly, should be combined. After all, the situational method also induces the student to isolate the particular communication units to be transmitted by a given word, phrase, or grammatical construction. Situations, however, lead to isolation of information in an inexplicit manner, teaching the student to operate by analogy, while the use of algorithms causes him to isolate communication units explicitly, and to proceed not simply by analogy, but with a clear understanding of what he wants to say. Algorithms can and should be taught situationally; and vice versa, teaching on the basis of situations should include their algorithmic analysis; how best to do this is another question.[6] There are two possibilities:

(a) first to lead the student (perhaps even using examples from his native language) to isolate communication units in a "pure" form, and then to show him how these units become apparent in various situations, or

(b) first to confront the student with situations, and then to isolate communication units from them in a "pure" form.

It would clearly be incorrect to consider one approach as being better than the other in all circumstances. Sometimes situations are "transparent" and communication units can be extracted easily from them (in these cases, probably, it is best to start with situations and perhaps to avoid algorithms altogether), but there are other instances in which it is difficult to extract communication units from situations, and in these cases it is better obviously to begin by isolating communication units in a "pure" form, and then to illustrate them by means of situations. Of course, the individual characteristics of the student are also important in deciding between these two approaches.

8. **Some Functions of Algorithms in
     Foreign Language Teaching**

In discussing the basic causes of mistakes which students make in perceiving and producing verbal communications, we noted that the most fundamental were that students do not consider the necessary factors, or fail to consider all of these factors, or fail to derive correct consequences from the factors which they have considered in order to devise a correct response.

The first function of algorithms is to indicate what must be considered, and how, in the process of perceiving and producing verbal messages. They provide models of those consecutive processes which must be developed in the student's mind at the first stages of studying corresponding language phenomena in order for these processes to gradually transform themselves into correct simultaneous or nearly simultaneous processes and, in the long run, turn into subconscious and automatized processes. Algorithms represent a specific program of those verbal-cognitive operations, performance of which should lead to the ability errorlessly and intuitively to understand and speak a foreign language. Algorithms make controllable the formation of the desired final structures of verbal-cognitive operations and processes.

The second function of algorithms in language teaching derives directly from the first. Since they constitute a model (program) of those processes which, at the first stages, should occur in the mind of the listener (reader) and the speaker (writer) in the course of solving specific communicational-verbal and verbal-communicational problems, algorithms at the same time suggest a program of the material which the student must be taught if he is to learn a foreign language, of what must be "put into" his head, in order for the required verbal-cognitive mechanism to be formed in his mind.

The third function of algorithms is to indicate the differentiations which the student must learn to make, the phenomena which must be compared in order to make these differentiations, and, therefore, what the content should be of the practice exercises which the student is given.

The fourth function of algorithms is to systematize and unify all phenomena relating to the solution of specific communicational-verbal and verbal-communicational problems, guaranteeing thereby the completeness of the system of operations by means of which these problems are solved.

The fifth function of algorithms is to indicate the most efficient order for teaching specific verbal (in particular, grammatical) phenomena, their attributes, and operations for detecting these attributes (for a more detailed discussion of this point, see Landa, 1966a).

The sixth function of algorithms is to serve as an effective means of control and self-control of the verbal-cognitive processes involved in the solving of communicational-verbal and verbal-communicational problems.

The seventh function of algorithms is to provide a specific diagnostic map for determining the psychological causes of student mistakes.

Does the above discussion imply that students should memorize algorithms? Of course, it is possible to teach in such a way that the student will learn to proceed correctly on the basis of lengthy memorized algorithmic instructions. But this approach is clearly not efficient (it is justified only under certain specific conditions). In principle, instruction should be structured in such a way that at each moment the student concentrates his attention on not more than one or two attributes and operations involving them (or communication units in the case of verbal productions); these attributes and operations should be "connected" to the attributes and communication units which the student has already assimilated and which he is already able to use simultaneously and automatically.

Moreover, the student may learn successfully without being fully aware of the algorithm which is governing his activity. It is primarily the teacher who needs algorithms in order to have a program for developing the appropriate operations in the student and to know the optimal sequence in which they should be taught. It is not so much algorithmic instructions which should be taught as algorithmic operations (processes); and this can be done without forcing the student to memorize algorithms.

The availability of a precise program for developing verbal-cognitive skills and habits permits the application in foreign language teaching of such programmed instruction techniques as programmed textbooks and teaching machines. It is true that, as a result of the limitations imposed by these techniques on exchange of information with the student, they are inadequate for solving many important problems in this area (Shenshev, 1965, 1966). These limitations, however, are not the principal shortcomings of programmed instruction, as many believe. They are shortcomings in the *current* approach to foreign language teaching with the aid of existing *contemporary* machines and the *current* state of instructional technology. An understanding of these shortcomings permits us to formulate the problem of designing teaching machines and systems of a fundamentally new type, capable of significantly improving the information-exchange between student and machine, and to assign to the machines functions which are usually performed by the teacher, thus effecting a closer approximation of machine-student to teacher-student interaction.

9. **Non-Algorithmic Processes in
    Foreign Language Teaching**

One may ask whether all processes in assimilation and usage of foreign language are algorithmic and, hence, may be algorithmized. This question must be answered negatively. Together with the algorithmic processes, non-algorithmic and, in particular, heuristic verbal-cognitive processes play a major role in the assimilation and usage of language. The difference between algorithmic and non-algorithmic processes is discussed in more detail in other chapters. Here we should like to stress the following.

The characteristic feature of algorithmic processes is the presence of uniform and *unambiguous* connections (*qua* logical relations, *Ed.*) between certain conditions (objects, their attributes, and relations) and certain operations and their outcomes. Different people acting according to an algorithm, with or without being aware of it, will arrive, under the same initial conditions, at the same outcome. An algorithmic process turns identical input data into identical output or results. In contrast to algorithmic processes, non-algorithmic processes turn identical input data into diverse outcomes in different cases. Non-algorithmic processes are characterized by the *ambiguous* connections between conditions, on the one hand, and actions and their outcomes, on the other hand, i.e., between input and output. That is why different people with in the same conditions may act differently and arrive at different outcomes. Moreover, one and the same person may, in identical conditions, act in one manner one time and in another manner some other time, and for various reasons.

About many verbal processes it can be said with certainty that they are of an algorithmic character, since they are determined by or may be put in accordance with certain unambiguous rules (algorithms) of which the speaker or reader may be aware or not aware, but which stipulate one single solution to communicational-verbal or verbal-communicational problems. Of this type are, for example, algorithms for determining a subject and predicate in a sentence, for determining which tense must be used to express certain communication units, and many others. About some verbal processes, however, it is impossible at this time to say definitely whether they are algorithmic or not.

The difficulty of establishing with which type of process we are dealing—algorithmic or non-algorithmic—is due to the fact that very often we do not know beforehand why a person, under the same conditions, sometimes performs action A, sometimes action B, and sometimes some other actions. Is this because elicitation of an action is conditioned (stipulated) by some new or random factors which "join" initial conditions and influence, in some random and unpredicted way, the changing character of the actions being taken? If this is the case, then the process is non-algorithmic. Or is this because there exist some additional but not observable and not conscious conditions whose presence (more precisely, presence of some subsets) unambiguously and uniformly determine the type of the speaker's action? In this case the process is of the algorithmic or algorithmoid type, but the algorithm in accordance with which the person proceeds and which may be put in conformity with the process he performs is not in his consciousness. This process, though algorithmic or algorithmoid, appears to be non-algorithmic, since its underlying algorithm is not known.

It may be thought that the more complex the verbal act is, i.e., the more factors (especially those which are difficult to consider and assess) determine and influence its genesis and progress, the less algorithmic it is. For example, the choice between the present continuous and the present indefinite tense is completely determined by a finite number of precisely known factors which can be precisely taken into account in each case, and which unequivocally specify the character of the verbal act in this respect. The connection between the factors involved and their corresponding verbal act can be stated in the form of unambiguous rules and their corresponding algorithms. The choice, however, between, say, different ways of addressing someone with a request: "will you give me a book," "would you be so kind as to give me a book," etc., is not determined unequivocally by a set of precisely discriminable and considered factors. It is difficult, if not impossible, to state a precise rule (algorithm) which would determine which expression of all possible ones should be used in any given case. Often there are a number of possible equivalent or nearly equivalent solutions, each of them being correct. In other words, factors to be considered by a speaker or writer in the process of generating the verbal act determine not a single solution, but some set of possible solutions.

Of course, one also might call prescriptions algorithmic which yield not just a single solution, but a number of possible (equivalent or approximately equivalent) solutions. However, since the actual, final solution presupposes a free choice of one specific possibility from a given set of possibilities, and this specific choice is not determined by a prescription, it would not be precise to refer to such prescriptions and their corresponding processes as algorithmic.

The degree of non-algorithmicity of such prescriptions and processes is not very high. The choice of any one possibility from among a given set of equivalent or nearly equivalent possibilities is an arbitrary act that is not determined.

The process is still less determined when only the field of possibilities is given (known), just as in preceding cases, but the possibilities are not quite equivalent and the criterion of choice is not given or known. (This is a typical situation in foreign language learning, when a learner knows, for instance, a number of words which seem to relate to what is to be expressed, but which are not quite equivalent, and he does not know which of them is best suited and should be chosen.)

Still less determined are the processes when the field of possibilities of choice is not given or known to a person and he has to determine the field itself. Such processes include not only processes of choice from given alternatives (after they have been determined) but processes of search for fields of these alternatives.

We shall refer to the preceding processes as semi-heuristic and heuristic (the distinction between them is made clear in other chapters).

Semi-heuristic and heuristic verbal processes take place in ordinary conversation in native as well as in foreign languages. An example is the situation in which someone is not satisfied with the way he is going to express his idea or thoughts (i.e., by words or expressions which came into his head) and he begins a feverish *search* for a better way. He may or may not find a better, more adequate, more expressive way. It is obvious, however, that we encounter here a typical search for a solution which, as with other search processes, may or may not bring the solution to a verbal problem.

Semi-heuristic and heuristic processes play a particularly important role in the work of writers' and poets. To find the most appropriate (adequate, expressive) word, phrase, or description is often a genuine creative and difficult problem, which may not be solved for weeks or months. Success in the solution of such a problem presupposes a highly developed and complex search process. Sometimes the result of the solution of a creative verbal problem may be not only finding one of the existing words or phrases but creating quite new verbal phenomena (a new word, phrase, etc.) which has not existed previously in the language. Such new language creations are analogous to new creations in science and technology and sometimes involve genuine discovery.

The diversity of types of communicational-verbal and verbal-communicational problems which a person encounters during his verbal activity requires different types of verbal-cognitive processes by means of which these problems can be solved. Clearly, different types of processes have different underlying compositions and structures of knowledge and operations. Thus, the successful solution of algorithmic verbal problems requires unambiguous associations between specific semantic and linguistic phenomena which ensure that some phenomenon at the input elicits some particular phenomenon at the output (both phenomena may be complex and made up of a number of components). Algorithmic verbal processes do not require associations of such a type that some phenomenon of the input elicits a number of possible reactions at the output. They do not also presuppose the ability to perform choice and search processes. Semi-algorithmic processes, however, require multiple associations, when one phenomenon at the input is able to elicit a number of phenomena at the output. They also require the ability to perform choice processes. Semi-heuristic and heuristic processes require still more complex structures of associations, the presence of evaluation criteria for the appropriateness (fitness) of certain words, grammatical constructions, expressions, etc., for the expression of certain communication units, as well as the ability to perform the search process.

It is clear that different inner compositions and structures of components underlying different verbal-cognitive processes require different content, means, conditions and procedures of teaching, including different types of exercises. But the problem of the correspondence between the types of processes to be formed and the ways in which they are to be formed is a special problem which should be the subject of a special discussion.

Notes

1. Scherba (1947) noted the distinction between directions of processes occurring in verbal perception and comprehension, on the one hand, and those occurring in verbal production, on the other, and considered it of great significance in foreign language teaching.

2. See Gurvich's (1965) cogent remarks on the limitations of the pattern-teaching approach in foreign language instruction.
3. This classification has never been introduced before, so far as we are aware. We note that we are discussing perception and production algorithms, and not analysis and synthesis algorithms. The processes of analysis and synthesis take place in verbal perception and comprehension as well as in verbal production. In fact, any act of verbal perception and comprehension involves analysis of the utterance into elements of linguistic form and synthesis of meaning from the information which these elements carry. On the other hand, any act of verbal production constitutes analysis (isolation) of the information which must be transmitted, and the synthesis of linguistic form from elements which can carry this information.
4. In the first section of this chapter, it was stated that it is possible to know an algorithmic process without knowing the corresponding algorithm and, vice versa, to know an algorithm and yet have poor control of the corresponding algorithmic operations.
5. It seems to be the case that advocates of the direct method also desire to teach (and do teach) by means of this or a similar method. In fact, however, this approach differs in a number of respects from the direct method, or, in any case, does not necessarily presuppose it. With regard to instruction by the direct method, it should be noted that the most diverse conceptions as to which operations should be developed in the student and whether they should be developed at all may underlie this approach. It is possible to teach by the direct method without being fully aware of all of the specific grammatical attributes and combinations of attributes of grammatical phenomena which students should consider in the process of perceiving and understanding verbal communications, or of all of the information which must be transmitted in the speaking (or writing) process. But it is possible to teach by the direct method in such a way that the teacher has a complete and precise picture of all the

attributes and information which students should consider, and in such a way that he is able, by choosing a specific sequence of examples, to teach this material in a systematic and purposeful way and so to develop in the student the required verbal-cognitive operations. A specific algorithm will underlie instruction along these lines, although it might not be recognized as such by the teacher. It is entirely possible that the success which often results from use of the direct method is due to the fact that it is frequently based on such unconscious algorithms.

6. In some instances, it is expedient to present students with algorithms in their final form, while in others it is preferable to teach students to arrive at the required algorithms independently (by devising or discovering them), and in yet other cases the best approach is not to give students algorithmic instructions at all, but rather to formulate algorithmic processes by means of a particular choice of situations and exercises and to develop algorithmic operations in the student without his awareness.

Chapter Eight

A General Cognitive Procedure for Problem-Solving

An important function of education is the teaching of general cognitive procedures, that is, generalized cognitive abilities. The student can be taught to solve any number of individual, particular problems without becoming capable of solving varied problems independently, unless he learns at the same time general techniques for analyzing problems, i.e., a general approach to problem-solving.

There is a pressing need to investigate the conditions which make instruction truly general, to determine the factors which transform given specific skills into more general capabilities.

The purpose of the investigation described here was to delineate the psychological outlines of a thinking procedure and also the instructional techniques which create the conditions for the more efficient development of certain problem-solving abilities.

One of the most important indicators of an individual's intellectual development is the generality of his knowledge, skills, and habits. It is this feature which makes possible the transfer of these abilities from one situation to another, the capacity to "see" in new situations factors which they have in common with previously encountered situations.[1] Generality of knowledge is expressed in the transfer of ideas and concepts from one group of phenomena to another (for example, the transfer of the properties of a particular parallelogram to *all* other parallelograms), while generality of skills and habits is expressed in the transfer of actions (physical and cognitive) from

233

one group of phenomena to another.*

There is a very close interaction between knowledge and action in the problem-solving process. Knowledge of the conditions of a problem recalls the actions involved in analyzing these conditions. Then these actions, in transforming this information— in revealing new aspects in it—create the prerequisites for the reflection of these new aspects, i.e., for the establishment of new knowledge. This new knowledge, in turn, elicits new actions, etc. Thinking cannot occur without the interaction of these two basic components—knowledge and action. The development of cognitive abilities presupposes the development of both the content of thought (knowledge) and the activity of thinking (operations) to a high level of generalization.[2]

The knowledge involved in cognitive activity may be divided into two broad categories: (1) knowledge of the objective properties and relations of objects and phenomena, and (2) knowledge of the ways of acting on (or with) these objects and phenomena.[3] The first category is divided in turn into two types: (a) knowledge which is obtained in perceiving the conditions of a problem, and (b) knowledge which is not given in the conditions of a problem but which is essential to the thinking process and is included in it, i.e., definitions, theorems, laws, knowledge of physical and chemical processes and phenomena, etc., as derived from past experience. Knowledge of the second type is necessary for the indirect (mediated, *Trans.*) reflection of reality in thought. The absence of this knowledge or failure to take it into account makes it impossible for us to go beyond the limits of that which we perceive directly or which is given in the conditions of a problem.

*It is evident that the generality of ideas and concepts with which actions are linked lies at the basis of the generality of actions. But if in the first case generality of ideas and concepts leads to their recall under varying conditions, in the second case this leads also to the recall of actions which become applicable to these varying conditions and make possible their trans- formation. Generality of actions is, thus, generality of their underlying images (images of actions themselves included) which regulate their recall, applica- tion, and execution.

Constant shifting from knowledge of the first type to that of the second and back occurs during the thinking process. But this shifting occurs not only in the form of direct associations (as when, for example, the word "triangle" in the conditions of a problem evokes by association knowledge of the criteria for the equality of triangles), but also through the medium of actions performed on knowledge of the first type.[4]

Any object that is reflected in imagination or is conceptualized has numerous aspects. The isolation of its various aspects will recall various elements of knowledge, i.e., will evoke various associations. But the elements of knowledge and the associations which will be recalled depend on the aspect of the object which is isolated, that is, on the actions which are performed on it. For example, the geometric figure shown in Figure 8.1 might recall the concept "triangle" (triangles ABC and ADC), or the concept "quadrangle" (ABCD), or the concept "chord" (if, for example, the segment AD is isolated and considered in relation to the circle), or other concepts. However, from a system of associations by itself it is impossible to determine why, of all the elements of knowledge possessed by an individual, certain ones and not others are recalled in the course of solving a problem. A system of associations can show only possible paths of recall. The actual path that is recalled, the specific dynamic of the activation of knowledge occurring during the thinking process, the new linkages which may be formed between

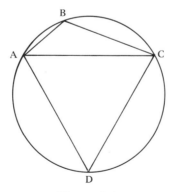

Figure 8.1

elements of knowledge—these depend on the actions which an individual performs on the conditions of a problem, i.e., on which of them he isolates and correlates.

Thus, the process of transition from knowledge of the first type (knowledge of the conditions of a problem) to knowledge of the second type (knowledge of definitions, theorems, etc.) which is necessary to establish the desired relations, are mediated by actions performed on the conditions of the problem. These actions constitute what is usually called analysis of the problem.*

The recall (elicitation) of knowledge is guided, consequently, by the analysis of the problem, and depends on the correlation of the content of the problem and actions directed toward this content. In instruction, speech is used to transmit not only the substantive content of human knowledge (concepts, judgments, opinions, theories, etc.), but also the actions comprised in this knowledge—the modes of action which have been compiled and checked by experience, including cognitive actions. These actions are not transmitted separately, but rather in conjunction with specific substantive content.

Thus, the acquisition of analytic-synthetic operations is equivalent, from the psychological point of view, to the development not only of internal mechanisms of action, but also of specific relations between actions and that substantive element to which these actions are applied. The significance of these relations consists of the fact that they permit substantive elements, under certain conditions, to recall the actions in question, thereby "evoking" analysis.

The thinking process includes, consequently, not only the recall of knowledge, but also the recall of operations, which is based on experientially stored relations between knowledge about objects and phenomena and actions involving these objects and phenomena. It is clear that the more are the number and diversity

*The term "analysis" is used here and in some other cases below in the broad sense of the breaking up of the given information of a problem into components and the transformation, comparison, etc., of these components; it includes, therefore, operations of synthesis as well as analysis in the narrow sense.

of objects with which certain actions have been connected in the past experience, the more general are these actions, and the easier they will be recalled under various conditions.

It is possible to explain in these terms a phenomenon which is often encountered in the classroom, namely, the fact that, although they possess all the knowledge required for the solution of a problem, students are often unable to solve it. The knowledge is present but is not recalled (elicited).

If it is true that recall of knowledge depends (provided that the knowledge is sufficiently generalized and systematized) on analysis, then clearly the cause of this failure of knowledge to "switch on" must be sought in analysis, i.e., in the character of the students' cognitive actions and in one or another of their correlations with the specific content of the problem. Success in solving one problem and failure to solve another indicate that the conditions of the first problem elicit operations which are necessary for its analysis, while the conditions of the second problem do not elicit these operations, i.e., that these operations are not evoked and applied in all conditions.

Knowledge of a truly general problem-solving method implies the ability to analyze successfully *any* problem, to apply the appropriate analytic-synthetic actions to any specific problem content. On the basis of the above discussion, it may be expected that this ability is guaranteed by a high level of generality and systematization of operations. In being associated during the instructional process with a variety of problem contents, operations acquire the property of being recallable in the most varied situations, and in being so recalled they create the preconditions for the recall in these situations of required knowledge as well.

Problem-solving, like any other activity, consists not of one operation, but of many. As in any other activity, these operations should be joined together in a particular way, applied in a particular order, and should possess a logic which reflects the logic of the problem in question. In other words, problem-solving should include a specific system of analysis. A thinking procedure for solving problems emerges, therefore, as a "putting together" of operations into a particular system and a subsequent generalization of this system.

Before we were able to proceed to the immediate goal of our investigation—that of finding effective means of forming in our subjects a general thinking procedure for solving problems in geometric proof—it was necessary to discover the state of their cognitive activity during the problem-solving process, to understand why they would succeed in solving some problems and fail to solve others, even when they possessed all of the knowledge required to solve the problems in question. In other words, it was necessary to discover what was lacking in their cognitive activity that made them unable to solve any and all problems put to them.

For this purpose, a preliminary, or, more correctly, a diagnostic experiment was performed.

The subjects of this experiment were 26 students of the eighth and ninth grades of three Leningrad secondary schools. Of the 14 ninth grade students, two were judged to be poor to fair problem-solvers, three fair to good, five good to excellent, and four excellent. These rankings were termed the first, second, third, and fourth groups, respectively. (In what follows we will introduce only data from experiments with ninth grade students.)

Twenty problems in geometric proof were administered to each subject individually—10 problems of intermediate difficulty and 10 easy problems, the diagrams associated with which evoked recall of the theorems needed to solve the problems. The solution of all of the problems required the application of theorems which the subjects had studied in the sixth and seventh grades and which they knew well (this was especially checked). The easy problems required for their solution the application of the same theorems as the difficult problems.

Students of whose ability to solve easy problems we were convinced were selected as subjects. Special attention was paid to the "equalization" of the subjects' knowledge.[5] They were asked to repeat all of the theorems required for the solution of the experimental problems. The subjects were also informed that, if while attempting to solve a problem they forgot the exact formulation of a theorem, they were permitted either to ask us or to refer to their textbooks.

They were requested to think aloud while working. The difficult problems were given first, then the easy ones.

The results were as follows: Group I solved 10 percent of the difficult problems and 80 percent of the easy ones; Group II solved 16.6 percent and 83.8 percent, respectively; Group III, 19 percent and 99 percent; and Group IV, 45 percent and 100 percent.

Why were even the *best* subjects unable to solve most of the difficult problems?

The basic reasons may be divided into two groups: those relating to shortcomings in knowledge and its organization, and those relating to inadequacies of cognitive operations.

We were not concerned with analysis of our subjects' knowledge, in particular, the state and degree of development of geometric concepts. However, both strong and weak students showed inadequate systematization of geometric knowledge.[6] In searching for the attributes (previously also called "indicative features," *Ed.*) of a geometric figure or relation, the student is frequently unable to find the one he needs because of a lack of systematization of these attributes in his mind. This is especially true of attributes which have been covered in different segments of a geometry course. Thus, the attributes which must be present for two triangles to be equal or the defining attributes of a parallelogram are as a rule systematized better than the attributes of equality of segments or angles. This is the case because the former are studied separately in special course units, while the latter are considered to be "obvious," and so teachers often do not devote time to systematizing them.

We have investigated the second group of reasons in somewhat greater detail.[7] They are:

(1) Lack of knowledge or incomplete knowledge of an operation (or a series of operations). Although he may know what to do and even how to do it, the student is often unable to perform the required operation itself.

(2) Insufficient generality of operations; a given operation is recalled in some cases but not in others.

(3) Lack of knowledge (especially in poor students) of the

correct system of operations. As our experiment showed, in many students this system is either completely absent, in which case the problem-solving process proceeds by means of chaotic, arbitrary trials, or the system by which they operate is incorrect. In either case, the student is usually unable to discover the required connections; and if he does manage to solve the problem, then this is due to a lucky guess, i.e., to randomly hitting upon the required figure or theorem.

(4) Lack of a system of operations which underlies a many-sided approach to an object and ensures many-aspected isolation of its diverse attributes. This lack expresses itself in a one-sided analysis and synthesis of the figures. For example, the student may correlate an element of a diagram with elements located to the right of it and fail to correlate it with elements located to the left of it or below it, and in this way fail to discover all of its properties. One-sideness appears also in actions involving concepts: the correlation of one concept with another is performed only in accordance with some randomly selected attributes.

(5) Insufficient generality of a system of operations. The correct system of operations is elicited by one element of a problem and is not elicited by another; as a result, some problems are solved while others are not (although the latter may be no more difficult than the former).

These shortcomings of cognitive activity were "distributed" unevenly in the subjects. The poor students showed them to a greater degree than the good students. The former showed lack of knowledge not only of system, but of various individual operations as well, while the latter more often showed that they did not possess a general system of operations (although there were instances in which good students also were unable to solve problems, because of a poor grasp of or failure to apply a particular operation). Each subject showed a highly individual combination of shortcomings in this regard.

A majority of the subjects showed an almost complete lack of understanding of the nature of proof, a lack of knowledge or incomplete knowledge of what it means to prove something, of what must be done with the conditions of a problem in order to demonstrate a proof. Many of the subjects had almost no knowledge of the actions-operations) required during this process.

It is important to note that the subjects also showed a poor grasp of those actions which they knew and which they actually applied during the problem-solving process, i.e., they showed only a vague awareness of their own cognitive activity. They generally were able to describe only incompletely and with difficulty (and in an undifferentiated manner) the actions which they performed in the course of solving a problem. They were totally unaware of many of these actions.

The experiment revealed what was lacking in the subjects' thinking and what had to be developed in them in order to raise the level of their analytic-synthetic activity to that of a truly general method.

Since many of our subjects did not know either a general method (i.e., a generalized system of operations) or simply a correct system of operations, or even the individual components of a correct system (i.e., those elements which constitute the prerequisites of a general method), it was necessary for the purposes of our experiment to form both a general method and preliminarily the primary elements.

1. Experimental Method

In developing our experimental method, we proceeded from the fact that actions (including cognitive actions) can be taught by demonstration, or by explanation, or by a combination of the two).[8] In the second case, the knowledge of actions obtainable by a human being makes it possible for him to have a clear awareness of them, and to deliberately recall and regulate them. This approach also promotes the generalization of actions, the clear awareness of some of the conditions of their application, and finally, makes possible the acquisition of some general principles of problem-solving.

A procedure for thinking, like any other system of actions, can be either conscious or unconscious (in the sense of *with* and *without* awareness, *Ed.*). It is possible to know and use such a procedure without being aware that one knows and uses it, or to know and use it and also realize that one knows and uses it. It is also possible to know what to do, but to be unable to do it.

Our experimental method involved teaching a procedure for thinking "from the top," beginning with the communication to the student of knowledge of actions, of how to think correctly while solving problems, and only later introducing training exercises for the purpose of creating the conditions necessary for the acquisition of practical skill in the use of these actions. In giving the subjects knowledge of actions, we simultaneously showed them what to do in order to solve problems and how to do it.

The principal significance of this method of forming a general thinking procedure lies in the fact that it gives the student the opportunity to perceive not only the problem, but to become aware also of his own thought processes, and in so doing allows him to control these processes.

But, before we were able to convey to our subjects knowledge of how to prove geometric propositions, we had to understand the structure of the cognitive activity which constitutes this process, to isolate the basic actions involved, to discover their systematic interrelationships, and then to express this structure in the form of a system of general rules.[9]

In developing such a system of rules, we took as our starting point an analysis of how adults and good students go about solving problems. In order to make such an analysis we performed an experiment using such individuals as subjects.

In formulating these rules, we did not attempt to comprise all of the actions involved. Rules were selected as a function of the level of mathematical development of the subjects, as well as the level of difficulty of the problems used in the experiment. The rules included only those actions which the subjects failed to perform while searching for a proof or did not perform always and under all conditions.

Of 18 ninth-graders, 10 were chosen to take part in the experiment; one from group I, two from group II, six from group III, and one from group IV. Subjects of the third and fourth groups showed a relatively high level of preparedness for learning the procedure. These subjects failed to solve a portion of the difficult problems largely because they did not know the correct reasoning procedure, or because their knowledge of this procedure was not sufficiently general.

The rules which we introduced during the instructional process were intended not only to facilitate becoming aware of the general analytic-synthetic operations which they used in solving problems, but also to provide a specific "inventory" of these operations (including an inventory of questions serving to "signal" operations), so that they would be able to consider all possible ways of approaching a problem, to recall deliberately the required operation, and thus would be able to move deliberately from one operation to another (to vary the analytical procedure) and to form various combinations of operations within a single system.

A system of rules for proving propositions may be regarded, therefore, as a system of signals for evoking all of the actions which must be performed on the conditions of a problem in order to arrive at the required proof, including actions that involve the posing of questions.

2. The Experiment

The experiment began with an explanation to the subjects of the basic nature of the process of proving something (we will describe this explanation only in very general terms).

We explained to the subjects that proving something, such as the equality of two triangles, means *finding* in these triangles attributes (indicative features) of equality which are previously known from theorems. If these attributes are given in the conditions of the problem, then the theorem is proved. If all of the required attributes are not present in the conditions of the problem, and it is known only that the triangles are equal on two *sides*, then it is necessary to prove that the angles formed by the sides of the triangles are equal, and this requires looking for the attributes of the equality of *angles*. We must continue the process of looking for such attributes until we arrive at that which is given in the conditions of the problem. This search for attributes, as the core of the process of proof, we illustrated by means of an example.

We explained in passing why the attributes of figures and relationships are studied in geometry (many of the subjects were unable to give reasons for studying these attributes). We stated that knowledge of attributes is necessary in order to establish the presence of particular figures or relations (for example, the equality of angles, segments, etc.).

We then indicated that geometric figures and relations (for the sake of brevity we will henceforth speak only of figures) possess, as a rule, not one attribute, but several, and that in order to prove the existence of a given figure it is not necessary to look for all of the known sufficient attributes of that figure, but rather only one of them. This point was illustrated by means of examples.

It was further emphasized that knowledge of all of the attributes sufficient to establish the presence of a given figure, i.e., the system formed by the attributes in question, is extremely important in the process of proving geometric statements. We noted that it is not always possible or expedient to prove the existence of a figure using any given attribute, and that it is often possible to use only a particular attribute or group of attributes. It is for this reason that, if the identity of a particular figure cannot be demonstrated by establishing the presence of one of its characteristic attributes, another of its sufficient attributes must be used. In order to find the required attribute, one must know all of the characteristic attributes of the figure in question, i.e., the system of such attributes. We illustrated all of these points by means of examples.

After explaining the importance of knowing systems of attributes, we asked the subjects to name the characteristic attributes of a number of geometric figures and relations. It proved to be the case, as a rule, that the subjects were unable to list all of the sufficient characteristic attributes of any given figure, that is, that they did not know the complete *system of sufficient attributes* of any given figure. We then assisted each subject in naming all of the theorems he knew as having something to do with the attributes of some figure, and these attributes were listed on a separate sheet of paper. The following is the beginning of one of these lists.

"Two arcs are equal: (1) if they are each equal to some third arc; (2) if they are composed of equal parts; (3) if they are equal parts of equal arcs, etc. (10 sufficient definitive-attributes in all)."

We then explained to the subjects that theorems can progress in two directions: from that which is given to that which must be proved, and the other way, from that which must be proved to that which is given. This point was illustrated by means of examples.

We further explained that, in solving easy, simple problems, it usually does not matter which direction is used, but that for difficult problems it is better to move from what must be proved to what is given and at the same time to draw conclusions from the given information in such a way as to approach that which is to be proved.

We then proceeded to the most important part of our discussion: an explanation of why one often is unable to solve a problem, even though one may know all of the theorems required for its solution and everything that must be done in order to arrive at this solution.

We explained that success in problem-solving depends on the performance of the correct actions and on reasoning correctly during the process of solving the problem. We said that a problem cannot be solved by a random, trial-and-error approach, though trials may be and often should be included in the process of search for a solution. The solution to a problem is made up of a specific order of actions, and to learn to solve problems it is necessary to know what actions to perform and often in what order. We then gave the subjects a set of rules which, we said, if followed, would permit them to solve problems in a rigorous, step-by-step manner. We illustrated each of these rules by means of one or two sample problems for which the rule in question was especially important and then trained students in its application, thus developing corresponding operations. Training was performed on the basis of solution of specially selected problems. Here are the rules:

1. Begin solving a problem by looking to see what is given and what is to be proved; separate the two.

2. Draw the most direct and obvious conclusions from the given information. For example, if the problem says "given an isosceles triangle," ask yourself the following questions: "What properties of isosceles triangles do we know?," recall these properties, and note the following: the angles formed by the base of the triangle and the sides are equal, and the bisector is both the median and equal in length to the height of the triangle. We emphasized that this rule had to be followed in order to connect the givens of the problem with that which was to be proved.

3. Now proceed to that which is to be proved, and ask yourself the question: "Which attributes are sufficient in order to prove that the given figure to be proved is such-and-such?"

4. Think over, to yourself, all of the sufficient attributes of the figure to be proved that you know; compare some or even each of them with the given information and with the diagram and then decide which of them seems to be best for proving what you need to prove. Then search among the sufficient attributes for the chosen attribute; then search among the sufficient attributes the next attribute; and so on. If one attribute does not work, or seems not to be promising, try another one.

5. Isolate from the diagram the figures and elements between which you must prove some relationship (for example, equality of angles or segments), include these elements into various relations with other possible elements, and keep asking yourself: "What are these elements and what else could they be at the same time?" Try to answer this question by looking for all possible relationships between the elements in question. We emphasized that this is what is meant by "seeing" or "looking at" a diagram. In showing the subjects a systematic approach to examining a diagram based on consecutively correlating each element with other elements and, thus, regarding it from all points of view, we at the same time showed them how to "rethink" or "reconsider" or "reconceptualize" it.

6. If the diagram contains none of the figures or elements which are necessary in order to use the attributes which you

thought of in (4) above, then construct the ones you need.

7. If the question: "What else could these elements be?" leads you to see certain elements as elements of a geometrical figure which is not in the given diagram, but the properties of which could be useful in your proof, then construct this figure.

8. While you are constructing these figures, draw all possible conclusions from them—use all of the attributes which result from these constructions.

9. Remember what was given in the conditions of the problem, and, in case of difficulty, check to see if you have forgotten something.

10. Since difficulties can also arise as a result of not following the rules, when you are having difficulties, refer again to the rules and check to see if you have forgotten to apply one of them.

It is easy to see that the cited prescription is not algorithmic, and this is not only because it does not prescribe a fixed sequence of operations (we will touch on this question below), but also because most of the instructions contain some degree of uncertainty and do not determine corresponding actions unambiguously. Some of the instructions are semi-algorithmic, while others are semi-heuristic or heuristic. This is why the prescription as a whole may be seen as heuristic (since it contains heuristic instructions, which are instructions of a higher order of uncertainty). It is known that for proof of geometric theorems assigned in school it is possible to devise an algorithm, but this algorithm would be an algorithm of exhaustive search. However, even in the case of school-level geometric problems, the volume of exhaustive search is so enormous that it would be impossible practically both to describe such an algorithm and to utilize it. That is why we have to decrease the "specification force" of the prescription, introducing into it instructions containing ambiguities such as: "decide which among the sufficient attributes seems to be best for a trial attempt at proving what you need to prove"; ask yourself: "what are these (isolated) elements and what else could they be at the same time constructing, if needed, new figures"; etc. Carrying out such instructions does not guarantee arriving at a solution, and presupposes the presence in a problem-solver of certain specific abilities, such as, for instance, the ability to estimate probabilistically which of all possible attributes is the most promising (i.e., may have a higher probability of leading to a solution), the ability to imagine into which figure some geometric element might be included in order to make some corresponding (geometric) construction, and so forth. Clearly these abilities are the result of students' past experience in solving problems, and they may be purposefully and deliberately formed in students during the teaching process. (For instance, one can increase the accuracy of the subjective probabilistic estimation of some specific attributes as more promising than others if one more frequently assigns problems—from among the whole body of problems put to students—where utilization of this attribute leads to success. In this way one can control operations underlying spatial imagination and train students in these operations, thus developing the ability just mentioned, etc.)

All this does not exclude the role of chance and luck in searching for a proof while acting in accordance with a heuristic prescription. When the field of search is large (even when it is predetermined, which is psychologically not always the case in solving geometric problems*) much depends on such random factors as whether the problem-solver was engaged in a search for a

---

*A problem-solver, while solving geometric problems, may find himself in an uncertain field of search. None of the formal propositions (axioms, theorems, etc.) recalled by the conditions of a problem, in particular, by attributes of a given figure, lead to a solution. In order to recall other suitable formal propositions, it is necessary to establish new properties in addition to those given in a diagram. For this purpose, it is necessary to know what rule (5) specificies, i.e., to isolate some elements of a diagram (which elements may be unknown) and to put them into some relation with some other elements (into which relation and with which elements may be also unknown). If the diagram is very complicated and the number of its constituent elements is very great, a problem-solver often does not know what to do, which elements to isolate, and with which elements to correlate the isolated ones. Being unable to make all possible isolations and correlations (some of them will not occur to him, which is a characteristic feature of an uncertain field of search) he really finds himself psychologically in a situation of an uncertain search

suitable attribute in an appropriate (for this specific case) subset among existing subsets of attributes (which subset among all existing ones is appropriate is unknown beforehand), whether he came across suitable attributes within the appropriate subset during given limits of time, whether he managed to correlate some geometric element of a diagram with suitable elements from all possible elements present in a diagram, etc. In short, acting upon the cited prescription does not eliminate all characteristics of heuristic and semi-heuristic search. Nevertheless, learning the operations underlying each instruction of the prescription and being guided by them may significantly increase the probability of arriving at a solution to a problem. First, it ensures that all operations will be carried out in the process of solution (as mentioned above, some problems are often not solved because the student did not apply all of the necessary operations). Second, since each operation will be performed more perfectly (per some instruction such as, "If one attribute does not work or seems not to be promising, try another one"), students often do find a solution to a problem, since they do refer to and test attributes other than those which came to their mind first.

We return now to the description of the procedure of experimental teaching.

We note once again that we did give the subjects only a few basic rules for regulating the process of analyzing the conditions of a problem and searching for a solution in order to create the basis of a system of reasoning, and did not give them rules involving actions (operations) which the subjects already knew how to perform. We also did not give them rules of the type which must

---

field. *For him* this field is uncertain, though it is before his eyes.

A more vivid illustration is the instance when exhaustive isolations and correlations of elements (when this is possible and has been done) have not led to obtaining those properties which stimulate recall of appropriate formal propositions, and it is necessary to resort to auxiliary constructions to follow the rules. But which constructions? It may not be evident. The number of possible constructions may be so great that many of them, if any, may not come to mind and a problem-solver finds himself in the situation of an uncertain field of search.

be applied during the solution of especially difficult problems.

In discussing the importance of applying all of the rules, we, at the same time, used concrete examples to show the subjects that the order in which some rules should be applied can vary as a function of the specific conditions of a problem, i.e., that the application of a system of operations does not imply a fixed sequence of actions. The ability to think so as to arrive at proofs, we emphasized, presupposes the ability to change the order of actions, to combine them in different ways, to approach problems in different ways, and to shift from one mode of action to another if one mode does not yield the required results.

It is easy to see that the latter instruction is also non-algorithmic. The reason is that it is hardly possible to establish and point out a sequence of rules (or operations) which would be applicable with equal success or optimally for every problem. In some cases it may prove to be more expedient to start (after having performed the first rule) with a reconception or reconstruction of the diagram, and only thereafter to begin the search for sufficient attributes. In other cases it may prove to be more expedient to follow a reverse order. It is characteristic that it is generally not possible to point out beforehand for problems of this type which order of application of rules is expedient or to be preferred. This is determined often only in the process of search for a solution itself, when one tries to use some operation in some kind of order and, thus, *develop* the order of operations in the process of solution itself. When some rule that is applied does not lead to progress in the solution, then some other rule is tried and tested and the first rule is applied again thereafter or in some other place. Of course, trials of rules and testing for their applicability at this specific point of the solution process are often not random or not completely random, since past experience frequently suggests which rule (or operation) should be applied in some specific situation, thus determining the order of rules or operations to be applied. But these suggestions may be only of a probabilistic nature, and there is never any guarantee that a sequence of actions suggested by past experience will lead to a success or to an efficient way of reaching a solution in the specific case.

Thus, we see that not only most individual rules contained in the prescription cited are non-algorithmic, but a rule as to the order of application of these rules, i.e., a meta-rule, or a rule of a second order, is also non-algorithmic.

We concluded this part of our instructions to the subjects with an additional rule: "If you are to prove that two angles or segments are equal or that two lines are parallel, it is useful to begin by asking yourself the question: 'What are these elements in relation to the other elements of the diagram?' " (i.e., in this case the subject should begin with rule [5]). If you are to prove the existence of a figure or of relationships between figures, then begin by asking yourself the question about sufficient attributes, i.e., rule (3). If analysis and "reconceptualizing" of the given diagram do not suggest the required attributes, then you must recall the entire system of attributes and try to find a suitable one from this system.

We directed the attention of the subjects to the fact that, if they could utilize various attributes of a figure in proving geometric propositions, they could solve the same problem in different ways, and we showed them how this could be done.

Students are often unable to solve problems in different ways because they do not understand that to solve a problem in a different way means to solve it using a different attribute. It is for this reason that it is very important to be able to shift, when necessary, from one attribute (or set of attributes) to another.

We also explained that it is not always correct to prove a theorem using the first attribute of a figure to be recalled. The ability to solve problems by the most efficient and sometimes also the most original means presupposes the ability to select attributes consciously and deliberately and to go easily from one attribute to another.

We gave special emphasis to the point that everything we had said regarding the principles of approaching a problem and the rules describing actions was applicable not just to one problem or group of problems, but to any and all problems in the problem set, so that these principles and rules constitute a general problem-solving method.

Providing them with explanations and rules and illustrating their application in problem-solving by means of examples followed by practice would, we assumed, permit the subjects:

(1) to understand the logical basis and structure of proof;

(2) to acquire a generalized knowledge of the fundamental analytic-synthetic operations utilized in this process;

(3) to become aware of the fact that these operations constitute a system, to see the basic structure of reasoning, and to realize that problem-solving cannot proceed blindly by random trial-and-error, though trials are not excluded from the solution process;

(4) to become aware of the significance of the flexibility of the system, of the necessity of varying methods of analysis, and of shifting from one operation to another;

(5) to understand that the principles and methods of approaching problems which differ in specific content are general, that one does not act and reason in one way while solving one problem of geometric proof and in another, fundamentally different way while solving a different problem;

(6) to realize the necessity of connecting the conditions of the problem with that which is to be proved, of proceeding "from both ends";

(7) to realize the necessity of analyzing the verbal component of the problem as well as the diagram from several points of view, while engaging in "rethinkings," "reconsiderations," and "reconceptualizations";

(8) to understand that when a different approach is required it is necessary to shift to other attributes and base the proof on these attributes rather than the old ones; and

(9) to realize that it is possible to get out of ruts by shifting to another attribute or another analytic-synthetic operation (another rule).

These explanations and rules were intended to give the subjects an idea of a general method of reasoning or a general method of approaching any problem of geometric proof, independently of its specific content.

Knowledge of actions, some of which were formulated

directly in the form of rules and which are the reflection of these actions in a secondary system of cues (i.e., what *to do* to analyze a problem of geometric proof, *Ed.*), should, according to our hypothesis, create the possibility of the deliberate recall of these actions during the problem-solving process and of the conscious "organization" of the analysis of a problem.

The subjects did not write down our explanations, but they did write down the rules, and we asked them not only to study them but as far as possible to memorize them at home. However, the major assimilation of the system of rules and of their underlying operations occurred not via rote memorization but during its application in the subsequent process of solution of practice problems. The student could refer to written rules at any moment of subsequent practice, if needed. But at some moment of training they became assimilated so well that the necessity to refer to them overtly disappeared.

The explanations and illustrations and practice of individual operations in the course of explanations and illustrations generally required three lesson periods.

In order to create the conditions for the generalization of the reasoning method which we were teaching, we deliberately selected illustrative problems which differed from one another in content (problems involving triangles, parallelograms, circles, etc.), i.e., we followed the principle of varying problem content.

After concluding the "explanatory" part of the experiment, the subjects solved 15 specially selected practice problems which differed from the criterion problems both in general formulation and with regard to the geometric figures involved (in order to exclude the possibility that subjects might solve the control problems by analogy with the practice problems). In addition, we took care to construct the practice problems in such a way that the theorems required for the solution of the criterion problems were not required for their solution.

This was done in order to demonstrate that, if as a result of instruction the subjects succeeded in solving the criterion problems, then this would not be due to their having been trained in the use of the required theorems, but rather to their having learned a general method for proving geometric propositions which permits the recall of any theorem, including theorems which the subjects had not previously encountered in the course of the experiment.

The major indicator of the acquisition of a method of reasoning must be, of course, not simply success in solving the criterion problems, but a change in the thinking process that occurs during their solution, which can be established only by a qualitative analysis of the reasoning process as it occurs both before and after instruction.

In presenting the practice problems, we explained to the subjects that, although these problems differed in their content, the method which they would use to solve them should be the same for all problems and would be determined by the rules which they had been given and which were applicable to all problems independently of the figures involved.

We solved the first two problems aloud for the subjects, indicating to them each step of our reasoning by referring to the corresponding rule ("showing" them, as it were, how to think). We then asked the subjects to solve the remaining problems on their own, using the rules in the manner indicated. Each subject's own written version of the rules lay in front of him, and he was permitted, as previously mentioned, to consult it whenever he wished.

After the introductory work (explanations of rules with examples of their use, learning the rules at home, and our demonstration of how to reason) most subjects had more or less thoroughly learned the procedure, and some began to solve the remaining problems without looking at the rules. All subjects, however, failed at the beginning to perform one or another operation and had to refer to their rule lists.

From the moment when the subjects began to solve problems on their own, our guidance consisted only in giving them hints of the sort: "You forgot to perform such-and-such a rule"; "You're doing it in the old way again"; "Look to see what the rules say you should do"; "The rules say: 'relate elements to other elements in all possible ways'—have you really tried all possible relations?";

etc. If a subject then proceeded correctly, we said "Good," "Right," "Correct," etc.

Our assistance to the subjects in solving the practice problems consisted, therefore, in stimulating them to refer to the rules and to use them in analyzing the conditions of a problem. Incorrect actions were stopped by telling the subject that he had not performed the actions specified in a given rule, while correct ones were reinforced by verbal approval.

Gradually we stopped telling the subjects that they had not followed a given rule and began to say instead: "Think—what rule have you forgotten to follow?"; and, looking for this rule in response to our question, the subject would find it and proceed.

Work on practice problems continued until we were convinced that the subjects had more or less learned the method and that they no longer forgot to perform the prescribed actions. If it proved to be the case that, after solving 15 practice problems, a subject had not mastered the procedure, we nevertheless terminated the practice session and tried to determine what progress in the acquisition of the procedure had already occurred and what was causing the subject the most difficulty.

The criterion measurement began after the solution of the practice problems.

During the criterion assessment part of the experiment the subjects were given the problems which they had been unable to solve in the diagnostic part. This was done in order to compare how the subjects reasoned before instruction with how they reasoned after instruction. This comparison was also expected to reveal any changes in the subjects' analytic-synthetic activity which might have resulted from the instruction.

3. Results

The subjects solved, on the average, 25 percent of the difficult problems before instruction and 87 percent of the same problems after instruction.

We will not introduce here the detailed data concerned with the subjects' acquisition of a new reasoning procedure. Some of these data, specifically those involving individual differences, are presented elsewhere (Landa, 1957). Let us examine the qualitative changes in the analytical process which occurred in the subjects as a result of the instruction which they were given.

The following is a description of how subject A.S. approached a problem* before instruction (I) and after instruction (II).

I. "Let's draw a line through the centers . . . (Figure 8.3). No. that's not right . . . . Let's draw a secant through one of the points of intersection (Figure 8.4). Let's try to join points C and D with point A (Figure 8.5). . . . Triangle CAD is isosceles . . . no, we don't know that yet. . . . Let's extend CA and DA as far as the intersection with the circle at points F and E (Figure 8.6). Angle C is measured by the half-difference of arcs FD and AB. . . . No, something is wrong. . . . Let's draw AB and prove that triangle CAD is isosceles (Figure 8.7). . . . No, we can't prove that. . . ."

At this point he drew a new diagram (Figure 8.8).

"Angle AON is a right angle, and so are the others. They are measured by the half-sum of the arcs."

He then attempted to prove that, if the angles are equal (like straight lines), then the arcs by which they are measured are also equal, but soon realized that the equality of arc half-sums does not prove that portions of these half-sums are equal.

This attempt to solve the problem was unsuccessful.

II. "What must be proved in order to prove that two arcs are equal? Well, for one thing, it's enough to prove that the angles subtending them are equal. Also, if the chords which they subtend are equal. . . . Well then, it's obvious. If I draw chord AB (Figure 8.9), then this chord is common to them, and so they are equal. That's it."

His attempted solution to the problem before instruction consisted of the following stages:

(1) a construction ("Let's draw a line through the centers . . .");

---

*"Two equal circles intersect at points A and B (see Figure 8.2). Show that the arcs lying between the points of intersection are equal" (see Figures 8.2-8.9).

(2) a construction ("Let's draw a secant . . .");

(3) a construction ("Let's try to join points C, D, and A . . .");

(4) analysis of the resulting figure, a triangle. The diagram led to the thought that the triangle was isosceles, but this idea was rejected, since it could not be proved;

(5) a construction ("Let's extend CA and DA as far as the intersection with the circle . . .");

(6) analysis of the resulting figure leading to a conclusion regarding the properties of the inscribed angles ("Angle C is measured by the half-difference of arcs FD and AB . . .");

(7) a construction ("Let's draw AB . . .");

(8) another attempt to prove that the triangle is isosceles;

(9) a construction (he connects the centers and draws chord AB); and

(10) conclusions regarding the properties of the resulting figures.

At this point, the subject gave up attempting to solve the problem. His successful attempt to solve this problem after instruction consisted essentially of the following stages:

(1) posing the question as to what attributes must be shown to be present in order to prove the equality of the two arcs;

(2) recalling the appropriate system of attributes;

(3) comparing each of them with the given diagram and selecting a suitable one ("Well, for one thing it's enough to prove that. . . . If the chords which they subtend are equal. . . . Well then, it's obvious");

(4) performing a supplementary construction for the purpose of obtaining the required attribute, a chord; and

(5) establishing the presence of the required attribute.

The subject's first attempt to solve the problem was characterized, as we saw, by the complete absence of a correct reasoning procedure. He simply engaged in a series of arbitrary and random trials in the hope that one of them might be successful.

He used essentially three operations during this process: (1) arbitrary supplementary constructions; (2) visual analysis of the resulting figures; and (3) conclusions regarding their properties.

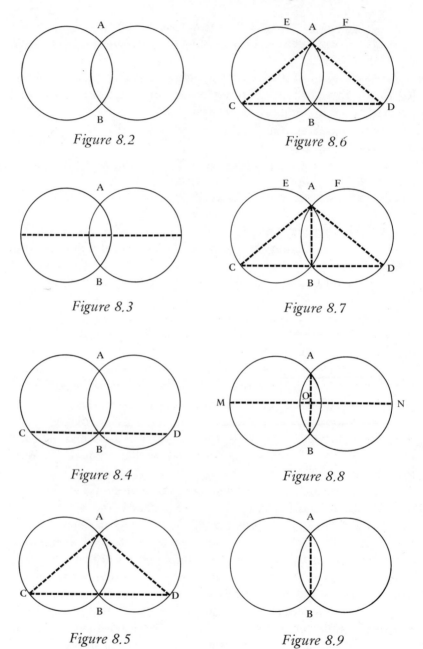

Figure 8.2

Figure 8.6

Figure 8.3

Figure 8.7

Figure 8.4

Figure 8.8

Figure 8.5

Figure 8.9

His attempts to solve the problem were based mainly on associations which the diagram evoked in him, and did not include such important operations as asking himself what attributes would be sufficient to demonstrate that which was to be proved, recalling systems of attributes, comparing them with the diagram, selecting an appropriate one, etc.

His attempt, after experimental instruction, on the other hand, showed that he was operating on the basis of a specific method of reasoning. He applied all or most of the analytic-synthetic operations which he had been taught (in complete accordance with the rules), and did this not in a random fashion, but systematically. He solved the problem in such a way that each successive step logically (literally, lawfully, properly, *Trans.*) flowed from the preceding one, and he did not perform any arbitrary actions (he performed six during his first attempt), all supplementary constructions being determined by a previously selected attribute and directed toward establishing the presence of this attribute. His supplementary constructions consequently showed a definite logic deriving from the conditions of the problem.

This subject showed a similar pattern of improved reasoning in solving all of the other problems, including the more difficult ones. His solutions to these problems showed that he had learned a specific method for approaching problems and that this method had reached a significant degree of generalization. He began to apply it to all of the problems which he was given to solve. Basically the same results were observed in all the other subjects as well. There developed in them a correct system of analytic-synthetic operations which achieved, as a function of the individual characteristics of the student, a greater or lesser level of generality. Both individual operations and systems of operations were now recalled under various circumstances, with the knowledge of a general problem-solving method now being the determining factor in this process rather than the given diagram or some specific element in the conditions of the problem. A system of operations was now recalled not only by the specific conditions of a problem, but also by the cues coming from the rules, which constitute a generalized reflection of what must be done in order to solve a problem. To the extent that the correct system of actions has been acquired, the rules "fall away," cease to be recalled, and operations begin to be executed in conformity with rules, as Shevaryov (1959) calls them.

It is clear that an important part of developmental instruction is the forming in the student of general methods of activity, showing him the general aspects not only of the things which he studies, but also of the actions which may be performed on or with these things, including cognitive actions. The development of cognitive capacities will proceed, clearly, more correctly and rapidly, if the general components of what at first sight appear to be individual and unrepeatable cognitive processes are isolated, and if the teaching of these general components becomes one of the specific functions of the teacher. The general factors in modes of cognitive functioning are more easily learned if they are isolated and formulated in such a way that the student can become aware of them and use them consciously.

Notes

1. S.L. Rubinstein has frequently noted the dependency of transfer on generality (1955a, 1955b).

2. In this chapter "cognitive action" and "cognitive operation" are used synonymously, although there is probably a basis for distinguishing between them, if "operations" are taken as conscious actions, that is, as actions the conditions for whose performance have become objects of awareness. Some other authors (e.g., Leontiev, 1947) distinguish between "action" and "operation" by considering operations to be components of an action. It is clear, however, that the difference between "action" and "operation" in this respect is relative. Some act regarded in relation to lesser acts which are included in it as its components is an action. The same act regarded in relation to greater acts of which it itself is a component is an operation.

3. In speaking of "knowledge of actions," we are referring not to actions themselves, but to knowledge of them, i.e., conceptualizations of them (literally, "awareness of them in concepts," *Trans.*).

4. Gal'perin (1957) assumes that direct associations between elements of knowledge are also mediated by cognitive actions, although these actions are highly reduced and automatized and therefore unconscious. This is, to our mind, no more than a hypothesis, which it is not yet clear how to prove.

5. The technique of equalization of subjects' knowledge has been used by Kabanova-Meller (1950).

6. The significance of the systematization of knowledge in the solution of geometric problems has been studied by Zykova (1950), Stepanov (1952), and others.

7. Menchinskaya (1955), Kalmykova (1955), and others, have investigated inadequacies of analytic-synthetic activity during the solution of arithmetic problems.

8. If actions are learned haphazardly, independently of instructional control, then they may arise, as A.N. Leontiev (1947) has noted, as a result of simple "adjustment" to conditions.

9. The idea that it is necessary to discover rules for regulating this process has been expressed by a number of mathematicians and methodologists (Hadamard, 1948; Osynskii, 1915; Polya, 1946; Sontsov, 1929). These authors have also attempted to formulate some rules of this sort.

Chapter Nine

Some Defects in the Cognitive Activity of Students Which Obstruct Independent Problem-Solving

Instruction which is aimed at developing in the student a capacity for independent thought must be based on precise knowledge of the mechanisms of thinking. The form and content of such instruction will depend, on the one hand, on the specific goals which it is intended to achieve or the abilities which are to be developed, and, on the other hand, on the conditions under which it is undertaken, in particular on the abilities which are already developed in the student and which may serve as a basis for further instruction. Therefore, one of the first stages in any didactic investigation should be the study of the student in order to discover the mechanisms and characteristics of his cognitive activity.

Two of the more frequently employed methods of studying the student are overall simultaneous observation of a large number of students and testing them. But as important as these methods are for providing a general idea of the skills and habits of students of a given age, they suffer from the shortcoming that the investigator is dealing only with the product of the student's cognitive activity, and is able only to a limited degree to trace the activity itself. Yet the student's performance depends on his cognitive processes, is determined by them; and instruction, in order to be effective, must mold these processes.

The study of the student's (overt, *Ed*.) classroom performance can only suggest an hypothesis as to the characteristics of his (covert, *Ed*.) cognitive activity and the sources of these characteristics. Such study yields only a general idea of what lies behind observable facts and phenomena. Precise knowledge of the processes which give rise to one kind of performance rather than another can be obtained only by studying these processes.

The best method for studying cognitive activity is the individual experiment, since only in this way is it possible to discern the subtle and, as a rule, hidden mechanisms which must be developed if instruction is to be effective.

Observations and experiments carried out by a number of authors (Gal'perin, 1957; Kabanova-Meller, 1950; Kalmykova, 1955; Menchinskaya, 1955; Slavina, 1958) show that defects in cognitive activity usually result from the fact that certain characteristics of this activity which are important for proper cognitive functioning are not being taken into account in the instructional process. This occurs not infrequently because the teacher does not know that these characteristics exist, which is in part inevitable, since many of them have never been studied.

Experience shows that students often have great difficulty solving problems, especially geometric problems. It has often been noted in the literature that students are frequently unable to solve problems independently, in spite of the fact that they possess all of the knowledge required in order to arrive at a solution. It is important to emphasize in this regard that the phenomenon in question is that of the students' inability to solve problems without assistance, since, on being given hints by the teacher or experimenter, they often succeed in solving problems which they were unable to solve on their own. For example, the following phenomenon noted by Stepanov (1952) and others is typical. Encountering a difficult problem, the student is unable to solve it because he cannot determine which axioms, theorems, and definitions to use. If this information is hinted to him, however, he solves the problem easily. His thinking is independent in some respects (the utilization of knowledge which he has been told is relevant), but in other respects (deciding what knowledge to use) it is dependent on outside assistance.

How can the student be taught independently to determine which elements of his knowledge to use in order to solve a problem? Effective teaching of this skill must be based on the structure of the skill itself, that is, on the cognitive operations of which it is composed. It is necessary, therefore, to first discover these operations.[1]

We have considered only a few of the defects in students' cognitive functioning which hamper independent thinking. Our experiments have shown that there are many such defects. The development of an effective instructional methodology requires detailed analysis of the factors which interfere with independent thinking during the problem-solving process and hamper students' analysis of a problem and their search for a solution.

The causes of the inability to solve problems (or of difficulty in solving them) may be divided roughly into two groups: those associated with defects of *knowledge,* and those associated with defects in thinking ability, i.e., ability to analyze a problem, to apply knowledge, that is, defects in analytic-synthetic *operations.* In order to prove, for example, that two triangles are equal, it is not enough to know the conditions of equality of triangles, it is necessary to find these conditions, to isolate them in the particular triangles in question. The triangles must be compared, related to one another, etc., procedures which are implemented by means of particular cognitive operations.

Thinking and knowledge are not identical, as noted earlier in this book, and problem-solving must be based on both. Thinking is the manipulation—the analysis and synthesis—of knowledge. Successful problem-solving requires the ability to operate not only with knowledge acquired in the past (such as theorems, rules, and laws), but also with knowledge of the givens and requirements of the problem under consideration. If a student who does not know how to begin the solution of a problem is asked what is causing him difficulty, he is likely to reply: "I don't know what to do." Cognitive activity fails to occur because the problem does not evoke from the student, and does not elicit from him, the analytic-synthetic operations required for its analysis.[2]

The process of solving a problem consists of an ordered series or a system of cognitive actions performed on the conditions of the problem and on the knowledge activated by these conditions. With the exception of the question of systematization of knowledge, we will not discuss in this chapter those difficulties in problem-solving which are due to defects in the student's knowledge. This problem has been discussed thoroughly by a number of authors. Kabanova-Meller (1950), Kalmykova (1958), Menchinskaya (1955), Samarin (1948), Shevaryov (1957), and Zykova (1950, 1955), for example, have shown that students often fail to solve problems because their conception of certain figures or geometrical relations is either too narrow or too broad, and/or because their understanding is not sufficiently systematized and generalized.

We will be concerned primarily with difficulties caused by defects in analytic-synthetic operations, that is, defects in problem analysis which prevent successful solution of a problem even in the presence of the required and correct knowledge. Defects of this sort are less evident to the teacher than defects in knowledge. Defects in a student's knowledge are more or less easy to detect in his responses to questions, but defects in his cognitive operations are not directly apparent. Special observation and analysis of his reasoning processes, i.e., of the flow of his thinking, are required in order to make them apparent.

Our investigation of the causes of difficulties in problem-solving was carried out experimentally. Our purpose was to discover the mechanisms of the cognitive activity of our subjects as they attempted to solve problems and then to elaborate, on the basis of this information, a more efficient methodology for teaching problem-solving.*

We remind the reader that (as noted in Chapter Eight) the subjects were given 10 problems of average or somewhat greater than average difficulty. We will refer to these problems as those of Group I. For purposes of comparison, 10 easy problems were also given, in which the diagrams strongly "hinted" at the theorems required for their solution. We will refer to these problems as those of Group II. Solution of all problems required knowledge of material normally covered in the seventh and eighth grades. The

---

*This methodology and the results of the experiment involving the teaching of it to students were presented in the preceding chapter.

subjects' knowledge of definitions, axioms, and theorems was checked before the experiment began. When we saw that a subject had forgotten a theorem, we reviewed it with him. This was done to ensure that the subjects possessed all of the knowledge necessary to solve the experimental problems, and to exclude the possibility that they might fail to solve a problem as a result of not knowing the necessary definitions, axioms, or theorems.

The problems of Group I were characterized by the fact that recall of knowledge was not directly elicited by the diagram, a more or less complex process of analysis being required in order to arrive at a solution. Problems requiring supplementary constructions for their solution fulfilled this condition. Observation of how a student solves problems of this type permits determination of the dependence of recall of knowledge on the flow of analysis and on the character of the analytic-synthetic activity of the student's thinking.

The experiment was performed outside of class with each subject undergoing the procedure individually. In the course of any one session, a subject was given not more than three or four problems, and was asked to "think out loud" while solving them. The experimenter asked the subject questions about how he was attempting to solve the problem. By comparing the subject's answers with the observed course of the solution process, we were able to trace the thinking process itself and to discover the characteristics of the subject's analytic-synthetic operations which were associated with successful problem-solving, as well as those which gave rise to difficulties. These difficulties were frequently of sufficient magnitude to prevent the subject from solving the problem.

What defects in the subjects' analytic-synthetic cognitive activity did the experiment reveal?

1. Inadequacies in the Composition and Comprehension of Analytic-Synthetic Operations

We have already noted that recall and *use* of knowledge depends to a significant degree on problem analysis. Operations of analysis and synthesis, by revealing in the object of thought particular properties and relations, bring about the recall of knowledge concerning these properties and relations. For example, we recall theorems about the properties of chords after we see a chord in a figure or read about a chord in the conditions of the problem. Recall of knowledge about the properties of chords occurs after the chord itself, or the concept of it, has been isolated by means of a specific analytical operation. (We will not be concerned here with other possible paths to the recall of knowledge.) From this it follows that one possible reason for the failure of knowledge to be recalled is to be sought in the character of these analytic-synthetic operations, in whether or not they have been fully mastered.

The experiment showed how difficulties in problem-solving depend on the nature of the operations which the student knows (or does not know).

Subject Tamara L., an average student, went about solving problem No. 4 as follows: *

(The subject looks at the diagram for a long time without saying anything.)

E. What are you thinking about?

S. I'm looking at this triangle (ABC).

E. What do you want to see in it?

S. I don't know ... (pause). Why is AB equal to BC? (Randomly traces the lines of the diagram with her pencil.) Maybe I should prove that angle DAB is a right angle. (Turns the diagram around and looks at it.) No, it's not a right angle ... (Draws OA and DB, Figure 9.1.) I have to prove that angle OAB is equal to angle ABD. That would prove that AB is equal to BC.

E. Would it? Is BC a complete side of triangle AOB?

S. No, it isn't.

E. Why did you draw OA and DB?

S. To get some triangles.

---

*Descriptions of the problem are given in the appendix to this chapter. We have included only those problems of *Group I* which are considered in this chapter. All of the diagrams given in the text are modified versions of the basic diagrams as given in the appendix. The modifications are supplementary constructions performed by the subjects and are shown by dotted lines.

Figure 9.1

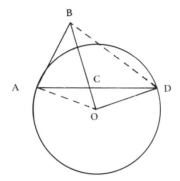

E. Why these in particular?

S. I don't know; I saw that I could construct them . . . (Long pause.)

E. What are you thinking about?

S. I don't know what to do . . . (Gives up.)

Analysis of this interaction shows that the only operations which the subject used were those involved in analyzing the diagram (isolating various figures in it) and constructing triangles. The result of these procedures was an attempt to demonstrate that the figures possess specific properties (that angle DAB is a right angle, that triangles OAB and ABD are equal); but the subject did not know how to do these things, that is, which operations to perform.

The subject did not analyze the verbal component of the problem at all,[3] and did not recall the attributes of any geometric figures or relations. Her analysis of the figure was entirely random and undirected; she did not know what she had to see in the diagram, did not use the "re-thinking" operation, etc. In other words, she did not perform the basic analytic-synthetic operations necessary for the recall of relevant knowledge, as pointed out in the foregoing chapter, and so was unable to utilize this knowledge in solving the problem. When random examination of the diagram and random supplementary constructions yielded nothing in the way of a solution, she gave up.

Here is how the same subject went about trying to solve problem No. 5.

(The subject notes in the diagram that the following pairs of segments are equal: AE and EB, BF and FC; CQ and QD; DH and HA. After a pause she draws diagonal EQ. See Figure 9.2.)

E. Why did you draw this diagonal?

S. I don't know, maybe it will yield something . . . (Pauses, looks at the diagram.) I don't know what to do. (Gives up.)

In attempting to solve problem No. 6 the subject did not even perform any supplementary constructions. After looking at the diagram and pausing, she said: "I don't know how to start," and gave up.

Figure 9.2

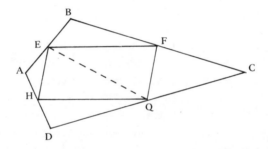

As these examples show, the subject was unable to solve the problems because they did not recall to her the required analytic-synthetic operations—she did not know what to do with the conditions of the problem in order to begin solving it.[4]

This does not mean that the subject knew no analytic-synthetic operations whatsoever. During the solution of easy problems, a large number of operations were recalled by her, but the experiment showed that this recall of operations occurs in this subject only under certain specific conditions, namely the perception of a familiar diagram. However, since the diagrams associated with the "difficult" problems of Group I did not prompt the solution—it was necessary first to add supplementary constructions, which required analysis of the verbal component of the problem conditions—it is not surprising that these problems proved to be insoluble for her. It was precisely these operations, those required for analysis of the verbal component of a problem, which she did not know. As a result, the knowledge necessary to solve the problem, which the subject possessed, was not recalled and applied.

Other subjects' attempts to solve the experimental problems showed that the level of mastery of different operations was not the same from subject to subject. Some subjects analyzed the verbal component of a problem, while others did not. For the most part they knew only operations for visual analysis of diagrams and so began with the diagram. Some subjects utilized the operation of searching for the attributes of a figure, some did not; some compared that which was to be proved with the given information, others did not, etc.

Inadequate ability or incomplete inability on the part of the student to perform operations is, therefore, one reason for the fact that the solution of problems which require the application of these operations proves to be difficult for him. He does not encounter these difficulties in solving problems which do not require utilization of these operations, and so is able to solve them.

Let us illustrate this point by means of an example. Subject Vladimir M., rated as an excellent student, went about solving problem No. 5 as follows:

S. I have to prove that this figure (EFQH) is a parallelogram (Figure 9.3). I have to use some property or other of the parallelogram. What about the one that says that the diagonals intersect at their midpoints? How can I prove that? Let's draw them and see. (Draws EQ and FH.)

When his attempt to prove that EFQH was a parallelogram by means of this indicative feature failed, he paused and said:

S. What about the fact that the sides are divided in half? How can I use that? (Pause.) What if I inscribe a circle? No, that's not right either. . . . In a quadrangle the sum of the angles is equal to 360 degrees, but that doesn't help. . . . The sum of the angles of triangle EOF is equal to 180 degrees, and so the sum of the angles of triangle HOQ is equal to 180 degrees.

He made several more attempts along the same lines but was unable to solve the problem.

Figure 9.3

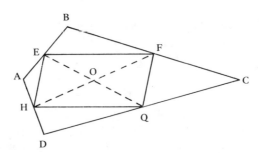

Analysis of this material shows that this subject used various kinds of operations. He tried to recall the attributes of the parallelogram and he used the "re-thinking" operation, relating EF and HQ to EO, OF, HO, and OZ, and drawing all possible conclusions from these relations. He further analyzed the given information (What about the fact that the sides are divided in half? . . .). Finally, he tried supplementary constructions, hoping to use the properties of the quadrangle. When this attempt failed, too, he turned to another component of the problem, the quadrangle, and recalled its attributes.

Nevertheless, he failed to solve the problem. Why? Because there was an important defect in his use of the operation of recalling attributes: he failed to recall *all* of the attributes of parallelness, although he knew them all. If he had recalled them all, he would have remembered and applied the theorem which states that two straight lines parallel to a third are parallel to each other. A supplementary construction (diagonal AC) would have given him the key to a rapid solution of the problem.

Let us consider another example.

Subject Lena K., a student rated as excellent, attempted to solve problem No. 1 as follows. She began correctly with the question: "What figures are segments MN and ND part of?" and used the correlation operation to answer it. But her grasp of this operation was inadequate. She related segments MN and ND only to elements located to the right of them and then, in order to obtain a triangle, drew NF and DC (Figure 9.4). This led her to an impasse. We suggested to her that she begin again, and she again began correctly by attempting to determine the figures of which segments MN and ND were a part.

Figure 9.4

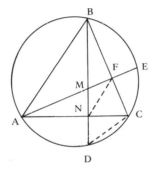

She stared at the diagram silently.

E. Well, what is MN part of? (Pause. She did not know.) Trace with your pencil all of the lines which are connected with this segment.

S. (Begins to trace the lines.) Oh, it's part of quadrangle NMFC. But that doesn't lead anywhere. . . . (Pause.)

E. What else is it part of?

S. Nothing.

E. Look harder. (She looks. Pause. She doesn't see any other figure of which MN is a part.) What triangle is it part of?

S. If I draw . . .

E. You don't have to draw anything. Keep tracing the lines connected with MN.

S. (Traces.) Oh, it's part of triangle MAN. (She now solves the problem without difficulty.)

We see that this subject's difficulty stemmed from the fact that she was unable to perform the correlation operation, although she knew that this was what she had to do. Having isolated segment MN, she related it only to elements located to the right of it.

As a result, she didn't "see" that segment MN is also a part of triangle MAN, and that segment ND is part of an imagined triangle NAD, which may be constructed by drawing AD.

The ability to "see" a diagram is the ability to perform certain operations. It is important in the instructional process that the cognitive operations which are the basis of "seeing" a diagram be clearly defined, so that they may be specifically and deliberately taught. Two such fundamental operations are the isolation of diagram elements from the context in which they are given, and the discovery of all relevant possible relations among these elements and other elements of the diagram by consecutive correlating of each element with the others. A student may "see" a diagram badly either because he is unable to isolate elements from the whole (especially when the diagram is complicated), or because he is unable to correlate them with other elements, or for both of these reasons. Only specific knowledge of which operations the student does not know or cannot perform adequately will enable the teacher to provide the proper exercises for developing these operations, and hence, the corresponding ability of "seeing" a diagram.

Everything that has been said above concerning defects in the operations underlying "seeing" a diagram applies equally to all other operations. An inadequate grasp of operations is a frequent cause of students' inability to solve problems and of their failure to utilize knowledge which they already possess.

Effective instruction requires understanding of why a student solves one problem but not another. Analysis of the problems which a given student solves and fails to solve, from the point of view of the operations required for their solution, permits us to determine the operations which he does not know or knows poorly. This knowledge, in turn, permits us to devote special attention to the development of these operations and the elimination of the defects in analytic-synthetic activity which prevent the student from being able to solve any and all problems.

2. Insufficient Generality of Analytic-Synthetic Operations

Another cause of difficulty in the utilization of knowledge is the fact that many operations are insufficiently generalized.

When a student is taught to solve problems, he is taught operations applied to a specific content. For example, in order to prove that two triangles are equal, it is necessary to: recall the (previously learned) sufficient attributes of equality of triangles, compare these attributes with the given information in order to select one of them for use as a basis for proof, etc. These and other operations are associated in the student's mind with a particular concept and visual content (triangles). These associations constitute the basis of the recall of operations in the student's mind when he perceives triangles within the conditions of a problem.

But these operations of recalling attributes, comparing them with given information, and others are equally applicable to the solution of problems not involving triangles. When the teacher teaches students how to solve "parallelogram" problems, "circle" problems, etc., the operations are associated with a different content. They become generalized, and this generalization permits the student to transcend past experience and transfer the operations to new conditions, such that they now can be recalled in various situations.

The degree to which operations have generalized is not the same from student to student. It depends both on the instructional methodology used to teach the operations and especially on the variety of content of problems assigned to students as exercises and on the individual characteristics of the student.

Insufficient generalization of operations is one of the reasons that students lack a general method for approaching problems. A particular manifestation of this lack of method is the fact that students only sometimes, rather than always, use a given operation when it is required.

For example, when the problem was to prove that two

triangles are equal or that a given figure is a parallelogram, the subjects usually began their solution with the operation of recalling the attributes of the equality of triangles or parallelograms. But when, as in problem No. 3, the problem was to prove that one chord is larger than another, this operation was seldom used. It is revealing that of the 13 good and excellent students, all began their attempts to prove that two triangles were equal by isolating sufficient conditions for the equality of two triangles, but that when trying to prove that a figure which was constructed is a parallelogram (problem No. 5), only 11 began with this operation as applied to parallelograms; and when trying to prove that two chords were unequal (problem No. 3), only four began by recalling the sufficient conditions (attributes) for the inequality of chords (most of this latter group recalled only one of these conditions: inequality of the arcs subtending the chords). This explains the seemingly incongruous result that problem No. 3—essentially one of the easiest problems of this group—gave the subjects more difficulty than any other problem. Of these 13 subjects, only two solved the problem, and one of them managed to do so only as a result of a successful random trial.

It proved to be the case, therefore, that students used one method to solve "triangle" and "parallelogram" problems, and another method to solve "chord" problems, although the same method should actually have been used for both types of problem, since the operation of recalling and selecting sufficient conditions is required in both cases. However, as we have seen, this operation has not been generalized in the minds of these students, such that it is recalled when they are working on problems involving some figures, but not recalled when other figures are involved. Thus, in spite of the fact that the subjects all knew the relevant theorems about triangles and chords equally well, the former were frequently recalled while the latter were not, so that the subjects solved "triangle" problems more easily (all other things being equal) than they did "chord" problems.

As mentioned previously, the degree of generalization of

operations may differ widely from student to student. As our experiments showed, there are students (the poorest) who use the operation of looking for sufficient conditions only when they are attempting to prove, for example, that two triangles are equal, and who, therefore, are able to solve only "triangle" problems. Other students apply this operation to triangles, inscribed angles, and parallelograms, but not to other figures and geometric relations; a few students apply it to most figures and relations.

Not one of our subjects, however, used this operation with regard to all geometrical figures and relations, thereby indicating that it was for them as general an operation as it would have to be if they were to be able to solve any problem, and not just problems involving a limited number of figures.

Insufficient generalization was observed with regard to all of the other operations as well.

The "reconceptualization" operation, for example, consists of the performance of active cognitive operations in order to isolate some element of a figure (a segment, for example) from the context in which it appears and to include it in different contexts, that is, to relate it to other elements than those of the context in which it was given. This process reveals other properties of the element in question. A given segment is revealed as a chord, as the side of a triangle, as a diagonal, etc.

Subject Lena K., an excellent student, always began an attempt to prove the equality of two segments with the question: "What is this segment part of?" This question recalled in her the recategorization operation. But this operation was not generalized in her, and so when she had to prove that two angles, rather than two segments, were equal, she did not pose this question and, therefore, did not apply the rethinking operation to these conditions.

Here is her attempt to solve problem No. 4.

S. I have to prove that triangle ABC is isosceles. That means I have to prove that the base angles are equal: angle

BAC should be equal to angle BCA. (Pause.) How can I do that? (Pause.) If BC is a tangent, then it would be equal to AB. But it isn't. . . . Angle BAC is a right angle . . . no, no, that's not true, because AC is not a radius. . . .

She continued in this trial-and-error fashion for a while but was unable to solve the problem.

We see that, when this subject was attempting to prove in problem No. 1 that segments MN and ND were equal, she used the reconception operation to see that these segments were the sides of a triangle; but when she was trying to prove that angles BAC and BCA in problem No. 4 were equal, this operation was not recalled, and the required knowledge was not applied.

Thus, reconception has not become a general operation in this subject's thinking, so as to lead always to the recall of the appropriate knowledge: in some cases the operation is recalled, in others not. As a result, she uses one approach to prove some geometric propositions and a different approach to prove others. She knows no general method applicable to all problems.

It is possible to specify situations, problems involving some type of angle, for example, in which the reconception operation is recalled in a student's mind, although in other very similar situations, for example, in problems involving a different type of angle, this operation is not recalled. Thus, in solving problem No. 1, subject Valery M., rated as a good student, "rethought" angles MAN and NAD of triangles MAN and NAD (Figure 9.5) as inscribed angles, but when he later ought to have seen other inscribed angles as the angles of triangles, the reconception operation failed to be recalled.

These observations reveal yet another cause of students' inability to solve any problem put before them: some figures and relations recall in them the required analysis and synthesis operations, thereby evoking the required knowledge, while other figures and relations do not recall these operations. Consequently, students analyze one problem correctly but are unable to analyze another one. The analysis operations have

Figure 9.5

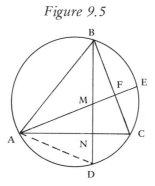

not become general and capable of being recalled under various conditions, that is, during the proof of various geometric propositions.

Differences occur as well in the degree of generalization of all other operations.

Thus, for example, subject Tanya F., rated as an excellent student, in attempting to prove that arcs DC and CE of problem No. 1 were equal, tried to use two conditions for the equality of arcs: equality of the chords subtending these arcs, and equality of the inscribed angles. When in problem No. 3 she had to prove that two chords were unequal, she tried to use only one condition, i.e., that chords are unequal if the arcs which they subtend are unequal, although she knew another condition perfectly well: chords are unequal if they are not equidistant from the center of the circle.

Recall of complete systems of conditions or attributes had not become, then, a general cognitive operation for this subject. In some cases, she recalled all relevant conditions; and in others, she did not.

Analysis of the subjects' attempts to solve the diagnostic problems shows that different operations can be generalized to different degrees in a student's mind. This explains the observation that a student will often, in the course of a generally inadequate approach to the solution of a problem during which he makes a large number of blind stabs, display a sudden "fragment" of correct reasoning. Or, conversely, a fragment of incorrect reasoning might "wedge" itself into a generally correct approach. The cause of these phenomena is the fact that the operations in question are generalized in the student's mind to different degrees. When dealing with one geometric figure or relation he uses one approach, and when dealing with a different figure or relation, a different approach.

So far we have considered difficulties in utilization of knowledge associated primarily with defects in the development of individual operations. Yet problems are never solved by means of a single operation, but rather by means of a system of operations. Considerations involving the student's degree of mastery of a system of operations and whether or not the system has developed properly in his mind also are important in determining whether knowledge will be successfully applied. Let us now consider the defects in the systematization of operations which we encountered in our subjects and which were responsible for their inability to solve all of the experimental problems.

3.   Defects in Systematization of
     Analytic-Synthetic Operations
     In the process of being taught how to solve problems the student forms associations not only between operations and specific elements of objective problem content, but also between operations themselves. Only when internal associations between operations have been formed is there the possibility that operations can be recalled, not only by the conditions of the problem, but also by other operations, one operation "evoking" another.

One of the characteristic features of problem-solving on the part of poor students is the fact that they often do not know the required system of operations, because this system has not been developed in them. As a result, after performing one or two operations, they stop and do not know how to proceed.

Here is how Sasha B., rated as a poor student, attempted to solve problem No. 4:

S. I am supposed to prove that AB is equal to BC—that this triangle is isosceles. So I'll prove that angle A is equal to angle BCA. (Pause. Looks at the figure for a long time.)

E. Well, what will you do next?

S. I don't know. . . I don't know what I should do. . . .

Having begun with the operation of isolating a sufficient condition for a triangle to be isosceles, he stopped and did not know what to do next. This operation did not provide the impetus for any others after it. Thus, lack of associations between operations and incomplete development of a system of operations was the cause of the fact that, several minutes after beginning the problem, the subject gave up, not knowing how to proceed.

However, students experience difficulty in solving problems not only in those situations in which they lack knowledge of an entire system of operations, but also in situations in which their knowledge of the system is limited or incorrect.

Here is how subject Ira K., rated as an average student, went about solving the same problem (No. 4):

S. Let's connect point E with point D and look at triangle EOD. (She connects the two points. See Figure 9.6.) It should be isosceles.

E. Why did you draw this line? What's your plan?

S. I don't know, I saw that I could connect the two points, so I did. . . . (Long pause.)

Figure 9.6

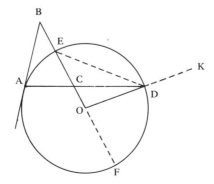

E. What are you going to do now?

S. Look at the triangle.... (Long pause.) If I could find some connection between triangle ABC and triangle EOD....

E. Why?

S. (Pause.) EC is a part of a side of both of them.

E. Well, if we showed that they're equal, what would that give us?

S. (Looks at the diagram.) Nothing, I guess....

E. Try to do it some other way.

S. If I extend OE until it intersects the circle at point F and then look at angle ABF (She extends it to point F. See Figure 9.6.).... Maybe the theorem about a chord perpendicular to a tangent would work here.... No, it wouldn't.... (Long pause.)

E. What now?

S. What's left to try? I've looked at angle ABF, I've looked at the triangles.... What if I extend OD (does so) and compare angles ABF and BOK.... No, I don't know what else to do....

E. What does the whole proof depend on, do you think?

S. On what you try. Sometimes you're lucky and try the right thing, sometimes you're not. (Gives up.)

The most characteristic feature of Ira K.'s attempt to solve this problem is the fact that she proceeded almost exclusively by means of blind trials. There was no correct system in her approach. Limited numbers of operations were directed toward arriving at a solution by random luck. She did not have a sound method for analyzing the problem, but she did have a method of sorts. Her method might be formulated as follows. "Find or construct figures in the diagram and draw conclusions about their properties. Maybe you will hit on the one which you need to solve the problem." The subject herself expressed the essence of this method very well when she said that success depends on what you try, on whether you hit on the right figure or not.

A number of subjects clearly showed this tendency to look for a figure which would suggest the required theorem and did not apply a number of other important operations. Subjects frequently answered the questions "Why did you draw that line?" or "What are you going to try to prove using that figure?" by saying "Maybe it'll show something."

The following is another example of this approach.

Subject Oleg S., an eighth grade student rated as average, was given an easy problem which could be solved on the basis of material covered in the seventh grade (Figure 9.7):

$$\text{given: AB} \perp \text{AD}$$
$$\text{CD} \perp \text{AD}$$
$$< 1 = < 2$$
$$\text{prove: BE = CE.}$$

S. Let's connect B and C. There's a theorem which says that triangles ABD and ACD are equal.

E. Try to do the problem without constructions.

S. OK. It's given that angle 1 is equal to angle 2, and angles BEA and CED are equal because they're vertices. . . . (Pause.)

Figure 9.7

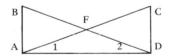

E. Why do you have to know that angle BEA is equal to angle CED?

S. I don't know yet, maybe I'll be able to use it. . . . (Pause.) Are these perpendiculars (AB and DC) equal?

E. I don't know. Are they given as equal?

S. No, so I can't use that. . . . Angles BEC and AED are equal because they're vertices.

E. Why do you have to know that they're equal?

S. To prove that triangle ABE is equal to triangle ECD.

E. Do you have to know that angle BEC is equal to

angle AED to prove that triangle ABE is equal to triangle ECD?

S. No, I don't. . . .

E. Then why did you mention that these angles are equal?

S. I thought it might yield something. . . .

Such an approach is justified when a problem-solver has exhausted all possibilities of finding a solution while acting in a systematic manner, i.e., when there are no ways left to accomplish a directed search. Then the problem-solver is forced to resort to blind trials and to look for "something" which could recall some (unknown beforehand) theorem which could prove to be useful and cue the field where the solution might reside. But such an approach is not justified at the very beginning when there is always a possibility that a solution may be found by utilization of operations which ensure systematic and directed analysis of a problem situation. But these operations are not included in the system of operations applied by certain categories of students while searching for a solution.

Some of the ninth grade subjects proceeded in a similar way when solving the more difficult problems. Visual analysis of the diagram was the basis of their approach, random "sorting" of figures appearing in the diagram or formed by construction, which recalled theorems about the properties of these figures. The subjects did not go from the conditions of a problem to the diagram, but from the diagram to the conditions. In this approach to problem-solving, recall of concepts concerning attributes (theorems) does not result from the analysis of the verbal component of the problem conditions, but only from the isolation or construction of specific figures. The objects which the student analyzes are not the concepts given in the verbal component of the problem, but the figures visible in the diagram, which he then considers in relation to the verbal information.

Therefore, the basic operations performed by the student who uses this method are visual analysis of the diagram, consisting of isolation and sorting of individual figures, supplementary constructions for the purpose of obtaining figures, and, frequently, reconception of the diagram. The student knows a system of operations, but this system is limited and unsuitable for the solution of difficult problems. It is adequate only for the solution of the simplest problems with "cueing" diagrams (which our subjects solved successfully), but is completely inadequate for the solution of problems in which the diagram does not cue specific theorems. This system does not include such extremely important operations as: analysis of the verbal component of the problem for the purpose of recalling a system of sufficient conditions, comparison of these attributes with each other and given information and selection of a suitable one, and others. It is not surprising that students using this approach find many problems insoluble.

The method in question is characterized by a large number of random trials which are usually of one of two types: "inspection" trials or "construction" trials.

The following is an attempt on the part of subject Andrei S., a ninth grader, rated as an excellent student, to solve problem No. 1.

S. Let's look at triangles MBF and NAM.

E. Why them?

S. Angles BMF and AMN are equal because they're vertices. . . . I don't think that gives us anything. . . . Only if arcs AD and BE are equal. . . . We're supposed to prove that MN equals ND. Angle AND is measured by arc AD and arc BC, and angle DNC is measured by arc AB and arc DC. But that's not right either. . . . Angle BNC is a right angle, and angle BNA is also a right angle. . . . If I try triangle NBC. . . . But that doesn't yield anything either. . . . What if I try to connect something. . . . A and D, maybe? (The student connects them as shown in Figure 9.8.) We get triangle DAM, in which angle AMD is measured by arc AD, and angle ADM is measured by arc AB. But it's obvious that arc AB is bigger than arc AD. No. . . it's measured by the half-sum of arcs AD and BE, and angle ADB is measured by arc AB. . . . If we look at triangles

NAM and DAN, we see that AN is common to them. . . . I have to prove that the legs are equal. . . . Aren't angles MAN and NAD equal? They're measured by arcs EC and CD. (Pause.) If I try to draw the bisector of angle C. . . (draws C). No, that doesn't lead anywhere either!

Figure 9.8

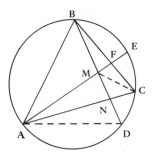

The subject made a few more trials and then gave up.

The use of inspection and construction trials to solve problems is characterized by the fact that these trials are arbitrary. The student does not know what he is supposed to obtain from them. He performs them in the hope that he will run across a figure which will recall knowledge of some theorem which, in turn, will serve as a basis for a solution to the problem.

Students use the "trial method" in solving problems because the instruction which they receive encourages this approach. It develops as a result of their being given practice problems with "cueing" diagrams, and is often never subsequently altered by the teacher. The students do not often learn a more developed system of analytic-synthetic operations which would be suitable for solving more difficult problems which require more than analysis of the diagram above for their solution.

This does not mean, however, that all trials are bad. They are, as was already mentioned, indispensable for creative thinking, and a necessary condition for the successful solution of difficult problems. Creative trials must be distinguished, however, from random, blind trials.

If the student, not knowing what to do, begins randomly to inspect any and all figures in the diagram and randomly to draw all possible supplementary constructions, he is proceeding by means of trials of the second sort. But if, knowing what he is trying to obtain, he begins to test possible means of achieving his goal (for example, various attributes of a given figure), then he is proceeding correctly—by means of trials of the first sort. In the first case, he is trying to guess the solution; in the second case, he is searching for it in a more or less systematic manner. The instructional process should teach the student to make creative trials and discourage blind trials based on guessing.

But in order to be able to freely use previously acquired knowledge to solve problems of a wide variety of types, it is not enough to have a complete and correct system of operations; it is necessary that this system be generalized. One of the reasons for the fact that even the best students were unable to solve all of the problems given them during the experiment was that they lacked a sufficiently generalized system of operations. They applied the correct system of operations to one problem but not to another. The system of operations had not been generalized; like the individual operations, it was associated in the students' minds only with more or less limited conditions and was recalled only when these conditions were present.

The following are solutions to two problems by subject Tanya F., rated as an excellent student.

First, problem No. 7.

S. Let's connect A and B, and B and C (Figure 9.9). We get triangle ABC. Let's prove that it's isosceles. To do this we have to prove that angle A is equal to angle C. Angle A is measured by half of arc BME, and angle C is measured by half of arc BNE. And these arcs are equal.

E. You have to prove that they're equal.

Figure 9.9

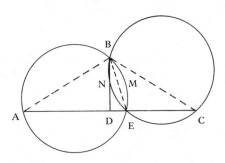

S. (Pause.) When are arcs equal? (Thinks.) If the chords are equal. . . . Let's draw the chord. (Draws BE.) This chord is common to them, so they're equal.

In solving this problem, the subject used an entire system of operations, including the reconceptualization operation, the operation of recalling the sufficient conditions for the equality of angles (angles A and C), the operation of recalling and selecting possible sufficient conditions for the equality of arcs ("When are arcs equal?"), and others. She also applied these operations in the correct order.

The following is her attempt to solve problem No. 3. She began by trying to prove that the chords were unequal by showing that their arcs were unequal, but did not succeed, and arrived at an impasse. At our suggestion, she made another attempt to solve the problem.

She looked intently at the diagram, drawing lines in the air with her pencil.

E. What are you thinking?

S. I'm thinking of drawing a construction. . . .

E. Why?

S. To get something.

E. What do you want to get?

S. Some figure. . . .

The subject, who used the correct system of analytic-synthetic operations in solving problem No. 7, did not use this system for problem No. 3. Instead she began making random trials, and thereby descended to the lower level of cognitive activity characteristic of our average and poor students.[5]

It sometimes happens that unusual problem conditions do not recall any analytic-synthetic operations whatever, and, in this case, even good students who have learned the correct system of operations find themselves in the situation of "not knowing what to do."

In order to develop in the student a generalized system of analytic-synthetic operations, it is necessary to teach him the correct method of analysis, using problems of the most varied content.

Finally, yet another source of the difficulties which our subjects encountered in problem-solving was insufficient flexibility in their systems of operations, such that they were unable to vary operations freely. This lack of flexibility was especially evident in those situations in which a subject had reached an impasse. Subjects frequently responded to the suggestion to try to approach the problem in a different way by saying, "I don't know how to do it any other way," and then proceeded to make a second attempt along the same lines as the first. They were unable to change their approach to a problem at will, i.e., to vary their analysis operation.

Any skill, including skill in thinking or in solving problems, presupposes the ability to select operations, to shift from one operation to another, and to vary analytical procedures. Only when the student's system of operations is flexible, when he is able to combine operations in various ways, is he able to solve difficult problems. An example will illustrate this point.

Subject Lena K., rated as an excellent student, solved problem No. 1 by proving that arcs DC and CE were equal, which she did by showing that the angles measured by these arcs (angles DNC and CFE) were equal, and by using arc AB.

After she had solved the problem by using angles DNC and CFE, we asked her to prove that the arcs were equal by a different method.

She looked up toward the ceiling and pondered.

E. What are you thinking about?

S. I'm trying to remember theorems having to do with arcs and angles.

E. How did you get the idea the first time to use angles DNC and EFC?

S. I just looked at the diagram to find out which angles had subtended arcs, and saw them.

Thus, in proving that the arcs were equal the first time she used one method—analyzing the diagram by isolating obvious conditions for the equality of arcs. The second time, she used a different method, a different operation—analyzing possible means of proving the equality of arcs by recalling theorems dealing with the relations between arcs and angles.

This variation in approaches indicates an ability to think about the problem and is a necessary condition for bringing various elements of knowledge to bear on the problem-solving process. The subject did not say: "I don't know what to do." Instead she used a new operation which would make it possible to approach the problem in a new way, to "grasp" it from another direction, to apply new knowledge. Overcoming the fixed, stereotyped associations between operations (the development of flexibility of associations) is a significant consideration and an important condition for the avoidance of difficulties in the solution of complex problems. The ability to approach problems from a new angle, to analyze them in new ways, must be specifically taught.

4.   **Incomplete and One-Sided Analysis of
     Geometric Relations as a Cause
     of Difficulty in Problem-Solving**

One of the more important causes of difficulty in problem-solving, and one which often makes a successful solution impossible, is incomplete, one-sided analysis of problem conditions.

Analytic-synthetic activity in problem-solving takes two forms: visual analysis of the diagram, and verbal-logical analysis of the concepts given in the verbal component of the problem conditions. Visual analysis has as its object the figures given in the diagram, as well as figures resulting from supplementary constructions. Verbal-logical analysis should be directed toward the given information as well as toward that which must be proved. Concepts which come into the problem-solver's mind in the course of reasoning should also be subjected to analysis.

Our experiment showed that, if a subject's analysis and synthesis activity was one-sided, if he did not consider all relevant associations and relations between geometric phenomena, the knowledge required to solve the problem was frequently not recalled and the problem proved insoluble for him.

The following is Lyuba Z.'s attempt to solve problem No. 2.

S. It's given that the straight lines are parallel. . . . What figures are AK and KC' part of? Triangles C'KM and AKN. Let's prove that these triangles are equal. Angle AKN and angle C'KM are equal as vertices, and angle ANK is measured by the half-sum of arcs AC' and A'B; angle C'MK is measured by the half-sum of arcs AC' and A'B; angle C'MK is measured by the half-sum of arcs AC' and CB'.

To prove that these angles are equal, we have to prove that arc CB' is equal to arc A'B. . . .

The subject continued for a considerable time to try to prove that segments AK and KC' were equal, using triangles C'KM and AKN, and then, unable to do this, gave up.

Her method of approaching the problem was, on the whole, correct, in that she used the correct system of operations, but she nevertheless failed to solve the problem, because her analysis of the figures of which segments AK and KC' were part was one-sided. If she had examined the diagram to see of which figures these segments are and could be elements and correlated them with various elements of the diagram, she would have seen that they could be also the sides of triangle AKC' if supplementary segment AC' is drawn (Figure 9.10). If she had related them to arcs AA' and CC', she would have seen that they were in addition the sides of triangles AKA' and CKC'.

In other words, the subject saw only one of the several relationships between AK and KC' and other elements of the diagram. If she had seen all of these relationships she would

Figure 9.10

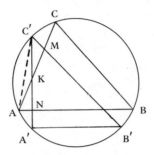

immediately have discovered two possible ways of solving the problem. She failed to see these relationships not because the operation of correlating elements was undeveloped in her, but because she did not know that she had to perform a complete analysis, to see *all* of the relationships between figures and elements. For her this was not a principle of problem-solving. She did not conceive of it as a general method of analyzing problems.

Failure to understand the need for consideration of all interrelations and attributes was also apparent in subjects' verbal-logical analysis of concepts. An example of this shortcoming is the fact that they frequently tried to solve a problem on the basis of the first attribute to come into their heads, without any attempt to recall, isolate, and utilize attributes.

Thus, subject Tanya F. began her solution of problem No. 3 by trying to prove that the chords were unequal on the basis of the fact that chords are unequal, if the arcs subtending them are unequal.

It is correct, in principle, to try to prove the inequality of chords by proving the inequality of the arcs which subtend them. The subject's mistake lies in the fact that, when this approach failed, she did not attempt to try to prove the inequality of the chords by means of another of the conditions (sufficient attri-butes) for the inequality of chords known to her, but rather began making random trials. She did not ask herself the question: "What other conditions for the inequality of chords do I know?" This indicates that she did not understand the significance of complete analysis.

There are two possible causes for the failure to perform a complete analysis of concepts. The first is that the set of theorems and other geometric propositions which students know is not amalgamated into a single system in many students' heads. The second is that they fail to use even that system of theorems which they know, because they do not realize that the process of searching for a solution to a problem requires recall of not just one attribute, not just one theorem, but of many, and perhaps all, of the attributes relevant to the figures or geometric relations under consideration.

Let us consider the first cause. In order for the student to be able to use a system of theorems which reflects all relevant geometric relations, it is first necessary that he be taught this system. The overwhelming majority of our subjects, although they knew all of the required theorems separately, did not know the system which these theorems constituted. This was true both of theorems explicitly covered in one of the usual divisions of a geometry course and especially of theorems touched on in various places and representing, thus, a comprehensive system of theorems.

Thus, for example, only three of 10 subjects were able to cite theorems dealing with all of the attributes of the parallelogram. Eight subjects of the 10, in naming the attributes of the isosceles triangle, failed to cite the theorem that the bisector of an isosceles triangle is simultaneously the median and the altitude, although they knew this theorem quite well and, in several instances, used it when cued by the diagram. But they did not see this theorem as one of a system of theorems dealing with the attributes of the isosceles triangle.

The situation, with regard to comprehensive systems of theorems, is even worse. For example, there are at least 15 theorems involving conditions for the equality of segments. These theorems are covered under "Triangles," as well as under "Parallelograms," "Circles," etc.

Of 10 subjects, one was able to name seven of these

conditions, two were able to name five, and seven named fewer than five.

The same is true with regard to the subjects' knowledge of the system of conditions for the equality of angles, for the parallelness of lines, etc. Here it was almost invariably the case that a theorem was recalled only when cued by the diagram, because the subjects did not know the required set of theorems as a system.

The situation with which we are concerned here is not that in which the problem-solver fails to recall a system of theorems because he does not know that it is necessary to recall it. Rather, we are considering the relatively infrequent situation in which the best students attempt to use various attributes of a figure or geometric relation, but are unable to find the one they need, because the system they know is incomplete.

Methodologists have long been aware of the fact that lack of knowledge of systems of attributes is a significant source of difficulty in problem-solving. In order to help the student find the required theorems in the course of solving a problem, American methodologists have proposed handing him these systems in the form of prepared "geometric instrumentariums" or "geometric keys." In the Soviet Union, this idea has received the support of Bernstein (1941). However, Gmurman (1949), Nemytov (1947), and others, have expressed criticism of the "geometric instrumentarium."

Without going into a detailed analysis of the debate over the significance of the "geometric instrumentarium," we will say only that it is wrong to regard the "geometric instrumentarium," that is, a system of theorems, as a panacea for all difficulties encountered by students in solving geometric problems, i.e., as a mechanical means for finding solutions. Knowledge of a system of theorems by itself is not sufficient. It is necessary to know in addition a system of analytic-synthetic operations, that is, to be able to analyze a problem in such a way as to be able to use this system. On the other hand, it is wrong to deny the importance of a system of theorems, since analysis of a problem will not lead to a solution, if it does not stimulate recall of the system of theorems which will permit recognition of all relevant properties of a given geometric figure or relation.

As we noted above, however, failure to perform a complete analysis may have causes other than lack of knowledge of a system of theorems. Inability to solve a problem is frequently the result of failure to realize that a particular system of theorems must be recalled, and often as completely as possible, in the course of search for a solution. Our subjects failed to solve a significant number of problems only because, having begun on the basis of the first attribute to come to mind, they reached an impasse and did not realize that, in order to make further progress, they had to use other attributes of the figures or relations in question, which is a condition of a more complete analysis of these figures or relations.

Our experiments showed that the first attributes to come to mind are those which are the most often used. As a result of their being used more frequently than others, the associations underlying their recall are stronger than those of other attributes. They are, therefore, recalled first during the problem-solving process. However, because students as a rule do not know that often several or sometimes even all attributes must be tried, their analysis shows that one-sidedness which makes solution of the problem impossible.

An extreme form of this one-sidedness was shown by students who attempted to prove the equality of segments and angles only by means of triangles, this being their only means of approaching this task.

The dominance of this attribute over others is not characteristic only of poor students. When we asked one of the good students, Lena K., why she had tried to prove that the two chords in problem No. 3 were unequal by using triangles AMC and DMB which she had constructed (Figure 9.11), without using the direct attributes for the inequality of chords which she knew, she replied: "I'm more used to using triangles—this is the way that usually comes to mind."

Why do students develop such a one-sided, stereotyped approach to problem analysis, which for some students becomes

Figure 9.11

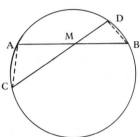

so entrenched that they attempt to prove everything using triangles?

The instructional cause of this one-sidedness is, it seems to us, an incorrect selection of practice problems. In order to develop in the student the habit of analyzing problem conditions completely, rather than one-sidedly, it is absolutely necessary to vary the practice problems which he is given, with regard to the attributes which must be used in order to solve them. The student should under no circumstances be permitted to develop the impression that use of triangles constitutes a universal method for proving geometric propositions. He should realize that this is only one way among many, though perhaps one which is more frequently used than others. And in order to develop in him the habit of complete analysis, he should be given more problems which require that he search for and select the required attribute from among all of the relevant attributes known to him. Solution of these problems will constitute training in comprehensive concept analysis.

It must be said that the development in students of a one-sided, stereotyped approach to problem-solving is, in many instances, the fault of the teacher, who, instead of teaching the student to recall and examine various attributes which might be used to prove a given proposition, intentionally or unintentionally leads him to believe that use of triangles is a universal method.

This approach is reflected even in methodological text-books—not only those published many years ago, but also some of the relatively recent publications. The following is an explanation of how to solve a problem taken from a methodological article by Golubovskaya (1935).

The problem is to prove that in an isosceles triangle the altitudes drawn to the equal sides are equal (Figure 9.12).

"Analysis: equality of segments is usually proved on the basis of the equality of the triangles of which these segments are corresponding elements. In the present case, triangles AFC and AEC fulfill these conditions. . . ."

Figure 9.12   *Figure 9.13*

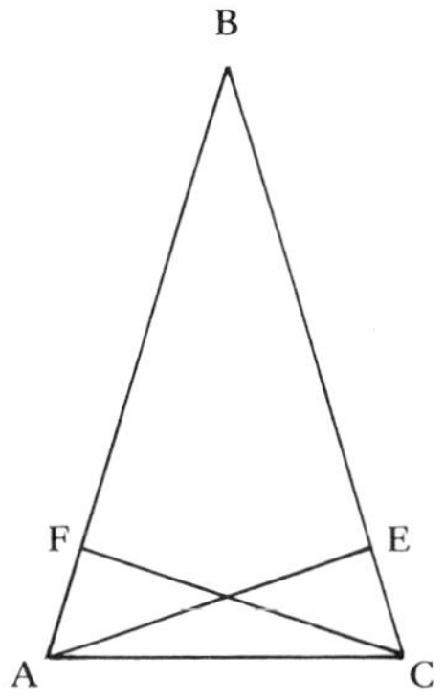

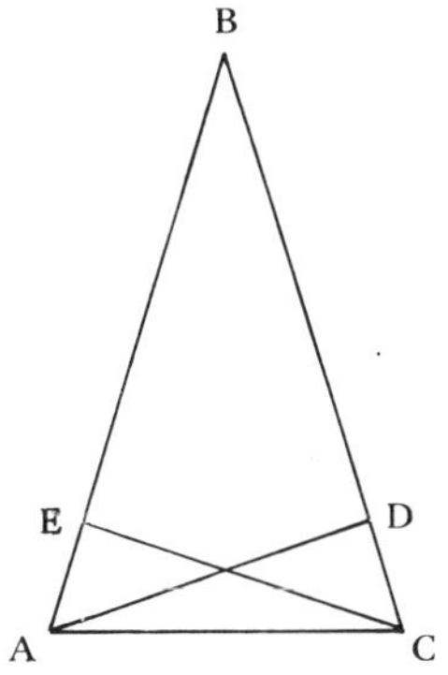

An analogous shortcoming is encountered in a number of other methodological texts, in particular in *Methods of Teaching Mathematics*, edited by S.E. Lyapin (1955), in which the following example of the teaching of analysis is given.

The problem is the same as in the previous example (Figure 9.13).

"In planning how to solve the problem, the student should analyze the given information as follows. To prove that segments AD and EC are equal, we find two triangles each having as one of its elements segment AD and segment EC, respectively. Having selected triangles ADC and AEC as meeting these conditions, he must now prove that they are equal. . . ."

Thus, instead of creating in the student an orientation toward comprehensive analysis, toward consideration of all relations between the elements under consideration and the other elements of the problem, some methodologists advise him to look only for triangles, that is, induce him to substitute mechanical use of one particular method for comprehensive analysis. It is not surprising, therefore, that many students begin their solution to a problem by looking for triangles, and by constructing them if there are none present, never thinking about what they are trying to prove or the means by which they will prove it, that is, without carrying out a comprehensive analysis of the conditions of the problem. When they cannot solve the problem using triangles, they often do not know what else to do and so give up.

Developing in the student a correct method of analyzing problems means teaching him general cognitive operations. It is clear that the instructional procedures cited above not only fail to teach him these operations, they prevent him from learning them. One of these general operations, as required, for example, in proving that two segments are equal, is the consideration, if needed, of all of the relations existing between these segments and other elements of the figure, and not only with those elements which form triangles. The student should be asked not to look for the *triangles* of which the given segments are a part, but more generally to look for the *figures* of which they are a part. He will then see not only the triangles of which the segments are a part, but any and all other figures of which they are a part as well.

Another manifestation of incompleteness of analysis is failure to consider all components of the conditions of a problem.

Thus, in solving the experimental problems, a subject occasionally analyzed only that part of the problem describing that which was to be proved, without considering the given information, or, after performing a supplementary construction and obtaining thereby some figure, he would fail to go on to determine all of the properties of this figure.

For example, subject Tolya G., a good student, in solving problem No. 1, performed a correct supplementary construction (he drew AD; see Figure 9.14), but forgot to draw conclusions from the given information. He analyzed only that which was to be proved, neglecting the given data.

Figure 9.14

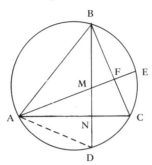

E. What is given in the problem? Have you forgotten?

S. No, I haven't, it's given that AF and BN are altitudes. I am supposed to prove that angle NDA is equal to angle NMA.

Having said that these segments were given as altitudes, the subject did not then proceed to recall and analyze the properties of altitudes, and so failed to realize that they formed right angles with the sides which they intersected, which was a necessary piece of information in the solution of the problem. His failure, at the very beginning, to get as a conclusion this fact was the cause of his inability to solve the problem.

Another example of this defect of reasoning on the part of a good student is subject Ira A.'s attempt to solve problem No. 6 (Figure 9.15). Having performed the right supplementary construction (radii OC, OK, O'K and O'B), the subject failed to

Figure 9.15

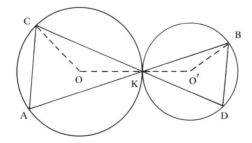

analyze the resulting figures. She did not see the two isosceles triangles with equal base angles. Having applied analytical operations to that which was to be proved and to that which was given, she failed to apply the same operations to the figures resulting from the supplementary constructions, and so was unable to solve the problem.

These and other observations indicate that many students lack a clear conception of what to do in order to solve a problem and when to do it. (For example, it is necessary to draw *all* relevant conclusions from the figures resulting from supplementary constructions.) Students often apply analytic-synthetic operations to some components of the problem conditions (for example, to that which is to be proved) but not to others (for example, to the given information or to the results of supplementary constructions, etc.). As a result, properties which should be realized from analysis of these components and used in solving the problem are not isolated, required knowledge is not recalled, and the problem remains unsolved.

Some subjects analyzed the conditions of some problems fully, but failed to analyze completely the conditions of other problems. In other words, comprehensive analysis of all of the components of a problem did not constitute for these students a general principle or method of problem-solving, and this hindered them in the application of their knowledge and resulted in their being unable to solve a number of the experimental problems.

5. Students' Awareness of the Logical
    Structure of Proof and of Their Own
    Cognitive Operations

All of the defects in the way students approach problems which we have considered are closely associated with a lack of understanding (or a poor understanding) of the nature of proof, of the logical structure of this process, and of a lack of generalized knowledge of the operations which should be performed in solving a problem of this type. It should be noted in this regard that the causes of these defects do not reduce to these factors alone.

The following are students' replies to questions asked them

after the conclusion of the experiment. Since the idea of studying how the subjects perceived the structure of proof and their own cognitive operations was somewhat of an afterthought, only 10 subjects were asked to reply to these questions.

First question: "You have been studying geometry and proving geometric propositions for several years now. Proving things is something you have to do in other areas besides geometry. How would you describe what it means to prove something?"

Answering this question was very difficult for all 10 subjects. Three of them were completely unable to give an answer. Five either said that proving something meant citing some fact or example (i.e., they did not reveal any knowledge of the nature of the deductive method), or gave some confused or unclear explanation. Only two subjects gave answers which indicated that they understood the nature of deductive proof more or less correctly and in a general way.

The following are some of the students' responses.

1. Subject Ira K., a ninth grader rated as an average student, answered the first question as follows.

S. What it means to prove something? (Pause.) I've never thought about it.

E. You've never thought about it? But you've been proving theorems for three years. Try to explain what you've been doing.

S. (Very perplexed. Pause.) Well, proving something is to prove it.

E. That's not an explanation.

S. Showing that two numbers are equal . . .?

E. In real life we prove other things than just that two numbers are equal.

S. I don't know. . . . I don't know how to explain it. I've never thought about it.

The following are some answers given by subjects who believe that to prove something means to establish it as a fact, to prove it as true in practice.

2. Subject Vera M., rated as a good student, answered the same question as follows.

S. To prove something means to show that it's true in practice. For example, that if one chord is parallel to another one, then this has to be proven in practice.

E. But what does proving something in practice mean?

S. It means to prove that it's a fact.

3. Subject Andrei S., rated as a good student, stated:

S. It means to show that a thing is the same as something else.

E. As what?

S. As an example of something.

E. Only as an example of something?

S. (Pause.) I don't know. . . .

E. Well, if we don't have an example of the thing we have in mind, can we still somehow prove it without using an example?

S. You can't prove it without using an example.

The following are answers given by subjects who understand more or less clearly or are coming to an understanding during the experiment of what proof is.

4. Subject Yura S., rated as a good student, said:

S. (Long pause.) It means to use certain things, theorems, things that we know are true.

E. Use them for what?

S. To find out other things.

5. Subject Tanya F., rated as an excellent student, stated:

S. I don't know how to explain it. . . . (Ponders.)

E. For example, someone says something, and someone else says, "Prove it!" What do they want him to do?

S. To show whether what he said is right or not?

E. And how can he do that?

S. By using facts.

E. And if there are no facts?

S. By using theorems.

E. But we don't prove things only in geometry.

S. (Pause.) By using what he knows to be true?

Similar difficulties were caused by the question "What does 'proving a theorem' mean?"

However, subjects' responses to the question "What does it

mean to prove that a given figure is a parallelogram?" were of a completely different character. This question caused difficulty for only two subjects; the other eight immediately began to cite the attributes of the parallelogram.

S. Ira K.: It means to prove that the opposite sides are either parallel or equal.

S. Sasha B.: You have to prove that its opposite sides are parallel.

Even the poor students who were unable to give an answer to the first question were able to answer this one.

After the subjects had indicated to us the attributes of the parallelogram, we asked them the following question: "How would you explain what it means to prove that a given figure is a parallelogram without referring to opposite sides being parallel or equal? How could you explain it in a more general way?"

Only Vera M. gave the correct answer: "It means to find one of its attributes."

We asked some of the subjects the following additional question: "What does it mean to prove that two chords are unequal?" It proved to be the case that three out of four of the subjects who had answered the question "What does it mean to prove that a given figure is a parallelogram?" by indicating the attributes of the parallelogram, failed to indicate any attributes for the inequality of chords; only one subject responded: "It means to prove that their arcs are unequal."

All of these observations indicate that a large majority of the subjects lacked generalized knowledge of the nature of proof, i.e., of its logic. They know what it means to prove that a figure is a parallelogram, but have difficulty answering the question: "What does it mean to prove that chords are unequal?" and they are completely unable to answer the questions (or answer by indicating only one approach): "What does it mean to prove something?" (that is, to prove something in general).

We stated above that many of our subjects were able to prove some geometric propositions, but not others, a fact which indicates that their system of analytic-synthetic operations lacks generality, which is to say that they do not know a general method of approaching problems.

Our experimental material shows that, although there is some correspondence between a student's practical approach to proving geometric propositions and his conception of the logical structure of proof, this correspondence is far from perfect. A significant proportion of those subjects who were unable to say what it means to prove something were reasonably competent in practice. Those subjects who said that to prove something means to cite some examples did refer, in the course of attempting to solve a problem, to theorems; that is, to general propositions, rather than to examples, but their responses to questions clearly indicated that they did this unconsciously.

Further studies, involving a significantly larger number of subjects, are required in order to determine more precisely the connection between practical ability to prove propositions and consciousness of the logical structure of proof. It is clear, however, that lack of generality of the system of analytic-synthetic operations is associated with lack of understanding of the general structure of proof. It is this factor which prevents the development of a conscious, generalized approach to problem-solving.

The second question was intended to determine whether or not the subjects knew what to do in order to prove something, and how they became aware of the operations which they performed in doing this. The question was formulated as follows: "How would you explain to someone who does not know how to prove a theorem what he should do in order to prove it? What is the first step you take when you are trying to prove something? What is the next thing you do?"

None of the subjects was able to answer these questions in a general way (what one must do in general in order to prove a theorem), but rather spoke about what they themselves do. This indicates that they did not possess a generalized knowledge of the principles of problem-solving in proof.

With regard to their perception of their own operations, comparison of the operations which they actually used in their attempts to solve problems with the operations which they cited in describing how they go about solving problems shows that there is frequently a significant discrepancy between the two. They used more operations when actually solving problems than they cited in these descriptions. Some subjects, on the contrary, cited operations which they frequently did not, in fact, use in situations in which their use was indispensable.

These discrepancies indicate, on the one hand, that the subjects were unaware of some of the operations which they actually used, and, on the other hand, that even if they were aware of an operation, they did not necessarily use it in solving problems. These operations were recalled only when the subject actually examined a diagram.

In order for a student to be able consciously and purposefully to search for a proof, he must consciously know the operations by means of which this process is effected, that is, the structure of proof. The more conscious the student is of the operations which he uses in solving problems, the better he knows how to proceed (knows not only in practice, but in theory), the more deliberately he is able to apply operations, and the better he is able to select and vary them. Knowledge of operations and how they fit together in systems, i.e., knowledge of the structure of proof, promotes in addition generalization of both individual operations and systems of operations.

The experimental data show, however, that knowledge of what to do in order to prove a proposition is not in itself sufficient to enable a student to solve problems, or to think. Training in the application of this knowledge is indispensable. In other words, training is required, not only in the application of knowledge of objective things and their relations in the external world (theorems, laws, etc.), but in the application of knowledge of actions which may be performed on these objects, i.e., in the application of the acquired method. Only as a result of such training can knowledge of operations regulate analytic activity, and only such training can eliminate situations in which the student knows an operation but does not use it. The strength of the associations between conceptual knowledge of actions and the actions themselves, more precisely, their images, is as important a condition for the use of this knowledge as strength of the associations between conceptual knowledge of specific objects and relations in the external world and images of these objects and relations.

As was noted above, this chapter discusses the results only of the first part of our experiment. Analysis of the mechanisms of cognitive activity and discovery of the sources of the difficulties which students have in solving problems constitute only the first stage (although a very important one) of the process of developing effective teaching methods. Knowledge of the student's difficulties, of the defects in his cognitive activity, of the reasons for his inability in some circumstances to solve a problem independently, provides necessary information for building a model of an ideal process of thinking to solve this sort of problem. It also makes possible the development of an instructional methodology and a system of exercises which will, on the one hand, prevent these difficulties from arising and lead to formation of a perfect process *de novo*, and on the other hand, provide a reliable means for eliminating them.

Our results show clearly that if, for example, some students are unable to solve a problem because they do not know certain cognitive operations, then an effective instructional methodology must include special provisions for the teaching of these operations. If students are able to solve some problems but not others as a result of insufficient generalization of cognitive operations, then an effective instructional methodology should include special exercises and practice problems for the purpose of ensuring that this generalization of operations will occur.

In other words, the pattern of difficulties and defects in the student's cognitive activity indicates the defects of the instructional methodology by means of which the student was taught, as well as the direction in which to proceed in order to develop the desired qualities as rapidly and efficiently as possible. Our procedures permitted us to develop an idea of the cognitive operations which must be developed during the instructional process, if it is to be successful in teaching the student how to solve problems (see the major operations cited in the foregoing chapter).

An important condition for independent use of operations is

the generalization and systematization of these operations. The teacher should, therefore, vary drill material in order to insure that each operation becomes associated in the student's mind with the most varied content. At the same time, it is necessary to develop associations between the operations themselves, and to include each operation in a system of operations. Only when each operation is associated both with the most varied objective content and with other operations will it be recalled in a wide variety of circumstances.

Awareness on the part of the student of his own cognitive operations is very important, as is knowledge of the general principles of problem analysis and of the nature of proof.

The defects in the subjects' cognitive activity, as exposed in the course of our experiment, have as their source defects in the instruction in geometry which they had received. Observation shows that, in teaching geometry (and this is true of teaching other subjects as well) teachers often do not set as their goal the teaching of specific cognitive operations and their systems, i.e., certain general procedures of thought, with the result that students learn them in a random fashion. If this serious shortcoming is to be eliminated, the results of the study of cognitive operations must be incorporated into teaching practice. Each teacher should have before him not only a program of the knowledge which he must transmit to the student, but also a program of the specific operations and their systems which he must teach him. The development of methods and procedures by means of which this may be accomplished is a subject for further research.

The issues discussed in this chapter have significance for areas other than the teaching of geometry. The study of cognitive operations should, in the future, precede the compilation of programs and methodological recommendations in any subject matter. It is for this reason that the elaboration of the principles of this study is the task not only of psychology, but of didactics as well.

Appendix

Experimental Problems

Problem No. 1

Figure 9.16

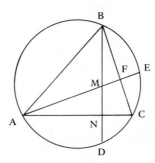

Two altitudes of a triangle ABC are drawn from points A and B, respectively (Figure 9.16), and extended until they intersect the circumference at points E and D, respectively. Prove that the segments of these straight lines from the orthocenter M to points E and D are divided in half by the sides of the triangle (prove that MN = ND and that MF = FE).

Problem 2

Figure 9.17

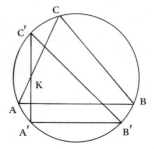

Chord AB of the circumference shown in Figure 9.17 is parallel to A'B' and chord BC is parallel to B'C'. Point C is linked with point A, while point C' is linked with point A'. Prove that segment AK is equal to segment KC'.

Problem No. 3

Figure 9.18

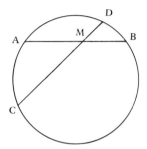

Point M is the midpoint of chord AB of the circumference shown in Figure 9.18. Prove that any other chord passing through point M is longer than chord AB (prove that CD > AB).

Problem No. 4

Figure 9.19

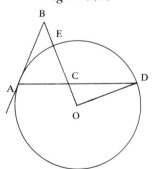

Chord AD is drawn in circumference with center O (Figure 9.19). A straight line is drawn from point D to the center O.

Radius OE is drawn perpendicular to OD and extended until it intersects, at point B, the tangent drawn through point A. Prove that AB = BC.

Problem No. 5

Figure 9.20

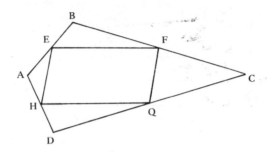

Prove that if the centers of all sides of a quadrangle are connected in sequence, the resulting figure is a parallelogram (Figure 9.20).

Problem No. 6

Figure 9.21

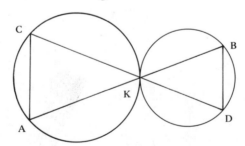

Two circumferences are tangent to one another at point K (Figure 9.21). Two secants, AB and CD, are drawn through point K until they intersect both of the circles. Prove that segments CA and BD are parallel (Figure 9.21).

Problem No. 7

Figure 9.22

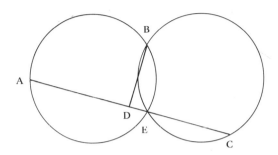

Two equal circumferences intersect at points B and E (Figure 9.22). A secant through point E intersects the circumference at points A and C. Prove that the perpendicular from point B to segment AC intersects it at its midpoint (point D).

Notes

1. The distinction between knowledge and operations is fundamental. Knowledge is always a reflection of objects and phenomena, as well as their interconnections in the form of images, concepts, and judgments. Operations, on the other hand, are actions (physical or mental) which transform the corresponding objects or their images, concepts, and judgments. It is one thing, for example, to imagine a cube or to have the concept of a cube, but quite another thing to mentally rotate it in space or to isolate its attributes. Imagining and conceiving of a cube constitute knowledge, while rotating it or isolating its attributes constitute cognitive operations.

2. Recall is the activation of knowledge or operations acquired in the past. It does not always occur when appropriate, however. One may possess knowledge, which will not necessarily "come into one's head" when it is needed. It

exists, as it were, as a potential in one's mind. The transformation of potential knowledge into actual knowledge, the excitation of the nerve pathways (literally, links, associations, *Trans.*) underlying knowledge and operations, is the process of recall.

3. The conditions of a problem are only the information given verbally in the text of the problem. But since operations involving diagrams are of great importance in the solution of geometric problems, and since the diagram of a problem is psychologically one of its conditions, we will for convenience speak of the analysis of the verbal component of the problem conditions and of the diagram.

4. Just as perception of an object can evoke actions directed toward it (for example, when one wishes to start an automobile, the sight of the controls evokes an entire system of actions directed toward this end), perception of and reflection on the conditions of a problem may evoke (recall) an entire system of cognitive operations directed toward analysis of these conditions. To a person who does not know how to drive a car, the sight of the car's controls does not recall the actions required for this activity; to a person who does not know how to solve problems, perception of the conditions of a problem does not recall the analytic-synthetic operations required for its solution. The recall of operations precedes the recall of knowledge (theorems, laws, etc.).

5. The idea of levels of cognitive activity is not absolute. As our experiments showed, a student may operate on a higher level of cognitive activity in solving one problem, and on a lower level of cognitive activity in solving another problem. The level of the student's thinking will depend, therefore, on the conditions with which he is working. This does not imply, of course, that a given level of cognitive activity will not be more typical and more stable for a given student than another.

Chapter Ten

Algorithms and Programmed Instruction: The Theory and Methodology of Programming

1. The Problem and Its Significance

The development of the theory and practice of instruction is entering a new stage with the introduction into the field of education of the techniques of automatic and semiautomatic control, which are effecting truly revolutionary transformations in almost all spheres of human activity.[1] The introduction of these new techniques into education is not, of course, an end in itself. They are only means for solving the basic problem, which is to improve regulation and control in the field of education, but they permit novel solutions to a number of problems in this area and promise to raise control (i.e., beneficial guidance, *Ed.*) of the instructional process to a new level.

The significance of algorithms in programmed instruction is, therefore, clear. As has been convincingly demonstrated in cybernetics, it is possible to establish effective automatic control of a process only by analyzing this process into elements or steps, discovering the interrelations of these elements or steps, and elucidating the initial, intermediate, and final stages of the process as well as the operative factors which determine its course at each stage. It is evident, therefore, that effective automatic control of a process requires knowledge of its structure and of the laws which it obeys, that is, an algorithmic description of the process and the design of corresponding instructions for controlling the process based on this description.

It should be noted in this regard that there is, in many cases, a tendency among workers in this field to focus attention on the

313

technology of programming, on the selection of one or another programming system (e.g., linear or nonlinear), one or another type of response (constructed or branching), etc., without taking into account the fact that programming systems have no independent significance. Programming techniques should be determined by the problems posed by the material to be programmed, as well as by our knowledge of the structure and laws of the process which is to be developed in the student with the aid of programmed instruction.

Cybernetics and many areas of applied science and technology have often had to deal with processes for which algorithmic descriptions are unobtainable or are very complex. These processes nevertheless must be controlled. Control of such processes is achieved by means of special algorithms which operate on the basis of the stochastic (probabilistic) nature of the processes in question and which involve self-instructional control systems. Such algorithms will play an important role in the field of instruction also, since many teaching-learning phenomena are stochastic in nature, are difficult to describe algorithmically, and must be controlled by means of self-instructional systems.[2] However, we will be concerned here primarily with instructional phenomena and processes which are amenable to algorithmic description and for which "ordinary" control algorithms, not involving self-instructional elements, may be written.[3] It is with processes of this sort that contemporary programmed instruction is primarily (though not exclusively) concerned. Most programs and machines are being designed for the control of such processes.

The great significance of programmed instruction lies in the fact that it first posed the problem of describing the instructional process algorithmically, and thereby stimulated the development of instructional theory in the direction of precise analysis of the instructional process. As long as the instructional process is conducted by the human teacher, it is possible to utilize approximate descriptions and general and often inadequately specified instructions (such as "Maintain a high level of active participation," or "Get the student to assimilate knowledge consciously," etc.). The teacher, being a rational and thinking being, is able to determine one way or another on the basis of experience and intuition when active participation is high and when it is low (and so needs to be raised), or when the student is assimilating knowledge consciously and when he is not (thereby making necessary a change in instructional technique in order to increase conscious assimilation). But instructions of this sort are totally inapplicable in programmed instruction, which is effected by means of programmed texts and teaching machines. A machine cannot control the student's active participation, i.e., raising and lowering it, if precise external manifestations of active participation are not indicated, and if absolutely precise criteria for judging the degree of active participation are not given. It is only on the basis of such criteria that a machine is able to alter its modes of responding to the student, i.e., its teaching strategy. Without these criteria it simply cannot operate. The same may be said with regard to the degree of consciousness (i.e., awareness, *Ed.*) with which the student assimilates knowledge and many other categories of information, which hitherto have remained at times so imprecise that no machine could operate with them. Even human teachers often operate unsatisfactorily on the basis of such formulations. The enormous significance of programmed instruction in its influence on education in general and on educational psychology derives from the fact that it poses the practical problem of analyzing instructional phenomena precisely, and describing them algorithmically, a problem which must be solved if programmed instruction is to bring about adequate control of the learning process and the student's activity. In this way programmed instruction raises these sciences to a fundamentally new level of development.

The question arises as to the relation between the concept of "instructional program" and that of the "instructional algorithm." These concepts are similar, but not identical. To write an instructional program in the sense of programmed instruction is to create an implementation (for instance, in the form of a programmed text or a program for a teaching machine) of an instructional algorithm, which is a *prescription* of how to conduct the instructional process and which precisely defines its content and goal (what and how something is to be taught, and what and how it is to be achieved as a result of this process). Further, in this prescription, the activity of both the teacher and the student (i.e., the actions which each must perform if the goal is to be reached) is analyzed into its component operations and specified precisely. This prescription should also specify when the instructional process proceeding according to a given algorithm, i.e., a process of programmed instruction or programmed learning, is to terminate. This occurs immediately upon reaching the goal.[4]

To further clarify the distinction between an instructional algorithm and an instructional program, an instructional algorithm may look somewhat as follows:

In order to form in students the concept of a parallelogram:
1.	Show them a diagram of a parallelogram.
2.	Tell them the attributes of a parallelogram.
3.	Ask them to find (to isolate) these attributes in the diagram.
(etc.)

This prescription presupposes that the teaching system knows how to perform these instructions. An instructional program is the *implementation of this algorithm*, in the sense that it executes (carries out) each of these instructions; it actually shows a diagram, actually articulates the attributes, etc.

If programmed instruction is imagined as a process similar to chess (the teacher makes a "move" in response to each "move" on the part of the student, the student responds with another move, and so on, until some terminal situation is achieved which is characterized by the required degree of assimilation on the student's part of some particular knowledge, skills, and habits), then an instructional program may be seen as a precise description of how to play this game, which "moves" to make in response to "moves" on the part of the student in order to arrive at the goal, to achieve the desired terminal situation.[5] Inasmuch as all "moves" in any form of instruction, both on the part of the teacher and that of the learner, have content (the student's actions, for example, cannot be performed independently of the specific material with which he is dealing), an instructional algorithm or program presupposes precise determination of the content which serves as the object of these actions.[6]

We have shown that the instructional program is a form of implementation of some instructional algorithm. But an instructional program may be implemented by various means. Thus, for example, instruction according to a given program may be effected by a teacher, another student, a programmed text, a teaching machine, etc. Programmed instruction has historically been understood as instruction in accordance with a program which the student follows independently, i.e., without the direct participation of a teacher and with the aid of programmed texts or teaching machines. The term "programmed instruction" has acquired a specific meaning. In this special meaning of the term, instruction in accordance with a program carried out by a human teacher is not programmed instruction; it refers only to instruction carried out by means of a programmed text or a teaching machine. The appropriateness of this limitation on the meaning of the term "programmed instruction" is questionable, since its literal meaning is any instruction implemented according to a precisely specified program-algorithm. If the term "programmed instruction" were used to denote any form of instruction conducted according to a particular program (including a human teacher), then it would be necessary to invent another term to denote the implementation of this program in the form of a programmed text or a teaching machine. After all, the principal innovation of programmed instruction is not simply the idea of instruction carried out in accordance with a precise program, but rather the idea of this sort of instruction implemented specifically by means of programmed texts and teaching machines.

Instruction in accordance with a precise program has always been known and practiced. Any experienced teacher, as a rule, knows how to conduct a class, how to respond to his students' errors, how to alter the course of the instructional process as a function of various learning indicators, etc.; he may know this so precisely that his teaching activity may in many instances be described algorithmically and regarded as the execution of the algorithm, which he "carries in his head," and sometimes in one form or another writes down. However, no one has ever called this activity programmed instruction. Also worthy of note in this regard are the widely used methodological lesson plans, which frequently prescribe to the teacher what he and sometimes his students should do in such detail that they approach being instructional programs. However, no one has ever called a lesson conducted by a teacher in accordance with a lesson plan programmed instruction. These considerations indicate that the term "programmed instruction" arose not in order to distinguish instruction conducted in accordance with a specific program (algorithm) from instruction not so conducted, but rather in order to designate a specific way of implementing a program (algorithm) with the aid of programmed texts and teaching machines. It is in this sense that we will use the term in this chapter.

The attributes of programmed instruction indicated above (conformance to an algorithm and implementation of this algorithm by means of a programmed text or teaching machine) are not, however, sufficient to distinguish programmed instruction from other forms of instruction. Programmed instruction is characterized by several features of the algorithm which determine the course of the instructional process, namely:

(a)   that this algorithm is one which presupposes operative feedback for both the teacher (or, more generally, the instructional agent) and the student or, at least for the student (there do exist instructional algorithms which have delayed feedback or no feedback at all, such as realized in lesson plans which precisely prescribe what the teacher is to do but not what the student is to do or how the teacher is to respond to the student's actions); and

(b)   that the algorithm is oriented toward interaction with individual students rather than toward the class as a whole (algorithms may be oriented toward a group of students or the class as a whole rather than toward the individual student).

We are not referring here to analysis of the instructional process into relatively small steps, since this attribute is inherent in the concept of the algorithm.

These remarks concerning the sense in which we will use the term programmed instruction, however, do not resolve the terminological difficulties. If we preserve the specific meaning of implementation of an instructional program with the aid of programmed texts or teaching machines, then we will have no term with which to designate instruction conducted in accordance with a specific program independently of who or what conducts it (i.e., the generic concept as opposed to the specific concept of "programmed instruction" in the narrow sense). This difficulty could be eliminated by terming such instruction, for example, program-based instruction. The terms programmed instruction and program-based instruction are easily confused at first, but are easy to learn and distinguish. Clearly, it is possible to find a better term to designate the generic concept, one which would not encourage confusion of the generic with the specific, but such a term does not as yet exist.

Figure 10.1 is a classification of the kinds of instruction denoted by the terms which we have been discussing:

Figure 10.1

Classification of Kinds of Instruction

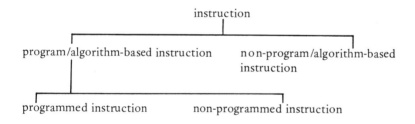

This diagram illustrates the fact that program-based instruction is more general (generic) than programmed instruction and includes both instruction conducted by a teacher in accordance with a program, and instruction with the aid of programmed texts and teaching machines.

The concept of programmed instruction must be distinguished not only from that of instruction conducted in accordance with a program-algorithm, but also from the concept of *automated* instruction, which is likewise broader than that of programmed instruction.[7] Film and magnetic tape can assume the function of transmitting knowledge without direct participation of a teacher, and so can replace him in this respect. This form of instruction will no doubt be automated,[8] but not programmed, since it does not normally include those attributes of the algorithm (operative feedback and individualization) which we discussed above. All programmed instruction is automated instruction (independent instruction with the aid of a programmed text, which is a form of teaching apparatus, may also be regarded as automated, or at least as semiautomated instruction), but not all automated instruction is programmed in the sense of programmed instruction. The use of devices as aids does not in itself constitute programmed instruction. In order for automated instruction to become programmed instruction, the algorithm in accordance with which such instruction is conducted must assume the attributes indicated above.

Programmed instruction has specific features not only because the implementation of a program (algorithm) of instruction with the aid of programmed texts or teaching machines lends the instructional process a number of novel and specific properties (for example, from a psychological point of view it is far from unimportant whether the student learns some given material or a given procedure from a teacher, or from a textbook, or a machine), but because the use of programmed texts and teaching machines in many instances permits implementation of instructional algorithms which a teacher is physically unable to implement under conditions of group or class instruction. For example, instructional algorithms which involve continual operation-by-operation control of the activity of each student presuppose adaptation of the form and tempo of instruction to the individual characteristics of each student. A teacher would be unable to execute such algorithms under conditions of group instruction, even if he knew them. Thus, programmed instruction is not simply a new means for implementing instructional algorithms through the use of programmed texts and teaching machines; it also offers new possibilities for improving control of the student's activity and, more generally, of his acquisition of knowledge, skills, and habits by means of control algorithms which could not be utilized and implemented without the devices which permit their automatization. These new possibilities (as well as the specific limitations which instruction with the aid of programmed texts and teaching machines entails) lend the instructional process new characteristics and require analysis in terms of new concepts.

From this it follows that the means by which an instructional algorithm is executed are important as regards both the student and the instructional process as a whole, since it creates possibilities for the design and utilization in teaching of such algorithms which could not be utilized without electronic and/or electromechanical devices. These considerations give rise to a new and specific field in instructional theory and practice, namely that of programmed instruction, which, as opposed to instruction conducted by a teacher in accordance with a program, possesses a number of specific features and constitutes a specific area for scientific instructional and psychological research.

2.   The Algorithmic Description of Processes

There exist various means for the algorithmic description of processes, some of which are appropriate for the writing of control programs (algorithms). Let us consider some of these means.

Let us consider, for purposes of illustration, the case of an operator of some sort of machine who must check his equipment before beginning work. First he must check to see if the equipment is connected to its power source. If it is not, then he must connect it. If it is connected, then he throws a switch and checks to see if a red light goes on. If it does, then the equipment is ready for operation and he may begin work. If the light does not go on, then the equipment is not functioning properly and a maintenance man must be called to repair it.

The relation between existing conditions and actions to be taken in this case is "stable." Under certain specific conditions (for example, whether or not the red light comes on) specific actions are performed (work is begun or a maintenance man is called). The operator's activity would be non-algorithmic in nature if in response to the lighting of the red light he were to perform randomly sometimes one action and sometimes the other.

The most widely used way of describing processes algorithmically is a verbal account. We have already given, in essence, an algorithmic description of the equipment operator's activity by specifying what he should do under various conditions. We can render these specifications in a more imperative form by writing them on separate lines and numbering them. Thus:

1. Check to see if the equipment is plugged in.
    If it is, proceed to Step 3.
    If it is not, then
2. Plug it in.
3. Throw the switch.
4. Check to see if the red light goes on.
    If it does, then proceed to Step 5.
    If it does not, then proceed to Step 6.
5. Begin work.
6. Call a maintenance man.

Operations 5 and 6 are terminal; activity as *prescribed* by the algorithm ceases with them as a function of the presence or absence of the preceding condition.

Lyapunov (1958) and Lyapunov and Shestopal (1957) have proposed a technique for symbolically describing control processes which are algorithmic in nature. For such description to be possible it is necessary, as we noted above, that the activity in question be analyzed into a series of elementary actions and that the conditions in response to which these actions are performed be determined. These actions (operations) are termed *elementary operators* and are denoted by the upper case letters A, B, C. . . . The conditions (attributes) which must be taken into account are termed *logical conditions* and are denoted by the lower case letters a, b, c,. . . . The order in which the conditions are checked and the actions are performed is recorded in the form of a logic diagram, which is an expression in terms of operators, logical conditions, and numerical indices arranged in a specific pattern. The operators and the logical conditions are the "elements" of the logic diagram.

Let us construct the logic diagram corresponding to the operator's activity:

Logical conditions:

a—the equipment is connected to its power source;

b—the red light is on.

Operators:

A—connecting the equipment to its power source;

B—throwing the switch;

C—beginning work;

D—calling a maintenance man.

A dot after an upper case letter will indicate cessation of activity, i.e., termination of the algorithm.

The operator's activity in checking his equipment may then be written as follows:

$$a \stackrel{1}{\uparrow} Bb \stackrel{2}{\uparrow} C. \stackrel{1}{\downarrow} ABb \stackrel{2}{\uparrow} C. \stackrel{2}{\downarrow} D.$$

The rules for reading the logic diagrams of algorithms are as follows:

The diagram is read from left to right. First of all, it is necessary to look at the first letter. In our case the first letter indicates a logical condition. Thus, the algorithm requires that this condition, whether or not the equipment is plugged in, be checked.

If it is plugged in (i.e., if the logical condition is fulfilled) then the arrow is ignored and the next letter is read (i.e., the action indicated by operator B is performed: the switch is thrown); if it is not plugged in (i.e., if the logical conditions is not fulfilled), then the letter indicated by the arrow is read;* it refers to operator A (connecting the equipment to its power source).

_____

*It should be noted that arrows occur in pairs of which one member (e.g., $\stackrel{1}{\uparrow}$) points "from" (e.g., a) and the other (e.g., $\stackrel{1}{\downarrow}$) points "to" (e.g., A) so that the numerical superscripts serve as pair indices, and arrow direction expresses "go to" (up) and "here" (down). (*Editor*.)

The next letter after A is then read (operator B—throwing the switch) and so on until a letter followed by a dot (period) or an unexecutable element is encountered (in our example there are no such elements).

In general: the algorithm begins with the leftmost element of the diagram.

First case. The letter under consideration is a *logical consideration*. There are then two possibilities:

(a)   the condition is fulfilled, in which case the arrow is ignored and the next letter is considered; and

(b)   the condition is not fulfilled, in which case the letter indicated by the arrow is considered.

Second case. The letter under consideration is an *operator*.

In this case the action indicated by the operator is performed and the next letter to the right is considered.

The execution proceeds in accordance with the algorithm until an operator immediately followed by a period or an unexecutable operator is encountered. After performance of the action indicated by such an operator, activity prescribed by the algorithm stops. There are some algorithms which continue indefinitely.

A third way of describing an algorithmic activity is the so-called graph or diagram. Figure 10.2 is a diagram of the activity in question.[9]

Figure 10.2

Diagram of Algorithm

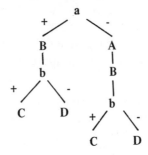

The arrows indicate the order in which attributes are checked and actions performed; the plus and minus signs indicate the presence or absence of attributes; the letters followed by periods indicate terminal actions. In this type of diagram attributes may be indicated not only symbolically, by letters, but also by means of words.

There are other ways of describing algorithmic processes than the three discussed above (for example, description in the form of normal algorithm diagrams or the functional diagrams of Turing machines). They are not convenient for instructional purposes, however. Block diagrams (see, for example, Smirnov, 1963) are also useful in this area.

As we noted above, in order to describe a particular activity algorithmically the activity must first be analyzed into elements (logical conditions and operations), and then the activity must be represented as a combination of these elements.[10] The general methodological significance of this method should be emphasized.

Algorithmic description can be regarded as one of the ways for representing the general method of advancing from the abstract to the concrete in cognition, which enables one to understand and represent the concrete as a specific synthesis of a number of general elements or abstractions. By focusing on the discovery of those elements of which the whole is composed, their functions and interrelations, this method permits a structural analysis and description of phenomena and processes. As soon as the basic elements of the whole have been found and their functions and interrelations elucidated, the description of phenomena and processes in the precise language of logic becomes possible. We note that describing the whole (i.e., what is general, *Ed.*) and the concrete (i.e., what is particular, *Ed.*) by means of a combination of elements does not mean reducing the whole to the sum of its elements, but that it may be understood only through analysis of its component elements, their functions and interrelations. These elements, moreover, are not to be regarded as static and unchanging; they must be regarded as changing and evolving.

It is not only the structure of the controlling activity as expressed in external, physical actions which may be described algorithmically; the logical structure of cognitive activity as expressed in (covert, *Ed.*) internal, cognitive actions which lead to the solution of a problem may also be described in this way.

We have presented an example of an algorithmic description of the controlling activity of an operator of a machine and indicated the possibility of describing algorithmically the cognitive activity associated with problem-solving.

What is the possibility of describing algorithmically the activity of the teacher (instructional activity) and of the compilation of algorithmic prescriptions for the instructional procedure (an instructional algorithm) on the basis of this description? Such description and compilation are possible whenever this activity is algorithmic in nature, on the basis of an analysis of the activity into its elements and its representation as a specific combination of these elements.

Instructional activity, like any other, is composed of specific instructional actions (operations) which are applied in a given sequence as a function of the conditions in which, and the plan according to which, the instruction proceeds (we will here consider the goal or task of instruction as given). It is clear from the preceding discussion what must be done in order to arrive at an algorithmic description and to write, on the basis of this description, algorithmic instructions (i.e., a detailed prescription, *Ed.*) as to instructional procedure (an instructional algorithm). It is necessary first to determine the conditions which are significant in the selection of given instructional actions (in the case of algorithmic descriptions these would be the logical conditions); second, the instructional actions themselves must be determined (in the case of algorithmic descriptions these would be the operators); third, their interrelations must be determined, i.e., a plan of instruction must be formulated (in the case of algorithmic descriptions the logic diagram of the algorithm would constitute the plan of instruction).

Let us design, as an example, an instructional algorithm which precisely programs the activity of the teacher (in directing the activity of the student) during the instructional process.

Let us assume that the goal of instruction is to acquaint the

Figure 10.3

Instructional Algorithm for the Concept "Circle"
(Schematic Representation)

1.   Give the class the definition of this concept and an illustrative diagram ("A circle is a curved, closed line, lying in a plane, all points of which are equidistant from a single point; this point is termed the center of the circle.").[11]

2.   Ask a student to find the attributes indicated in the definition and to name them.

If the student finds all of the attributes, then	If the student fails to find all of the attributes, then

3.   Ask him to name the logical connective which associates them.

3.   Draw the figure possessing the attributes named by the student (this figure will not, of course, be a circle).[12]

4.   Write down all of the attributes along with their logical interrelations.

If the student corrects his mistake, then	If the student fails to correct his mistake, then

4.   Ask him to name the logical connective which associates them.

4.   Call on another student.

5.   Write down all of the attributes along with their logical interrelations.

5.   Ask him to correct the mistake.

6.   Ask him to name the logical connective which associates the attributes.

7.   Write down all of the attributes along with their logical interrelations.

student with a new concept, namely, the circle. This could be done in various ways. The way which we will select may be expressed in the form of the following algorithmic instructions (see Figure 10.3).

It is apparent that these algorithmic instructions constitute a definite program of the teacher's actions, which in their turn assume specific actions on the part of the students.[13] In order to be able to describe this program in the form of a diagram in which logical conditions and operators are designated by means of symbols (see Figure 10.4), and in the form of an algorithmic logic diagram, we introduce the following designations:

Logical Conditions:

a—the student finds all of the attributes;

b—the student corrects his mistake.

Operators:

A—formulating the definition of the concept and drawing the figure;

B—asking the student to find the attributes indicated in the definition and to name them;

C—asking the student to name the logical connective which associates the attributes;

D—drawing a diagram possessing the attributes named by the student but not corresponding to the figure in question;

E—calling on another student;

F—asking him to correct the first student's mistake;

J—writing down the attributes along with their logical interrelations.

The diagram of the algorithm in question is shown in Figure 10.4.

The logic diagram of this algorithm in operator notation would be the following:

$$\overset{1}{ABa} \uparrow \overset{1}{CJ.} \downarrow \overset{2}{Db} \uparrow \overset{2}{CJ.} \downarrow EFCJ.$$

It is clear that the order of the teacher's actions will vary as a function of the logical conditions which are fulfilled in various

Figure 10.4

Teaching Algorithm for the Concept "Circle"
(Diagramatic Representation)

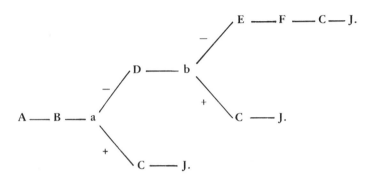

circumstances (the student might find all of the attributes or not find them all; he might correct his mistake or fail to correct it). There is an "inflexible" relation between the logical conditions and the teacher's actions (each condition requires a specific action), but there is no "inflexible" relation between the actions themselves.[14] Since the combination of conditions in different cases may be different, the combination of actions may be different as well. But a given combination of actions always corresponds to a given combination of conditions.

Let us consider the possible combinations of conditions.

(1) Neither condition *a* nor condition *b* is fulfilled, that is, the student fails to find all of the attributes and does not correct his mistake (this state of affairs may be expressed symbolically as follows: $a = O, b = 0$);

(2) condition *a* is not fulfilled but condition *b* is ($a = 0, b = 1$);

(3) condition *a* is fulfilled but condition *b* is not ($a = 1, b = 0$);

(4) both conditions are fulfilled ($a = 1, b = 1$).

The dependence of combinations of actions on combinations of conditions is shown in Table 10.1.

Table 10.1

Value of the Logical Conditions		Order of Actions
a	*b*	
0	0	A B D E F C J
0	1	A B D C J
1	0	A B C J
1	1	A B C J

3. Teaching Algorithms and the Teaching of Algorithms

The concept of the instructional or teaching algorithm should be clearly distinguished from that of the teaching of algorithms, since they are often confused. Instructional algorithms are programs for guiding the student in which the actions of the teacher (human or non-human) are considered as operators and the results of the student's actions as logical conditions. If the instructional algorithm is a program which guides the teacher (indicating which actions he should perform in response to various actions on the part of the student), then the teaching of an algorithm is the teaching of a program by which the student should be guided (indicating which actions he should perform as a function of the results of previous actions). An example of an algorithm intended to guide the student would be the algorithm described above for checking equipment. If the operator of this equipment did not know the algorithm, then the problem of teaching it to him would arise. In this case the operator would be a student who is to be taught an algorithm, and the transmission of the knowledge of how to operate the equipment in question and the development of the corresponding operations would constitute the teaching of the algorithm. The teacher might be guided by a precise set of instructions as to how to teach the algorithm, or he might not have such instructions and so might instruct on the basis of experience and intuition, permitting himself to use trial and error, with changes in the course of the instructional process as a function of thoughts and hypotheses arising during the instructional process itself. In the first case the teacher would be using an algorithm to teach an algorithm, in the second case he would not. There is in addition a third possibility, that of the teacher using an algorithm to teach a non-algorithmic process.

Thus, it is possible to teach an algorithm either with the aid of an algorithm or without it. On the other hand, an instructional algorithm may be directed, both, toward teaching an algorithm and toward teaching non-algorithmic processes. It is easy to see that if, in an algorithm intended for the teacher's use (i.e., an instructional algorithm), the student's actions and their results are considered as logical conditions, then in an algorithm intended for the student, the same actions are considered as operators, and the logical conditions in this case are the changes in the (logical, *Ed.*) objects toward which these actions are directed (for example, the coming on of the red light or its failure to light).

It is clear then that an instructional or teaching program in programmed instruction is always a relation of an instructional algorithm, but that this algorithm may or may not be used to teach an algorithm. Programmed instruction, of necessity, is based on instructional algorithms, but does not, of necessity, entail the teaching of algorithms. The fundamental problem in programmed instruction is that of instructional algorithms, and not that of the teaching of algorithms, although programmed instruction does not in any way exclude (and good programmed instruction even assumes) the teaching of algorithms.[15] The problem of the teaching of algorithms is discussed in detail in *Algorithmization in Learning and Instruction* (Landa, 1974). This chapter is devoted primarily to the problem of instructional algorithms.

The question arises as to the degree to which it is possible to algorithmize the instructional process, indeed, as to the possibility of creating a universal instructional algorithm.

This question is similar to that regarding the possibilities and limits of programmed instruction, namely, whether it is possible to program any instructional process totally, in order that it might be fully implemented in a closed "student-teaching device" system[16] and always, in all cases and under all conditions, achieve the goals set for it. "Total programming" here refers to a description of the instructional process as a system of unambiguously performed operations, carried out in a sequence which is unambiguously determined by the controlling logical conditions. This question in turn arises naturally from the proposition, demonstrated by cybernetics, that any process which may be algorithmized in the sense intended here, in principle, may be automated, i.e., its control may be shifted to a machine (see, e.g., Glushkov, 1962).[17]

It is sufficient to pose this question to realize that it must be answered negatively. The impossibility of creating a universal instructional algorithm follows from the fact that the writing of such an algorithm would require an absolutely exhaustive knowledge of all of the conditions of the instructional process, all possible reactions of the student to all possible external and internal influences, all possible actions on the part of the teacher, and all possible consequences of each of these actions. In other words, the writing of a universal algorithm would require absolute knowledge of all psychological phenomena and processes of significance in instruction. This is impossible even in principle, since the acquisition of knowledge is a developing and inexhaustible process, and at any given moment our knowledge of the objects and processes of the external world and even of ourselves is incomplete. It is important to note in this regard that it is not only our knowledge of internal and external objects and processes which develops and changes, but the objects and processes themselves.

In fact, it is never possible to foresee all of the answers which a student might give to all of the problems which he is given to solve, since there will always be students who in various unpredictable circumstances will give unpredictable answers. It is never possible to be certain that current instructional procedures will be effective for all students and always achieve the expected results. There will always be students for whom these procedures will prove ineffective and for whom new ones will have to be discovered, and the discovery of these new procedures is a creative process. Their character cannot be predicted and embodied in an algorithm.

It is impossible to write a universal instructional algorithm for the same reason it is impossible to write a universal algorithm for solving all mathematical problems (c.f. Goedel's, 1931, theorem on the impossibility of fully formalizing even the arithmetic of natural numbers). The algorithmization of instruction is always associated with its formalization (formalization, of course, in the logico-mathematical sense, not in the sense of an instructional formalism). Does this mean that the algorithmization of instruction is totally impossible? Of course not. The standard, general problems of instruction can be solved by algorithmization, and, as instructional theory and practice develop, the number of these problems continually increases. The possibility of algorithmizing instruction at any given moment of history is determined directly by the degree to which its specific laws are known, and, in particular, by the degree to which it is possible to take into account the fundamental determining factors on which the course of the instructional process depends, in order to include adequate control of these factors in the algorithm.

The sphere of application of algorithmization in education widens even further if instructional algorithms are used which do not comprehensively control the student's activity and which effect this control by shifting much of the burden of guidance and control onto the student himself, relying on his self-organization and self-control (i.e., of his internal, cognitive processes, *Ed.*). In this case it cannot be said that the instructional process has been fully programmed in the sense indicated above. Since such algorithms are based on the assumption that the student will arrive at an understanding of certain things on his own, they cannot guarantee that the goal of instruction will be achieved and that all students will in fact come to understand what they are supposed to understand (for example, that they will discover independently a method for solving problems of some given type). This situation is somewhat analogous to one which arises in mathematics and mathematical logic in which an algorithm under some conditions does not achieve its intended goal, because it either halts without result or continues to operate indefinitely.[18] It is clearly necessary to attempt to write instructional algorithms which are calculated to evoke maximum independence, self-organization, and self-guidance on the part of the student, but which at the same time ensure against the possibility of failure. This means that the student must be given the opportunity to achieve on his own that which is required, but that if he is unable to do it—if self-guidance does not "click"—the program will assume control and lead the student without fail to the goal. However, the writing of such a program presupposes the possibility in each given case of total programming of the instructional process in the sense specified above.

It must be said that current programmed texts and machine-aided instructional programs (which always implement a specific instructional algorithm) very frequently fail to take into account some important factors which now may be taken into account, often without great difficulty, with the result that these programs are flawed and fail to guarantee the required guidance of the student's activity. Programmed instruction as a closed "student-teaching device" process breaks down and the student is forced to turn to the teacher for assistance.

We wish to emphasize that we, like most others working in the field of programmed instruction, are far from believing that programmed instruction should supersede all other forms of instruction and that the teacher should be fully replaced by a programmed text or teaching machine. This would be wrong and harmful. Moreover, in indicating the impossibility of total formalization and automatization of the instructional process, we at the same time indicated the impossibility in principle of excluding the human element from the educational process and converting the process as a whole into a closed "student-teaching device" system. Distinguishing areas in which it is expedient to use programmed instruction, i.e., programmed texts and teaching machines in a closed "student-teaching device" system, from areas in which it is more expedient to use a human teacher, i.e., to break this closed system, is a different question, and one which goes beyond the scope of this chapter. We wish to note only that these areas are not separate, are not independent of one another, and often can and should intersect. Programmed instruction should be combined with methods involving a human teacher. The teacher moreover organizes and supervises the administration of programmed instruction. In speaking of "flaws" in algorithms which disrupt programmed instruction as a closed "student-teaching device" process, we are not referring to those instances in which it is appropriate to include the teacher in the instructional process, but rather to those instances in which it is appropriate to use programmed texts and teaching machines, but in which this is impossible as a result of poorly written instructional programs (algorithms). In these cases the teacher is included in the instructional process not because it is appropriate by definition for him to be included, but because the program does not work by itself.

Let us consider two examples of such program defects.

Example 1

The following paragraph appears in a mathematics program on the subject of logarithms.[19]

Frame 153. The decimal logarithm of a number expressed as the number one followed by zeros is equal to the number of zeros:

$$\log 10 = 1$$
$$\log 100 = 2$$
$$\log 1000 = 3 \text{ etc.}$$

What is log 1000000000?

Answer	see Frame
9	154
8	155

One wonders in reading this paragraph why only one wrong answer (i.e., "8") is given. The reasons why the student might make such an error are clear, but he might also make another error, giving the answer "10." Why is this possible error not taken into account? Let us suppose that in solving this problem the student "miscalculates" and arrives at the answer 10. What should he do? The program has failed to foresee this possibility and the student must either break the rules for using the program, i.e., its logic, and refer to the frames indicated for the answers 9 and 8, or ask the teacher for assistance. The closed "student-teaching device" instructional process is broken. But if the algorithm had been written correctly and all likely errors taken into account, then no intervention by the teacher would have been required. The program would have "coped" with the student by itself.

Example 2

The following problem appears in the same textbook.

Frame 62. Solve the equation $2^{x-2} = 1$.

Answer	see Frame
3	64
2	65

Here the author gives the student a choice of only two answers, assuming not only that he will arrive at an answer but that his answer will be one of these two. As regards the number of anticipated answers, the same considerations apply here as in the previous example. (What is the student to do if he obtains some answer other than the two specified?) But let us assume that a third answer is improbable. It is nevertheless entirely possible that some student will *fail to obtain any answer at all* because he does not know how to solve the problem. What is he to do then? He does not know, since this possibility has not been foreseen. If it should occur it will result in the program's losing control of the student and either will force the student to break the rules for working with the program (destroy its logic), or it will make intervention on the part of the teacher necessary. As in the preceding case there would be no fundamental reasons for such intervention, only a flaw in the algorithm in question.

4. The Correct Use of the Concept of the Algorithm with Regard to Instructional Phenomena

The writing of effective instructional algorithms must be based on a precise understanding and correct use of the term "algorithm." Unfortunately, this term is frequently used incorrectly in current literature on programmed instruction, as well as in literature on educational psychology and didactics. It is applied equally to the content of a curriculum or subject-matter ("curriculum algorithm," "subject-matter algorithm"), a plan for presenting material in a book ("presentation algorithm"), a plan for responding to a question, a procedure for solving creative (non-algorithmic) problems, grammatical rules, physical laws, etc. This incorrect use of the term "algorithm" not only discredits an important and quite precise concept (as well as the idea of introducing precise methods into education and psychology), but also confuses the formulation and solution of instructional problems. This process may not be immediately obvious, since discussion of these topics proceeds in current scientific terminology and even utilizes logical and mathematical formulas. The following is from a manuscript in which the author poses the task of writing a general (essentially universal) algorithm for classroom instruction (an insoluble problem, as we indicated above).

"Let us compile a diagram describing classroom instruction. Operators:

A—output of information to be assimilated (lectures, pages of a textbook, instructional films and tapes, etc.);

B—assimilation and reinforcement of information received (repetition from a summary or textbook, reading of supplementary literature, memorization, synopsis, etc.);

C—development of habits of use of the assimilated and reinforced information for the purpose of explaining phenomena of the outside world, solving problems, etc.;

D—development of a skill;

E—consultation (instructions, advice, hints, etc.);

F—termination of instruction.

Logical conditions:

p—checking assimilation of information;

q—checking development of habits of use of assimilated information;

r—checking skill.

The logic diagram of classroom instruction will then have the form:

$$\overset{1}{A} \downarrow \overset{1\ 2}{Bp} \uparrow \downarrow \overset{2\ 3}{ECq} \uparrow \downarrow \overset{3}{Dr} \uparrow F."$$

All of this seems correct at first glance. However, it is sufficient to recall that *an algorithm presupposes analysis of a process into acts or operations which are sufficiently elementary to be performed by all users of the algorithm, as well as unambiguous instructions rigorously determining the manner in which they are to be performed*, to realize that operators such as "delivering a lecture," "consulting," "development of habits," "assimilation and reinforcement of information received," etc., are non-algorithmic. These are not elementary acts but rather extremely complex processes, which themselves require algorithmic description. It is indeed not clear whether such description is possible for some of them. The author's "algorithm" is formally correct, but we have only to imagine giving a teacher such instructions as "deliver a lecture," "show a film," "develop a skill," "consult with the student," etc., to realize the complete uselessness of such an "algorithm." The fundamental problem after all is how to design and deliver a lecture, how to design an instructional film and how and when to use it in the teaching process, how to develop skills, etc. But the author does not attempt to analyze these very complex processes and to describe them algorithmically, taking them instead as "elementary operations." All algorithms are written, ultimately, for the purpose of controlling the process—the ordered set of activities—which they describe. This algorithm, however, though correct in form, in practice cannot control anything. The author simply stated in algorithmic form and described by means of a formula the commonplace fact that the instructional process consists of reading lectures to the students, showing them films, developing their skills, consultations with them, etc.; this formulation yields nothing new or useful.

The question arises as to which operations are sufficiently elementary, and what is the criterion of elementarity. This is a very complex issue and we will not be able to discuss it in any detail here.[20] It should be noted only that the concept of the elementary operation, though relative (an operation may be elementary for one system or person but non-elementary for another), at least assumes the possibility that an operation may be correctly and unambiguously performed.

All algorithms consist, of course, of a series of instructions concerning the performance of some system of operations in a particular order. Instructions are algorithmic if they evoke, from those to whom they are addressed, unambiguous, strictly determined, identical operations, and are not algorithmic if they do not evoke such operations. These attributes of algorithmic operations lend to the algorithm one of its most important characteristics, that of specificity. A set of instructions constitutes an algorithm only when it fully determines some process, i.e., specifically prescribes the activity, and when a given set of initial data always leads to the same final result or outcome. It is, therefore, clear why instructions to students of the following sort, for example, do not constitute an algorithm: (1) analyze the conditions of the problem; (2) compare the given information with that which is to be proved; (3) apply theorems; (4) draw conclusions; etc. None of these instructions is specific and none determines the student's activity unambiguously. Different students could easily fulfill the same instruction in different ways and arrive at different results. Moreover, many students would probably not know what to do in response to the instruction "analyze the conditions of the problem" and so would fail to solve the problem.[21]

This does not mean that an algorithm cannot address itself to complex (compound) operations and that such operations cannot be regarded under some conditions as elementary. But a necessary condition for regarding a complex operation as elementary is knowledge of the system (person or machine, *Ed.*) to whom the instruction to perform it is addressed, and of its ability to perform it unambiguously and without error.[22]

It is extremely important for the success of the instructional process, especially for the success of programmed instruction, that complex (compound) operations be broken up where necessary into more elementary operations, and that they, in turn, be broken up into still more elementary operations, and so on, until the operations arrived at are so elementary that they can *always* be performed unambiguously by everyone instructed to perform them. When this is done it becomes possible to change the level of complexity of the instruction, adapting it to the level of development of the operations in the student. In other words, when it is necessary to analyze complex operations into more elementary ones, it is very important that it be possible to write an algorithm for performing these complex operations. The basic algorithm may then be regarded as an algorithm governing the use of algorithms, or as an algorithm of a higher order.

Thus, for example, it is possible to write an algorithm for analyzing sentences into their component parts of speech, in which operations such as recognition of nouns, verbs, pronouns, adjectives, and other parts of speech will be regarded as elementary operations. This can be done only if the student can perform these operations as elementary, can analyze each of them, if needed, into their component parts or into simpler, more elementary operations, and if an algorithm for performing them can be stated (for example, an algorithm for recognizing nouns, an algorithm for recognizing verbs, etc.). This is necessary, for example, in case the student should make a mistake in recognizing some part of speech, in which case the recognition process would not be for him a unitary act which always "clicks."

It is therefore clear why the instructions introduced above on how to teach a concept (of the circle, *Ed.*) may be considered as an algorithm (for most teachers the indicated operations are elementary, and, if necessary, each of them may be reduced easily to a system of more elementary operations which in turn may be described algorithmically) and why the instructions cited above concerning a general system of classroom instruction including such "operations" as "delivering lectures," "giving consultations," etc., do not constitute an algorithm.

5. Sufficiently Elementary Operation and
    Step Size in Programmed Instruction

As is generally recognized, design of an instructional algorithm in programmed instruction should proceed in such a way as to analyze the activity of both teacher (whether human or mechanical) and learner into "sufficiently elementary" steps or operations. (If a "step" on the part of the teacher is the transmission to the student of some quantity of information, then such a step is often termed a "chunk.") In the language of programmed instruction this issue is often formulated as the problem of "chunk size" or "step size."

Both in the Soviet Union and abroad, an intensive search is being conducted for criteria which will permit determination of step size in programmed instruction. These criteria are often thought of as formal measures which would make it possible to determine theoretically, without experiment, on the basis of certain formal characteristics of the material to be taught, the optimal step size for a given programmed text. From the above discussion of the concept of the elementary operation it is clear that such a formulation of the problem is incorrect. It is not possible to find formal criteria of optimal step size in programmed instruction, because step size depends, on the one hand, on the content which "fills" the step and the specific goals of the instructional process, and, on the other hand, on the level of development of the operations in the student to whom the step in question is "addressed." A given chunk of information, a given step, may be optimal for one student, for another student too large, and for a third too small, as a function of their knowledge and skills, their level of development, and the degree to which specific concepts and cognitive operations have been developed in them. Formal criteria for optimal chunk size which are independent of the character and level of development of the student do not and cannot exist.

But how can programming of the instructional process occur

if formal criteria do not and cannot exist? Some general conditions under which the instructional process occurs and some general maturational features in students cause students of the same age and grade to possess, in common, certain characteristics, such as a similar level of development of concepts, ideas, cognitive operations, and other cognitive processes. Specific analysis of the character and level of development of these cognitive processes will make it possible to judge what is difficult for students and what is easy, what chunk sizes of the material to be taught they can assimilate immediately in the desired manner and which chunk sizes they cannot assimilate, thereby making necessary analysis of the chunks into smaller segments. Only analysis based on consideration of the cognitive processes in question can give the program writer the information concerning the development in the student of specific cognitive processes which he must have in order to determine the chunk size appropriate to the material which he is programming.

But data obtained as a result of such analysis are valid only on the average, i.e., statistically. They characterize the average level of development of the students of a given age and grade. This is insufficient for programmed instruction, since most students will deviate from the norm. Programmed instruction should take into account the individual characteristics of the student, and chunk size should be adapted to the level of development of each student. How is this to be accomplished, if analysis of the average level of development of the students of a given age and grade yields only an average chunk size, which in principle may be less than optimal for all or most students?

The first possible way to solve this problem is to administer diagnostic tests before beginning instruction for the purpose of discovering the level of knowledge and development of each student, so that chunk size may be adjusted to this level.[23] This is the preliminary adaptation approach.

Another approach, one which does not exclude the first, is to include in the program as an initial datum an average chunk size and then, during the instructional process itself, by analyzing how each individual student assimilates the material, to change the size (and perhaps the content as well) of these chunks, i.e., dynamically adapting them to each student's level of development and individual characteristics.[24] In other words, an ideal instructional program should operate as adaptively as an experienced teacher, or more precisely tutor, who has only a general idea of the level of development of the students with whom he is working (derived from working with other students of the same age and grade, i.e., from average data) and who discovers during the instructional process itself the particular level of development of each individual student, and on the basis of this information adapts the content and technique of instruction (including step size) to the student.

We see, therefore, that the problem of chunk (or step) size, if approached with due consideration for the relativity of the concept of the elementary operation, is not at all a problem of formal criteria, but rather a problem of the analysis of content and level of the knowledge possessed by the student to whom the programmed material is addressed. It is a problem of dynamic adaptation of the instructional process to the student's characteristic mode of assimilating knowledge, and it is finally a problem of the technological resources by means of which these adaptive algorithms may be implemented.

6. The Concept of the Didactic Problem
   and the Algorithm for Solving It

As was noted above, design of an instructional program presupposes the writing of a specific instructional algorithm.[25] An instructional algorithm, like any algorithm, is directed toward the solution of a specific problem. And if, for example, a mathematical algorithm is directed toward the solution of a mathematical problem, then an instructional algorithm is directed toward the solution of an instructional or didactic problem (as the problem facing the teacher may be designated).

What is the nature of the didactic problem and what is the nature of an algorithm for its solution? These concepts are understood easily by comparing them with those of the mathematical problem and the algorithm for its solution.

In any mathematical problem (or any other type of problem)

there are some initial data (or conditions) and some requirements, i.e., some things which are to be obtained. The process of solving the problem consists of transforming the initial data into the final data. The final data are termed the solution or answer to the problem.[26] A solution algorithm (if the problem can be solved by means of an algorithm) is a set of instructions or rules which specify what to do with the initial data and how to do it—how to transform them—in order to satisfy the requirements of the problem and to obtain an answer. A simple example would be the problem of squaring a binomial (for example, 2a + 4b). The initial datum in this case is the mathematical object 2a + 4b, and the final datum is that which is to be obtained as a result of solving the problem; the solution process consists of transforming the initial data into the final data in accordance with specific rules (a specific algorithm) which are well known and which therefore need not be repeated here. As a result of solving the problem, i.e., of transforming the initial mathematical object in accordance with a particular algorithm, we obtain the final mathematical object $4a^2 + 16ab + 16b^2$ as the solution or answer to the problem.[27]

The solution of didactic problems is analogous to the solution of mathematical problems, except that the objects which are transformed are not numbers and letters but rather cognitive processes, actions, and personality characteristics; the transformations, moreover, are of a different sort.[28] In fact, in any didactic problem there are initial data or conditions (which are the current state and level of the student's knowledge, skills, habits, and personality characteristics)[29] and requirements, usually termed in education the instructional goals or tasks (the new states and levels of the student's knowledge, skills, habits, and personality characteristics which are to be obtained as a result of the instructional process).[30] The instructional process is the process of solving didactic problems and is, in essence, the transformation of the initial data of each didactic problem (i.e., the student's initial state and level of knowledge, skills, and habits) into the final state defined by the requirements (goals) of instruction. If this transformation is brought about by the teacher in accordance with strict and unambiguous rules analogous to the rules for squaring a binomial, then these rules may be considered as constituting an algorithm for solving a didactic problem or, equivalently, an instructional algorithm. (Didactic problems may also be solved non-algorithmically, as was noted above, by trial and error based on experience and intuition, as is the case frequently in practice.[31])

For a deeper understanding of the nature and essence of didactic problems and of ways of writing algorithms for solving them (and this is the cardinal issue in the theory of programmed instruction) it is useful to consider the instructional process in the light of some cybernetic concepts, primarily those of the state of a system and transformation from state to state, especially as outlined by Ashby.[32] The application of these concepts to instructional phenomena permits a somewhat new approach to and a new interpretation of the instructional process, which in turn give rise to new approaches to the solution of a number of instructional problems, including problems in programmed instruction.

7. Instruction as a State Transformation Process

Each object or phenomenon possesses an infinite number of characteristics or attributes of which only a few are isolated for purposes of investigation and/or control. If specific numbers may be assigned to these characteristics or attributes in accordance with some rules, they are termed variables.[33] Thus, for example, variables associated with the human body which may be isolated for purposes of investigation and/or body control are temperature, blood pressure, oxygen content of the blood, etc. The values of these variables change over time as a function of various conditions. Any aggregate of variables selected for purposes of investigation or control is termed a system. The state of this system at a given point in time, according to Ashby, is the set of the numerical values of its variables.

All of these concepts are easily illustrated by example. Let us consider a human being from this point of view. A person has an infinite number of characteristics (physical, physiological, psychological, etc.), which assume various numerical values and therefore are variables (for example, body weight, height, body temperature, degree of fatigue, visual activity, etc.). A set of characteristics (variables) isolated for purposes of analysis and control from the infinite number of such characteristics would constitute a system. Thus, a person may be considered as a physical body (system), as an object of chemical, physiological, psychological, etc., investigation. In this instance, an individual person is considered as different systems. Let us assume that we consider a person from a medical point of view and are interested in the system defined by such variables as temperature, blood pressure, and heart rate. The specific values which these variables assume at a given moment will constitute the individual's state as defined by these variables. Thus, the state of a healthy person may be characterized by a set of numbers such as the following: temperature—98.6 degrees, blood pressure—140/70, pulse—70.[34] The state of a sick person would be characterized by a different set of values of these variables, for example: temperature—101.3 degrees, blood pressure—190/95, pulse—80.

The set of numbers constituting the values of a set of variables is termed a vector. Thus, the state of a person's health at any given moment may be described by the vector consisting of the variables indicated above. In Table 10.2 the top line represents the state vector of a healthy person, while the lower line represents the state vector of a sick person.

Table 10.2

Vectors of a Healthy and a Sick Person

Body Temperature	Blood Pressure	Pulse
98.6 degrees	140/70	70
101.3 degrees	190/95	80

Let us now suppose that a physician is called and that he detects the state described by the second vector. Since this state is abnormal, i.e., pathological, the physician's task, once he has established a diagnosis, is to bring about a cure; and bringing about a cure means to subject the patient to those therapeutic influences which will result in a change in the values of the variables indicated in the second vector in the direction of the values indicated in the first vector. In other words, the therapeutic process consists in the doctor's transforming, by means of particular therapeutic measures, an initial pathological state into a final normal one. For this purpose the doctor has at his disposal a wide range of possible procedures. For example, he might first use medication A, which rapidly lowers temperature, and then medications B and C, which lower blood pressure and heart rate; or he might use a medication or group of medications which act simultaneously on all of the variables in question, but which alter them in the direction of normalcy gradually. There are other approaches in addition to these.[35]

It is evident that the transition of the variables from one set of values to another will occur in different orders and at different rates, i.e., through different transitional states, as a function of the therapeutic measures selected by the doctor and the combinations and the sequence in which he applies them. The sequence of states through which the system moves and the time intervals between them may be described in various ways, for example, in tabular form, as the movement of a point in phase space, etc. It is clear that the various ways or procedures for changing the patient's state from pathological to normal are determined to a significant degree by the character of the therapeutic measures chosen by the physician, and there is a wide variety of such measures available, as we have seen. The physician's choice of therapeutic measures resulting in one or another path of transition of the patient from one state to another may be termed a therapeutic strategy. As a rule a physician has various possible therapeutic strategies from which to choose. The selection of one of these as a procedural guide or, what is the same thing, as a precise prescription as to therapeutic procedure, constitutes the adoption of a specific procedural algorithm.

It is difficult to draw a rigorous distinction between the

concept of a strategy (in its precise cybernetic and mathematical sense) and that of an algorithm. The strategy concept is frequently used, however, in a wider sense as including the possibility of random actions, which, by definition, cannot occur in an algorithm. On the other hand, a strategy may be regarded as a prescription of *possible* (i.e., permissible) procedures, while the algorithm is a prescription of an *imperative* character. It might be said that a strategy is a possible algorithm, while an algorithm is a particular chosen strategy. This distinction between these two concepts is not important in the present context, however, and so we will use them synonymously.

It is clear that a physician in treating a patient is facing a problem which is in a number of respects analogous to the mathematical problems discussed above. In both cases the problem-solver (in the first case the mathematician, in the second case the physician) faces an initial situation which he must transform into some final situation constituting the solution to the problem. If the physician, like the mathematician, has precise and unambiguous instructions as to how to bring about this transformation, then it is possible to speak of a solution algorithm for the therapeutic problem (as we will term the problem facing the physician). It is further quite clear that the therapeutic problem is analogous to the didactic problem, in which there is always an initial state (the student's knowledge, skills, and habits), a final state defined by the objectives of instruction (that which is to be achieved as a result of the instructional process), and a means for transforming the initial state into the final state, which the teacher (human or non-human) must find and use and which constitutes a system of instructional (analogous to therapeutic) influences (or instrumentalities, or operators, i.e., means to effecting the series of transformations, *Ed.*). This system of instructional influences may sometimes be described and rendered algorithmically, that is, as an algorithm for transforming the initial state of the student into the desired final state.[36]

In order to turn programmed instruction from an art into a science (some leading American theorists in the field of programmed instruction have noted that programmed instruction hitherto has been to a significant degree more an art than a science), it is necessary for us to learn to formulate and describe didactic problems precisely, to classify them, and to find ways of writing algorithms for solving them. Only in this way can the problems associated with programmed instruction be formulated in a rigorously scientific manner and rigorously scientific methods found for their solution.

We shall attempt to indicate some approaches to the solution of these problems (at this stage it is possible to speak only of approaches to the solution of problems in this area, since they have not as yet been clearly formulated). The following discussion may be considered also as a general and incomplete description of the stages in the writing of instructional algorithms, i.e., as a rough draft of a methodology for the writing of instructional programs.

8. **Stages in the Writing of Instructional Algorithms (Programs)**
   First Stage—Determining the Content and Goal of Instruction

Before beginning to program instructional material and the student's activity, it is necessary to determine the content and goal of instruction, i.e., what we want to teach the student, the knowledge, skills, and habits that we wish to develop in him. This is a self-evident requirement, but fulfilling it correctly is not easy. The basic difficulty encountered here is the necessity of maximally specifying the goal of instruction, which means representing it as a state in the form of a set of variables possessing, where possible, specific numerical values. Where this is not possible, qualitative attributes should be indicated which permit precise characterization of each variable and its representation as a standard by which the development (literally, formation, *Trans.*) or lack of development of knowledge, skills, and habits may be unambiguously determined.[37] (Where it is possible, one should use quantitative values; but where this is not possible, one must use qualitative standards.) In other words, determining the goal of instruction means representing it in the form of a final state vector; without such representation it is impossible to design good programs.

In order to specify a final state vector it is necessary to analyze the cognitive activity or processes which are to be developed as a result of instruction (we will henceforth refer to the knowledge, skills, and habits developed during the instructional process as cognitive activity or cognitive processes) into their elements and to define the variables which will serve as the objects (i.e., operands, *Ed.*) to be influenced (i.e., changed due to the influence of operators, *Ed.*). Next, the level of development of each variable which must be obtained at a given stage of instruction, in the course of solving a given didactic problem, must be determined. It is quite evident in this regard, as noted earlier, that definitions of the goal of instruction of the sort which are frequently encountered (for example, to teach the student to speak a foreign language, to teach the student to read a foreign language, to teach the ability to think, to teach the student to analyze phenomena, to develop ingenuity in the student, etc.) are inadequate for programmed instruction. It is necessary to analyze each of these processes into an aggregate of elements which are sufficiently simple to be precisely and unambiguously represented in the form of a set of variables. Thus, for example, if the objective is to teach the student to count in French from one to ten, then this objective—"ability to count in French from one to ten"—may be analyzed into the following skills:

1. The ability to recognize the acoustic pattern of each number (aural comprehension).
2. The ability to recognize the written form of each number (reading comprehension).
3. The ability to reproduce the acoustic pattern of each number (oral reproduction ability).
4. The ability to reproduce the written form of each number (written reproduction ability).

We have defined the components, or variables, of which the "ability to count in French" consists. These components may be represented in tabular form as indicated in Table 10.3.

But this is not sufficient to specify a final state vector. A means must be found for measuring the *degree* of development of these skills (for example, what does "recognition of the aural

Table 10.3

Components of Ability

ability to com-prehend acoustic patterns	ability to com-prehend written forms	ability to render numerals orally	ability to render numerals in written form

pattern of a number" or "aural comprehension" mean? How can we determine whether or not the student can recognize these forms?). Next, the numerical value of each variable must be determined. For example, what level of development of aural comprehension will we consider sufficient? If the student understands slowly and with difficulty—and what are the criteria for this?—will we be satisfied that he has acquired "aural comprehension"? At this point we encounter two of the most important problems faced by the programmer, problems which are among the most complex in the psychology and theory of instruction. The first is the problem of methods of identification, or diagnosis, of the degree of development in the student of a given cognitive process, in particular, with regard to tests, if diagnosis is effected by this means. The second is the problem of the level at which development of a process is to be considered complete. This is the question of the criteria for evaluating the degree to which a process is developed and of the means for measuring such development.

We will discuss each of these problems briefly. We begin with the problem of identifying, or diagnosing, cognitive processes. The discovery of means of effecting such diagnosis constitutes the second stage of the programming process.

Second Stage—Analysis or
Diagnosis of Cognitive Processes
Landsberg has written: "Any concept introduced into physics takes on concrete significance only when and if there is

associated with it a specific procedure for observation and measurement, without which this concept cannot find any application in the investigation of concrete physical phenomena" (Landsberg, 1956). This statement is valid not only in physics but for all other sciences as well, including psychology and education. To speak of the development (literally, completed formation, *Trans.*) of cognitive processes in the absence of any means for analyzing or diagnosing these processes is pointless. It is for this reason that the development of analytic procedures is such an important stage in the programming of instruction. Instruction can proceed purposefully (rather than blindly) only if the degree of development of the cognitive capabilities in question can be determined at each stage of the instructional process.

Although many physical phenomena and processes may be observed directly, cognitive processes can be observed only indirectly. How? All cognitive processes manifest themselves externally, in external reactions and behavior,[38] and so the only means of obtaining knowledge of them is through the analysis of behavior.[39] However, it is difficult to determine precisely which behavioral acts are manifestations of a given process and, therefore, which acts to use to arrive at judgments concerning this process. The problem is to find behavioral acts which are indicators of particular cognitive processes. This difficulty is aggravated, on the one hand, by the fact that the same processes are usually manifested in the most varied behavioral acts, and, on the other hand, by the fact that the same behavioral act may be indicative of cognitive processes (for example, a mistake in problem-solving may be the result of any one of several defects in cognitive activity). There is often no mutually unambiguous relation between cognitive processes and particular behavioral acts.

This is not the place for a detailed discussion of this problem. We wish to note only that the fundamental shortcoming of testing theory in the form that is being developed by many psychologists and educational scientists is the fact that the behavioral acts which are selected as indicators of specific cognitive processes are not such in fact, or are not unambiguous indicators of these processes. Similar errors are often made by teachers, although those who make these errors often do not share the theories on which such testing procedures are based. Such errors are often completely unrelated to any explicit theoretical position.

Judgments as to whether or not a student has learned a given concept are frequently made in practice on the basis of the student's ability to give a definition of this concept. Yet a behavioral act of this sort does not unambiguously indicate understanding of the concept: it is possible to formulate a correct definition of a concept (for example, by memorizing it) without understanding it or, conversely, to understand a concept and yet define it clumsily or even incorrectly. Lately psychologists and educational scientists have emphasized, with complete justification, that to know a concept means to be able to use it. But here, too, the matter is not so simple, since not every act of applying a concept is an indication of a full understanding of it. The question arises as to which acts of applying a concept indicate that the individual performing this act understands the concept completely, and which do not. For example, a student correctly identifies the subject in the sentences "The construction crew built the house," "Someone entered the room," and "Skis are sold in sporting-goods stores." May we conclude that he understands the concept of the subject of a sentence? These behavioral acts (identifying which word in a sentence is the subject is a behavioral act) are not sufficient to indicate full understanding of the concept in question. The information which they give is insufficient to justify this conclusion. The student may correctly recognize the subject in these sentences and yet fail to recognize it in other sentences (for example, in the sentence "Thousands of wild geese were making their way south," the student might identify "geese" as the subject because it refers to an active being).[40] The student might correctly identify the subject in a series of sentences by considering incorrect, inadequate, or accidental attributes, and this would not only *not* indicate a correct understanding of the concept, but, on the contrary, would mask his incorrect understanding of it.

We encounter examples of such masking in schools and institutions of higher education every day. Teachers draw the conclusion on the basis of a few correct answers (including answers to problems involving the application of concepts) that the student understands a concept, although in fact he may understand it imperfectly or even incorrectly. In many instances, the completeness of a given cognitive process may be judged only by an entire aggregate or system of behavioral acts, and the problem in making such judgments is to find (analytically, *Ed.*) this system, and then to find and formulate a system of exercises which will *require performance of all of these behavioral acts* and which will permit accurate and unambiguous judgments concerning the cognitive processes in question. This system of exercises should be included in the instructional program, since without it the program cannot correctly discriminate the level of development of the student's capabilities and adaptively alter the course of the instructional process.

It must be said that analysis of existing programmed materials indicates that in many cases performance tests administered to students for the purpose of determining their degree of mastery of knowledge, skills, and habits are inadequate and do not yield this information. This is especially true of tests which are based on the multiple-choice method. Although in many circumstances the multiple-choice approach permits adequate elucidation of the degree of development of specific cognitive processes, in many other circumstances it does not, yet is utilized for this purpose (the question as to the circumstances under which this technique is applicable warrants separate consideration).

Let us return to the example of mastering the French numerals and attempt to define behavioral acts which could be considered as manifestations of the skills of which this ability is "composed."

(1) The student must show that he is able to comprehend the numerals in acoustic form, for example, by indicating a set of objects whose number corresponds to the French number heard, or by indicating the written form of this number, or by indicating the corresponding form in his native language.

These behavioral acts could serve as the basis for a test for the presence of this skill. For example: the student listens to numbers spoken in French and is required to indicate a set of objects whose number corresponds to each number which he hears, or the corresponding number in Arabic numerals, or in his native language.[41]

(2) The student must show that he is able to comprehend the numerals in the written form (i.e., manifests reading comprehension), for example, by indicating, in response to reading the verbal form of a number, a set of objects whose number corresponds to the number read, or the corresponding number in Arabic numerals or in his native language.

Again, these behavioral acts could serve as the basis for a test for the presence of the skill in question: the student is given a list of number-words written in French and is asked to indicate the set of objects, Arabic numeral, or native-language form corresponding to each of them.

(3) The student must show that he is able to orally render a number by pronouncing it in response to the perception, for example, of a set of objects, an Arabic numeral, or the native-language form of the number.

It is obvious how these behaviors might serve as the basis of a test for the skill in question.

(4) The behaviors manifesting the ability to render numerals in written form will be evident to the reader by analogy with the preceding examples, as will a procedure for testing for the presence of this skill.

We have attempted to show by means of this simple example how behavioral acts may be found which manifest the cognitive processes and properties (in this case skills) which are being developed or measured and how tests for elucidating and discriminating these processes may be constructed.

This is not sufficient, however, for the construction of a final state vector. Numerical values for the isolated variables must be assigned, if possible. To do this we must define criteria of "knowing the French numerals." The assignment of numerical values to the final state variables is the third stage of the programming process.

Third Stage—Assignment of Numerical Values to the
Variables of the Final State Vector

The behavioral acts which express the ability to comprehend the acoustic and written (verbal) forms of numerals and the ability to render numerals in these forms are easily measured. It is also not difficult to define precise criteria for the level to which these skills must be developed in the student for him to be considered as "knowing the French numerals." For example, we may assume that the student has learned the French numerals from one to ten if he is able 100 percent of the time to indicate the correct number upon perceiving the acoustic or written form of a number in French, to say the correct French form upon perceiving a number in Arabic numerals or in his native language, etc. But knowledge of the French numerals is expressed not only in the correctness of the student's reactions to a given form, but also in the time which these reactions take.[42] Thus, statistical data from observations of the reaction times of people who know French well can be used as a criterion of knowledge of the French numerals (such reaction times might be, for example, 0.7-0.9 seconds for recognition, 1.0-1.5 seconds for speaking, and 2.0-4.0 seconds for writing).[43] With this information it becomes possible to describe the goal of instruction and to express it in the form of a final state vector with specific numerical values assigned to the variables (see Table 10.4).

A vector of this sort must be constructed for each number from one to ten (since the student might learn some numbers faster than others). It describes the final state, the objective which is to be achieved as a result of solving the didactic problem of teaching the student the French numerals from one to ten.

Fourth Stage—Assigning Numerical Values
to the Initial State Vectors

The initial states of these same variables may be described in an analogous manner. They constitute the conditions (the givens) of the didactic problem of which the instructional process is the solution. For example, if instruction must start from the very beginning, with the student having absolutely no knowledge of the

Table 10.4

Reception Skills				Production Skills			
Comprehension of Acoustic Form of Numerals		Comprehension of Written Form of Numerals		Aural Reproduction of Acoustic Form of Numerals		Written Reproduction of Written Form of Numerals	
Percent Correct	Time	Percent Correct	Time	Percent Correct	Time	Percent Correct	Time
100	0.7 - 0.9 secs.	100	0.7 - 0.9 secs.	100	1.0 - 1.5 secs.	100	2.0 - 4.0 secs.

material to be taught, then all of the variables of the initial state vector will have a value of zero. On the other hand, if the student already has some knowledge of the material, then the variables for one or more numbers will have some non-zero value (see Table 10.5).

The purpose of the instructional process is to change the student from his initial state to a desired final state, i.e., to cause the initial values of the relevant variables to shift to the values indicated in the final state vector. When this has been accomplished the didactic problem may be considered solved.

We have indicated two criteria by which to judge the degree of development of the skills in question, but these criteria are insufficient even for the simple problem of teaching the French numerals from one to ten. The student can be considered to have this ability only when he is able to say the appropriate French form with a sufficiently short reaction time after being given a stimulus to say it, *and* to pronounce this form correctly. This variable—correct pronunciation—cannot be assigned a numerical value (at least not yet), but it can be included in the final state vector as a standard against which the student's pronunciation may be compared at each level of ability which he attains. When his pronunciation comes to approximate this standard satisfactorily, the objective of instruction for this stage may be considered achieved and the didactic problem solved.

The variables indicated above are clearly adequate for purposes of teaching the French numerals. Many more variables (and criteria) would be required to achieve more complex instructional goals. Such variables might be, for example, the degree to which knowledge or verbal-cognitive operations have been generalized, their stability, etc. The more completely and precisely the fundamental variables and values relevant at each stage of the instructional process are defined, the more effective and reliable will be the instructional programs based on them. Without being able to determine at each step what the student has learned (and what he has not learned) a teaching device cannot "know" how to conduct successive stages of the instructional process. (We are speaking here, of course, about adaptive teaching

Table 10.5

	Reception Skills				Production Skills			
	Comprehension of Acoustic Form of Numerals		Comprehension of Written Form of Numerals		Aural Reproduction of Acoustic Form of Numerals		Written Reproduction of Written Form of Numerals	
	Percent Correct	Time	Percent Correct	Time	Percent Correct	Time	Percent Correct	Time
	80	2.0 secs.	60	1.5 secs.	30	1.6 secs.	10	6.0 secs.

devices operating in accordance with a flexible, adaptive algorithm; the future belongs to such devices, and instructional theory
must take them into account.)

We have indicated several problems which must be solved in
the course of writing an instructional program (defining the initial
and final states of the students and describing them in vector
form, developing procedures for elucidating the corresponding
cognitive processes, selecting behavioral acts which may serve as a
basis for judging the degree to which these processes have
developed, and formulating criteria by which to determine when
this development is complete). The above discussion, however, is
only a formulation of the didactic problem and a definition of
means for evaluating attempts to solve it (whether or not the
student achieved the desired final state). The performance of the
steps indicated above yields only a precise description of what the
student is to be taught (the final state vector) and the point at
which the instructional process must begin (the initial state
vector). The actual solution of the didactic problem consists of
finding and using instructional procedures, i.e., means of influencing the student, which will transform the initial state into the final
state.[44] If this transformation can be made to happen by means of
an instructional algorithm, then the writing and application of this
transformation algorithm will constitute a solution to the didactic
problem.

There are few problems which can be solved only in one way,
and problems which are solvable algorithmically can usually be
solved by means of more than one algorithm. This applies to
didactic problems as well. It is clear that the transformation from
one state (the initial) to another (the final) may be brought about
in the most varied ways, by means of the most diverse algorithms.
One of the basic problems arising during the programming process
consists, therefore, of finding an instructional algorithm which will
solve the problem of state-to-state transformation in the most
efficient and, in particular, in the fastest and easiest way possible,
with the least expenditure of time and energy on the part of both
the teacher and the student.

The efficiency of an instructional algorithm cannot be

evaluated, however, solely on the basis of the time and energy required to transform the student's initial state into the desired final state. This is so, because any instructional algorithm produces not only direct results in the form of "leading" the student to the desired state, but also indirect results (which are sometimes more important than the direct results for achieving the goals of the instructional process) in the form of the development in him of particular abilities, of interest in knowledge *per se* and in studying, etc., which cannot be measured (at least not at present) precisely and represented as variables with specific numerical values. Two algorithms which are equally effective from the point of view of the development of the variables constituting the immediate objective of instruction (the development in the student of specific knowledges, skills, and habits), may not be equally effective from the point of view of the development of more general aspects of the student's personality. For example, one algorithm might develop the desire to learn to a greater degree than another. Such considerations must enter into the selection and design of algorithms. The development of the desire to learn could, of course, simply be included in the final state vector as a variable, but at the present time this would be difficult to do, since there are no precise qualitative criteria (to say nothing of quantitative criteria) by which to judge whether or not, for example, the student's desire to learn has reached the required level. At this point it is easier to use a simpler approach: not to include in the final state vector development of qualities such as desire to learn (especially since this characteristic is dependent on other variables and is developed along with them as one of their general aspects), but to consider the capability of stimulating the desire to learn as a characteristic of the instructional algorithm, i.e., as a requirement which it must satisfy. The instructional algorithm, besides guaranteeing transformation of the initial state into the final state, must possess the capability (property) of developing in the student such qualities as the desire to learn. Such capabilities or properties and the degree to which they are expressed should be included in the criteria by which the effectiveness of the algorithm is evaluated.

The writing of an effective instructional algorithm entails the solving of a number of problems, two of which we will consider here: determination of the sequence of states through which the student should move in order to make the transition as quickly and easily as possible from the initial state to the final state, and determination of those types of activity which he should perform in order to effect this transformation. The solution of the first of these problems may be considered as the fifth stage of the programming process.

Fifth Stage—Determination of the Sequence of
Intermediate States Between the Initial State
and the Final State

As has been noted already, the transformation from the initial state to the final state in the solution of almost any problem (including didactic problems) may be accomplished in various ways, that is, through various transitional or intermediate states. In order to write an instructional algorithm (program) it is necessary to determine precisely the transitional states through which the student must pass in order to reach the final state as quickly and easily as possible. It is clear that this problem is that of analyzing the over-all didactic problem into a series of subproblems, analyzing the instructional process into a series of steps, and analyzing the instructional algorithm into a series of subalgorithms. In everyday terms this problem might be termed that of defining the sequence or course of the instructional process.

In speaking of the sequence of the instructional process it is necessary to keep in mind that there are at least two aspects to this problem. The first is content—the question of the order in which topics, concepts, methods, etc., should be studied. The other is the question of how instruction on a given topic is to be divided into stages. (For example, we wish to teach the student the French numeral "eight." In what sequence will we develop the skills which constitute this knowledge?)

Let us dwell briefly on the first aspect and examine this question as it applies to large segments of the instructional process (didactic problems differ in the "distances" between their initial and final states).

In the literature on programmed instruction one of the characteristics of this approach is usually considered to be analysis of the material to be taught into chunks (segments, steps, *Ed.*) and its rendering in a strict, logical sequence. A more detailed analysis of a "strict, logical sequence" might show, however, that this concept is frequently insufficiently precise, and in some situations simply devoid of precise meaning. What, in fact, is a "strict, logical sequence?" Apparently it is a sequence which is determined in accordance with the logic, or more precisely the system, of the science, or in accordance with the developmental logic of the concepts of a given science. As is generally recognized, however, in many sciences or in the relations between their divisions the concept "logic" is inadequately defined,[45] and moreover a science can have several "logics," all of them correct;[46] finally, in many instances the logic (system) of instruction does not correspond (and should not correspond) to the logic (system) of science.[47]

One of the serious shortcomings of many textbooks (and these shortcomings are usually transferred to programmed texts) is the fact that, in determining the expository logic (sequence) of the instructional material, authors take as their sole starting point the logic (system) of the science in question, basing their exposition on the manner in which the subject is presented in scientific works (for example, in an academic grammar of the Russian language) and fail completely to consider the psychology of the assimilation of this material, i.e., how it is perceived and stored in the student's head. The consequences of such an approach can be illustrated in one simple example.

In academic grammars of the Russian language, simple sentences are discussed in one section and complex sentences in another. This expository logic has been transferred to school textbooks, with the result that students have great difficulty with the punctuation of complex sentences. The punctuation of a sentence containing the conjunction "and" may serve as an example. In Russian grammar, when a single "and" connects homogeneous parts of a simple sentence, commas are not inserted before it, but when it is used as a conjunction to connect clauses in a complex sentence, a comma is inserted. When the topic "simple sentences" is being covered, a great deal of energy is devoted to developing in the student the habit of not putting commas before a single "and." When the topic "complex sentences" is being covered, the same energy is devoted to break this habit and to form another habit of putting a comma before a single "and." The more firmly established the habit becomes of not inserting commas before a single "and," the more difficult it is later, when the topic "complex sentences" is covered, to develop the habit of putting commas before "and" used as a conjunction to connect two clauses. The association already formed in the student's mind is extremely difficult to break.[48] This difficulty is lessened if the order in which these topics are covered, i.e., the one used in scientific treatments of Russian grammar, is changed so that these topics are studied simultaneously rather than sequentially and in correlation with one another, involving comparisons. This approach is used by many experienced teachers and is recommended in a number of methodological handbooks.[49]

This example clearly illustrates the necessity of writing instructional programs not solely on the basis of the logic of the material to be taught, i.e., on its exposition in scientific treatments of the topic, but on the psychology of its assimilation by students as well. The student's success in learning a topic and perceiving its logic depends on such a consideration of the psychology of its assimilation.[50]

As to the logic (sequence) of the stages in the study of material within a given topic, it is often in no way determined by the logic of its scientific treatment, but depends entirely on the psychological considerations involved in its assimilation by the student, that is on the question of which sequence is the most efficient from the point of view of the time and effort required to achieve the goal of the instructional process. Indeed, in the teaching of French numerals, neither the logic of French grammar nor the logic of mathematics (since the French words in question denote numbers) will suggest to us whether we should teach aural comprehension of the French forms first, for example, and then reading comprehension, or vice versa. Logic is irrelevant to these questions.

We will now consider the second of the problems indicated above, namely that of determining the types of activity which the student should perform in order to move from an initial to a final state. The solution of this problem constitutes the sixth stage of the programming process.

Sixth Stage—Determination of Types of
Student Activity Which Will Guarantee
Transformation from One State to Another

Instruction is distinguished from many other forms of control in that the transformation of one state of a human being (level of knowledge, skills, and habits) into another does not occur directly as the result of external influences exerted by the teacher, but indirectly, as a result of the student's own activity. Knowledge, skills, and habits cannot be simply inserted full-blown into the student's head; they must be assimilated and processed, and processing means the performance of a specific processing activity, or in other words, of specific cognitive and/or physical operations. In any well-organized instructional process the teacher or program should not simply transmit (substantive, *Ed.*) information; it should organize the student's activity for processing and assimilation of the transmitted information.

This idea has been expressed frequently and is well-known.[51] The problem, however, is to determine precisely which activity to use and how to organize it in such a way that it will lead to the development of the required cognitive processes and at the same time guarantee that the objective of instruction will be achieved. Since the most frequently employed means of organizing the student's activity is to give him specific problems and exercises together with instructions as to how to do them, the question arises as to which problems and exercises to select and how to present them to the student at each step of the instructional process, as each intermediate state is reached, so as to evoke the activity which will lead to the development of the desired processes.

At this point the program writer must solve the following problems:

1. He must discover types of activity which will develop each of the required cognitive processes, i.e., each required variable, and thereby permit attainment of the level of development of these cognitive processes defined by the vector of the state closest to the student's current state (this is the problem of finding forms of activity which generate a given cognitive process and cause it to develop).

2. He must analyze this activity into its component operations.

3. He must determine an appropriate sequence for the performance and development of these operations (the sequence in which they are performed and the sequence in which the student learns them may not coincide).

4. He must determine which exercises will evoke the required operations and activity as a whole and at the same time generate the required cognitive processes, guaranteeing the successful transformation from one state to another. Analysis of a number of programmed textbooks and methodological guides shows that these problems are frequently solved incorrectly, that the authors of programmed as well as other instructional materials in many cases either do not concern themselves at all about finding forms of activity which lead to the development of the required cognitive processes (thinking that knowledge or information can be simply transmitted), or give the student exercises and evoke in him activity which does not lead to the development of the required processes or which leads to the development of some other processes. The following examples illustrate this point.

Example 1

The following appears in a programmed text in arithmetic:

    I.   The Concept of the Fraction

    1.   Up to now you have been studying the characteristics of natural numbers.

2. A long time ago when people first began counting objects they came to the idea of _____ numbers.

Natural (answer)

In leaving a blank for the student to fill in, the author hopes to evoke in the student a specific activity. But exactly what activity will this procedure evoke, and what processes will it develop in the student? Will it develop processes that the author wants? What processes does the author want to develop? The answers to these questions are not evident. It is clear, however, that this activity does not pose any cognitive problem to the student. In order to fill in the blank correctly the student has only to use a word from the preceding segment (the word "natural"). He could do this mechanically, without knowing what a "natural number" is. It could be the case, of course, that the author wished to fix the student's attention on the word "natural," but surely this would be better accomplished by including use of this word in a problem which would require the student to operate with the *concept* of the natural number! After all, the author is not teaching grammar. This at least would prevent a sudden influx of unthinking, mechanical responses into the student's efforts.[52]

Example 2

In a programmed text on the Russian language the student is told that in compound nominal predicates, which he has been studying up to this point, only two verbs may be used as copulas: "to be" and "to become." "But you may encounter others," says the author. "Write in your notebook the most frequently used of these." A list of verbs follows: to be, to become, to serve, to appear, to seem, to be considered, to be made.

What is the purpose of the assignment—to write down these verbs? Why is the activity which the student is hereby asked to perform necessary? What process does it develop in him? This is not clear. Perhaps it facilitates better understanding, assimilation, and retention of the material? This cannot be said to be the case, since the activity of "writing down" bears no relation to the solution of the problem of isolating the "most frequently used" copulas (they must be isolated before they can be written down), while the student can, of course, perform the act of writing itself in a purely mechanical manner without learning anything whatsoever, which would be a complete waste of time. The assignment in question requires the performance of a specific external activity, but requires no internal activity, no internal active involvement, and so causes a considerable expenditure of time and effort without developing any useful processes. In giving the student this task to perform, the author addresses himself only to the student's external actions and shows that he does not have a clear idea of the internal actions which are to be evoked by the performance of this task, or of the psychological problem which is to be solved, or the psychological functions which these external actions are to perform.

Consideration of these examples leads to an important conclusion. One of the frequently cited attributes and virtues of programmed instruction is the fact that it requires constant active involvement on the part of the student, constant independent activity, and so increases the preparation of active, as opposed to passive, learning activity during the instructional process. This is true, but are all forms of active involvement useful? Does independent work always develop independence? The examples cited above show that the answer to these questions is no. Active involvement may be external (and only external), or internal: it can involve thinking or be purely mechanical.[53] Independent work can develop independence, but it can also do the opposite, if the tasks which the student is given to solve independently require mechanical copying of models, blind rewriting of definitions, quotations, etc. Programmed instruction creates the possibility of developing active involvement and independence, but in order for these possibilities to be realized, the student must be given tasks which require internal active involvement and independence, which develop the required cognitive processes and characteristics. Active involvement and independence are not, after all, objectives in themselves. They are only means for developing specific cognitive processes and characteristics, among which are active involvement and independence as personality characteristics.

We have cited examples illustrating how an inadequately thought-out approach to the selection of forms of activity intended to lead to the development of certain cognitive processes in the student (or the inability to find such forms of activity) gives rise to serious defects in programs based on these activities. This takes the form of effort which is unnecessary and time-wasting, and which, moreover, develops habits of mechanical responding. It happens, not infrequently, however, that program authors give the student problems and evoke in him activity which causes incorrect development of the cognitive processes in question and under some conditions actually hinder the correct development of knowledge, skills, and habits. Instructional programs frequently contain (not, of course, by design) outmoded and incorrect methodological conceptions, and the extension of these conceptions to programmed instruction and their embodiment in programmed texts and even teaching machines actually has the effect of making instruction less, rather than more, effective.

For example, let us consider a machine constructed for the purpose of teaching reading. The machine operates in the following way. A picture of an object (a house, for example) appears on a screen in front of the student and he types the first letter of the word denoting this object. If the student types the correct letter (in the case of a house, the letter "h"), another picture appears and he proceeds as before. If he types the wrong letter, an error light goes on and he tries again; if he again fails to type the correct letter, that letter appears on the screen.

Contemporary study of reading[54] has shown that (in Russian, *Ed.*) the individual letters of the alphabet should be taught after phonological analysis of words is undertaken, i.e., isolation of phonemes (the actual sounds denoted by a given letter in different words written with this letter are not identical, but they are all manifestations of one and the same phoneme). Letters should be associated with phonemes, yet in the approach to the teaching of reading described above they are associated with the specific sounds occurring in a particular word, not with the phonemes represented by these letters. This approach hampers the development of correct reading habits. The situation becomes worse when the student makes an error and must correct it by typing the correct letter. In so doing he operates to a significant degree by trial and error, and even if he finds the correct letter and the machine registers a correct response, this correct response does not in any way demonstrate that a correct reading habit is developing. The student has not learned the most important thing, namely the phonemic analysis of words.[55] If he is unable to find the correct letter by himself, and the machine "helps" him by revealing it to him, then the results may be even more undesirable. The student simply forms an association between the picture of the object and the form of the letter without learning anything in the way of phonological analysis. This way of responding to student errors not only does not lead to the objectives of the instructional process (i.e., does not develop the operations involved in the phonological analysis of words) but actually leads away from them by developing associations which are detrimental to the teaching of reading.

This example shows that programmed instruction can actually be detrimental as well as useful, if it is used as the vehicle for an incorrect methodology or encourages carelessness with regard to the forms of activity which should be evoked in the student and the cognitive processes which develop as a result of this activity. Carelessness of this sort, which frequently characterizes the writing of instructional programs and the design of teaching machines, is detrimental to the educational process and can only discredit programmed instruction.

Seventh Stage—Specification of Exercises
Which Guarantee Performance of the
Required Activity

We have discussed the importance of a correct selection of types of activity for developing particular cognitive processes and for bringing about the transformation from one state to another. It is clear, however, that for the student to be able to perform an activity it must be organized, i.e., he must be given the information necessary for the performance of the activity in the form of specific instructions, exercises, etc. In other words, it is necessary to find instructional influences which will evoke the required activity and thereby lead to the development of the required cognitive processes.

A detailed discussion of the question of how to select and devise instructional influences which meet these requirements would go beyond the scope of this chapter. We wish to note only that the program writer faces the following problems in this regard:

1. He must find instructional influences (in particular, exercises) which evoke in the student precisely the activity and the cognitive processes which are required. In order to do this:

2. He must know all of the instructional capabilities of each of the procedures, i.e., the psychological "effects" which each procedure is capable of evoking. We will term these "effects" of instructional influences, their didactic properties.

3. He must compare the didactic properties of various types of instructional procedures with the objectives that he wishes to achieve by using them and on this basis select the one which, first, solves the instructional problem immediately at hand and, second, evokes the largest number of useful psychological effects. The influence which meets these conditions will be the one which is most effective in solving the didactic problem or subproblem in question.[56]

4. If none of the existing instructional procedures possesses the required didactic properties, the program writer must develop new ones. In particular, he must develop new types of exercises which will evoke the required activity and cognitive processes.

As we noted in characterizing the problems involved in the preceding stage, writers of instructional programs frequently use instructional procedures (exercises, for example) which do not evoke in the student the required types of activity and do not develop the required processes. They also often select instructional procedures possessing less than optimal didactic properties. A more detailed analysis of these questions, however, is not possible here.

Eighth Stage—Determination of Means of
Responding to the Student's Actions and
Their Results, Especially Mistakes

When the program writer has solved the problems described above, he can proceed to design the instructional algorithm. Design of an instructional algorithm presupposes not only a specification of the content of instruction, the initial and final state vectors, the sequence of intermediate states, the types of activity to be evoked in the student, and the instructional procedures for influencing him so as to guarantee his transformation from each intermediate state to the next, but also a specification of means for responding to the student's actions and the results of these actions during his assimilation of knowledge and his attempts to solve problems, specifically, to his incorrect responses. Control of the instructional process consists of leading the student to the goal, i.e., to the final state, with the most varied responses on his part to the instructional influences to which he is subjected (he may learn or not learn, respond correctly, or make an error). The writing of an instructional algorithm requires that not only the instructional influences but also the student's possible responses be taken into account, as well as the teacher's responses to these responses on the part of the student, and so on until the goal of instruction is reached and the student "arrives" at the final state. In other words, the writing of an instructional algorithm requires the writing of instructions describing the teacher's responses in a situation in which various "moves" on the student's part may be made in response to each "move" on the teacher's part, and in which the teacher will respond to each possible "move" on the student's part in a way which will lead him to the desired final state.

Before going on to the question of how to write such an algorithm and the considerations to be guided by in selecting ways of responding to various actions on the student's part and their results, we must consider a fundamental question of a more general character.

The theory of programmed instruction is an instructional model, or more precisely a set of instructional models, having in common the feature of requiring that the instructional process be analyzed into "steps," that the student be asked a question (literally, given a task, *Trans.*) at each step, and that his answer be responded to in such a way that, if he made a mistake, he be able to recognize and correct it before going on to the next "step." If the student is regarded as a system which is being controlled,[57] then control of the student in the process of programmed instruction (as in any other form of instruction) is effected in two ways: (a) by providing the student with information followed by problems and specific directions on how to solve them (this is control of the "input" to the controlled system/student), and (b) by analyzing the student's answers and responding to them (control of the "outputs" of the controlled system/student). Programmed instruction requires control of both the inputs and the outputs of the controlled system/student and the bringing to bear of appropriate influences on them. "Input" and output" are external phenomena which initiate cognitive activity (the instructional material and the corresponding problems and instructions) and terminate it (a response in the form of a particular physical action). "Input" and "output" are the initial and final links of the chain whose middle link is the cognitive processes which convert the input information into the output information.

The question immediately arises as to the degree to which control of the initial and final links in this chain ensures control of the "middle link," of the development of cognitive processes and personality characteristics.[58] It is not possible to give a simple and unambiguous answer to this question, since in one case the "input" and "output" may be influenced in such a way as to lead to control of the intermediate states (there is no other means of controlling the intermediate states than by affecting the "input" and "output"), while in another case the "input" and "output" may be influenced in such a way as not to lead to control of the intermediate states. Which of these possibilities occurs depends on the content and nature of the influences applied.

This point may be illustrated by means of a simple example. If a student attempts to solve a difficult problem, arrives at an incorrect answer, and is informed that his answer is wrong (i.e., we control the "output" by bringing to bear on it a specific influence), then our manipulation of the "output" may have an insignificant effect on the intermediate states, that is, it will not in itself teach the student the correct way of thinking in order to solve the problem. It will not teach him a method for searching for an answer independently, although it will stimulate him to look for such a method. If we, upon discovering that the student has made a mistake, not only inform him that he has made a mistake but also give him indications as to how to think in order to keep mistakes from reoccurring, then this influence on the "output" will facilitate the development of correct methods of thinking, i.e., will exert control over the intermediate states.

The principles of programmed instruction require that influences on the "input" and "output" be discrete (the principle of step-by-step instruction) and exerted with sufficient frequency to insure assimilation (the principle of operative feedback), but they say nothing about the nature of the influences themselves. In other words the (Skinnerian, *Ed.*) principles of programmed instruction require control of the "input" and "output" (of external information and physical actions), but leave open the question of how to effect this control in such a way as to control the intermediate states. Programmed instruction, therefore, may control the intermediate states (i.e., link) well or poorly, depending precisely on the means by which control of the "input" and "output" is effected. In the form in which it was originally developed in the United States, the theory of programmed instruction, which arose as an approach having the goal of radical improvement in the control process, has solved this problem only in part. It has indicated principles and means for improving control of the external factors in instruction ("inputs" and "outputs," the presentation of information and the external activity of the student in response to this information), leaving room for the application of the most varied theories and procedures (both effective and ineffective) for controlling the intermediate states.

Evidence for the correctness of this view lies in the fact that theorists holding views on how best to control the intermediate states which are in a number of respects diametrically opposite,

Skinner and Crowder, for example, are both considered as proponents of the theory of programmed instruction. No author can avoid the question of how to control the intermediate states. This problem is central in any instructional theory; its solution also determines the external forms which are imparted to material during the programming process. For us, however, it is at the moment important only to note that these opposing views may be embodied in programmed texts which, though differing in form, have in common a number of features reflecting some general principles of programmed instruction.

Thus, Skinner and his followers attempt to structure the instructional process in such a way that each step of the program shapes within the student one simple verbal association or one simple action. For example, the student is told that a circle is a closed, curved line lying in a plane, all points of which are equidistant from a single point, termed the center. Then he is given the following problem: the attributes of the circle are listed, and he is asked to name the geometric figure possessing these attributes (he then immediately proceeds to compare his answer with the correct one). This particular type of exercise can be useful in some situations, but if the entire instructional process is structured in accordance with this principle, then the question arises as to whether control of the intermediate states is taking place here. In one sense such control is certainly present, since Skinner and his followers very skillfully evoke in the student the desired associations, but in another sense it is not present, since the problems involved in shaping cognitive activity cannot be reduced to the development of some simple associations. In taking this approach Skinner and his followers fail to control the development of complex conceptual processes or of complex forms of cognitive activity.

In fact, little or no cognitive effort is required in order to answer a simple question by filling in a blank. Answering such a question *often does not require the performance of any system of cognitive operations.* It requires only the activation of an elementary association, and this is facilitated by an entire system of specially developed clues and hints. In other words, Skinner and his followers organize the "input" and "output" in such a way that there is nothing between them but the simplest type of associative bond; the intermediate states are practically regarded as unnecessary and are discarded entirely.

If we consider the sorts of problems which people are actually called upon to solve in life, we see that there are relatively few which require for their solution the activation of only one simple association, i.e., in which the connection between "input" and "output" consists of one single, simple link.[59] Most problems are such that the connection between "input" and "output" consists of many links or stages, and there often exist not one but several or even many paths leading from the "input" to the "output." The solution of such problems requires more than the simple activation of individual, pre-interconnected associations; it requires search, testing, the establishment of new associations, the checking of results in accordance with specific criteria, the inhibition of inadequate associations and actions, etc. Yet it is precisely this sort of activity for which programs of the Skinnerian type do not prepare the student; these programs do not develop processes of this type, i.e., do not control them. If such processes do develop in the student in the course of his independent activity, then this occurs not because of the program, but independently of it.

Unlike Skinner and his followers, Crowder makes the connection between "input" and "output" in programmed instruction significantly more "distant," hence the considerably larger informational chunk size in Crowderian programs as compared to programs of the Skinnerian type. If Skinner solves the problem of controlling the intermediate states by practically eliminating it from the instructional process, Crowder does not do this. He believes that the student should be given tasks which require thought, search, and testing. But Crowder deliberately avoids direct control of these processes; he does not even make any attempt to discover their structure. In one article Crowder implies that he does not pretend to know how to teach anyone anything. He wants to know only whether or not the student is making mistakes, and if he is, what the nature of these mistakes is so that his responses to the mistakes will be such as to lead the student to a correct understanding of the material and a correct solution to the problem.

It is, of course, possible, by means of a proper response to a mistake, in particular by means of a response based on an analysis of its cause, to control the processes (the intermediate states) which led to this mistake, but this is retrospective control, so to speak, control by correction. Such control is moreover to a significant degree blind, since Crowder, not being interested in how the individual learns, in the structure of the processes which lead to a correct solution or to a mistake, is unable always to influence these processes in a deliberate and goal-directed manner. Crowder explicitly takes the position that the student is to be considered as a "black box." Only the "input" to and the "output" from the "black box" are known—nothing is known of the interior states which connect them. The most important point in this regard is that Crowder, in proposing the requirement of differentiated response to mistakes (mistake-based control), indicates no principles regarding how to respond to mistakes in order to control the intermediate states.[60] The effect of a response to a mistake, however, whether or not it leads to the development of the required cognitive processes, whether or not it exerts control over the intermediate states, depends on the content and manner of the response. But Crowder does not propose any theory of "methods of responding" (or, incidentally, any theory of the exposition of material), proceeding from the fact that the design of good programs is as yet more of an art than a science.

These examples show that the theory of programmed instruction, in requiring step-wise instruction through the control of "input" and "output," does not solve the problem of the control of the intermediate states or, more precisely, permits utilization of the most varied control techniques based on the most varied conceptions of the instructional process, including those developed by Soviet psychologists and educational scientists.

Let us now move to a more detailed consideration of the principles and techniques for responding to the student's actions and their results from the point of view of control of the intermediate states. The question of techniques of responding to the student's errors will be of particular interest in this regard.

In many programmed texts, response to student mistakes is frequently effected in such a way as not to lead to control of the intermediate states. Though such programs (algorithms) exert good control over the student's external activity, they often exert very little control over his internal, cognitive activity. In this respect, too, programmed instruction as implemented in programs of this sort does not differ greatly from non-programmed instruction. The examples discussed below are taken from programs of this sort.

Figure 10.6 is a representation of a format commonly used in programmed instruction.

Figure 10.6

Commonly Used Format of
Programmed Instruction

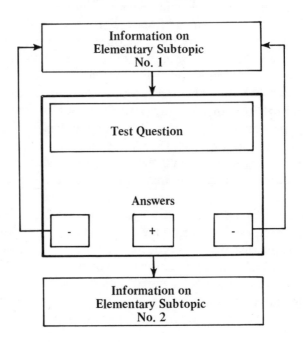

The essence of this format is as follows: if the student answers the question correctly, he is told to proceed to the next chunk of information (step); if he makes a mistake, he is told to go back to the preceding chunk, to read it again, and to select another answer.[61] The following is an example of how this arrangement is implemented in one programmed text.

In Paragraph 21 the definition of a logarithm is given along with several examples of logarithms of specific numbers. The student is then given a problem to solve:

What is $\log_4 16$?

Answer	see Paragraph
4	22
2	23

Let us assume that the student chooses the first answer (4) and refers to Paragraph 22. There he reads:

"Paragraph 22. Your answer was 4, that is, you think that $\log_4 16 = 4$. But from the definition of a logarithm we see that this would mean that $4^4 = 16$, which is incorrect. Carefully read the definition again, then study the examples until you understand them, and then give the correct answer."

We see that if the student makes a mistake, he is told to reread the same definition and to study the same examples again. We are not concerned here with the possibility that the student might select the correct answer in a purely mechanical manner and go on to the next step without having understood why $\log_4 16 = 2$ and perhaps without even having thought about it at all (in this text one of the two answers is always wrong and the other right). This possibility exists in any programmed text, and constitutes the principal defect of such texts relative to teaching machines. The question is, does a second reading of the material develop the ability to solve the problem? The author believes that it does, as is clear from his subsequent responses to student errors.

When the student chooses the correct answer and turns to

Paragraph 23, he is told that his answer is correct and is given another problem of the same type to solve.

What is $\log_3 27$?

Answer	see Paragraph
3	24
9	25

Let us assume that the student decides that $\log_3 27 = 9$ and turns to Paragraph 25. He reads:

"Paragraph 25. Your answer was 9. It is incorrect, since it would mean that according to the definition of a logarithm $3^9 = 27$, which of course is wrong. Study the definition of a logarithm again, turn to Paragraph 23 and choose the correct answer."

We have seen that if the student solves the problem incorrectly the first time, he is referred back to the definition of the logarithm. If he gets the wrong answer again, then once again he is sent back to the same definition. The program is designed in such a way that, if the student fails to solve the problem on his third and fourth tries he is sent back a third and fourth time to the definition. The fourth and last referral reads as follows:

"Paragraph 27. Your answer was 5. It is wrong, since $5^5 \neq 1$. Read the definition of a logarithm given in Paragraph 21 again, and then turn to Paragraph 24 and choose the correct answer."

The author assumes that, if the student reads the definition a fourth time he will finally understand how to solve the problem. This is unlikely, however, since it is quite clear that the student is failing to solve the problem not because he has not understood or does not remember the definition of a logarithm, but because he has no problem-solving method. He does not know the operations which he must perform in order to find the logarithm of a number to a given base. This system of operations follows from the definition of a logarithm, but is not contained in it directly, and not all students are able to deduce it on their own. It is precisely a method, or a system of operations for solving problems, which the author fails to teach the student, and to which he does not even lead him, by always sending him back to a definition which does not contain this method in a clear form.[62] The author, therefore, exerts no direct control over the development of a method of thinking, or a system of operations for solving problems. The student who, as a result of making many mistakes and reading the definition many times, eventually does manage to discover such a method, will learn it, and the student who does not manage to discover it will not (we are referring here to independent discovery, not discovery with the aid of the teacher).

Standard instruction also very often proceeds in this way when it is poorly conducted. The student who is unable to solve a problem or who makes a mistake in writing is frequently told to "study the rules and definitions," although the cause of his difficulties is most often not that he does not know the rules and definitions, but that he does not know how to apply them, does not know the thinking procedures required to solve the problem, or does not know them very well. These methods are frequently not taught. This is another example of programmed instruction being modeled after poor standard instruction. The program on logarithms quoted above follows a rigorous instructional algorithm, but this algorithm controls only the student's external actions (if he makes an error, he is told precisely what to do—to read the definition again), but it does not control the internal cognitive processes, the intermediate states, which must be influenced in the proper way if the student is to learn how to solve problems.

What considerations should guide the program author in selecting a response to an error which will control not only the student's external actions, but the intermediate states as well?

Briefly, there are three such considerations:

1. Understanding of the psychological cause of the mistake.

2. Understanding of the psychological mechanism of the correct means (method) for solving problems of the type in question, i.e., the thinking procedure which must be followed in order to solve such problems, or the set of cognitive operations which must be performed.

3. Understanding of how to teach these thinking procedures (methods), i.e., of *what* to do and *how* to do it in order to develop in the student the required system of cognitive operations.

When we consider Skinnerian linear programs, which are the most widely used ones, and Crowderian branched programs, which are less widely used, we see that neither type, as a rule, takes into account the fact that a given student's mistake can have any one or any combination of causes and that it is impossible to respond adequately to mistakes and to develop a correct thinking procedure (i.e., to construct an instructional algorithm which controls the intermediate states) without first discovering the psychological cause of the mistake.

No competent physician would think of prescribing a medication for a patient complaining of a headache without first discovering the cause of the headache, i.e., without first establishing a diagnosis. The medication (and the therapeutic procedures in general) prescribed for headache due to flu, high blood pressure, fatigue, a stomach ulcer, etc., are quite different. Yet teachers, especially writers of programmed instruction materials, frequently "treat" without diagnosis, responding to student errors as though a given error could have only one possible cause. We saw the results of this approach in the preceding example: the student was unable to solve a problem which involved finding the logarithm of a number, because he did not know the method for solving it, i.e., the operations to be performed. Yet the "disease" for which the author of the program "treated" him was not knowing the definition of a logarithm, or not remembering it precisely. Figuratively speaking, the student was sick with the flu, but was treated for a stomach ulcer. The therapeutic system was extremely inflexible and unadaptive. After the second "treatment" (the second referral back to the definition) it should have been clear that since this "medication" did not help, the student was "sick" with another "disease" and so the medication should be changed; this, however, was not done. The medication was ineffective, but the physician continued to administer it. It is not surprising that this approach, though applied in a programmed format, proves ineffective in "curing" the patient, and if some of the patients nevertheless get

well under this treatment, they do so not because the "medication" was the right one, but because as organisms they were strong
and capable of healing themselves.

The inadequate control of the intermediate states characteristic of most current instructional programs is explained by the
fact that for the most part they strive to inculcate knowledge and
spend too little time and effort in teaching methods of thinking.[63]
Most program writers concentrate primarily (and sometimes exclusively) on getting the student to give the correct answer to the
questions put to him, without being concerned about *how* he
arrives at his answers, how he thinks, reasons, and operates in
order to produce an answer. Yet it is possible to arrive at the right
answer by an incorrect method, and if the program writer fails to
take this fact into account and accepts such a correct answer and
reinforces it positively, then he simply reinforces the incorrect
method which the student used to obtain this answer.[64]

In many instances, the authors of programmed texts do not
simply send the student back to the segment containing the relevant definition and/or examples and instruct him to read the segment again and to select another answer, but also explain to him
the reason for his mistake. It would appear that with this procedure the student would learn the correct method for solving the
problems in question, but in fact this is not the case or it is not
always the case. If the student is told that $\log_3 27$ is not equal to 9
because 3^9 is not equal to 27, then he will understand only why
his answer was wrong, but not (at least not necessarily) what the
flaw in his problem-solving method was or, what is more important, how to proceed correctly in order to arrive at the correct
answer.[65]

Some authors do not simply analyze the student's erroneous
answer, but also indicate the mistake in reasoning which caused
him to arrive at this answer. Such responses would seemingly,
without fail, teach the student the correct method for solving the
problems, but it proves to be the case that they do not do this in
any direct way.

In a certain programmed Russian text, if the student makes
the mistake of writing "sdelanyi" (it should be "sdelannyi," with

two n's) he is told that he did not take into account the fact that this word is a prefixed participle (and in such cases the word is written with two n's); if his answer to another question is "kozhannyi" (it should have only one n), he is told that he forgot that this is an adjective formed from a noun by addition of the suffix -an-, and therefore is written with only one n; in another case, if he writes "rvannyi" (it should have only one n) he is told that he forgot that this word is an adjective formed from a perfective verb and so should be written with one n, etc.

This way of responding is based on direct analysis of errors in the student's reasoning (what he did not take into account, the attributes he did not look for and, consequently, the operations he did not perform). Nevertheless, it fails to teach a correct and general procedure, because it does not clarify for the student what he should take into account in *any* given situation, the things he should pay attention to when he encounters a new word ending in *nyi* (and the sequence in which he should consider them) in order always to be able to determine whether it is written with two n's or one. The capable student, of course, will be able to arrive at the required general system of operations even with this kind of analysis of his mistake and to discover a general procedure for solving problems of this type, but in this case success is due not to the program nor to the instructional techniques employed, but to the student's own competence. A given student will either discover the method or not discover it, but the program does not ensure that every student will discover and assimilate a correct and general procedure, since it does not control this process directly.

Does this mean that this commonly used approach (algorithm) to programmed instruction ("if you made an error, go back to the preceding segment, read it again, and select another answer") is totally wrong and ought never to be used? Must a program always diagnose the cause of a mistake before responding to it? Of course not.

It is frequently sensible as a first response to a mistake simply to tell the student that he has made a mistake and to send him back to the preceding segment. This procedure forces the student to think about the cause of his mistake, mobilizes his attention and motivation during the second reading of the material or attempt to solve the problem, and stimulates him to take a new approach to what he just finished doing incorrectly. However, this sort of response to mistakes is inappropriate when it is the only one used, as is the case in many programmed texts and teaching machine programs. The student is told again and again that he has made a mistake and is referred again and again to the preceding segment, even when his "internal resources" with regard to the material or problem in question are exhausted and he is unable to achieve an understanding of the material or to discover a method for solving the problem on his own. The only thing left for him to do in this situation is to select another answer mechanically, which teaches him nothing or actually develops in him the habit of not thinking or of pretending to know the answer when actually he does not.

Although it is often unnecessary in the initial responses to a mistake to diagnose its causes (relying on student's "self-organization" to enable him to cope with the material or to find the correct procedure for solving the problem), when reliance on "self-organization" proves unjustified the instructional algorithm should foresee and specify a change in control which will exert direct influence on the intermediate states. If a given mistake can have only one cause and this cause is known, then the cause is unambiguous and no diagnosis is necessary. If, however, a mistake may have any one or a combination of several causes, and the response depends on the cause, then good control requires diagnosis. The first case requires one instructional algorithm, the second another.[66]

Let us consider several conditions (not all possible ones by any means) in which the "go back to the preceding segment, read it again, and select another answer" approach is appropriate, in general, and not merely as an initial response. In order to do this we must consider the possible causes of erroneous problem solutions. We will examine only a few such possible causes.

The student may fail to solve a problem or arrive at an erroneous solution because:

1. He did not understand, or understood incorrectly the explanation given in the segement in question.

There are at least two fundamental possible causes for such a failure to understand:

  (a)   the explanation is poor, difficult, or incompatible with the student's level of preparation or development, or

  (b)   the student's attention wandered while he was reading the explanation (causing him to read a word incorrectly, to miss a word, or a punctuation mark, etc.).

2. He did not know a method for solving the problem or did not know it sufficiently well.

3. He allowed his attention to wander during his attempt to solve the problem (writing the wrong letter or sign while solving an algebraic problem, for example).

Under which conditions will sending the student back to the preceding segment have a high probability of eliminating the cause of his mistake and achieving the required instructional effect? Clearly, yes, under conditions 1b and 3. Under conditions 1a and 2, sending the student back is, in most cases, useless. The probability that repeated reading of an explanation which is poorly written, difficult to understand, or inappropriate to the student's level of development will cause him to understand it, and, moreover, learn a method not contained in this segment, is very small.[67]

How, then, are we to determine which of these conditions is present in a given instructional situation? One of the most accurate and reliable means of doing this is to diagnose during the instructional process itself, as discussed above. But it is frequently possible to make this determination earlier, on the basis of analysis of the task in question and a psychological analysis of the means by which it may be performed, or the appropriate problem-solving procedure or method, if the task is a cognitive one.[68] The following is an example of this approach.

In Paragraph 14 of the textbook on logarithms cited above, there is a discussion of base-10 logarithms—of numbers consisting of the number one followed by zeros:

Paragraph 14. Consider these equations:

$$10^1 = 10 \qquad\qquad 10^4 = 10000$$

$$10^2 = 100 \qquad\qquad 10^5 = 100000$$

$$10^3 = 1000 \qquad\qquad \text{etc.}$$

Thus, if we square the number 10 we obtain the number indicated by the number one followed by two zeros. If we cube the number 10, we obtain the number given by the number one followed by three zeros, etc., the number of zeros in the resulting number being equal to the power to which we raise the number 10.

To what power must we raise the number 10 in order to obtain 1,000,000?

Answer	see Paragraph
5	15
6	16

Turning to Paragraph 15, we read:

"Paragraph 15. Your answer was 5. It is not correct, since $10^5 = 100,000$, i.e., 10^5 gives a number which is written as the number one followed by five zeros. Recall that we wanted to obtain 1,000,000. Turn to Paragraph 14 and select the correct answer."

Was it appropriate in this case to refer the student back to the initial paragraph? Yes, as the following considerations show.

Let us attempt to determine the probable cause of the student's mistake.

Could (1) above be the cause, i.e., not understanding the explanation? This is unlikely, since the rule in question is very easy to understand.

Could (2) be the cause, i.e., not understanding the method? This is also unlikely, since the procedure is clearly described in the explanation and is in addition quite simple.

Clearly the cause of the student's mistake was (3), i.e., he simply "miscounted" the number of zeros, and in such a case, as we attempted to show above, it is appropriate to refer the student back to the preceding segment. The student has only to be more attentive in counting the number of zeros.

It should be noted, however, that mistakes due to inattentiveness, although they occur frequently, do not constitute the most difficult category of mistakes. Data from psychological experiments indicate that the basic cause of poor problem-solving (i.e., of the mistakes students make in attempting to solve problems) is the student's not knowing how to think, his ignorance of general problem-solving methods, and of general methods of thinking. But it is precisely this most important, fundamental, and typical cause of mistakes which programs based on the "go back to the preceding segment . . . ." approach fail to eliminate. It is also not dealt with in many currently employed branched programs of the Crowderian type, since these programs are constructed on the basis of consideration of only the character of the student's mistakes, not of their causes (in cases in which a given mistake may have more than one cause). These programs diagnose only the symptoms of the disease rather than the disease itself. Continuing the analogy, these programs establish that the student has a headache rather than an earache, but do not establish why his head aches, and proceed to "treat" him accordingly. A programmed text can give the student either aspirin or a medication which acts to remove the most probable cause of the ailment, but neither of these two procedures will cure the patient reliably and without fail. In the first case, the "treatment" removes only the external manifestations of the disease (the headache) without eliminating its cause, i.e., without curing the disease, and, in the second case, the treatment proceeds on the basis of guesswork, since the cause of a given student's headache may be different from the one which the physician assumes is present on the basis of statistical data.[69] All these factors account for the fact that the currently most widely used programs, which successfully control the student's external activity, exert inadequate and often poor control over the intermediate states. Effective control of the intermediate states usually requires not only that the character of the student's mistakes be known and taken into account, but that their psychological causes be known and taken into account as well, which in turn requires adaptive diagnostic programs.[70]

Are these the principal shortcomings of contemporary programmed instruction? This question must be answered in the negative.[71] As a rule, the present shortcomings of programmed instruction are the result of shortcomings in the educational theories by which the authors of many existing programmed materials were guided, and also the result of the weak preparation of these authors in the field of psychology and their lack of understanding of the fact that a good instructional algorithm (program) can be written only on the basis of an extensive knowledge of the psychological mechanisms in the processes which an instructional program must control, as well as extensive knowledge of the methods and mechanisms by which this control may be effected.

This concludes our discussion of the basic stages in the writing of an instructional algorithm (program). Lack of space prevents us from considering the principles governing selection of optimal means for implementing an algorithm with the aid of various possible teaching devices. This is a separate and important question requiring special consideration. We will conclude with a short discussion of the question of the effectiveness of programmed instruction.

9. Some Considerations Concerning the
    Effectiveness of Programmed Instruction
    The problem of the effectiveness of programmed instruction is often posed as follows: is programmed instruction more effective than ordinary instruction? It is clear from the above discussion that programmed instruction may be both more effective than ordinary instruction and less effective. The most important factor in this regard is the material which is taught with the aid of instructional programs (algorithms) and the methods by which it is taught, that is, what is put into the programs, although the

way in which the program itself is designed (step size, reinforcement frequency, etc.) is also very important. It is not surprising, therefore, that instruction which is programmed in form, but is poor from the point of view of content and method, proves significantly less effective than non-programmed instruction based on good content and methods. On the other hand, programmed instruction based on good content and good methods may be significantly more effective than non-programmed instruction based on the same content and methods, to say nothing of non-programmed instruction based on poor content and poor methods.

As we noted earlier, programmed instruction only *creates the possibility* of high effectiveness of instruction under some conditions (and these conditions are also a subject requiring separate consideration). Translation into reality of the possibility that a given instructional program will be more effective than a teacher working under normal conditions depends (1) on how this program is designed, or on the effectiveness of the instructional algorithm chosen for implementation in the program, and (2) on the teacher with whom the program is being compared. A particular teaching program may teach better than a poorly qualified, inexperienced teacher, but worse than a highly qualified and experienced one. The administrators of an educational institution are faced with the problem of deciding, on the basis of the quality of available instructional programs and the qualifications of available teaching personnel, when to use each mode of instruction. There are, however, situations in which programmed instruction (if the programs are of high quality) is *always* more effective than non-programmed instruction administered by even the most experienced teachers, and situations in which non-programmed instruction administered by teachers of sufficient experience is *always* more effective than programmed instruction. The elucidation of these situations, the determination of their attributes and characteristics, is a task for future scientific research.

10. Conclusions

Instructional theory and practice are currently undergoing considerable change. This is due not only, or even primarily as yet, to the introduction into education of new cybernetic technology, as it is to the introduction into education and psychology of new ideas and the revision of educational concepts. Everything of value which has been accumulated by education and psychology throughout their long history should be utilized in this revision, although unfortunately this is not always done.

Psychoeducational science has always faced the task of transforming education (and child rearing) from an art into a science. Never before, however, has education come so close to the rigorous formulation of many of the problems which it faces and the development of rigorous methods for solving them. It is clear that these problems will not be solved quickly, but the enormous effort and the new scientific methods now being applied to this task all over the world guarantee that they will be solved.

Notes

1. Programmed texts also fulfill a number of semi-automatic control functions, thereby permitting some degree of adaptive instruction without the direct participation of a human teacher, although they have a number of limitations as compared to teaching machines. Specifically, programmed texts may semi-automatically accommodate the flow of the instructional process to the flow of the student's assimilation of knowledge, skills, and habits, provided that the control function is fulfilled by the student himself (programmed texts "work" on the basis of self-checking on the part of the student). Teaching machines, however, can take over automatic checking functions as well.
2. The stochastic nature of instructional phenomena and processes is examined in detail, for example, in Itel'son (1964).
3. The sense in which the concept of algorithm is used in this book does not fully correspond with the mathematical concept, but the difference between them is not significant for our purposes, especially since the sense in which we use it preserves the most important features of the mathematical

concept and is applied widely in the most diverse areas of scientific investigation. (See Chapter 2 in Landa, 1974.)

4. An instructional program in the sense of implementation of an instructional algorithm should not be confused either with a program of study (in the sense of curriculum, for example, a program of studies in Russian in a secondary school) or a program or course of studies in mathematics (in college or a university).

5. There are also significant differences between chess and programmed instruction. One such difference is the fact that in chess the interests of the players are opposed, each wishing to place the other into a terminal situation (checkmate) and to avoid being placed in this position by the other, while in programmed instruction the interests of the participants are identical. They (the teacher and the student) wish to achieve the same terminal situation as quickly as possible; this situation being, as we have already noted, a particular level of assimilation by the student of the knowledge, skills, and habits which constitute the goal of the instructional process.

6. Just as there must be an objective, precise, unambiguous description of the activities (operations) to be performed by the student and by the teacher in order to attain a given set of instructional objectives, so must there be an objective, precise, unambiguous description of the subject-matter (content) at hand. Both are fundamental requirements for the possibility of effective and efficient regulation of the instructional process. Without a specification of the structure of the subject-matter content, the formulation of an unambiguous instructional algorithm becomes impossible, and, hence, effective guidance of the instructional process (toward the specified goals) becomes impossible. For a preliminary discussion of this point see Kingsley, Kopstein, and Seidel (1971), also Stelzer and Kingsley (1975). (*Editor.*)

7. The idea of differentiating types of instruction was developed by our colleague at the Programmed Instruction Laboratory of the Institute of General and Educational Psychology, L.V. Shenshev, and has been discussed frequently at meetings

there. The position that programmed instruction is automated instruction (in the United States, for example, the terms "programmed instruction" and "automated instruction" often are used synonymously) was developed by Shenshev in a paper read before the Academic Council of the Institute. It should be emphasized that automatization is not the essence of programmed instruction, but rather a means for implementing it and for improving control of the instructional process.

8. Automatization, as is well-known, is the performance of human functions by devices.

9. The diagrams which are used to describe algorithms are often termed algorithmic diagrams. Algorithmic diagrams representing the logical structure of an activity resemble structure formulae in chemistry, which represent the chemical structure of substances. Such diagrams are evidence of the rigor and precision which may now be attained in the scientific description of the structure of activity.

10. If the symbols designating logical conditions, operations, and their interrelations are regarded as the letters of an alphabet, then any given algorithmic process may be represented as a word in this alphabet.

11. We assume that the teacher makes use of this common definition.

12. Vorobev (1963) has termed this procedure the "counterform procedure."

13. We do not claim that this is the best possible program, only that it is a possible one. The purpose of this example is not to recommend a particular instructional program, but to illustrate a method for describing instructional programs in general. Such methods are important for the description of poor programs as well as good ones, since poor programs also must be analyzed scientifically.

14. All good algorithms are simultaneously flexible and inflexible: they are flexible because they prescribe different actions under different circumstances (and in this sense adapt to circumstances); they are inflexible because they always pre-

scribe the same action whenever a given set of circumstances arises.

15. This refers, of course, only to circumstances in which the teaching of algorithms is appropriate.

16. We will use this term to include programmed texts as well as teaching machines, since, relative to ordinary textbooks, programmed texts may be regarded as "devices."

17. We are concerned here only with the possibility of complete automatization of those instructional processes which can be automatized, and not with the desirability of such automatization, which is a separate question. We wish to note here that the possibility of automatization does not imply its desirability. There are many processes in various fields of human activity which could be but have not been algorithmized and automatized, since for various reasons this would be undesirable.

18. See Uspenskii (1960) for a discussion of outcomes of this sort in the functioning of algorithms.

19. In view of the fact that we are not concerned with analysis of particular programs, but rather with analysis of some common defects occurring in programs of various types, we will not cite the authors of the programmed materials from which these examples are drawn, especially since many of these programs are classified as experimental material, or have not been published. We wish to note in addition that the presence of these defects does not mean that the program as a whole is "bad."

20. This problem is discussed in Landa (1974). Some basic approaches to its solution are outlined in Landa (1962).

21. This certainly does not mean that the student should be given instructions only of an algorithmic type, i.e., that he should be taught only algorithms. In many instances it is necessary to provide instructions of a non-algorithmic type, characterized by some degree of indefiniteness and thus not fully determining the student's activity. We merely wish to say here that to term instruction of this sort algorithms only

confuses the characterization of educational and psychological phenomena.

22. The degree of automatization, i.e., the performance of a component operation as a single operation, is also important psychologically, but this requires a specific criterion of automatization, such as, for example, the time taken to perform the operation in question.

23. Adaptation to the student's level of knowledge and development is necessary in order subsequently to be able to raise this level.

24. It is easy to see that the problem of determining optimal chunk size is, in this case, a typical search problem and should, therefore, be solved by the search method.

25. We use the terms "instructional algorithm" and "teaching algorithm" as synonyms, using two terms only for stylistic reasons. The same is true of the terms "instructional program" and "teaching program."

26. The word "solution" has two meanings in this context: the process of searching for an answer and the result of this process, i.e., the answer itself. Context will make it clear which meaning is intended.

27. Another example, somewhat different from this one, but in some sense closer to the conditions which interest us, is the problem of deriving one mathematical (or logical) expression from another, in which the initial and final expressions are given from the first, the solution process consisting of the step-by-step transformation of the first expression into the second, in accordance with specific rules.

28. One of the ways in which instructional transformation algorithms differ from the transformation algorithms by which mathematical problems are solved is that transformations in mathematics always have an unambiguous result (a mathematical operation applied, for example, to a number, always transforms it into one and the same number), while most transformation operations in teaching have probabilistic results (an instructional instrumentality evokes different responses from different students and even from the same

student at different times). This means that instructional transformation algorithms must take into account the possibility of different student reactions to a given instructional instrumentality (i.e., operator, *Ed.*) and therefore that various responses to these student reactions must be foreseen in the program.

29. For the sake of brevity we will speak henceforth only of knowledge, skills, and habits. The conditions of the didactic task include also some other psychological phenomena as well as the external conditions in which instruction proceeds and which must be taken into account in the selection of instructional influences, but we will not examine these conditions here, considering them as givens.

30. All of these considerations with regard to didactic problems apply equally to problems of upbringing.

31. Many teachers operate not only on the basis of experience and intuition, trial and error, but also, one might say, on the basis of unconscious algorithms. Their solution of didactic problems has a stable and uniform, i.e., algorithmic, character, but they are unaware of the rules governing their actions (in the same way that people are often unaware of the grammatical rules governing their use of language or the logical rules governing their solution of the logical problems which they encounter in daily life). The algorithms by means of which experienced teachers solve didactic problems and the algorithmic description of the techniques which they use are of great scientific interest. The discovery of these algorithms should constitute a significant part of the scientific study of educational experience. This experience should not simply be described, but described algorithmically, since only algorithmic description exposes the regularities of the teacher's activity, i.e., the structure of his instructional procedures. Algorithmic description presents this structure in a pure form, separated from the external and often accidental form which a given procedure takes for the solution of a particular didactic problem. This is the great cognitive significance of the algorithmic description of instructional activity

and of activity in general. Description of the structure of such procedures in a pure form is the only means by which these procedures may be shifted to other situations and applied to the solution of other, analogous problems.

32. See, e.g., Ashby (1959, 1964).

33. Ashby states that in situations in which variables cannot be measured and expressed numerically, they nevertheless may be assigned numerical values having ordinal, rather than quantitative, values and which may be used as labels (Ashby, 1959). Concerning various forms of measurement in education see, e.g., Itel'son (1964).

34. In general the values of variables in this case may be rendered in the form of numerical intervals (normal temperatures, blood pressure, etc., fluctuate within specific limits both in one person as a function of time and in different people simultaneously), but for the sake of simplicity we will use specific values rather than intervals in this example.

35. These examples, of course, have no actual medical significance.

36. In educational terminology, systems of instructional influences are the component parts of instructional procedures and methods. Unfortunately, in education, instructional procedures and methods are usually not defined as systems of instructional influences leading to the solution of a given type of didactic problem, and so these concepts remain imprecise and give rise to controversy as to how they are to be interpreted (thus, for example, some educational textbooks describe more instructional methods than others; a process which one author considers to be a method is not so considered by another author, etc.).

37. An example of this would be the correctness of pronunciation of a given phoneme in a foreign language. It is difficult to measure this variable quantitatively, but it is possible to indicate a standard of pronunciation for a comparison which will always permit the teacher to determine more or less precisely whether the student has learned the correct pronunciation or not.

38. I.M. Sechenov (1953) has written: "Human mental activity is accompanied by external signs (literally, is expressed by, or by means of external signs, *Trans.*), and all people, uneducated and learned, naturalists and those concerned with the spirit, normally interpret the former by means of the latter."

39. This has nothing in common with behaviorism, since behaviorism asserts that cognitive processes either do not exist (only behavior exists) or are unknowable, leaving only behavior as a possible object of knowledge. We, however, assume the epistemological position that covert cognitive processes exist and are cognizable, but that they may be cognized only through the medium of external phenomena, i.e., behavior. There does not and cannot exist any other medium for the objective cognition of these processes. This position, it should be noted, is not specific to psychology. In all fields of knowledge the internal is known through the external, i.e., in essence through its (behavioral, *Ed.*) manifestations.

40. Many examples of a similar sort are given in Orlova (1950). We have obtained analogous data in our own experiments.

41. It is clear that for the solution of this diagnostic problem the multiple-choice technique is completely adequate.

42. The time of reaction shows, specifically, such characteristics of the mastery of the numerals (as well as the language in general) as the ability to comprehend and to reproduce language phenomena directly, i.e., without translation.

43. These numbers are arbitrary.

44. The concept of a solution to a didactic problem has three possible meanings: (1) the search for instructional techniques or procedures capable of transforming a given initial state into a given final state. This search is performed "in the mind" and so is a cognitive problem for the teacher. (2) The application of these techniques or procedures and the practical transformation of one state of the student into another. Solution in this sense is a practical problem, i.e., that of the implementation of the procedures found as a result of the cognitive search process. (3) The solution requires both the

search for instructional techniques and their use. The first two senses of the term are only stages of solution in the third sense. In the following discussion, context will make clear the sense in which we speak of the solution of a didactic problem.

45. If, for example, it is clear that the participle should be placed in the course of study after the verb, because the verb is the initial form and the participle the derivative form ("initial" and "derivative" refer to objective relations which are taken into account in the construction of a system [of a scientific logic]), then the sequence in which certain types of subordinate clause should be studied is considerably less clear; for example, should complex sentences containing subordinate clauses of purpose or those containing subordinate clauses of cause be studied first?

46. Thus, for example, if the logic of geometry is understood as the sequence in which geometric concepts are developed on the basis of some system of axioms, then there may be more than one "geometric logic" as a function of the system of axioms adopted in a given instance, that is, as a function of which propositions are considered as axioms and which as theorems.

47. The author's original comment cited the often noted difference between the logic of the investigation of some subject-matter and the logic of its exposition. The latter has been the object of experimental investigation (Pask, 1971; Pask and Scott, 1972), and of an axiomatic development (Stelzer and Kingsley, 1975). Both approaches confirm and elaborate the author's original point. (*Editor.*)

48. The teacher A.P. Sidelkovskii makes this point in his paper (Sidelkovskii, 1964).

49. The simultaneous, comparative study of different topics is discussed in Balashova (1964).

50. It would be more accurate to speak here not of the exposition of material in a rigorous logical sequence, but of its exposition in an efficient sequence, one which takes into account both logical and psychological factors.

51. The significance of organization of the student's activity is emphasized in particular by Leontiev (1945), Gal'perin (1957), and Talyzina (1960). They have developed a number of techniques for organizing this activity as regards the assimilation of concepts and certain other problems.

52. The problem given the student here is also inappropriate logically. In the sentence "In ancient times people arrived at the concept of the _____ number" the blank may be filled either with the word "natural" or one of a number of other appropriate words, for example, "negative," or with no word at all, since in ancient times people arrived not only at the concept of the natural numbers, but at the concept of number *per se*. This absence of logic and precision and the consequent multiplicity of correct solutions are yet another indication of the fact that this problem encourages purely mechanical, unthinking activity in the student. The word "natural" is the correct one only because it was used in the preceding segment. Other, more serious and profound reasons for choosing this word are lacking. Its selection is not determined by any logic, or by any thinking or reasoning process.

53. Discussion of this question in the literature has already been noted. See, for example, Mashbits and Bondarovskaya (1964).

54. See, for example, El'konin (1962).

55. A correct answer does not imply of necessity the complete and correct assimilation of the required activity. There are many instances in which a correct answer may be arrived at by incorrect means, and in such cases a correct answer is harmful rather than helpful, since it conceals defects in the student's understanding of the corresponding concepts and actions, creating the appearance of proper assimilation of the material where it does not exist. This situation, however, is not only harmful because the teacher receives the wrong feedback information, but also because incorrect concepts and cognitive procedures are positively reinforced. Thus, a correct answer frequently proves nothing, or rather it may indicate either correct assimilation of the concepts and opera-

tions in question, or incorrect assimilation of them. It is, therefore, often necessary to control not only the student's answer, but also the means by which he arrives at it.

56. Many instructional procedures possess undesirable as well as useful properties, and exert negative psychological effects as well as positive ones. In such cases the positive and negative features must be compared in order to determine which predominates.

57. A student, of course, is also a self-controlled and self-organizing system, and the development of these properties is one of the most important tasks of education and upbringing. The student must be guided in such a way that he eventually ceases to need guidance and is able to operate independently. But the development of self-control must itself be controlled, and in this sense the student (i.e., so long as the individual remains in a student status, *Ed.*) may be regarded as a controlled system.

58. This idea may be expressed somewhat differently by saying that the major goal of instruction is not to teach the student a set of answers to a set of problems, but to teach him to arrive at these answers on his own, or rather to arrive at the answer to any problem (of the given type, *Ed.*) which he may encounter.

59. Skinner's approach is entirely suited, generally speaking, to teaching the ability to solve problems of this sort.

60. This does not mean that Crowder in general responds incorrectly to mistakes (his textbooks are interestingly and ably written). The issue here is the scientific, theoretical principles of responding to mistakes, which Crowder has not clearly formulated.

61. Sometimes the student is not referred to the preceding chunk of information, but is simply asked to select another answer. In this case the arrows associated with the incorrect answers in Figure 10.6 go to the upper half of the middle box. For an example of such a diagram, see Ivanov (1964).

62. Even if it is assumed that the student solved the problem incorrectly because he did not understand the definition of

the logarithm, it would nevertheless be naive to suppose that, having failed to understand a relatively easy definition, perhaps even after a second reading, he will succeed in understanding it by reading it four times, although in principle some things may have to be read four times before they are understood.

63. Some critics of programmed instruction both abroad and in the Soviet Union believe that the inability to develop cognitive abilities is a fundamental shortcoming of programmed instruction. This shortcoming is not a fundamental characteristic of programmed instruction, however, only of existing programmed texts and methods for writing programs.

64. Many examples could be cited of a correct answer being obtainable by incorrect means. We gave one such example in the course of our discussion of the machine for teaching reading. Here are two more examples. (1) Commas in a written sentence (in Russian, *Ed.*) frequently correspond with the intonation of the spoken form of the sentence. In such cases it is possible to place punctuation marks correctly on the basis of an incorrect method, namely by using intonation. Many students do this. (2) Students frequently identify the subject of a sentence by looking for words which answer the question "what?"; this may be done because such words are indeed frequently the subject of the sentence in which they appear. However, they are not by any means always the subject, and so when the student successfully uses this method he is correctly identifying the subject by means of an incorrect method.

65. This is analogous to the following situation. A person who has a poor sense of direction is trying to reach some place and at some point in his search is told that his present location is not his destination. The local inhabitants are able to explain how his present "erroneous" location differs from the "correct" location and prove that the former is indeed not his destination. But will their doing this cause the person in question to acquire a good sense of direction, i.e., will it teach him a method by which he will always arrive at the

"correct" location? It is clear that it will not teach him this ability directly, although it will help him to learn it on his own *by trial and error*. But *how* and *what* he will learn is not controlled by this mode of teaching. It also cannot guarantee that the individual in question will discover independently and teach himself a correct, let alone an efficient, procedure. The time required by this approach is another disadvantage.

66. In articles and scientific conferences the question of the advantages of a given system of programming (for example, linear or branched), or of a given type of response (for example, constructed or multiple-choice), or of procedures for writing programs, is often posed in an abstract way. Yet a given system of programming, type of response, procedure, etc., may be appropriate under some conditions and inappropriate under others. The problem is to define precisely the conditions in which a given system or procedure is adequate and expedient.

67. There are at least two other situations in which referral back to the preceding segmment for the purpose of correcting a mistake is appropriate: (1) when the student's task is simply to memorize something but he fails to remember the material or remembers it incorrectly; and (2) when the teacher's task (the didactic problem) is to teach the student to "learn from his mistakes" (it is important to teach this ability as well). However, in order to solve this didactic problem it is not sufficient simply to send the student back to the preceding segment. He must be taught to extract information from his mistakes, to analyze his procedure and the possible causes of his mistake, and appropriate responses must be provided in case he is unable to do this on his own after having his mistake pointed out to him and being referred back to the preceding segment.

68. The solution to this problem will almost always be probabilistic in nature; it is possible to determine which condition obtains only to some degree of probability. Instruction, however, is a field in which the solutions to many problems are probabilistic in nature, since it is almost never possible to

take into account all of the causes and conditions which can give rise to a given instructional phenomenon.

69. Let us assume, for example, that a given symptom (headache, to use our example) can have one of four causes: A, B, C, and D. Let us assume further that statistical data have shown that A is the cause of 30 percent of all headaches, that B is the cause of 25 percent, that C is the cause of 22 percent, and that D is the cause of 20 percent. If the physician treats without diagnosis and administers a medication which acts on the most probable cause (i.e., cause A), he will have only a 30 percent chance of being right.

70. Such programs are being written both abroad and in the Soviet Union. Specifically, at the Programmed Instruction Laboratory of the Institute of General and Educational Psychology, we, together with G.N. Protasova, have written part of a program of this type to teach a portion of the sixth grade English course. This program takes into account not only the nature of the student's mistakes, but also their causes; it does this by means of diagnostic tests. The programmed text based on this program is not only a teaching device, but a unique diagnostic device as well.

71. Many opponents of programmed instruction who criticize this approach and note its shortcomings (and this criticism is frequently justified) assume that these shortcomings are inherent in programmed instruction. As a rule, however, they are inherent only in some contemporary forms of programmed instruction, in some specific programmed materials written by some authors operating on the basis of certain theories and ideas about teaching and learning. The particular shortcomings of some programmed materials and teaching machines prevent these critics from seeing the fundamental possibilities and prospects of this approach.

Chapter Eleven

Diagnostics and
Programmed Instruction

Designing Adaptive Teaching
Programs and Raising the Effectiveness of
Programmed Instruction

It is often stated that instructional programs should be directed toward the establishment of specific terminal behavior in the student, and that this behavior should be precisely defined and should direct the instructional process. In its general form this idea is, of course, correct, depending on how "terminal behavior" is defined. For example, the problem of teaching someone to press certain buttons in response to the coming on of indicator lights on a panel (a problem arising in the training of operators of complex machinery), or of teaching someone to type, or to associate a word in a foreign language with a particular object, implies a definition of terminal behavior which consists of specifying a set of *sufficiently** elementary external responses to specific *sufficiently* elementary stimuli, the relation between them being direct, *one-link* associations. It must be defined differently, however, if the problem is to teach someone to solve complex problems, to say nothing of problems requiring creative solutions. In this case to define terminal behavior by saying that it should consist of specific solution-responses to specific problem-stimuli is, in essence, to say nothing at all. In teaching problem-solving of this sort we must teach, generally speaking, not *external* responses (operations) involving presentation of solutions (it is not difficult for a person who knows how to read and write to communicate his solution to a problem), but rather *internal* processes, *internal*

---

*Sufficient, that is, for each student in a defined population to respond as specified, when the specified stimulus is presented. (*Editor.*)

operations for transforming information (problem-stimuli) into solutions (answers), since in these cases there is, as a rule, no direct, *one-link* association between the initial information (stimuli) and the final responses (answers), and there may exist dozens or even hundreds of ways of going from one to the other. It is often impossible in the instructional process to elaborate a single, predetermined chain of associations which will guarantee the transition from stimulus to response. In short, it is impossible to teach the ability to solve complex problems by teaching a series of specific transitions from the conditions of a concrete problem to its specific solution, although this is often attempted in practice (for example, students are required to learn specific proofs of particular theorems instead of being taught general methods of reasoning applicable to the proof of any theorem).

What should be the subject-matter of instruction aimed at developing the ability to solve problems of this sort, and what should be the terminal behavior that it is designed to establish? It is clear that the subject-matter and terminal behavior of instruction of this sort will be completely different from that involved in the first case. It will not consist of direct associations between stimuli at the "input" and responses at the "output," but rather of the internal processes which mediate between "input" and "output," i.e., the "intermediate states." Of course, the operations involved in the internal processes may also be termed behavioral acts, and the processes themselves may be termed internal behavior. The term "terminal behavior" may therefore be applied not only to external responses, to external behavioral acts, but also to internal processes, internal mediating behavioral acts; in this case, however, it is clear that the description of terminal behavior understood as internal cognitive processes is different from the description of terminal behavior as a collection of terminal external responses (behavioral acts) to specific stimuli-problems. These are different, though related, things—different "terminal behaviors."[1]

From the above it follows that, in writing programs, it is very important that the author clarify what he wishes to achieve as a result of instruction, i.e., that he specify the desired terminal behavior in whatever sense it interests him. Does he define terminal behavior only in terms of how a person should act in particular situations, or does he include a specification of how he should think or reason in order to select the appropriate operations, i.e., of the internal behavior, the cognitive processes, which should lead to the appropriate external actions? On these considerations depend not only the characteristics (i.e., attributes, *Ed.*) by means of which terminal behavior will be described, but also, to a significant degree, the instructional methodology by means of which the terminal behavior will be achieved.

We assume that, if those situations are to be considered as typical, major, and general they are not those in which there is a direct, one-link association between stimulus and response (such as responding to the lighting of a light, typing, or verbal responses in a foreign language to specific objects), but are, rather, those situations in which there is extended mediation between stimulus and response involving dozens or hundreds of internal, cognitive (as we will henceforth term them) operations,[2] then the goal of instruction (terminal behavior) should consist not only of specification of external responses to particular stimulus-problems, but also specification of the cognitive processes and their properties and internal mechanisms, which mediate the association between stimulus and response. In order to devise an effective teaching procedure, therefore, it is insufficient to know how the student should behave in specific situations; it is necessary to know precisely which psychological mechanisms ensure this behavior, give rise to it, and, consequently, which psychological mechanisms should be developed through instruction, if we assume, as we do, that the development of these mechanisms is the most important objective of instruction. This requires, however, that these mechanisms first be discovered, that the structure of the "intermediate states" be elucidated, and that precise methods for describing and controlling it be developed.

In other words, before proceeding to write an instructional program, it is necessary to have a precise knowledge of the structure of the internal cognitive processes which must be developed during instruction and to describe these processes in the form of a model of how the student is to reason in solving problems or of the cognitive operations he should perform, etc.[3] This model should serve as a pattern of the processes which are to be developed in the student's mind during instruction. If, for example, the student is to be taught *how* to think in order to solve problems of a particular class, the teacher must possess a model which is accurate enough to specify how the student's thinking processes should proceed in solving these problems, how he should reason, which cognitive operations he should perform, etc.

The design of a model of the student's internal cognitive activity which is accurate and which satisfies specific requirements, is particularly important because it is possible, of course, to produce a given pattern of external behavior in the student by various means, through the development of various internal psychological mechanisms, although these mechanisms will not be of identical effectiveness or value from the point of view of the student's further education and general development.

Examples may be found everywhere. Thus, the correct solution to a problem might be achieved not as a result of rigorous reasoning (when this is possible), but rather as the result of a fortunate blind guess, or by relying on a purely external analogy, etc. It is possible to answer questions correctly, and thus produce the required behavior, without having any understanding at all of why the answers are correct (by rote learning, reasoning stereotypes, etc.). It is, therefore, far from a matter of indifference, in the organization of the instructional process, how the student proceeds to the correct external response, which internal psychological processes he uses to achieve the correct answer or the desired behavior in general. Moreover, failure to solve a problem or making a mistake (i.e., incorrect external behavior), provided that the student is proceeding, in general, in the correct way, is often more useful than a correct solution of the problem, achieved by means of an incorrect or inefficient internal procedure, for example, as the result of a blind guess. It should be noted in this regard that the characteristics of the *procedure* used to solve a problem (how the student reasoned) are often more important in teaching than the *outcomes* of this procedure (whether or not he got the right answer).[4] Stated in a more general form: in instruction, as in life, it is often not actions themselves which are important, so much as that which evokes these actions or how they are produced, i.e., the process leading to them. The teacher's (and the programmer's) attention should be focused, therefore, not simply on creating, evoking, and reinforcing a particular behavior (for example, correct answers), but on developing processes (mechanisms) which are sufficiently general and effective to guarantee the production of this behavior.

The question arises as to the degree to which contemporary programmed instruction takes the above considerations into account. The answer to this question must be, unfortunately, that it frequently fails to take them into account. In controlling the "inputs" and "outputs" of the controlled system—the student— and in evoking in him the required external behavior, program authors do not always consider the internal psychological (cognitive) mechanisms which are *developed* by the behavioral control methods which they apply and do not always pose the question as to whether the psychological mechanisms which are shaped in this way will be capable in the future of guaranteeing a high level of *independent and creative* activity under various conditions. In addition, analysis of instruction by standard methods as well as instruction based on programmed textbooks and teaching machines shows that, in achieving the desired external behavior on the part of the student, instructors unwittingly often not only fail to develop the correct internal psychological mechanisms, but in many instances even develop incorrect or ineffective mechanisms, the negative aspects of which remain hidden and reveal themselves only later by giving rise to difficulties when the student tries to assimilate knowledge, skills, and habits.

Let us consider an example from standard teaching procedure which bears a direct relation to the manner in which some teaching programs for elementary schools and higher educational institutions are designed.[5]

The student is given the following geometric problem of proof.

"Chord AD is drawn in a circle centered at O. A straight line

Figure 11.1

Geometric Problem of Proof

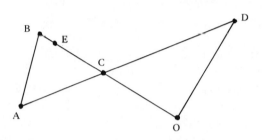

connects points D and O. Radius OE, at right angles to OD, is extended until it intersects, at point B, a line tangent to the circle at point A. Prove that AB = BC."

The student tries every approach he can think of and draws all possible supplementary constructions, but cannot find the solution. Then the teacher begins to question him, intending to put him on the right path and to teach him how to solve problems in general.

Teacher: What figure are segments AB and BC part of?

Student: Triangle ABC.

Teacher: Under what conditions are AB and BC in triangle ABC equal?

Student: If the triangle is an isosceles triangle.

Teacher: And what must be established in order to prove that the triangle is isosceles?

Student: That angle BAC is equal to angle BCA.

Teacher: How can we prove the equality of these angles?

Student: (silence)

Teacher: Look, can't we use the theorem which says that two quantities are equal if they are both equal to a third quantity? What would we have to prove in order to show this?

Student: That angle BAC is equal to angle DCO. . .

Thus, step by step, in answering the teacher's questions, the student solves the problem.

Let us suppose that, a little later on, the student is unable to solve another problem (see Figure 11.2):

"Prove that if the centers of the sides of any tetragon are sequentially connected, the resulting figure is a parallelogram."

The teacher again interrupts the student's work and begins to ask him questions with the same purpose as before—to help him solve the problem and learn how to solve problems in general.

Teacher: To prove that tetragon EFGH is a parallelogram, what properties must segments EF and HG and segments EH and FG possess?

Figure 11.2

A Second Geometric Problem of Proof

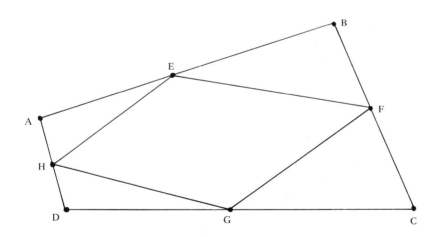

Student: They should be parallel.

Teacher: Can't we use the theorem: "two straight lines are parallel if they are each parallel to a third straight line"?

Student: No, there is no such straight line here.

Teacher: But can't we construct one?

Student: Yes. . . .

Once again, in answering the teacher's questions and using a supplementary construction—segment AC—the student solves the problem.

At first glance it seems that the teacher has succeeded in achieving his goal. He has managed to get the student to solve the problems; he has evoked the required terminal behavior. In using his questions to direct the student's thinking along the right channel, he showed him how to reason, to think, during the process of solving a problem. But this is true only at first glance. In actual fact, this sort of instruction does not teach general problem-solving ability, since it does not develop in the student (at least not directly) the internal psychological mechanisms which underlie the ability to think independently.

That this is the case can easily be shown as follows. First, we list the questions which the teacher asked the student in our first example (see Figure 11.1):

What figure are segments AB and BC part of?

Under what conditions are the sides AB and BC of triangle ABC equal?

What must be established in order to prove that triangle ABC is isosceles?

How can the equality of these angles (BAC and BCA) be proved?

Can't we use the theorem which says that two quantities are equal if they are each equal to a third quantity?

Now let us list the questions which the teacher asked the student in our second example (see Figure 11.2):

What properties must segments EF and HG and EH and FG possess?

Can't we use the theorem which says that two straight lines are parallel if they are each parallel to a third straight line?

Can't we construct such a straight line?

We see, in comparing these two sets of questions, that they are not equivalent. In one case the search for a solution begins with the question: "What figure are segments AB and BC part of?," while in the other case it begins, "What properties should segments EF and HG and segments EH and FG possess?" In the first instance the second question was, "Under what conditions are sides AB and BC of triangle ABC equal?," while in the second instance it was, "How can we prove the equality of angles BAC and BCA?," etc.

What is the correct way to reason in solving problems? What questions should one ask oneself? Why, in one instance, does the attempt to solve a problem begin with question *a*, and in another instance with question *b*? Why, in one case, do the questions follow one another in sequence *A*, and in another case in sequence *B*? These are the things that the student fails to understand clearly. He does not see and is unable to see any regularity (constancy, *Ed.*) in the formulation of questions or any general method of approaching the problem. When he encounters a third, new problem, he will not know what to do, what questions to ask (himself), and which aspects of the given information to pay attention to, since he did not know these things when he tried to solve the first two problems.

It would seem that the instructional method used by the teacher in our example proved to be ineffective and useless to the student because, in leading him to the solutions of the above two specific problems, it failed to teach him how to approach problems in general. But to say that this method was simply of no use is not enough. It actually did harm. This harm lies in the fact that, as a result of this instruction, the student formed the opinion (and possibly the conviction) that there exist no regularities in the process of searching for the solution to problems, that everything depends on lucky random trials (lucky random questions, construction, etc.) and that the essence of problem-solving is random trials of this sort. A study which we performed a number of years ago (see Chapter Nine of this volume) showed that this is the case and that a rather large proportion of students solve problems by the method of random and even blind trials, often simply trying to guess the solution.[6]

Analysis of a number of contemporary programmed textbooks shows that they utilize precisely this sort of instructional technique. "Helping" the student permits him to answer a given particular question or solve a given particular problem (i.e., evokes, in each particular case, the correct behavior), but does not teach him how to solve problems in general and does not develop the ability to think *per se*. This is due to the fact that such aid is not based on a clear conception of the psychological mechanisms which underlie the ability to think about problems and which ensure that the student will solve them independently. In designing instructional programs, authors often do not design a preliminary model of the psychological process which they should develop in the student—they do not determine the structure of the psychological mechanisms which ensure independent problem solution and which must be "assembled in the student's head" during the instructional process.

From all that has been said above concerning the structure of the cognitive processes which are to be developed and the design of models of them in order to permit the writing of effective teaching programs, it is clear that there is a need in education generally and in programmed instruction in particular for diagnostics. Only diagnostics can provide a solid foundation for adaptive teaching and adaptive instructional programs.

Control of the learning process in the present state of programmed instruction is based, in most instances, on the final outcome of the student's activity (whether he correctly solved a given problem or the nature of his mistake). As was emphasized above, however, different processes can lead to this outcome, and instructional programs fail to discriminate between these processes. The program knows how the student *answered*, but does not know how he *thought* while he was looking for the answer, how he reasoned, which processes took place "in his mind" and led him to the answer. It is precisely these processes, as we have said, that are the most important factor in instruction. If it does not know how the student thought, or how he reasoned, a program cannot define an effective or at least an efficient means of responding to the student's answers and actions. After all, the important factor in this regard is not to correct each individual mistake, but to eliminate its psychological cause and at the same time to lower the probability that such mistakes will recur.

A simple example from the area of native (i.e., Russian, *Ed.*) language instruction will illustrate what has been said above regarding the impossibility of precisely defining an adequate means of responding to the student's errors without diagnosis of their psychological causes.

Let us assume that a student is given the problem of punctuating several sentences, such as: "The river-bank was overgrown with grass thick and rich"; "Exhausted she could not go on"; "Snow which does not melt even during the warmest summers covers the high peaks"; but that he is unable to solve some of these grammatical problems and makes a number of mistakes. How should the teacher respond to these mistakes? How should the relevant sections of an instructional program be structured?

These questions cannot be answered until the psychological causes of these errors have been discovered (diagnosed), i.e., until it is known what did not "click" (or "clicked" incorrectly) in the student's head. But in order to understand the malfunctioning of a mechanism, its working principles—the elements of which it is composed and their structure, i.e., how they are interconnected and how they interact—must be known first. Discovery of the principles by which this psychological mechanism functions constitutes the design of a model; without such a model it is impossible to know how the mechanism might malfunction, which, in turn, would make it impossible to recognize defects when they occur.

Analysis of grammatical rules and of how people who write correctly proceed permits us to form a rather clear conception of what should occur in the head of a person in order for him to write sentences of a particular type (in our case, sentences with inflected modifiers*) correctly. He must isolate certain specific attributes

---

*Most modifiers in Russian agree with the word modified in gender, number, and case. (*Translator.*)

which these sentences possess, determine their logical structure (the logical connective by means of which they are associated), and then, as a function of the presence or absence of relevant attributes, insert punctuation marks. When this skill is developed to a higher degree, the isolation of attributes and determination of their logical structure occurs automatically, without conscious recognition of the attributes and without conscious awareness of the operations by means of which they are recognized; these operations are nevertheless performed.

The attributes in question and their logical structure are given by grammatical rules, which may be expressed in the implicative form: "if. . ., then. . .;" for example: "If an inflected modifier modifies a noun, and is dual or extended, and comes after the modified word, then this modifier is set off by commas;" "if an inflected modifier modifies a pronoun, then this modifier is set off by commas;" "if an inflected modifier modifies a noun, and is not purely attributive in meaning, then this modifier is set off by commas;" "if an inflected modifier modifies a noun, and is purely attributive in meaning, and consists of only one word, then this modifier is not set off by commas," etc.

Let us denote these expressions as follows:

an inflected modifier modifies a pronoun $-a$	an inflected modifier does not modify a pronoun, i.e., modifies a noun* $-\overline{a}$**
an inflected modifier has purely attributive meaning $-b$	an inflected modifier does not have purely attributive meaning $-\overline{b}$
an inflected modifier consists of only one word $-c$	an inflected modifier does not consist of only one word, i.e., is dual or extended $-\overline{c}$

*Other parts of speech may function as nouns.

**A line above a symbol indicates negation of the proposition represented by that symbol.

an inflected modifier comes after the word being modified −d	an inflected modifier does not come after the word being modified, i.e., comes before it $-\overline{d}$

We may now write the rules for isolating inflected modifiers in the language of mathematical logic, denoting, in accordance with its conventions, the possession of an attribute a by object x by means of the expression $a(x)$, the logical connective "and" by the symbol &, the logical connective "or" by the symbol V, and association of the "if-then" type (the logical connective "if... then,...") by the symbol →. The expression "The inflected modifier is set off by commas" we represent by the symbol $A(x)$.

We may now write the rules for setting off inflected modifiers by commas as follows:

1) $\overline{a(x)}$ & $\overline{c(x)}$ & $d(x) \to A(x);$*
2) $a(x) \to A(x);$
3) $\overline{a(x)}$ & $\overline{b(x)} \to A(x);$
4) $\overline{a(x)}$ & $b(x)$ & $c(x) \to A(x).$

The rules for not setting off inflected modifiers by commas may be derived from these.

It is easily seen that rules specifying the conditions under which inflected modifiers are or are not set off by commas do not simultaneously specify an efficient system of operations for testing for these conditions, i.e., for punctuating a sentence. In other words, rules which specify the attributes which must be present for a modifier to be set off by commas do not specify the process by means of which these attributes are to be recognized for the purpose of solving the grammatical problem in question. The rules themselves do not clarify the structure (mechanism) of the psychological process, the means of solving the problem, or the system of operations by means of which one may efficiently

---

*$\overline{a(x)}$ means that attribute a is not possessed by object x; similarly for $\overline{b(x)}$, $c(x)$, etc. (*Editor.*)

determine whether a modifier is to be set off by commas in a given sentence or not.

This structure (mechanism) may be discovered through analysis of rules and some other factors, and described in the form of an algorithm which constitutes a model of the process which must occur in a person's head if he is to accurately place punctuation marks in a sentence.

Here is the algorithm.

Algorithm

1. Having located an inflected modifier, find the word being modified and see if it is

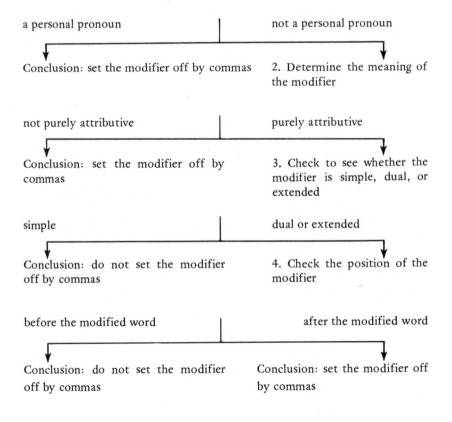

a personal pronoun | not a personal pronoun

Conclusion: set the modifier off by commas

2. Determine the meaning of the modifier

not purely attributive | purely attributive

Conclusion: set the modifier off by commas

3. Check to see whether the modifier is simple, dual, or extended

simple | dual or extended

Conclusion: do not set the modifier off by commas

4. Check the position of the modifier

before the modified word | after the modified word

Conclusion: do not set the modifier off by commas

Conclusion: set the modifier off by commas

After the structure (mechanism) of the problem-solving process has been established and a model of it has been designed, it becomes possible to find truly adequate means of responding to the student's mistakes on the basis of a diagnosis of their psychological causes and thereby to bring about truly adaptive instruction.

If the student makes a mistake because he does not know the appropriate grammatical rules, then one response is required (to teach him the rules); if he knows the rules but does not know the procedural algorithm or is not good at using it, then a different response is called for (the development of the appropriate cognitive operations). In this case, the student's mistake may be due to the fact that he failed to perform (or performed incorrectly) the first operation in the left branch of the algorithm, or the first operation in the right branch, or the second operation in the right branch, or the first and second operations in the right branch, or the third operation in the right branch, or the first and third operations of the right branch, etc. It is clear that even in this not very complex example there may be several dozen sources of error. Any way of responding to a mistake which is not based on a preceding diagnosis of its psychological cause is liable to prove to be either inadequate or inefficient.

Thus, suppose the student habitually makes mistakes, because he does not know or does not perform operation No. 3 in the right branch of the algorithm. If the program responds to his mistake without preceding diagnosis of its psychological causes, it may well happen that it will direct its response not toward that section of the algorithm which is the source of the mistake, but toward a different one (for example, operation No. 4) and will then—to use an analogy with medicine—treat the patient for influenza when in fact a bacterial infection of the blood was the real cause of his symptoms. Another means of responding to a mistake without establishing a diagnosis is to begin anew and teach *all* the operations, the entire algorithm, again. This procedure would probably remove the cause of the student's error, but would be similar—continuing the analogy with medicine—to a physician's observing a symptom in a patient and, knowing that it might be caused by any one of 10 diseases, treating him for all 10 simultaneously instead of trying to determine which of the 10 he actually has. By this means the physician would succeed, of course, in curing the patient, but could such a procedure be considered efficient?

Analysis of instruction in both secondary schools and universities shows that one of its most serious shortcomings is the fact that it is, as a rule, non-diagnostic. The means used for influencing the student during instruction are very seldom based on precise knowledge of the psychological causes of the difficulties in assimilation of knowledge and problem-solving which the student experiences, i.e., on a preliminary determination of the processes and operations which were not performed or performed incorrectly. In the absence of this knowledge it is possible to influence the student only blindly and haphazardly, often treating him for one disease when in fact he is suffering from a quite different one. This explains why many unsuccessful students so often fail over a long period of time to "get on their feet," in spite of the supplementary individual instruction which they receive. (It is to be noted in this regard that individualization of instruction does not in itself guarantee success, since individualized instruction may also be non-diagnostic.)

We tested these ideas regarding the significance of diagnostics in making education more effective in a series of experimental studies as noted earlier in this book. These experiments involved the teaching of mathematics, more specifically, the solving of problems in geometric proof, to secondary-school students. The subjects of this experiment were students in grades 7-9 who had a good knowledge of all relevant formal propositions (definitions, rules, theorems, etc.), who were highly motivated and studied hard, but who were unable to solve problems because, according to their teachers, they "reasoned poorly" or "didn't know how to think." Remedial work with some of these students carried out by the teachers over a period of one to two years failed to have any noticeable effect; the students continued to be poor at solving problems.

By studying how skillful problem-solvers, both children and

adults (including mathematicians) go about solving problems, we designed a model of the cognitive activity involved in proving geometric theorems, i.e., we isolated the basic operations which one must carry out in order to arrive at such a proof, and determined some of the structures by means of which they are related. (We note that this model was not an algorithm, but heuristic in character, in that it did not guarantee that a proof would be obtained through its use; however, since the operations included in the model were, for the students involved in the experiment, either sufficiently elementary to begin with or were taught to them during the course of the experiment, use of this model was in most cases sufficient to arrive at the required proof.) The model describing how to search for a proof was formulated as a procedure (set of instructions, system of rules) which specified what to do with the conditions (givens) and requirements of the problem, i.e., which operations to perform (and, in some cases, the order in which they were to be performed), in order to solve the problem. In other words, the procedure gave instructions regarding *how to think* while solving the problem or *how to reason* in order to arrive at the required proof. This model (procedure) constituted a representation of the mechanism which had to be developed "in the student's head" if his attempt to prove the theorem was to be successful.[7]

After we had designed the model describing what should happen in the head of a person if he is successfully to prove a theorem, we analyzed what was actually occurring in the heads of the students in whom we were interested, i.e., those who were unable to think properly, or to reason, in solving problems. We carried out a special diagnostic experiment the purpose of which was to discover which of the required operations the students were not performing or were performing poorly, that is, to discover what was not "clicking" in their cognitive mechanisms. It proved to be the case that the psychological causes of the inability to solve problems *differed from student to student*.

As soon as the diagnosis was made it became clear precisely what was required in each student's case, what the defects were in his cognitive apparatus which had to be eliminated. A short course of differentiated instruction on the basis of this diagnosis permitted us to correct these defects. (We note in this regard that the question here is not one of eliminating gaps in knowledge [ideas, concepts] [8] which Lewis [1963] for example, emphasizes, and which is, of course, also necessary and of great significance, but of eliminating defects in the actual mechanisms of cognitive activity, in cognitive operations and their structure.) A short course (two to three weeks) of therapeutic instruction on the basis of the sources of difficulty established during the diagnostic process was sufficient to get students "on their feet" who had been "persistent" failures in geometry and who had been considered lacking in ability. It became understandable why supplementary individual instruction over a period of one to two years had not had any noticeable effect. The teachers did not know the psychological causes of the students' difficulties and had not directed their instruction toward the elimination of these causes; they did not know from what "disease" the students were suffering and, therefore, did not know what to treat so that they could be "cured."

If we pose the question as to whether contemporary programmed instruction is diagnostic, then we must answer, on the whole, in the negative. In the overwhelming majority of cases it is not diagnostic. In formulating the problem of how, in programmed instruction, to simulate the interaction between a teacher and an individual student as fully and flexibly as possible, most program authors take as their model the sort of procedures which involve a simple drilling of the student, i.e., they simulate non-diagnostic instruction. One of the most serious shortcomings of traditional instruction is thereby carried over into programmed instruction.

In fact, reactions to the student's responses in a linear program, as has often been noted in the literature, do not depend on the character of these responses, and certainly not on their psychological causes. Instrinsically programmed, branched programs do react as a function of the character of the student's responses (the program reacts differently to different responses), but do not, in general, depend on the psychological causes of the response. Such a program reacts differently to different symptoms (to a headache in one way, to a chest pain in another way), but also reacts in the same way to similar symptoms. Yet it is clear, that, in general, it is necessary to react to identical symptoms in different ways, since such symptoms may have different causes and may indicate different diseases. Of course, this is not the case in those instances in which a response (a mistake, for example) may have only one cause (i.e., in which there exists a unique, *one-to-one* relation between the mistake and its psychological cause), but such instances arise only in relatively elementary instructional situations in which the student is solving relatively simple problems and are, therefore, exceptional. In general, solving a problem requires execution of a multistage process, the performance of a series of cognitive operations, and in such cases mistakes usually indicate nothing regarding their psychological cause (or causes). We note that intrinsic programming attempts to overcome the difficulties which arise with this method by directing the student, when necessary, through several branches: from an initial frame the student, upon choosing an incorrect answer, is directed to page *a*, then, if he answers incorrectly again, to page *b*, then, in case of a third wrong answer, to page *c*, etc., until he has selected all possible incorrect answers and finally chooses the correct one. (In principle, this technique permits him to choose the correct answer without having understood why it is correct, and, moreover, without having learned to reason properly.) Instruction of this sort is like medical treatment in which the doctor, having observed the symptoms of the disease without having made a diagnosis, tries every drug he can think of, one after the other: if the first does not help, he tries the second; if that fails, he tries the third, etc. Of course he may, in utilizing this procedure, find the right drug. It is clear, however, that this method of treatment is not, in general, the most reliable or the most efficient. Of course, with branched programs the "drugs" are not tried on a purely random basis, but on the basis of probable sources of error;[9] to the extent that errors may have more than one possible cause, however, the probability that a program's responses will be adequate will be lower the more possible causes there are.

So-called extrinsic programming opens significantly greater possibilities in this regard, in that the character of the program's reactions to the student's responses (in particular, to his mistakes) is determined not simply by his most recent response, but by several of his previous responses. It should be noted, however, that by itself the fact of taking into account previous responses in reacting to a mistake or in determining the strategy of subsequent instruction does not make such instruction diagnostic. It is possible to pose questions (problems) to the student and assess his responses to them (for example, mistakes) in such a way that these questions and responses will not permit any conclusions regarding the psychological causes of his mistakes or any diagnosis with regard to his cognitive activity. Consequently, extrinsic programming, like intrinsic programming, creates only the possibility of diagnostic instruction. Whether this possibility is realized depends, first, on the degree to which the structures of the relevant types of cognitive (in particular, conceptual) learning and problem-solving activity have been correctly identified; second, on the correctness of the models of these forms of cognitive activity which have been constructed on the basis of these structures; third, on the effectiveness of attempts to develop methods for penetrating into the internal structure (mechanisms) of these types of activity (i.e., methods of psycho-educational diagnostics); and, finally, the degree to which these methods can be put into practice in programmed instruction, i.e., the degree to which they can be integrated or are in fact integrated into teaching programs.

It is true that current instructional programs include programs for observing the student (in studies carried out via teaching machines, especially computers, much information concerning the number of student mistakes, the character of these mistakes, the time which students need to answer a question, the number of requests for aid, diagrams of students' paths through the program, etc., is being accumulated), but all of this diverse and in many ways valuable information, such as information regarding the student's responses to the last few preceding frames, does not, in itself, permit diagnosis of the psychological causes of the student's mistakes, if the conditions indicated above are not fulfilled and if observation of the student is not directed specifically toward diagnosis of these psychological causes, which would require that special *diagnostic* programs be included in the *instructional* program.

It should be noted that the problem of diagnostics is not a new one in psychology and education. The entire science of testing is, in essence, a science of diagnostics, but the diagnostics we are speaking of is a quite specific type of diagnostics as compared with the diagnostics in the sense of visual testing. Classical psychometrics is concerned primarily with the construction of tests for identifying and measuring knowledges, skills, and habits on the one hand (achievement tests), and intellectual development and abilities on the other (intelligence and ability tests).

In noting the importance in programmed instruction, of determining the nature and level of the student's knowledge, skills, and habits, as well as his cognitive development (although serious objections could be raised to the methods of testing cognitive abilities utilized in a number of countries), it should be emphasized that the diagnostics discussed here does not involve measurement of cognitive processes, but rather identification of the composition and structure of mechanisms by which these processes operate, especially disturbances in these mechanisms. Such diagnostics may be termed *structural*. The diagnosis made on the basis of such a diagnostics is similar to diagnosis in medicine, in which the causes and mechanisms of specific pathological disturbances in the organism* are determined, or to diagnosis involving troubleshooting in complex electronic systems. It involves a search for defects in the mechanisms of the student's intellectual activity (it might be termed a search for psychological defects or "psychological troubleshooting"), but it is not limited to defects. In solving problems the student may reason correctly, but inefficiently: he may arrive at the right answer by a less than

---

*Although in the case of instruction it is not a question of pathological disturbances, but of incomplete or improper development of normally occurring processes.

optimal path. All of this must be established (diagnosed) if the optimum teaching strategy is to be established.

Diagnosis of psychological defects or "psychological trouble-shooting" permits organization of instruction in such a way as both to eliminate these defects and to prevent them from re-occurring. Identification of the psychological causes of mistakes, of specific "defects" in the student's mechanisms of cognitive activity, should therefore serve as the basis for defining a teaching strategy at every stage, and in some cases at every step, of the instructional process.

Contemporary programmed instruction has adopted and developed further everything that has been developed in psychology and education in the diagnostics of knowledges, skills, and habits (see, e.g., Pask, 1960a; Stolurow, 1961; Stolurow and Davis, 1965), and has managed to construct adaptive programs which operate on the basis of such diagnostics. The problem now consists of basing teaching programs not only on diagnosis of the nature and level of development of the student's knowledges, skills, and habits, but on diagnosis of the psychological mechanisms or of cognitive processes, and, in particular, on diagnosis of the psychological causes of mistakes and elimination of "psychological troubleshooting."

We will proceed now to pose and discuss a very frequently encountered psycho-educational problem, one which is solvable with the aid of mathematical logic and computers, as well as computer-based teaching machines for the presentation of diagnostic programs.

The enormous number of actions which constitute behavior in the broad sense of the term are governed by rules which prescribe the actions to be performed under a given set of conditions, which thereby control the behavior. All such rules may be expressed in the implicational, or "if . . . then . . ." form: $a \nabla b \nabla c \nabla \ldots \nabla n \rightarrow A$, where the left side of the expression indicates the properties of objects which determine which actions are to be performed on them, and the right side indicates the operations (behavioral acts) themselves.* The symbol ∇ serves as a dummy

---

*It would be more accurate to say "statements regarding" these properties and actions, but for the sake of simplicity we will speak simply of the properties and actions themselves.

variable for which the logical operators "and" or "or" may be substituted (along with brackets where necessary).

We encounter rules of this sort everywhere; they literally permeate our lives. *If* we hear short beeps when making a telephone call, *then* we know that the number is busy; *if* the indicator on a gauge moves into the red region of the scale, *then* we know that a dangerous situation has arisen and that certain measures must be taken, etc. We recall the rule presented above for isolating an inflected modifier: "If an inflected modifier modifies a noun (attribute $\bar{a}$), and is dual or extended (attribute $\bar{c}$), and comes after the modified word (attribute d), then it is set off by commas (operation A)." We wrote this rule above in the language of predicate logic. Now let us write it in the language of propositional logic:

$$\bar{a} \,\&\, \bar{c} \,\&\, d \to A.$$

It is easily seen that rules (in the broad sense of the term) describing how specific phenomena are related at the same time describe and, as it were, prescribe the structure of the processes which must be assembled and functioning in a person's head if he is to be able to operate correctly (in accordance with the rules) with respect to these phenomena and thereby solve the problem in question. In fact, failure to isolate all of the relevant attributes of an object or to take into account the nature of their interconnections (for example, by taking a disjunctive relation to be conjunctive) is, in general, sufficient to cause the action being performed to be incorrect. The same result is normally obtained when irrelevant attributes are included in the conditions defining the actions in question.

The rules describing objective properties of and relations among objects may thus be considered at the same time a description of the corresponding internal images of these objects and of operations with them, and also as a description of the way these images and operations are interrelated and interact, i.e., as rules to which a person's cognitive activity should conform. In other words, they may be considered as rules defining required

cognitive activity, as description of the relations existing among
required cognitive (and in particular conceptual) processes.

Thus, if we consider the above rule to be a description of
grammatical phenomena, the letter *a* would designate a specific
attribute possessed by a grammatical object; if the rule were a
description of the structure of cognitive processes, then this same
letter would be treated as a designation of the image of this
attribute or of the corresponding cognitive operation by means of
which its presence or absence may be determined. If the symbol &
denotes a particular relation between two attributes (namely that
of conjunction) when the rule is interpreted as a description of
grammatical phenomena, then the same symbol may be considered
as representing the operation of relating these attributes in a
particular way when the rule is interpreted as a description of the
structure of the corresponding cognitive processes, and so on.

The validity of this dual interpretation of rules derives from
the fact that a person's mental images (i.e., internally used pictures
and concepts) and his actions must correspond to the *objective
properties and structure* of the phenomena which they reflect and
transform (if only on the conceptual plane), or, put another way,
that the structure of a person's internal, cognitive activity must
model the structure of those objects of the external world toward
whose reflection and transformation it is directed. This permits a
rule of the type $a \vee b \vee c \vee \ldots \vee n \rightarrow A$ to be reviewed as one which
describes both the structure of objects in the external world, and
the cognitive (conceptual) activity by which it reflects and
transforms these objects.

An important conclusion follows from this. It is quite clear
that if, using the language of symbolic logic, it is possible to
describe the structure of cognitive processes which results in
correct actions (behavior) under particular conditions, (i.e.,
"correct structure") then it is also possible, using the same
apparatus, to describe the structure of these processes which
results in incorrect actions (i.e., "incorrect structure"). This fact
opens broad possibilities for introducing into psychology precise
methods for describing and analyzing the structure of cognitive
processes and permits the creation of a logico-mathematical

method for establishing the structure of these processes. We now turn to the description of such a method.[10]

Let us assume, for the sake of concreteness, that human actions in a particular situation are determined by the rule a & b & $c \Leftrightarrow A$. This formula indicates that, in order to perform correctly in this situation, one must isolate the indicated attributes in the corresponding objects by means of cognitive operations (which may be either conscious or unconscious). In this case action A is to be performed only if all three attributes, a, b, and c are present in the object. If it should happen that any of these attributes is absent, then action A is not to be performed (or, what is the same thing, action not -A ($\overline{A}$) is to be performed).

Analysis of mistakes made by people, especially school-children, in solving various types of problems indicates that the causes of these mistakes lie in the following fundamental flaws in the structure of the operations involved in isolating attributes:

1. Students do not take into account *all* of the attributes (conditions) required for the correct performance of a given action.

For example, attributes a, b, and c must all be taken into account in the performance of action A, but students might take into consideration only attributes a and b which are insufficient. Hence the structure of the operations for isolating attributes and the corresponding structure of the relations (associations) among the images of the attributes and the action indicated on the right side of the formula will be in them a & $b \Leftrightarrow A$ instead of a & b & $c \Leftrightarrow A$.*

2. Students take into account *superfluous* attributes, i.e., are oriented not only toward essential attributes but toward non-essential ones, which, under certain circumstances, lead to mistakes.

---

*For the sake of brevity we will henceforth use the terms "process structure" or "associative structure" instead of the lengthy expression "structure of the operations for isolating attributes and the corresponding structure of the relations (associations) among the images of the attributes and the action indicated on the right side of the formula."

For example, students might take into consideration, besides attributes *a, b,* and *c,* attribute *d,* which then begins to exert a deleterious influence on their actions. The process structure in this case would be, accordingly, $a \& b \& c \& d \Leftrightarrow A$ instead of $a \& b \& c \Leftrightarrow A$.

3. Students take into account attributes *other than* the required ones, at least some of them. The process structures in this case may vary greatly, such as, for example, $a \& b \& g \Leftrightarrow A, g \& k \Leftrightarrow A$, etc., instead of $a \& b \& c \Leftrightarrow A$.

4. Correct attributes are caused to be associated in the student's mind with actions *other than the required ones,* for example, $a \& b \& c \Leftrightarrow B$ instead of $a \& b \& c \Leftrightarrow A$.

5. *Erroneous* logical associations between attributes are established in the student's mind,* for example $(a \& b) \lor c \Leftrightarrow A$ instead of $a \& b \& c \Leftrightarrow A$.

6. A given set of attributes and their structure *sometimes* evoke correct actions and sometimes erroneous ones, i.e., $a \& b \& c \Leftrightarrow A$ alternating with $a \& b \& c \Leftrightarrow \bar{A}$.

We have described several of the possible incorrect process structures which may for one reason or another occur in a person's mind and condition his actions in some situations in such a way as to give rise to mistakes. Yet, how are we to determine which of the possible incorrect (defective) structures is present in a particular person's mind while he is attempting to solve a particular problem, if he is unable to tell us because he is unaware of these structures? How, in particular, are we to determine (diagnose) the structure of his cognitive processes, or to establish those internal relations which mediate between "input" and "output"?

Let us turn now to a description of the method which we propose for solving this problem. We note that this method permits, in principle, solution of the problem even when the individual is unaware of the attributes which he is isolating and

*The use of this term is simply a convenient shorthand and does not betoken a mentalistic conception. "Consciousness" or "awareness" might be regarded as synonymous. (*Editor.*)

which are determining the character of his actions.

The following example illustrates what is meant here. Let us assume that a person is to punctuate a sentence. He often does not know why a dash, for example, should be inserted in a sentence, that is, he is unaware of the properties (attributes) of a sentence which evoke in him the desire to insert this punctuation mark. He simply says: "I think that a dash should be inserted here, but I don't know why." His "feeling" in such cases is not without foundation; it is evoked by specific properties (attributes) of the sentence which he perceives unconsciously. The method proposed here permits elucidation, under specific conditions, of the unperceived attributes which impel a person to particular actions and which he himself is unable to perceive. For the sake of clarity in the following account we will take this example as a model.

The problem is as follows. A person is given a collection of objects as "input" (for example, a list of sentences) to which he is to respond in a particular manner (for example, by inserting punctuation marks in the sentences). We are to determine, from the "output" (i.e., the sentences which he punctuates correctly and those in which he makes mistakes), the algorithm governing his activity, i.e., the functional dependence of "output" on "input," or the structure of relations which determines the character of his actions in a given situation (for example, how he punctuates each of the sentences). The problem may also be formulated in a somewhat different way. If a person were to perform the correct action in all circumstances, then it could be said that he was guided by the "correct" rule (which is known). If, on the other hand, he makes mistakes, then he is being guided by a different, incorrect rule, of which he himself may be unaware and which he may be unable to formulate. What is the rule which he follows, even if unconsciously?

The essence of the problem, the idea of the method for discovery of the rule, and some other points may be also illustrated by a playful example.

Let us assume there exists a young man who often falls in love with different (but not all) girls. He cannot answer the question why is he taken with some girls and is not taken with others, and what are the girls' attributes which attract him. He is unaware of these attributes. He knows only one thing: whether he likes some particular girl or not, whether she attracts him or does not attract him. The problem is as follows: on the basis of a set of girls presented to a young man and his reactions toward each of them (whether one attracts him or not) to discover the attributes (and their structure) which are attractive for him, i.e., to discover what "he likes them for." If his preferences are stable, then the task may be viewed as a task to elaborate a method for identifying (diagnosing) a law or a rule or an algorithm which is, as it were, incorporated in his processes, by which he is unconsciously guided in his preferences (reactions). This incorporated rule, often a number of rules, or algorithm determines which attributes and which of their sets and their structures the young man isolates in a girl as her relevant features and how he reacts toward them. The rules may be, for instance, as follows:

$$a \rightarrow \text{Attraction}$$
$$a \,\&\, b \rightarrow \text{Attraction}$$
$$a \,\&\, b \,\&\, c \rightarrow \text{Attraction}$$

Possible interpretation: let a designate that the girl is beautiful, b that she is clever, and c that she is rich or belongs to a prestigious stratum of society. Then the structure of the young man's feelings is as follows: If a girl is beautiful (this may be the first attribute which the young man isolates in a girl), then attraction begins. Beauty is a sufficient condition for evoking attraction. If this feature is lacking and a girl is not beautiful $(\bar{a})$, then another attribute (b) begins to play a role, namely cleverness. Attraction is also evoked when a girl is not beautiful $(\bar{a})$, but clever (b). When a girl fails to be either beautiful or clever $(\bar{a} \,\&\, \bar{b})$, then the next attribute (c) begins to play a role.

The cited set of separate rules may be joined in a single united (complex) rule which will read as follows:

$$a \lor (\bar{a} \,\&\, b) \lor (\bar{a} \,\&\, \bar{b} \,\&\, c) \Leftrightarrow \text{Attraction}.$$

If for the arising of a feeling any conjunction of attributes is not only sufficient but has the same subjective significance (subjective weight) and the young man, while coming across a girl, does not isolate her attributes in a definite succession, then the last formula describes an algorithmoid process in the man. When a successive isolation of a girl's attributes takes place (because of the fact that the young man attaches more weight to one set of attributes than to another), then the sequence of his checking actions may be presented in an algorithmic form which will reflect this sequence. This may be, for example, the following algorithm:

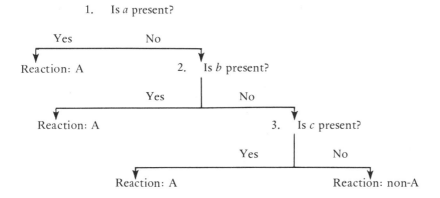

The task consists of creating a method (procedure) which will enable one to discover, without addressing a person and observing only input objects and output reactions toward these objects, which are the attributes and their structure that are relevant for a person and determine the character of his reactions. Stated in another way: what is the basis for the orientation of a person's actions, or toward which attributes in an object does he orient himself, or which attributes does he isolate in an object, and how do the isolated relevant attributes determine the character of his actions?

It is clear that to answer these questions means to discover the rule (or the algorithm when the order of the person's isolating actions directed toward an object play a role) which guides corresponding processes and of which a person may be unaware. In the last case, a person does not know the rule which directs his processes, as we have already mentioned, and the rule is, as it were, incorporated in the process, emerging as its specific form of organization. The rule in the usual sense of the word, i.e., as a statement about some connection between certain phenomena, must be extracted from the structure (organization) of processes. When we speak below of discovering rules (or algorithms) which guide a person's activity, we will have in mind not the statements about regularities underlying some process which, being in one's awareness, direct the person's activity (the person may not know or be aware of rules in this sense and may not be guided by them), but regularities themselves as a form of inner organization of the objectively proceeding process, which often are not in the awareness of the acting person.

It should be noted that the method described below is unable to solve the above mentioned problem of recognizing the precise law or rule determining the genesis of feelings such as sympathy, love, and the like, because (1) it is usually not possible to take into account *all* the possible attributes of a girl which may be attractive (or not attractive) for some young man and bring about or contribute to some nuance of his feelings; (2) the attributes are, in most cases, not discrete and, therefore, there are usually no means for their precise recognition and unambiguous evaluation (they are far from being constructive objects in the sense of mathematical logic*); (3) a person's reactions toward some attribute or particular attribute sets are often very unstable (changeable, fluctuating) and oscillate extensively, depending on many external and internal random factors; (4) each attribute has certain, and for different persons different, subjective "weight," and is usually assessed on the basis of a many-valued rather than binary scale of

---

*A constructive object is an idealization accepted in constructive mathematics (e.g., Markov, 1954) and denotes an object which is clearly distinguishable, unambiguously identifiable and, therefore, permits operating with it according to unambiguously understandable rules. Real objects approximate constructive objects to varying degrees.

assessments, each assessment being often fuzzy and not clearly distinguishable from other assessments (it should be added that assessments themselves of attributes in question are also not stable and are sometimes subject to considerable fluctuations and even changes); (5) as well as the attributes to be recognized and assessed and the assessments themselves, the final reactions also are often fuzzy and non-binary.

These five stated reasons make the evocation and genesis of most feelings normally non-algorithmic, and this makes the proposed method inapplicable for the discovery of the precise rules governing the behavior of a person in such situations and while solving such problems. There are, however, many algorithmic problems and situations which require algorithmic processes (as, for instance, in solving many mathematical, grammatical, and other problems). The method is applicable, in principle, to the discovery of the behavior of a person in these kinds of situations.

We have illustrated our point by the identification of the law (rule) which might guide the genesis of attraction in one person toward some other person, in order, first, to provide a simple and clear example of the type of problem which can be solved by the method to be developed as well as the idea of the method itself; and, second, to show to which conditions this method may and to which it may not be applied, i.e., the area of its applicability. Algorithmic processes are of a type in which the objects to be recognized (their attributes) can be feasibly made constructive and where the reactions toward these objects are fully specified and relatively stable.

Our solution to the problem of creating a method for discovering the structure (and its corresponding rules or algorithm) of the hidden and, often unconscious processes, underlying someone's overt actions or decisions is analyzable into twelve stages:

1. From the "correct" rule the attributes which define the required action are isolated; then the logical operators (or connectives, *Ed.*) joining these attributes are isolated (i.e., the logical structure of the attributes is determined) and each attribute is assigned a specific symbol so that their logical structure and the

rule as a whole can be written in the language of propositional logic.

Above we introduced the rule $a \ \& \ b \ \& \ c \Leftrightarrow A$ as an example of such a "correct" rule.

2. Typical errors committed by people (henceforth referred to as subjects) attempting to solve problems requiring application of the rule in question are investigated, and from this information a hypothesis is formed as to which relevant attributes the subjects are not isolating, noticing, or taking into account, and which irrelevant attributes the subjects regard as important. These irrelevant attributes are noted along with the relevant ones and are assigned specific symbols.* In this manner we form a complete inventory of the attributes which are likely to be thought of as significant or relevant by the subjects (different subjects will consider different attributes as significant), and toward which they will orient themselves in attempting to solve problems.

Let us assume that our example involves only one irrelevant attribute, and let us denote it by the letter d.

3. The letters representing attributes are then combined into words** in such a way that each attribute (letter) or its negation (denoted by the letter with a line over it) appears in each word, but not both together; each attribute or its negation, will, therefore, appear only once in each word. All possible combinations of attributes (letters) and their negations are formed. These combinations (words) are then listed (for example, in column form):

$$
\begin{array}{cccc}
a & b & c & d \\
a & b & c & \bar{d} \\
a & b & \bar{c} & d \\
a & b & \bar{c} & \bar{d} \\
  &   & \cdot &   \\
  &   & \cdot &   \\
  &   & \cdot &   \\
\bar{a} & \bar{b} & \bar{c} & \bar{d}
\end{array}
$$

*We will term the set of letters denoting isolated attributes the alphabet of attributes.

**A "word" is here any string of symbols (letters) from some alphabet.

For n independent attributes, of course, the number of possible combinations is 2^n.

4. Since all possible attributes which objects may possess cannot occur together in reality (the list represents all abstractly possible combinations), each word in the list is checked to determine whether the combination represented by the word is possible or not. Words which represent impossible (non-existent) combinations are then deleted from the list.

5. The remaining words are considered as standards (matrices) in accordance with which the objects (for example, sentences) which possess a given combination of attributes are selected or constructed. At least two objects corresponding to each combination are selected.

The purpose of this procedure is to permit determination, in the experiment which will be discussed below, whether or not the experimenter has taken into account all of the attributes toward which the subject is oriented, and whether or not the latter's responses are regular or stable or consistent. Thus, let two sentences be selected which possess the combination of attributes $abc\overline{d}$. Let us assume that the experiment shows that the subject responded in one way to one sentence, (punctuating it correctly, for example) and in another way to the other sentence (punctuating it incorrectly). This result would permit us to assume either that the experimenter had failed to take into account attributes toward which the subject is oriented or that the subject's responses are not consistent. If fewer than two objects (sentences) possessing the given combination of attributes had been used, it would have been impossible to discover that this was the case.

6. Since at least two objects are selected for each word, identical words to which different objects correspond are indexed in order to distinguish them: $abc\overline{d}_1$, $abc\overline{d}_2$.

After appropriate objects (in this case, sentences) have been selected or constructed, each combination of letters (word) may be considered as a symbolic description of (or code for) the corresponding object. Between an object and its description there exists an unambiguous (but not reciprocally unambiguous) correspondence: to each object there corresponds one and only one description (word) in a given alphabet of attributes (letters), but to each word there may correspond many, sometimes infinitely many, objects possessing that set of attributes.

Let the letter *b* indicate that an inflected modifier modifying a noun has purely attributive meaning; let the letter *c* indicate that the modifier is single (consists of only one word), and the letter *d* that the modifier comes after the word it modifies. Then the sentences corresponding to different combinations of these attributes might be of the following form:*

    $b \; c \; d$ —a house divided cannot stand
    $b \; c \; \bar{d}$ —a divided house cannot stand
    $b \; \bar{c} \; d$ —a house, divided by strife, cannot stand
    $b \; \bar{c} \; \bar{d}$ —a divided by strife house cannot stand
    $\bar{b} \; c \; d$ —a house, divided, cannot stand
    $\bar{b} \; c \; \bar{d}$ —divided, a house cannot stand
    $\bar{b} \; \bar{c} \; d$ —a house, divided by strife, cannot stand
    $\bar{b} \; \bar{c} \; \bar{d}$ —divided by strife, a house cannot stand

7. From the objects (sentences) which have been constructed so as to represent all possible combinations of the selected attributes, a test is constructed and administered to the subjects. The subjects are instructed to perform the required actions (punctuation) on the objects included in the test (sentences).

8. The results of the experiment (the correctness or incorrectness of the subjects' actions) are determined and the combinations of attributes (words) which correspond to objects eliciting positive responses (actions) are marked.[11]

9. It is determined whether, among identical words with different indices, some are marked as eliciting positive responses and others are not so marked, i.e., whether there are instances in which certain objects corresponding to a particular set of attributes elicit one type of response (positive) while others,

---

*These examples are the closest parallels which can substitute for the original Russian ones. Obviously, the fourth variation is not proper English, but suggestive of the Russian form. (*Translator.*)

corresponding to the same set of attributes, elicit different responses (negative).

If such instances are discovered, then either the subject's responses are of a random character or the experimenter has failed to take into account attributes with regard to which the objects in question differ from one another and which are influencing the subject's responses. It is expedient to begin by checking the last assumption and asking the subject why he responded differently to the objects in question.* If he responds by indicating an attribute by which the objects differ and which evoked different responses on his part to these objects, then the problem is solved and this attribute must be included in the alphabet of attributes and the entire procedure repeated. If he cannot answer because he is not aware of the reason for his different responses to these objects, then the experimenter must compare the objects in order to discover how they differ from one another and, having determined the attributes in which the objects differ, include one of them in the alphabet of attributes. The hypothesis that this attribute influences the subject's responses should be tested by means of the procedure described above. If the hypothesis proves to be correct and the ambiguity in the subject's responses is eliminated, the experimenter should proceed to point 10. If the hypothesis should prove to be incorrect, then another attribute must be tried and another hypothesis devised and tested in the manner described above.

The devising and testing of hypotheses continues until either the required attribute is found or the ability to devise hypotheses has been exhausted. If the attribute is found, then the experimenter proceeds to point 10; if not, then it remains unknown whether the discrepancy in the subject's responses arose as a result of the experimenter's inability to discover the attribute which differentiates the objects from one another, or as a result of

---

*This issue may also be resolved in a purely objective way which does not involve questioning the subject, as will be shown below; however, it is always more efficient to begin with the simpler of the two means of solving a problem.

randomness in the subject's response patterns. In this case the problem is insoluble by algorithmic means.

If the subject responds in the same way to objects described by a given set of attributes, then the experimenter proceeds to point 10.

10. Combinations of attributes (words) to which a given subject responds positively are written (without indices, as yet) on a separate line with the sign of logical disjunction (V) between them. The resulting expression represents a disjunction of conjunctions and is called a perfect disjunctive normal form (*pdnf*).[12]

Such an entry might take the following form:

$$abcd \lor ab\overline{c}d \lor \overline{abc}d \lor \overline{abcd} \Leftrightarrow A.$$

The meaning of this formula is as follows: if the objects (sentences, in our example) possessed the combination of attributes *abcd*, or *abcd*, or *abcd* or *abcd*, then the subject performed positive actions on them (and, therefore, performed negative actions on all other objects). However, it is not clear from this formula which attributes from these combinations of attributes are significant for any individual subject, that is, which ones he isolates. Every term of this expression contains attributes which may be isolated in various combinations by different subjects, since every term contains all of the possible attributes taken into account before the experiment was carried out with any given subject. Further, the formula fails to specify the attribute structure toward which the subject is oriented. (As we noted above, mistakes can result not only from the subject's failure to orient himself toward the necessary attributes, but also from his failure to recognize how they are related to each other, i.e., their structure.) At this point the question arises as to how to transform this logical expression in such a way as to isolate, by purely formal procedures, those attributes and structures which determine the character of the subject's actions. In other words, the problem is, on the one hand, to separate, by means of a purely formal transformation of the *pdnf* expression, those attributes which are significant for a given subject from those which are not significant for him, and on the other hand, to determine the structure which the subject assumes to be correct, although it may in fact not correspond to the correct structure. These transformations should yield an expression describing the combinations of attributes which the subject isolates (perhaps unconsciously) in the object and which determine the character of his responses to it.

11. The solution of the problem of separating those attributes which are significant for the subject from those which are not requires the transformation of the perfect disjunctive normal form (*pdnf*) into the reduced disjunctive normal form (*rdnf*). This transformation may be accomplished as follows. The disjunctive terms of the expression are sequentially compared with each other and, using the rule $Ax \lor A\bar{x} = A$, the single term A is substituted for the two terms Ax and $A\bar{x}$. A disjunction is formed between the resulting terms, and the remaining unsubstituted terms are disjunctively joined to it. The same procedure is applied to the resulting set of disjunctive terms until an expression is obtained to which the procedure is not applicable. This expression will be the *rdnf*.

The procedure of transforming the *pdnf* into the *rdnf* is intended to screen out those attributes which are not significant for a given subject and to isolate those which he utilizes (consciously or unconsciously) to determine his responses. Thus, the *rdnf* may be regarded for our purposes as that statement in the language of propositional logic in which are represented only those attributes, from among those selected by the experimenter as possibly significant for various subjects, which are significant for a given subject (although those attributes which are significant for the subject may not in fact correspond to the attributes which are objectively significant according to the "correct" rules governing the phenomena in question). The *rdnf* also reveals the inter-attribute relationships toward which the subject is oriented. The *rdnf* does not, however, indicate that minimal set of combinations of attributes which is capable of producing a positive response in the subject.

12. In order to arrive at this minimal set of combinations of attributes, the experimenter must apply to the *rdnf* one of the

procedures, well-known in symbolic logic, for minimizing logical expressions (see, e.g., Yablonsky, 1958; Voishvillo, 1958). Minimization yields a formula which describes the desired minimal set of combinations of attributes, i.e., the rule on the basis of which the input of information may be transformed by the subject into an output of responses.

In our example this rule has the form:

$$a \& b \Leftrightarrow A.^*$$

Several minimal normal forms may correspond to one and the same reduced normal forms. If the *rdnf* reveals to us the complete set of minimal combinations of attributes, that is, all possible minimal combinations to which a subject responds in a particular way, then the minimal normal forms yield those minimal sets of combinations which can guarantee a response to the relevant phenomena which is characteristic for a subject. Minimal normal forms describe, therefore, all possible minimal rules by which a subject may be guided in solving problems, but they do not indicate the specific rule, from among all of the possible equivalent rules (including the rule of which the left side is the *rdnf*), which is guiding him. An additional experiment is required to obtain this information.

The method which we have described above permits, therefore, discovery of all possible combinations of attributes which evoke a particular response in any given subject (provided that all the attributes toward which the subjects might, in general, orient themselves are known or have been discovered beforehand) and description of the relation between these attributes and the subject's responses (the "input" and "output") in the form of a specific rule (the left side of which will be in the *rdnf*). The method also permits discovery of all the minimal equivalent rules which a subject might follow and which determine the character of his responses to the objects in question (the left sides of these

---

*In the specific case under consideration here this formula is obtained at the earlier stage of the transformation of the *pdnf* to the *rdnf*.

formulas will be in the minimal normal form).

Comparison of the left side of the rule describing all minimal combinations of attributes evoking a positive response from a subject (the student's *rdnf*) with the "correct" rule, reduced to the *rdnf*, will immediately show how they differ and will permit diagnosis of the causes of his mistakes. This comparison reveals defects in the structure of the processes occurring in the student's mind or in the relation linking "input" and "output." This information permits not only quite precise prediction of the situations in which a student will perform the correct actions and those in which he will make mistakes, but also identification of those elements in the structure of his cognitive processes (associations and operations), which must be corrected in order to eliminate the cause of his mistakes and establish the correct mode of action.

Above, we have mentioned some conditions under which the method described is applicable and the restrictions it imposes. We note here only that, when a large number of attributes is involved, transformation of the formulae becomes laborious and time-consuming. However, since the part of the method involving the transformation of formulae can be represented in the form of a rigorous algorithm, it becomes possible to do all of the transformations by computer. This creates the possibility of automating some aspects of psychological cognition and psychological diagnostics and provides programmed instruction, it appears, with a powerful means of implementing highly adaptive instruction. Diagnostic programs, when made integral components of instructional programs, will permit, especially in conjunction with computers, instruction to proceed on the basis of continuous psychological diagnosis of the causes of students' mistakes and of dynamic change in the flow and strategy of instruction as a function of the results of this diagnosis.

Another question is that of the ways of improving the method described and, first of all, how to go about making it more efficient. There may be different lines, not excluding each other, along which the method can be made more efficient.

One of these is the possible minimization of the amount of

an object's attributes which are used as hypothetical reasons for students' mistakes, as tried out in the experiments described earlier in this chapter. This may be done on the basis of gathering massive experimental data concerning the scope of attributes toward which students may erroneously orient themselves. This may be termed the *a priori* minimization of possible alternatives.

Another way which may follow the preceding one is the collecting of experimental statistical data as to the probabilities of orienting the students toward each of the irrelevant attributes. Having available such data, one may improve the strategy of diagnostic searching for the irrelevant attributes which may erroneously determine some student's action. Starting diagnostic trials with most probable attributes, one will minimize the overall number of trials.

The third way consists of diminishing the number of hypothesized attributes at the expense of decreasing the certainty of the diagnostic conclusions derived from these trials, i.e., at the expense of the fact that diagnostic conclusions will acquire a more probabilistic character than earlier, when greater numbers of attributes were taken into account and verified.

The fourth, and one of the very important ways, consists of going from a non-dialogue to a dialogue mode of diagnostics, where each subsequent diagnostic action depends on a student's response to a preceding diagnostic action. Non-dialogue procedures must be included as a component in dialogue procedures, fulfilling their special functions. The dialogue mode of diagnostics makes the procedure adaptive and makes possible a more efficient procedure.

We note that a variant of the dialogue structure-psychological diagnostic procedure has been developed in our laboratory by O.N. Yudina. It has a number of common features with our method of "psychological troubleshooting," mentioned above. This procedure was applied in our experiments directed at establishing the psychological reasons for students' inability to think successfully or for experiencing difficulties in thinking while solving problems of geometric proof. However, Yudina's procedure also has some specific features which need to be mentioned.

One of the features common to both procedures, worth mentioning in connection with the examination of non-diagnostic procedure described above, is the following.

In contrast to the non-dialogue procedure described in this chapter, neither of the two dialogue procedures permitted the discovery of the erroneous rules which guided students' actions but, to make up for it, made possible the establishment of some other important psychological phenomena. Specifically it can be determined whether the student has made a mistake because he did not know the corresponding rule or because, though knowing the rule, he was not skilled in applying it. This determination in each particular case should influence the selection of strategy for subsequent remedial instructional actions, which must be different in each different case.

There are some other differences in psycho-educational capabilities of the non-dialogue as compared with the dialogue diagnostic procedures. Each has its strong as well as its weak features, and the task consists of combining them rather than choosing between them, because only their combination can increase their diagnostic potentials and make them stronger diagnostically.

On the basis of Yudina's procedure, a structuro-diagnostic instructional program on Russian grammar has been designed and tested. It has demonstrated that teaching on the basis of structural diagnostics of the psychological reasons for students' errors may be implemented even by means of a textbook. A structuro-diagnostic programmed textbook reacts to a student's responses, depending not only on the character of the response (whether it is correct or not and, if not, which was the character of the mistake). It takes into account also psychological reasons for each mistake. After establishing the character of the mistake, and before reacting to it, the program executes a diagnostic procedure aimed at discovering psychological reasons for each particular mistake. Only thereafter does it react to the mistake, the character of the mistake, and its psychological reason. Thus, as opposed to the usual branched programs of the Crowderian type, where the program reacts to identical mistakes by means of identical reactions, the structuro-diagnostic branched program being described can react to one and the same erroneous response in different ways, depending on the psychological reasons for this response, which may be different in different students.

It should be noted that implementation of a structural psycho-diagnostic approach to instruction in the form of a programmed textbook requires far more pages than the usual branched textbook. Moreover, utilization of such texts does present students with a greater inconvenience. The more adequate and convenient form of implementation of structural psycho-diagnostic programs takes the form of teaching machines, and especially computers. In conclusion, a conviction might be expressed that the structural psycho-diagnostic approach to instruction in general and to programmed instruction in particular may open a new stage in the process of increasing the adaptivity of instruction; and, quite probably, will significantly increase its effectiveness.

Notes

1. In speaking of internal behavioral acts, we have in mind operations involving transformation not of real objects in the external world (as in the case of external behavioral acts), but of their images and concepts. (The actual turning of a chair through 180 degrees is an external behavioral act involving transformation of a material object, while rotating the chair in the imagination, "in the mind," is an internal behavioral act involving transformation of an *image* of a chair; it begins as one image and ends up as another.) In other words, if external behavioral acts are operations involving transformation of actual objects, then internal acts involve transformation of information about actual objects. This, incidentally, does not mean that internal behavioral acts cannot be expressed externally (for example, in the form of slight eye movements, internal speech, etc.). It is simply that it is important to distinguish terminal behavioral acts which are

the result of internal processing of information from *mediating* behavioral acts which themselves constitute a processing of information and which determine these terminal acts.

2. It is situations of precisely this sort that we are most often faced with in schools and institutions of higher education.

3. K. Steinbuch (1959, 1961) speaks of internal models in a completely different sense. A teaching (or, more precisely, a self-teaching) system, according to him, in order to teach successfully, should continually construct an internal model of the external world. This conclusion is extremely important for the theory of self-teaching systems and for cybernetic theory, as well as, more generally, for the theory of human instruction. However, the models of cognitive activity which we are discussing are not the models of the external world which a self-teaching system builds in order to orient itself and operate, but models of cognitive activity which are designed to be taught to the student.

4. In real life, of course, results generally are more important than anything else. But it is possible to guarantee stable results only by developing, through instruction, sound, general, and effective procedures for achieving these results even if, for whatever reasons, the development of these correct procedures produces mistakes in solving problems during the process of their formation.

5. Although the examples adduced here and below are taken from secondary school curricula, the problems considered in this chapter are significant at all levels of education. Analogous examples could be adduced from the field of higher education.

6. This is not to say that tentative trials play no role in problem solution. On the contrary. But they are truly effective only when they are part of a system of *directed* problem analysis and *directed* search for a solution. For a more detailed discussion of this question see Landa (1974).

7. For example, an analogous project involving analysis of the psychological mechanisms involved in proving propositions (although with a different purpose—computer modeling of

these mechanisms) was begun in the U.S. simultaneously with, but independently of our project. See, for example, Newell and Simon (1956).

8. All the students taking part in the experiment either already possessed the required knowledge, which was tested before the experiment was carried out, or were provided this knowledge as required in each individual case. The purpose of this procedure was to exclude the possibility that students might fail to solve problems as a result of a lack of knowledge of formal propositions (definitions, theorems, etc.) and to ensure that all students had the same information at the beginning of the experiment.

9. This point is made, for example, by Stolurow (1961).

10. The author wishes to thank E.K. Voishvillo, Associate Professor of Mathematical Logic at Moscow State University, for his valuable suggestions regarding this section of the chapter.

11. A positive response would be, for example, insertion of a comma at a particular place in a sentence, while a negative response might be failure to insert a comma at this place. However, positive responses do not always coincide with correct ones. Thus, if the subject inserted commas into all those sentences which did not require commas and did not insert commas into all those sentences which did require commas, then all his positive responses would be incorrect. It is more often the case, of course, that some of a subject's positive responses will be correct and some incorrect.

12. For further discussion of the *pdnf*, consult any work on mathematical logic.

Chapter Twelve

Current Problems
in Instructional Technology

1. Programmed Instruction: A Natural Stage in the
    Development of Instructional Theory and Practice
    In spite of the enormous amount of research in the field of
programmed instruction, it still has its opponents (as noted in
earlier chapters), and skeptics continue to ask whether it is a
necessary development in education. They believe that instruction
with the aid of programmed texts and teaching machines is a fad
which, though somewhat prolonged, will eventually pass, as have
many other educational enthusiasms.

These criticisms may be answered with assurance: programmed instruction is not a fad, and will not "pass." On the
contrary, it will continue to develop intensively, and will be an
indispensable part of educational methodology in the future.

How can we be certain that this prognosis is correct? Because
it is based on a scientific and, above all, cybernetic analysis of
existing educational methods.

---

*The author's title for this chapter was translated as "Current Problems in
Programmed Instruction." The author's intent in this discussion, however,
clearly transcends programmed instruction in its present, commonly accepted
sense. Thus a change in the title was deemed necessary; no changes were made
in the body of the text, because of potential ambiguities or distortions.
Readers should look for a broader significance whenever the phrase
"programmed instruction" is used. (*Editor.*)

Cybernetics has formulated a set of general requirements which must be met if effective control of the instructional process is to be achieved.

These requirements, as stated in earlier chapters, are:

1. The goal of the control process must be specified precisely.

2. The controlling system must operate according to a precise control program.

3. The controlling system must have complete and operative information on the state of the system being controlled.

4. The controlling system must adapt to the states and characteristics of the system being controlled.

Examination of contemporary education from the point of view of these requirements shows that it does not satisfy any of them.

It fails particularly with regard to the third and fourth requirements, which have to do directly with the exchange of information between teacher and student.

Much has been said in recent years about the significance of operative feedback in education. Research has shown that if the teacher does not receive sufficient feedback information from the student, he or she is forced to conduct the instructional process blindly, which results in the random and uncontrolled development of knowledge, skills, and habits in the student. This research, however, deals for the most part with only one aspect of the question: insufficiently frequent feedback. There is another aspect: incomplete feedback.

Today much attention is devoted to the problem of obtaining information about the state of the student's knowledge, skills, and habits. Yet it is important to have information about other parameters as well, e.g., the student's motives, his memory, thinking processes and capabilities, how he goes about solving a given type of problem, his resistance to fatigue or boredom, etc. Instruction cannot be fully effective without information about these parameters. Yet the teacher frequently does not receive such information from the student, and its significance is frequently not recognized by workers in the field of programmed instruction.

The significance of diagnostic information concerning the

psychological mechanisms by means of which the student assimilates knowledge, skills, and habits and solves problems is worthy of special emphasis.

The problem, of course, consists of the fact that even the most frequently updated information about the student's activity does not in itself give the teacher knowledge about the psychological mechanisms underlying this activity. Effective instruction depends not only, and perhaps not so much, on the results of the student's cognitive activity (for example, whether he solved a particular problem or failed to solve it), as on the processes leading to this result, i.e., how he went about solving the problem. This is the case, because the most effective means of influencing the outcome of an activity is to influence the processes which give rise to it. It is precisely information about those processes which must be controlled if instruction is to be effective that the teacher often does not receive.

It is possible to correct mistakes, for example, and to prevent them from occurring in the future only if their psychological causes are known and if these causes can be removed. This requires that they be discovered, i.e., that a psychological diagnosis be established. As a rule, however, the teacher does not have such diagnostic information. Not having discovered the psychological cause of a mistake, not having uncovered the "psychological defect" underlying it, in other words, not having established a psychological diagnosis, he finds it difficult, if not impossible, to proceed in a correct and effective manner so as to prevent the same or a similar mistake from occurring again.

Psychological analysis shows that a given mistake may have many (up to a dozen or more) psychological causes, and teachers frequently do not even suspect the existence of many of them. If this is the case, however, then it is understandable why teachers often spend months and even years attempting to bring poor students up to grade level. Not knowing the psychological causes of the student's difficulties and mistakes, not having established a *psychological diagnosis*, they treat the student for diseases he does not have in many instances. This failure to diagnose is one of the most serious shortcomings of contemporary instruction.

Thus, the third requirement for good control—that the controlling system (the teacher) should receive not only frequent but also (reasonably) *complete* information regarding the state of the system being controlled—is not fulfilled in contemporary instruction.

The same may be said regarding the fourth requirement as well—adaptation of the controlling system to the states and characteristics of the controlled system, i.e., individualization of instruction.

The teacher is physically unable to adapt the instructional process to the needs of each individual student, i.e., to say one thing to one student, while at the same time saying something else to another student, to give five exercises to one student and 10 to another, to teach one student by one method and another student by another method, etc. Yet investigation of the individual characteristics of students by diverse authors has shown the enormous variability of student characteristics.

Studies in our laboratory at the Institute of General and Educational Psychology have shown that one student may take approximately three hours to go through a fragment of instructional material while another student may take more than 14 hours, i.e., almost five times as long. One student needs one or two hours to develop a grammatical habit, while another needs 10 to 12 hours, six to 10 times as long. There are significant differences among students with respect to their abstract and concrete modes of thinking, or in the means by which they assimilate knowledge most easily. Some students learn best by going from specific examples to general propositions, others by going from the general to the specific. There are a number of important individual differences which the teacher would be physically unable to take into account even if he knew of them.

It is now firmly established that the absence of adaptation (individualization) is one of the most important causes of learning difficulties in the classroom. How, indeed, can a student succeed in learning material which is presented at a tempo which is too fast for him, or which is not sufficiently drilled, or which is explained in a way which is inappropriate and therefore difficult for him?

It may be said that in spite of the overburdening of students with mental work, the information requirements of each individual student are not satisfied. The student does not receive all of the information which he personally needs in order to achieve the goal of the instructional process (different students require different information in order to reach the same goal). The information which is given to the student is often inappropriate for him, which leads to the paradoxical situation of the student's being forced to take in an enormous quantity of information while at the same time suffering from "information hunger." The need for information, like any other need, cannot be fulfilled simply by large amounts of the relevant commodity; the commodity must not only be supplied in sufficient quantity, it must be suitable also in quality and structure, and these properties are always individual. Just as a man who has, let us say, an unusually high protein requirement will experience hunger no matter how much bread and fruit he eats, the student who has a high need for rote repetition in order to assimilate knowledge and develop the corresponding skills and habits, will experience information hunger if he does not have the opportunity to repeat the material a sufficient number of times, no matter how much information of other sorts he receives.

We see, therefore, that the fourth requirement for good control of the instructional process is also not fulfilled. In order to be effective, the teacher must, on the one hand, receive immeasurably more information from the student than he now receives, and, on the other hand, give the student more information than he does at present, with this information being tailored to the individual student. Improvement in the quality of control of the instructional process presupposes and demands a sharp increase in information flow both from the student to the teacher, and from the teacher to the student.

Is it possible to increase information flow under standard classroom conditions? This question has only to be asked for the answer to become obvious: no.

The teacher is physically incapable of taking in information from many students at the same time, let alone responding individually to the information received from each student.

Thus arises the contradiction which has been noted often in the literature. In order to improve the quality of instruction, it is necessary to sharply increase the flow of information between the teacher and the student. Yet, even an insignificant increase in the information coming to the teacher makes it impossible for him to perceive and process it, let alone make a differentiated response to it.

Until recently, the theory of instruction concerned itself for the most part with what the teacher *should* do in order to teach effectively. The cybernetic approach to the instructional process, however, has raised the important question of what he is *able* to do, and has shown that he is able to do significantly less that he should (be able) do. What he should do in order to teach effectively is considerably in excess of his psycho-physiological capabilities.

A similar contradiction is encountered in all other fields of human activity, and the means by which it is resolved is well-known—transfer of a portion of the information reception and processing functions to special automatic devices—computers—or, stated in a different way, automatization of the control processes.

It is because of the wide application of this approach that the idea of the partial automatization of instruction is not simply a passing fashion. It is based on profound analysis of the instructional process in terms of modern science and the discovery of its objective characteristics, laws, and tendencies.

The branch of psychology and education which has been concerning itself with the problem of how to transfer part of the task of receiving and processing psychological and instructional information to special devices—programmed texts and teaching machines—has come to be called the theory of programmed instruction. Programmed instruction arose as a response to profound educational needs and is a natural stage in the development of psychology and education. Although there is currently a great deal of controversy as to what constitutes "programmed instruction" (many consider, not without reason, that programmed instruction covers a greater range of problems than does the field of automatization of education), one thing is unarguable: these new instructional techniques, principles, and methods require their own designation and their own theory. We believe that programmed instruction is not simply a new direction in education. It is a new system of techniques, principles, and methods, and, therefore, a new and distinct field of investigation. This new field of investigation gives rise to its own theory and leads to the development of new branches of psychology and education. And just as the theory underlying the helicopter does not supplant the theory underlying the airplane, the theory of programmed instruction does not supplant the theory of classical instruction. Each of these theories has its own objects of study, its own fields of application, and each is a component of educational theory in general, relying on it as a general base. But it is precisely because the theory of programmed instruction has its own object of study—instruction with the aid of programmed texts and teaching machines—that it is possible to speak of the development of a separate theory, i.e., the theory of programmed instruction, within psychology and education.

It should be noted, however, that the appearance of programmed instruction and the theory of programmed instruction did not simply create a new branch of classical educational theory. It reconstructed, or should reconstruct, the general educational theory influencing it and changing it. If previously the general instructional theory was practically the theory of instruction with the aid of a live teacher, now such an instruction is only a particular case of instruction. Thus the general instructional theory must now become a theory which embraces instruction both with the aid of a teacher and a teaching device. It should reveal regularities common to both types of instruction which will heighten the degree of its generality.

The above analysis showed that contemporary classical classroom instruction does not meet any of the requirements for good control and cannot possibly be sufficiently effective. The first two requirements are not fulfilled mainly as a result of the shortcomings of instructional science, whereas failure to fulfill the last two is rooted in the organization of classical instruction itself.

If the basic task of programmed instruction is that of shifting some of the functions of receiving and processing information to teaching devices, then the question arises as to how best to divide these functions between the teacher, on the one hand, and the machine and the student on the other, in order to maximize the effectiveness of the instructional process. This question is all the more important for the fact that many of the shortcomings of contemporary programmed instruction are due to an incorrect allocation of functions. Before proceeding to a more detailed examination of this question, however, we should introduce and examine the concept of the instructional model.

2.   The Attributive Instructional Model. The
      Implementation of Ideal Models as an
      Important Function of Programmed Instruction

The instructional process, like any other object or process, possesses specific properties. It may be explanatory-illustrative or problem-oriented, diagnostic or non-diagnostic, individualized or non-individualized, etc. Each specific approach to the instructional process, therefore, may be characterized by the set of properties which it possesses. An instructional method described by means of a set of properties may be termed an attributive instructional model.*

If the properties defining a model are expressed symbolically by means of the letters of some alphabet, then the model may be represented as a "word" in this alphabet ("word" in the logico-mathematical sense). Thus, instruction according to model A might be explanatory-illustrative in nature (property a), diagnostic (property b), and individualized (property c), in which case model A would be described by the word *abc*. Instruction according to a model B, on the other hand, might be explanatory-illustrative (*a*) like model A, but, unlike model A, non-diagnostic

---

*For the sake of brevity, attributive models will be referred to below as models. This does not mean, of course, that attributive models are the only type of models. There do exist functional models and other types of models.

(property $\overline{b}$) and non-individualized (property $\overline{c}$). Model B, therefore, would be described by the word $\overline{abc}$. If the set of properties indicated above is considered as defining a property space, then any model may be described as a vector in this space.

The fact that the instructional process (like any other object) possesses more properties than can be included in any model indicates that a model is always a less than perfect reflection of reality (the original process). Since one model of a given object may reflect more of its properties than another model, however, some models will be better than others.

If the properties of a given object are examined and compared, it will be noticed that they stand in specific logical relations to each other. Let us consider the phrase: "the brightly shining star." The word "star" is a noun denoting an object, "shining" is a property of this object, and "brightly" is a property of this property of the object. If we call "shiningness" a property of the first order, then "brightness" (that is, the property of this property) will be a property of the second order. If we consider the phrase "a very brightly shining star," then "very" will be a property of "brightly," i.e., a third-order property.

It may be said that every property of a higher order is (in a philosophical sense, *Ed.*) a form relative to a lower-order property. Thus, "shining" can appear in the form "brightly" or in the form "not brightly." "Brightly" in turn can appear in the form "very" or in the form "not very," etc.

A description of an object as a set of first-order properties may be termed a first-order model, as a set of second-order properties, a second-order model, etc.

If the properties (attributes) of programmed instruction are considered from this point of view, they may be said to be second-order properties. Thus, for example, if the explanatory-illustrative characteristic is considered as a first-order property, then this property may appear in an individualized form or in a non-individualized form, i.e., in a form in which a human teacher presents the material or in which the material is presented by machine, etc. It is, therefore, useful to consider models of programmed instruction as second-order models, although sometimes the distinction between first- and second-order properties as applied to the instructional process is relative, depending on the "reference point" to which they are related.

If the results of cybernetic analysis of the instructional process are formulated in terms of models, it may be said that the cardinal defect in education, as currently organized, is the fact that it does not permit implementation of adequate first- and second-order models, that it sets definite limits on the attainment of effective instructional models.

Thus, ordinary instruction does not permit implementation of adaptive models, diagnostic models, and several other types of models. The basic problem facing programmed instruction is the creation of the conditions for implementation of better and more effective models, i.e., to remove the limitations imposed by the way instruction is normally organized on the implementation of good models.

Programmed instruction is able to implement better models of the instructional process only with the aid of teaching devices, however, which take over from the teacher some of the burden of receiving and processing psychological and educational (instructional) information.*

If this is so, then practical attainment (implementation) of adequate (sufficiently complex) instructional models depends on the psychologico-didactic functions which teaching devices are able to perform, and these in turn are determined by the operating capabilities of the devices.

To what degree do modern teaching devices possess the capabilities required for the implementation of complex models? How well can they imitate the human teacher, who possesses the most varied capabilities and skills and who under some conditions (for example, when working with óne student) is able to do a great deal?

---

*We will use the term "teaching device" to include not only teaching machines, but also programmed texts, which are, relative to ordinary texts, "devices" of a sort, even though they happen to be made of paper. Programmed texts are sometimes referred to as "paper machines."

The operating capabilities of existing machines determine which instructional models are practically implementable today with the aid of programmed instruction and which are not. The operating capabilities of such machines and thereby their psychological and didactic functions determine, on the one hand, the potential of programmmed instruction, and, on the other hand, impose definite limitations on programmed instruction.

However, if teaching devices, as a result of their limitations, are unable to implement all desirable instructional models and perform all desirable psychologico-didactic functions (and at the present time they are able to perform for the most part only rather simple functions), then the important question arises as to which functions to leave to the human teacher, which to shift to the student himself, and which to shift to the teaching device, i.e., how to distribute these functions in the best way in order to implement the best instructional models. This problem is one of the basic ones facing programmed instruction, one to which a considerable number of publications have already been devoted. Let us consider this problem.

3.   Optimal Distribution of Functions Among
      Teacher, Teaching Device, and Student in
      Programmed Instruction

Let us begin with the distribution of functions between teacher and teaching device. The distribution of these functions depends on a number of conditions: on what the student is to be taught and how he is to be taught it, on what the teacher is able to do and knows how to do, on the teaching aids available to him and what they are able to do, etc.

The distribution of functions in a given case is always a specific problem which must be solved. Like many other problems, it can be solved in various ways, and adequate, general methods for arriving at an optimal solution must be developed.

Let us attempt to outline the stages in the solution of this problem.

Design of an ideal instructional model. Before the problem of assigning functions can be solved, it is necessary to determine what the student is to be taught and how this can best be done, assuming ideal conditions. This stage may be termed design of an "ideal instruction model" (a model of an ideal instructional process).

Design of a model of this sort requires that the limited capabilities of both teacher and existing teaching devices be ignored, and that the assumption be made that the conditions under which the teacher operates are the best that could be wished for, such that he is able to do everything required to teach in the most effective manner. It must then be determined what the teacher must do, i.e., what functions he must perform, in order to solve the instructional problem in question in the best way. A list of such functions must be compiled. In other words, it is necessary to imagine the characteristics which the instructional process should have in order to be maximally effective (for example, it should take into account not only the student's knowledge, skills, and habits, but also his motives, cognitive style, the dynamics of his perseverance, etc.). The functions which the ideal instructional model fulfills are the desired ones.

Analysis of the conditions of instruction and discovery of the real capabilities of the teacher and teaching devices. The ideal instructional model determines, in essence, what the teacher (and the student) should do in order for the instructional process to proceed in the most effective manner, and also the conditions required for this, i.e., it formulates the problems which the teacher must solve and the functions which he must fulfill in order to solve them.

The question now arises as to which problems the teacher and the technical resources at his disposal are *able* to solve, which functions they are *able* to fulfill (in principle and in reality under specific conditions).

In order to determine this, the actual conditions under which the instructional process proceeds must be analyzed; the *possible* functions can then be compared with the *desired* functions as determined during the process of designing the ideal model.

Comparison of the real capabilities (functions) and the ideal (desired) ones permits us to distinguish the following categories of functions.

Functions which neither a human teacher nor a teaching device can perform. There is no point in attempting to perform these functions. By ignoring them it is possible to transform an ideal instructional model into an implementable one. An ideal model reflects desired functions, while an implementable model reflects functions which are, in principle, fulfillable (not exceeding human and technological capabilities at a given point in time).

But fulfillable functions are also of different types. Let us consider each type separately.

Functions fulfillable by a human teacher, but not (at least at the present time), by teaching devices. Examples of functions of this sort would be creative problem-solving in situations which have not been foreseen by an instructional program, the super-vision of cooperative work on the part of students at specific stages of the instructional process, the conducting of discussions, and the influence on an individual student by means of the teacher's own example.

If machines cannot fulfill these functions, then they must, of course, be left to the human teacher.

Functions fulfillable by a teaching device, but not a human teacher. An example of a function of this type would be the uninterrupted monitoring of the development of habits by means of a set of parameters, analysis of these parameters, and subsequent dynamic adaptation of the instructional process to their rapidly changing values. This problem can be successfully solved by certain machines, but cannot be solved by a human teacher.

Functions which a machine can fulfill, but which a human being cannot fulfill, should, of course, be shifted to the machine.

If, however, the teacher does not have such a machine at his disposal, he must avoid these functions altogether, thereby weakening his instructional model and causing it to approximate more closely a real model by which the instructional process may actually be conducted.

Functions fulfillable either by a human teacher or by a teaching device. These functions should be assigned to whichever agent, the human or the machine, performs them better. In doing this, it is necessary to take into account the fact that there are tasks which machines, under some conditions, perform better than human teachers, in spite of the fact that, in general, these tasks are performed better by human beings. In such cases the functions in question should be shifted to a machine.

The method described here for solving the problem of optimal distribution of functions between the human teacher and teaching devices assumes that there are problems which under some conditions are best solved by the human teacher, and problems which under some conditions are best solved by a teaching device, although there are also, of course, problems which under any conditions are best solved (at least at the present time) either by the human teacher or by a teaching device, as well as problems which neither is able to solve. If this is so, then practical solution to the problem of optimal distribution of functions between the human teacher and the teaching machines consists of giving to the human teacher the functions which he is best able to do, and to the machine the functions which it is best able to do. As was stated above, it is wrong to proceed on the basis of whether the human teacher or the machine is *in general* best able to fulfill the function. Functions should be assigned on the basis of whether they are best fulfilled under *specific* conditions by the human teacher or by a teaching device.

The most important factor influencing the expedient (i.e., optimal, *Ed.*) distribution of functions is the economic one.

At the present time it is possible to construct powerful teaching machines which are capable of assuming a number of rather complex instructional functions, but which frequently prove to be excessively costly.

The essence of this question is that broadening the functions performed during the instructional process (i.e., improving the instructional model) increases its effectiveness, but at the same time requires an increase in material expenditure (for example, the purchase of teaching machines, the replacing of less efficient machines by more efficient ones, etc.). Does the increase in the effectiveness of instruction justify this increased expenditure? If it does not, then clearly the increased expenditure would be impractical; if it does, then such expenditure is appropriate.

Neglect of the economic factors of educational resources and methods (models) is one of the reasons why little work is done in the Soviet Union on the development of economic criteria of effectiveness for instructional models. We do not even discuss the fact that, as a result of neglect of this problem in educational practice, the models which we use are often not as effective as they might be (from the point of view of the relation between didactic functions and economic factors), which results in the inefficient expenditure of public resources allocated to education.

Up to this point we have been discussing the distribution of functions between the human teacher and the teaching device. There is, however, an additional problem: the distribution of functions between the teaching device and the student.

The essence of this problem may be stated as follows. Since the student is not only a controlled, but also a self-controlled system, which, specifically, is capable of performing certain functions having to do with control of the learning process on its own, the question arises as to whether it is not appropriate to shift some of these functions to the student, and if so, then which ones.

The importance of shifting some functions to the student himself derives, first, from the fact that the teacher is relieved of some of the functions which teaching devices cannot perform, but which he cannot perform very well either because they exceed his psycho-physiological capabilities.

It is clear, then, that shifting certain functions to the student is in some respects entirely desirable and offers definite advantages.

It entails, however, some disadvantages as well, and these are frequently quite significant.

Several questions immediately arise with regard to the shifting of control functions to the student: (1) will the student wish to perform them (and will he perform them); (2) will he be able to perform them properly; and (3) will performance of these functions not interfere with the student's main problem, namely the assimilation of knowledge, the development of skills, habits, etc.

Thus, an important function of guidance in the instructional process is, of course, to communicate to the student a correct answer only after he has attempted to answer the question or solve the problem on his own. This function can be automatized, shifted to an automatic teaching device, but it can also be handled in another way, by using a programmed text and asking the student to refer to the correct answer after he gives his own, independent answer. But will the student always perform this function diligently? Will he not experience the temptation to look up the correct answer before trying to produce his own? There can never be any guarantee that he will not do this.

This example shows that changing one instructional para-meter (using cheaper teaching devices) in order to achieve some advantages entails disadvantages with regard to another (decreased reliability of control or guidance), and vice versa. A number of conditions determine whether programmed texts or teaching machines are to be preferred in designing a specific instructional procedure. If teaching machines are available which perform this function automatically, then they are to be preferred. If no such machines are available (or if the funds by which they could be acquired are better spent on other things), then programmed texts should be used instead, with full recognition of the fact that use of programmed texts entails a decrease in the reliability of control and in the adequacy of the model governing the instructional process. There are, in addition, several other factors which must be taken into account in determining an effective distribution of functions in this respect.

The second of the questions posed above is whether the student is able to perform the control functions which might be transferred to him, assuming that he wishes to perform them.

The significance of this question may be illustrated by using the example of the checking or verifying function.

Let us assume that in going through a programmed course a student is asked a question to which the correct answer is "artillery." He writes this word with a spelling mistake ("artil-ery"). He then compares his version with the correct one and decides that they are the same. He frequently refers to the correct answer only after giving his own, as required, but he is simply not very good at comparing them, and often fails to see that his answer does not coincide with the correct one. The reliability of the control function decreases when it is shifted to the student, therefore, and regulation of the learning process deteriorates.

This is the same situation which arose in the preceding case. The automatization of control functions requires more expensive devices and, consequently, greater material expenditure, but decreasing expenditure for devices and shifting control functions to the student (i.e., switching from automatic control to self-control) results in a lowering of the reliability of control and of the quality of instruction. The general approach to the solution of the problem of whether to opt for larger expenditure in order to improve control is the same as in the preceding case.

The third question is whether shifting control of the learning processes to the student will hinder him in the performance of his basic task—the assimilation of knowledge and the development of skills and habits.

The essential factor in this regard is that any control in the instructional process fulfills a secondary function with regard to this basic task, and if the student is required to perform too many of these secondary functions, he is distracted from it.

Experience shows that control functions which are imposed on the student are often poorly executed, giving rise to a decrease in the quality and reliability of control of the learning process.

The problem of the distribution of functions among teacher, teaching device, and student is a typical optimization problem, the solution of which is achieved by shifting functions to whichever agent is best able to perform them—the teacher, the student, or the machine. The distribution of functions which under specific conditions permits the best possible performance of the maximum number of functions will be the optimal one (for those conditions). The optimal distribution of functions for a given set of conditions, therefore, is the one which permits performance of the greatest number of functions, in the best possible manner, at the least cost, thereby making possible the implementation of the most effective instructional model for the conditions in question.

Shortcomings in the distribution of functions among teacher, teaching device, and student in contemporary programmed instruction. The above-described approach to optimizing the distribution of functions among teacher, teaching device, and student permits a clearer understanding of the shortcomings in the solution of this problem which are encountered in practice. Let us enumerate these shortcomings.

a. Shifting to teaching devices of functions which these devices perform poorly, or at least worse than the human teacher, with no compensating improvement in the teacher's performance of other functions.

b. Shifting to teaching devices of functions which they perform worse than the human teacher, with the teacher having to oversee the operation of these devices and therefore not being free to perform other, higher-order functions.

c. Using relatively complex and expensive devices to perform functions which simpler and cheaper devices could perform just as well.

d. Shifting to the student control functions which he cannot be relied upon to perform, and thereby lowering the reliability of control.

e. Transferring to the student control functions on which he must expend considerable effort to perform, thereby having less time and energy for the solution of the basic learning task—the assimilation of knowledge, skills, and habits.

All of these shortcomings in the distribution of functions discredit programmed instruction. Any incorrect distribution of functions causes some functions to be performed poorly or not at all, which in turn causes inefficient utilization of available instructional capabilities and engenders waste of time, effort, and resources; and if all possible instructional functions are not utilized or are utilized in a suboptimal manner, the result is a deterioration of the model governing the instructional process and a lowering of the over-all effectiveness of this process.

Ways to expand the potential of programmed instruction and to improve teaching machines. We have considered the question of the optimum distribution of functions among teacher, teaching device, and student, taking into account the fact that at any given stage in the development of science and technology the technological and instructional capabilities of teaching devices have definite limits and that these devices cannot do more than they can do. Since at the present time, however, teaching devices are able to do significantly less than would be (ideally, *Ed.*) desirable, the possibilities for using them are limited, and this places corresponding limitations on the sphere of application of programmed instruction. Even an optimal distribution of functions among teacher, teaching device, and student does not permit implementation of instructional models which are as good as those which would be (ideally, *Ed.*) desirable.

Indeed, if a teaching device is not capable of executing psychologico-diagnostic procedures, for example, then it is capable of implementing only non-diagnostic (and therefore less than perfect) instructional models. The imperfection of technological aids places definite limits on the utilization of good instructional models. Stating this in a more general form: the capabilities of technological aids (i.e., electro-mechanical, electronic, *Ed.*) to education directly determine the degree of adequacy of the instructional models which can be used at any given stage in the development of science and technology.

If this is so, then one of the most important means of creating the conditions for the use of better instructional models is the development of teaching devices which will be capable of performing more complex psychologico-didactic (i.e., instructional, *Ed.*) functions and thereby of implementing better models.

At present, considerable concern is being expressed about machine-aided education, and, moreover, hostility toward machines in education is intensifying in various countries. Even professionals assert that the experiments with automated, machine-aided instruction has proven unsuccessful and that the benefits of teaching machines do not justify their cost.

This assertion is not without foundation. It is to some degree justified by the current state of affairs in the field of machine-aided instruction and by certain difficulties which have been encountered in this area, although the conclusions drawn from the existence of these difficulties are not always correct.

There are at least two causes for this pessimistic evaluation of the role of machines in education.

The first is that most of the teaching machines existing today perform such rudimentary psychologico-didactic functions that they cannot solve many of the complex problems which arise within the instructional process. The functions which the machines currently in use are able to perform are extremely rudimentary relative to those which it would be desirable for them to perform. Moreover, in many instances machines perform these functions worse than the human teacher.

The other source of doubt as to the value of machines in education is that they are not always used intelligently in practice; they are expected to perform functions which, at the current level of educational technology, are didactically (instructionally) or economically inappropriate for them. In addition, it frequently happens that expensive and complex machines are used to solve problems which could be solved using inexpensive and simple devices. All of this discredits the idea of machine-aided instruction in the eyes of many educators.

The fact that current machines are often inadequate, or that some unduly enthusiastic proponents of programmed instruction use them inappropriately frequently serves as the basis for the incorrect conclusion that machines are unsuited to, or unnecessary, in the instructional process. A similar, and equally incorrect, conclusion was drawn by many observers at the beginning of the automobile age to the effect that automobiles were unnecessary, because they performed the function of transportation worse than did the horse. This observation was correct, of course, only with regard to the automobiles existing *at that time*.

The problem of perfecting the (hardware, *Ed.*) technology and thereby the psychologico-didactic functions of teaching machines is, therefore, an important one. One of the paths which programmed instruction has taken is that of developing individual teaching machines and of supplying each student with his own, personal machine, if not several of his own machines.

It is quite clear that this approach is unsound from the

economic point of view, and thus untenable in the long run. It involves expenditures which increase in proportion to the number of students, although the situation should be precisely the opposite. The cost of instructing each student not only should *not* increase as the number of students increases, but it should actually decrease.

Supplying each student with one or more machines for individual instruction is thus not practicable; rather, the creation of centralized teaching systems which are capable of teaching many students simultaneously is the course which should be followed.

The obvious expediency of this latter approach has stimulated the development of teaching systems in which one device serves several or many students at the same time. Classes in which the students sit in individual booths connected to a central tape recorder are an example of this type of system; the teacher asks the students questions, they answer individually, their answers being recorded by the central machine, and the teacher then provides reinforcement as required. Useful as such systems may be in stimulating the process of assimilating knowledge, instruction carried on with the aid of these devices is not programmed, since it does not provide individualized instruction, not even individualization of the rate at which the students progress through the material.

Another direction in the creation of centralized teaching systems is the use of electronic computers.

There is no doubt that computers possess immeasurably richer logical and adaptive capabilities than any other type of machine used for instructional purposes. It may be supposed, however, that the use of computers is nevertheless not the fundamental solution to the problem of automatizing education. First, the large-scale use of computers for educational purposes is so far rather expensive, and will continue to be expensive even as computer costs go down. Second, there are many problems which cannot be solved even by the speed and memory capacity of computers. Third, many problems which are often thought to be soluble only by means of computers, are, in fact, soluble by simpler and less expensive means.

There is one other extremely important consideration in this regard. One of the major shortcomings of all existing teaching machines, including computers, is that they do not understand natural human speech and can communicate with the student only in the artificial language of codes. This seriously restricts the possibilities of student-machine communication and places limits on the adequacy of the models which may be used in the instructional process. The possibility exists, of course, of using input devices capable of understanding natural human speech, if only in written form, and automatically coding it into a language understandable to the machine. Such devices are as yet very imperfect, however, and they increase even further the cost of instruction which the use of computers, to begin with, makes excessively high.

The computer, therefore, even with its large memory and powerful logical (adaptive) capabilities, cannot solve (at least not as yet) the central problem in the automatization of education—that of student-machine communication, of natural means of exchanging information between them. Yet it is extremely important for the solution of many problems in education that a machine possessing a memory and logic capacity approaching that of the computer be able, on the one hand, to speak in natural human language—be able to talk, in other words—and on the other hand, to understand the student's natural speech (even if only in written form).

The problem of creating an instructional system which would be centralized (i.e., able to teach hundreds of students simultaneously), adaptive (i.e., able to adjust its approach to the character and dynamics of the learning process), and capable of natural-language communication with the student (even if only in written form) has now been formulated and the technological feasibility of such a system has been demonstrated. It is reasonable to suppose that the use of teaching systems of this sort will help to eliminate many of the shortcomings of contemporary programmed instruction, shortcomings which greatly restrict its use in educational practice. Also, they will create the possibility of significantly broadening the scope and potential of programmed instruction, as well as its effectiveness, thereby increasing the effectiveness of education in general. At the present time, it is important to define the most promising lines of development of programmed instruction, i.e., to take the long-range view. It is reasonable to suppose that its potential will be most fully realized through the creation of centralized adaptive instructional systems capable of communicating with the student in natural human (written) language and, therefore, able to imitate more closely the communication which takes place between a student and a human teacher. These considerations do not in any way diminish the importance of programmed texts, which can be (and even now often are) more effective than ordinary textbooks. The need for them apparently does not disappear even in the face of highly developed educational technology.

Some problems in the writing of instructional programs. So far we have discussed, for the most part, teaching devices which provide only the possibility of implementing one or another instructional model. In order for an instructional model to be implemented in practice, however, an instructional program possessing the properties of the model must be designed.

There are two approaches to the writing of instructional programs.

The first is to take material which has already been compiled and a method which is already in use and use them to write an instructional program. An example of this procedure would be the writing of programmed texts on the basis of standard (non-programmed) texts.

The second approach is to first improve existing material and methods, creating an improved first-order model, and then to program it, putting it into the form of a programmed text or teaching machine program.

The first approach is significantly faster and easier, but it has one important disadvantage: all of the defects of the initial first-order model are transferred to the instructional program (for example, if the expository sequence of the original material in the standard text was suboptimal, then it will not improve by being recast in programmed form).

The second approach is much more difficult, requiring the expenditure of more time and energy, but the resulting instructional program will be of significantly higher quality than with the first approach, and the effectiveness of programmed instruction written in this way is incomparably greater than that of standard instruction.

It should be noted that the first method of writing instructional programs is the more widely used at the present time, at least among teachers. Program writers do not as a rule systematically develop the instructional models which they incorporate in their programs (whether programmed texts or machine programs), but rather create programmed materials on the basis of experience, i.e., on the basis of the models which they use in their own teaching. In using this approach, they create programs which imitate their own teaching style, which teach the material which they teach in the classroom, and which teach this material by the methods which they use in the classroom. However, since different teachers have different ideas about how to teach (and, in fact, teach in different ways), programmed materials created in this way will embody different (first-order) instructional models. This to a large degree explains the differences in programmed materials written by different authors, but dealing with the same subject-matter, as well as their differing effectiveness. Programmed materials of this sort, although they may prove somewhat more effective than standard texts (as a result of the relative independence of the programmed form and its relatively independent influence on the learning process), nevertheless do not constitute the fundamental solution to the problem of making instruction more effective. Effective programming must imply the solution of tasks which are specific not only for programmed instruction but for the theory of instruction in general. One of the advantages of programmed instruction is that it permits more effective implementation of first-order instructional models, but in order that this advantage is to be secured as fully as possible, the quality of these first-order models must be quite high.

An extremely important conclusion follows from these

considerations. In order to make programmed instruction effective, it is not enough to solve only the problems involved in designing the second-order models which are specific to programmed instruction (i.e., problems having to do with how best to program a given first-order instructional model, such as how to divide it into "steps," how to provide operative feedback, etc.). Rather, it is necessary to design and perfect the underlying first-order models. But this task goes beyond the scope of programmed instruction and requires the solution of many problems lying in the areas of educational psychology, instruction, and related methodology.

Of particular significance in this regard is the design and use in programmed instruction of models which presuppose development in the student not only of *algorithmic*, but also of *heuristic* (creative) processes. Programmed instruction is sufficiently powerful to effect without great difficulty the transmission of knowledge to the student and to develop ideas and concepts in him, as well as the algorithmic processes which underly skills and habits. To implement instructional models which presuppose the development of heuristic processes, however, is significantly more difficult. The problem is not so much that we are not always able to algorithmize and program the development of heuristic processes as much as that with the aid of currently existing teaching devices (programmed texts and teaching machines) it is difficult to implement instructional models which presuppose the development of heuristic processes.

All true heuristic processes, as opposed to algorithmic processes, involve search in some undefined field. It is difficult to control a search process which is not unambiguously determined by the conditions of the problem, since it is never possible to know beforehand the region in which the problem-solver will look for a solution, and thus to program instructional responses to his actions. Although it is not possible to know with certainty what the problem-solver will do, it is possible to predict probabilistically what he will do to some degree, since it is possible to establish statistically beforehand, by means of observation and experiment, the probable actions which problem-solvers perform in trying to solve problems of a particular type. This creates the possibility of programming some instructional responses to these actions. In principle, it is also possible to program instructional responses to unforeseen actions as well (responses such as "try a different approach"), although these responses are not always adequate. Authors of algorithms for developing heuristic processes clearly will always have to take into account the fact that adequate instructional responses in such algorithms will always be approximate and probabilistic in nature.

Programmed instruction and instruction in problem-solving are frequently presented as opposites. This is not the case, although most of the instructional programs in use at the present time do not, in fact, develop heuristic processes in the student. The shortcomings of current instructional programs, however, should not be regarded as shortcomings of programmed instruction in general, and it should not be thought that programmed instruction is incapable, in principle, of developing heuristic processes in the student, i.e., of teaching him to think creatively, as noted earlier in this volume.

The real task is not merely to discover the weaknesses and shortcomings of contemporary programmed instruction and to continue to emphasize the differences between it and instruction in problem-solving, but to remove these weaknesses and shortcomings and to develop ways of making programmed instruction capable of teaching problem-solving. Programmed instruction today, in most cases, does not teach this ability and does not implement problem-solving instructional models. As the experience of a number of authors shows, however, programmed instruction can be used to implement (at least within limits) not only the explanatory-illustrative, but also the problem-solving method of instruction, and thus to develop in the student the ability to think independently and creatively when solving problems.

Given that programmed instruction can, in principle, implement various instructional models (although not all models to the same degree and with equal ease), there are several points to be made with regard to the problem of the effectiveness of programmed instruction.

The question as to which format is more effective—standard or programmed instruction—has hitherto been one of the major issues in the theory of programmed instruction. As a number of authors have noted, however, it is wrong to pose this question in such a general form, and impossible to arrive at an unambiguous answer to it. Everything depends on the model governing the instructional process and the conditions under which instruction is conducted, in particular the means, the hardware technology, available for implementation of the model.

It is quite clear that if programmed instruction is based on a poor first-order model (for example, if only the explanatory-illustrative method is used so that knowledge is presented to the student in a final or "ready-made" form and no attempt is made to teach him methods for cognitive enterprise, etc.), then giving this model a programmed form will not significantly raise the effectiveness of the instructional process. Since it is possible to program poor instructional content and methods as well as good content and methods, the programmed form in itself does not guarantee high effectiveness.

Programmed instruction will be highly effective or ineffective as a function of the first-order models which it implements, and there is nothing surprising in the fact that programmed instruction based on a poor first-order model proves less effective than non-programmed instruction based on a good first-order model. A poor instructional model does not become an effective teaching instrument by being programmed. Moreover, the negative influence on the student of a poor instructional model (for example, a model which teaches mechanical [rote, *Ed.*] rather than intelligent assimilation of material) can be intensified by being programmed.

In general, however, there is no doubt that instruction in which there is good feedback, for example, is more effective, all things being equal, than instruction in which feedback is poor. It is clear, too, that instruction which takes into account the individual characteristics of the student is more effective than instruction which does not. The most important point to be made here is that improving only these parameters of the instructional process will not increase its effectiveness in any fundamental way. In other words, it is not sufficient to program the instructional process to guarantee that it will be of high quality.

Indeed, material which is presented in a way which is difficult to comprehend (as it frequently is in standard textbooks) will not be assimilated significantly better by being programmed, although some improvement may occur. This improvement is due to the division of the material into steps or chunks and the fact that the student is asked questions after each chunk which force him to deal with the material in a more active way, to analyze it more deeply, etc. It is for this reason that the effectiveness of instruction is frequently increased even when poor, ineffective instructional models are programmed. It is important to note, however, that replacing an ineffective first-order model with a more effective first-order model in standard, non-programmed instruction can increase effectiveness more than giving programmed form to an ineffective first-order model. On the other hand, giving programmed form to a highly effective (good) first-order model can very significantly increase the effectiveness of instruction. Moreover, it is reasonable to suppose that programmed instruction is capable of increasing the effectiveness of a good first-order model to a significantly greater degree than it is capable of increasing the effectiveness of a poor first-order model. If a poor model is not simply ineffective, but in some respects actually harmful (e.g., by developing in the student incorrect concepts, inadequate methods of approach to cognitive efforts, etc.), then programming it is likely to cause an "adverse increase" in its effectiveness, i.e., to strengthen its negative effects. The possibility of programming poor instructional content and methods as well as good ones makes programmed instruction not only a useful tool, but also a dangerous one which must be used carefully.

Another factor on which the effectiveness of programmed instruction depends to a significant degree is the capabilities of the devices used to implement it.

Programmed instruction will be more effective than standard instruction if these devices permit implementation of adequately sophisticated instructional models, and less effective if they do not.

Many of the experiments conducted both abroad and in the Soviet Union for the purpose of comparing the effectiveness of programmed with standard instruction are flawed by the fact that, although the instruction in question is conducted on the basis of particular models and administered by means of particular teaching devices, the conclusions drawn are considered to be true of the relative effectiveness of the two approaches in general. This methodological error distorts the true state of affairs and conceals the fact that the relative effectiveness of programmed and standard instruction depends on certain specific factors determining the effectiveness of each approach.

The important role which effective first-order models can play in increasing the effectiveness of programmed instruction requires that serious attention be devoted to the content and methods embodied in instructional programs.

For purposes of illustration, we cite below the stages through which work on Russian (i.e., native, *Ed.*) language instructional programs proceeds when the aim is to design both an effective first-order model and an effective second-order model. (The programs were developed by G.G. Granik, O.N. Yudina, E.D. Bozhovich, L.A. Kontseva, and S.M. Bondarenko at the Programmed Instruction Laboratory of the Institute of General and Educational Psychology).

First stage—analysis of existing instructional content and methodology:

(a)   analysis of content (in this case linguistic content),
(b)   logical analysis,
(c)   psychological analysis, and
(d)   methodological analysis.

Analysis of current content and methodology of Russian language instruction in the school has shown that the linguistic basis of this instruction is frequently inadequate (from the point of view of contemporary linguistics, a number of grammatical concepts are handled incorrectly), that it contains a number of errors and shortcomings of a logical character (both with regard to specific concepts and with regard to presentation of the material), that the psychological mechanisms by means of which the student learns many concepts and grammatical habits are not well-understood, and that there is considerable discrepancy in the instructional methodology used by different authors to teach the same concepts, skills, and habits.

Second stage—removal of the shortcomings discovered in stage one and design of an ideal instructional model.

This stage entails the solution of a number of complex content (in this case, linguistic content), logical, psychological, and methodological problems, in order that the content and basic principles of instruction (i.e., what to teach and how to teach it so as to achieve the desired results as quickly, reliably, and efficiently as possible) may be determined precisely. This involves clarification or reformulation of the linguistic content of the course, determination of the optimal sequence for presentation of material, definition of the basic principles which will underly the instructional process, i.e., its fundamental characteristics (for example, will it be diagnostic, individualized, adaptive, etc.), definition of the requirements on drills, elaboration of effective means for controlling the student's cognitive processes, etc.

Third stage—construction of an implementable model.

This stage entails analysis of the conditions which may be established for the instructional process, and determination of which of the problems posed in stage two are solvable. In those instances in which existing conditions do not permit satisfactory solution of these problems, an attempt is made to adapt the means available for solving them to actual conditions. If this is impossible, the decision is made to defer performance of some instructional tasks, and to accept an instructional model which is less than ideal with regard to some of its parameters.

Fourth stage—design of a realistic instructional model and an instructional program which will enable the teacher to implement it.

This stage entails the development of a precise plan for the course as a whole, including a formulation of the procedure for each lesson which specifies how the teacher is to conduct it. The goal here is to develop the skeleton of the future program, its content, and the principles embodied in it, before proceeding to the actual writing of the programmed text or machine program.

Fifth stage—experimental testing and fleshing out of the skeleton of the future program.

This stage consists of the step-by-step experimental testing, both on an individual and a teacher-conducted class basis, of the content and procedure developed in the previous stages. The teacher simulates (imitates) the future instructional device (the programmed text or teaching machine) piecemeal. On the basis of this experimental test of the future program the changes, corrections, additions, etc., which are necessary to insure that it will "work" are made.

Sixth stage—writing the program in the form of a programmed text or machine program.

Seventh stage—the step-by-step experimental checking and completion of the program both on an individual and a group (class) basis.

Eighth stage—writing the second, perfected version of the program and checking it by means of a large-scale experiment.

Ninth stage—analyzing the results of the experiment carried out in the previous stage, making appropriate corrections, and writing the final version of the program.

An effort on this scale requires, of course, a team consisting of specialists from various fields: a specialist in the subject-matter being taught, a psychologist, a logician, a mathematician, teachers, an editor, and an artist. The authors of programmed texts and machine programs frequently do not have such specialists at their disposal, which can have only a negative effect on the quality of the programs they produce. This, however, is a practical problem in the organization of the production of programmed instructional materials.

Bibliography

Anan'ev, B.G. "Man as a General Problem of Contemporary Science." *Leningrad University Bulletin*, 1957, Vol. 2, No. 11.

Anokhin, P.K. "Anticipatory Reflection of Reality." *Problems of Philosophy*, 1962, No. 7.

Ashby, W.R. *Introduction to Cybernetics*. Moscow, 1959.

Ashby, W.R. "What Is an Intelligent Machine?" *Science and Life*, 1962, No. 8.

Ashby, W.R. *The Structure of the Brain*. Moscow, 1964.

Balashova, L.I. "Simultaneous Study of Related Topics." *Soviet Pedagogy*, 1964, No. 1.

Barkhydarov, S.G., and Kryuchkov, S.E. *Textbook of the Russian Language: Part 1*. Moscow, 1965.

Belopol'skaya, A.R. "An Experiment in the Use of Instructional Algorithms." *High School Bulletin*, 1963.

Belopol'skaya, A.R., and Krylova, V.A. "First Algorithms, Then Machines." *High School Bulletin*, 1964, No. 8.

Belopol'skaya, A.R., and Landa, L.N. "Translating from the German into a Russian Teaching Film." Leningrad, Scientific and Popular Film Studio, 1962. See also: "Films in Teaching Translation." In *The Application of Audio-Visual Aids and Programmed Instruction in High Schools and Colleges (Vol. II)*. Moscow, 1963.

Belyaev, B.V. *The Psychological Basis for Learning the Lexicon of a Foreign Language. A Manual for Teachers and Students*. Moscow, 1964.

Belyaev, B.V. *Notes on the Psychology of Foreign Language Teaching. A Manual for Teachers and Students.* Moscow, 1965.

Bernstein, M.S. "Recent Progress in the Teaching of Geometry." *Mathematics in the School*, 1941, No. 2.

Bung, K. "A Model for the Construction and Use of Adaptive Algorithmic Language Programmes." Paper read at the National Programmed Learning Conference held in Birmingham, England from March 31 to April 3, 1967.

Carroll, J.B. "Linguistic Relativity, Contrastive Linguistics, and Language Learning." *International Review of Applied Linguistics*, 1963, Vol. 1, No. 1.

Correll, W. *Programmed Learning and Creative Thinking.* Munich, Ernst Reinhardt Verlag, 1965.

Dunker, K.A. "Qualitative (Experimental and Theoretical) Study of Productive Thinking (Solving of Comprehensible Problems)." *Journal of Genetic Psychology*, 1926.

Edwards, K.S. "Algorithms and the Teaching of Grammar." *Audio-Visual Language Journal*, 1967, Vol. 5, No. 1.

Eiger, G.V., and Hochlerner, M.M. "Reinforcing Grammatical Models by Means of Algorithms." *Foreign Languages in the School*, 1964, No. 3.

El'konin, D.B. "An Experimental Analysis of the First Stage in the Teaching of Reading." *Problems in the Psychology of the School Activity of the Child.* Moscow, 1962.

Feigenbaum, E.A., and Feldman, J. *Computers and Thought.* New York, McGraw-Hill, 1963.

Frank, H. "Teaching Machines for Individual and Group Instruction." *Cybernetic and Pedagogical Aspects of Teaching Machines.* Stuttgart, Klett-Verlag, 1965.

Gal'perin, P. Ya. "On the Formation of Sensory Images and Concepts." Proceedings of the Conference on Psychology, Moscow, July 1955.

Gal'perin, P. Ya. "On the Formation of Cognitive Actions and Concepts. *The Moscow University Herald*, 1956, No. 4.

Gal'perin, P. Ya. "Cognitive Actions as the Basis of the Development of Thinking and Imagery." *Problems of Psychology*, 1957, No. 6.

Gelernter, H.L. "A Geometry Theorem-Proving Machine." *Proceedings of the International Conference on Information Processing.* Paris, UNESCO, 1959.

Gelernter, H.L., and Rochester, N. "Intelligent Behavior in Problem-Solving Machines." *IBM Journal*, October, 1958.

Gentilhomme, I. "Optimization of Teaching Algorithms." *Cybernetic Pedagogy*, 1964, No. 4.

Glushkov, V.M. *Synthesis of Numerical Automata.* Moscow, 1962.

Gmurman, V.E. *Proof Problems in Secondary School Plane Geometry Courses.* Dissertation, Moscow, 1949.

Golubovskaya, A. "Solving Geometrical Problems in Secondary School." *The Solution of Mathematical Problems.* Leningrad, 1935.

Granik, G.G. "Cognitive Work Techniques in the Learning of Orthography." *Psychology of Activization of Teaching in Evening Secondary School.* Edited by D.N. Bogoyalenskii. Moscow, 1943.

Granik, G.G. *Developing Cognitive Procedures in School-Children During the Acquisition of Orthographical Habits.* Dissertation, Moscow, 1965.

Granik, G.G. "Repetition of Punctuation in Higher Classes." *The Russian Language in School*, 1966, No. 2.

Gunther, K. "Algorithms as a Means for Efficient Teaching of the Russian Language." *Foreign Language Teaching*, 1965.

Gurvich, P.B. "Positive and Negative Aspects of the Structural Approach to Foreign Language Teaching." *Foreign Languages in High School*, 1965.

Hadamard, J. *Elementary Geometry, Part I.* Moscow, 1948.

Itel'son, L.B. *Mathematical and Cybernetic Methods in Pedagogy.* Moscow, 1964.

Ivanov, A.A. *The Use of Teaching Machines.* Odessa, 1964.

Izvestia. "Shortcomings in the Cognitive Activity of Students Who Have Difficulty in Solving Problems Independently," 1961.

Kabanova-Meller, E.N. "A Psychological Analysis of the Application of Geographic Concepts and Laws." *Transactions of the APS of the RSFSR*, 1950.

Kabanova-Meller, E.N. *The Psychology of the Development of*

Knowledge and Habits in Elementary School Pupils. Moscow, 1962.

Kalmykova, Z.I. "Processes of Analysis and Synthesis in Problem-Solving." *Transactions of the APS of the RSFSR*, 1955.

Kalmykova, Z.I. "Levels of the Application of Knowledge During the Solution of Psysics Problems." *The Psychology of Applying Knowledge to the Solution of School Problems*, Edited by N.A. Menchinskaya. Moscow, 1958.

Kelbert, H.A. "The Application of Lyapunov's Algorithms in Professional Pedagogy." *Mathematical and Technical Problems in Cybernetics.* Berlin, 1963.

Kelbert, H.A. "A Cybernetic Model for the Use of a Branched Programmed Text." *Cybernetic and Pedagogical Aspects of Teaching Machines.* Munich, Oldenbourg-Verlag, 1964.

Kingsley, E., Kopstein, F.F., and Seidel, R.J. Graph Theory as a Meta-Language of Communicable Knowledge. *Man in Systems.* Edited by M. Rubin. New York: Gordon and Breach, 1971.

Kostyuk, G.S. "The Interaction of Up-Bringing and Personality Development." *Problems of Psychology*, 1956, No. 5.

Kostyuk, G.S. "Upbringing and Development in the Child." *Soviet Pedagogy*, 1956, No. 12.

Krupatkin, Y.B. "Teaching Translation Using Analysis: Methodological Notes for a Course in Teaching Foreign Languages in an Institution of Higher Learning." Moscow, 1965.

Landa, L.N. "Search Trials in the Thinking Process." *Proceedings of the Conference on Problems in the Psychology of Perception*, Moscow, May 20-22, 1957a.

Landa, L.N. "Some Data on the Development of Cognitive Capactities." *Transactions of the APS of the RSFSR*, 1957b.

Landa, L.N. Teaching a General Thinking Procedure for Problem-Solving. *Problems of Psychology*, 1959, No. 3.

Landa, L.N. "On a Method of Increasing the Efficiency of the Learning-Teaching Process and of the Prevention of Pupils' Failure." *Abstracts of Papers Submitted to the Conference on Didactics.* Moscow, 1960.

Landa, L.N. "Some Shortcomings in the Cognitive Activity of

Students Who Have Difficulty in Solving Problems Independently." *Transactions of the APS of the RSFSR*, 1961a, No. 115.

Landa, L.N. "The Teaching of Methods of Efficient Thought and the Problem of Algorithms." *Problems of Psychology*, 1961b, No. 1.

Landa, L.N. "On the Cybernetic Approach to Instructional Theory." *Problems of Philosophy*, 1962.

Landa, L.N. *Algorithmization in Learning and Instruction.* Moscow, 1966.

Landa, L.N. *Algorithmization in Learning and Instruction.* Englewood Cliffs, New Jersey: Educational Technology Publications, 1974.

Landa, L.N., and A.R. Belopol'skaya. "On the Formation in Students of General Schemes of Cognitive Actions as a Prerequisite for Efficient Teaching of Methods of Cognitive Activity." *Abstracts of Papers Presented at the Congress of the Psychological Society of the USSR*, Moscow, 1959.

Landa, L.N., and Khlebnikov, S.P. "The Tutor I Teaching Device." *Technological Aids in Teaching: Bulletin of the Academy of Pedagogical Sciences of the RSFSR*, 1963.

Landa, L.N., Orlova, A.M., and Granik, G.G. "Principles of Programmed Russian Language Instruction." *The Russian Language in School*, 1965, Nos. 3, 4, and 5.

Landsberg, G.S. Foreword to *Elementary Textbook of Physics.* Moscow, 1956.

Leites, N.S. *Intellectual Giftedness.* Moscow, 1960.

Leontiev, A.N. "On the Theory of Development of the Child's Psyche." *Soviet Education*, 1945, No. 4.

Leontiev, A.N. On Awareness in Learning. *Transactions of the APS of the RSFSR*, 1947, No. 7.

Lewis, B.N. *The Rationale of Adaptive Machines: Mechanization in the Classroom.* Edited by M. Goldsmith. London, Souvenir Press, 1963.

Lewis, B., and Edwards, K. "Short Cuts to Problem Solving." *New Society,* Oct. 20, 1966.

Lyapin, S.E. *Methods of Teaching Mathematics.* Moscow, 1955.

Lyapunov, A.A. Some General Problems in Cybernetics. *Problems of Cybernetics*, Moscow, 1958.

Lyapunov, A.A., and Shestopal, G.A. "The Algorithmic Description of Control Processes." *Mathematical Education*, 1957, No. 2.

Malir, F. "The Russian Imperative." *Foreign Language Teaching*, 1967.

Markov, A.A. "The Theory of Algorithms." *Transactions of the V.A. Steklov Mathematical Institute*, 1954.

Mashbits, E.I., and Bondarovskaya, V.M. *Foreign Conceptions of Programmed Instruction*. Kiev, 1964.

Menchinskaya, N.A. "More on the Problems of the Psychology of Mastering Knowledges." *Transactions of the APS of the RSFSR*, No. 61, 1955.

Miller, G.A., Galanter, E., and Pribram, K. *Plans and the Structure of Behavior*. New York, Holt, 1960.

Minsky, M. "Steps Toward Artificial Intelligence." *Proceedings of the Institute of Radio Engineers*, January, 1961.

Nebylitsyn, V.D. *Basic Properties of the Nervous System*. Moscow, 1966.

Nemytov, P.A. *Methods of Proving Geometric Theorems in the Seven-Year School*. Dissertation, 1947.

Newell, A., and Shaw, J.C. "Elements of a Theory of Human Problem Solving." *Psychological Review*, 1958, Vol. 65, No. 3.

Newell, A., Shaw, J.C., and Simon, H.A. "Empirical Explorations of the Logic Theory Machine." *Proceedings, Western Joint Computer Conference*, 1957.

Newell, A., Shaw, J.C., and Simon, H.A. "Report on a General Problem-Solving Program." *Information Processing: Proceedings of the International Conference on Information Processing*. Paris, UNESCO, 1959.

Newell, A., Shaw, J.C., and Simon, H.A. "A Variety of Intelligent Learning in a General Problem Solver." *Self-Organizing Systems*. Edited by M. Yovits and S. Cameron. New York, Spartan Press, 1960.

Newell, A., Shaw, J.C., and Simon, H.A. "Computer Simulation of Human Thinking." *Science*, Dec. 22, 1961.

Newell, A., Shaw, J.C., and Simon, H.A. "Empirical Exploration with the Logic Theory Machine: A Case Study in Heuristics." In *Computers and Thought*, edited by E. Feigenbaum and J. Feldman. New York, McGraw-Hill, 1963.

Newell, A., Shaw, J.C., and Simon, H.A. *The Processes of Creative Thinking: A Symposium Held at the University of Colorado*. Edited by H.E. Gruber, G. Terrell, and M. Wertheimer. New York, Atherton Press, 1963.

Newell, A., and Simon, H.A. "The Logic Theory Machine." *IRE Transactions on Information Theory*, 1956, Vol. 3.

Novikova, P.S. *Elements of Mathematical Logic*. Moscow, 1959.

Orlova, A.M. The Psychology of the Acquisition of the Subject Concept." *Transactions of the APS of the RSFSR*, 1950.

Osynskii, M.D. "Guiding Elements in Mathematical Research." Paper read before the Second All-Russian Conference of Mathematics Teachers in Moscow, 1915.

Pask, G. Electronic Keyboard Teaching Machines. *Teaching Machines and Programmed Learning: A Source Book*. Edited by A.A. Lumsdaine and R. Glaser. Washington, D.C., NEA, 1960a.

Pask, G. Adaptive Teaching with Adaptive Machines. *Teaching Machines and Programmed Learning: A Source Book*. Edited by A.A. Lumsdaine and R. Glaser. Washington, D.C., NEA, 1960b.

Pask, G., and Lewis, B.N. "An Adaptive Automaton for Teaching Small Groups." *Perceptual and Motor Skills*, 1962, No. 14.

Pask, G. "Learning Strategies, Memories, and Individuals." *Cybernetics, Artificial Intelligence, and Ecology*. Edited by H. Robinson and D. Knight. New York, Spartan Press, 1971.

Pask, G., and Scott, B.C.E. Uncertainty Regulation in Learning Applied to Procedures for Teaching Concepts of Probability. Final Scientific Report. System Research, Richmond, Surrey, UK, January, 1972.

Polya, G. *How to Solve It*. Princeton, 1942.

Polya, G. *How to Solve It*. Princeton, 1946.

Polya, G. *How to Solve It*. Princeton, 1972.

Porter, D. "Teaching Machines." *Harvard Graduate School of Education Reviews*, 1958, Vol. 3, No. 1.

Pushkin, V.N. "The Psychology of Supervision of Railroad Transport." *Problems of Psychology*, 1959, No. 3.

Pushkin, V.N. Towards an Understanding of Heuristic Activity in Cybernetics and Psychology." *Problems of Psychology*, 1965.

Revzin, I.I., and Rosenzweig, V.Y. "Fundamentals of General and Machine Translation." *High School*, 1964.

Retsker, Y.I. Regular Correspondences in Translating Into One's Native Language. *The Theory and Practice of Translation*. Moscow, 1950.

Rubinstein, S.L. "The Psychological Ideas of I.M. Sechenov and Soviet Psychological Science." *Problems of Psychology*, 1955a.

Rubinstein, S.L. "Problems of Psychological Theory." *Problems of Psychology*, 1955b.

Rubinstein, S.L. *Approaches to the Investigation of Thinking*, Moscow, 1958.

Samarin, Yu. A. "Older Students' Style of Cognitive Effort." *Transactions of the APS of the RSFSR*, 1948, No. 17.

Samarin, Yu.A. *Outline of a Psychology of Intelligence*. Moscow, 1962.

Sapir, E. "Conceptual Categories in Primitive Languages." *Science*, 1931, Vol. 74.

Scherba, L.V. *Foreign Language Teaching in High School: General Problems in Methodology*. Moscow, 1947.

Sechenov, I.M. *Selected Works*. Moscow, 1953.

Shenshev, L.V. "General Features of Thinking in the Learning of Mathematics and Foreign Languages." *Problems of Psychology*, 1960, No. 4.

Shenshev, L.V. "Implementation of the Principles of Programmed Instruction in Foreign Language Teaching." *Technological Aids and Programmed Instruction in High School*. Novosibirsk, 1965.

Shenshev, L.V. *The Role of Teaching Machines in a Programmed Instruction System*. Moscow, 1966.

Shevaryov, P.A. "Observations on the Problem of Associations." *Transactions of the APS of the RSFSR*, 1957, No. 80.

Shevaryov, P.A. *Generalized Associations in School-Children*. Moscow, 1959.

Shevaryov, P.A. *Generalized Associations in a Student's School Work*. Moscow, 1959.

Sidelkovskii, A.P. "The Algorithmic Approach to the Analysis of Instructional Processes Is Correct." *Problems of Psychology*, 1964, No. 5.

Slavina, L.S. *The Individual Approach to Backward and Undisciplined Students*. Moscow, 1958.

Smirnov, B.A. "Algorithms and the Algorithmic Logic Diagram." *Problems of Logic*. Moscow, 1963.

Sontsov, A. "Teaching the Student to Find Proofs Consciously." *Bulletin of the Gorky Pedagogical Institute*, 1929.

Steinbuch, K. Lernende Automaten. *Elektronische Rechenanlagen*, 1959.

Steinbuch, K. *Automat und Mensch*. Berlin, 1961.

Stelzer, J., and Kingsley, E. Axiomatics as a Paradigm for Structuring Subject-Matter. *Instructional Science*, 1975.

Stepanov, A.V. *The Development of Mathematical Abilities in Children*. Dissertation, Moscow, 1952.

Stolurow, L.M. *Teaching by Machine*. Washington, D.C., U.S. Office of Education, 1961.

Stolurow, L.M. "Model the Master Teacher or Master the Teaching Model." *Learning and the Educational Process*. Edited by J.D. Krumboltz. Chicago, Rand McNally, 1965.

Stolurow, L.M. *Machine-Aided Instruction*. Moscow, 1965.

Stolurow, L.M., and Davis, D. "Teaching Machines and Computer-Based Systems." *Teaching Machines and Programmed Learning: Data and Directions*. Edited by R. Glaser. Washington, D.C., NEA, 1965.

Talyzina, N.F. "Ways to Form Elementary Scientific Concepts." *Transactions of the APS of the RSFSR*, 1960.

Teplov, B.M. *Individual Differences*. Moscow, 1961.

Tonge, F.M. "Summary of a Heuristic Line Balancing Procedure." *Computers and Thought*. Edited by E.A. Feigenbaum and J. Feldman. New York, McGraw-Hill, 1963.

Trakhtenbrot, B.A. *Algorithms and the Mechanical Solution of Problems*. Moscow, 1957.

Uspenskii, B.A. *Lectures on Computable Functions*. Moscow, 1960.

Voishvillo, E.K. "A Method for Simplifying Truth-Functions in Russian." *Philosophical Sciences*, 1958, No. 2.

Vorobev, G.V. "A Method for Making Concept Acquisition More Precise." *Teaching Secondary School Students Techniques for Independent Work*. Edited by M.A. Danilov and B.I. Esipiv. Moscow, 1963.

Vygotsky, L.S. *Collected Psychological Research*. Moscow, 1956.

Weisgerber, R.A. (Ed.) *Perspectives in Individualized Learning*. Itasca, Illinois: F.E. Peacock Publishers, Inc., 1971.

Whorf, B.L. *Language, Thought, and Reality*. Cambridge, MIT Press, 1956.

Yablonsky, S.V. "Functional Structures in K-Valued Logic." *Proceedings of the V.A. Steklov Mathematical Institute*, 1958.

Zadeh, L.A. "Fuzzy Sets." *Information and Control*, 1965, Vol. 8.

Zankov, L.V. (Ed.) *Combining Oral Instruction and Visual Aids in Teaching*. Moscow, 1958.

Zykova, V.I. "Operating with Concepts in the Solution of Geometric Problems." *Transactions of the APS of the RSFSR*, 1950, No. 28.

Zykova, V.I. *The Psychology of Assimilating Introductory Geometrical Knowledge: An Outline*. Moscow, 1955.

Index

Names

A
Anan'ev, B.G., 208
Anokhin, P.K., 90
Ashby, W.R., 116, 345, 397

B
Balashova, L.I., 399
Belopol'skaya, A.R., 173, 213
Belyaev, B.V., 207, 208
Bernstein, M.S., 294
Bondarenko, S.M., 477
Bondarovskaya, V.M., 400
Bozhovich, E.D., 477
Bung, K., 213

C
Carroll, J.B., 207
Crowder, N., 375, 376, 377, 401

D
Davis, D., 426
Dunker, K.A., 118

E
Edwards, K.S., 213
Eiger, G.V., 213

F
Feigenbaum, E.A., 105, 116
Feldman, J., 105, 116
Frank, H., 4

G
Galanter, E.H., 106, 117, 184, 186, 188
Gal'perin, P. Ya., 261, 264, 400
Gelernter, H., 106
Gentilhomme, I., 173
Glushkov, V.M., 113, 332
Gmurman, V.E., 294
Goedel, K., 333
Golubovskaya, A., 297
Granik, G.G., 173, 477
Gunther, K., 213
Gurvich, P.B., 230

Sechenov, I.M., 398
Seidel, R.J., 392
Shaw, J.C., 102, 105, 107
Shenshev, L.V., 192, 207, 208, 225, 392
Shestopal, G.A., 322
Shevaryov, P.A., 194, 260, 266
Sholomii, M.M., 168
Sidelkovskii, A.P., 399
Simon, H.A., 102, 105, 107, 448
Skinner, B.F., 375, 376, 401
Slavina, L.S., 264
Smirnev, B.A., 325
Sontsov, A., 261
Steinbuch, K., 447
Stelzer, J., 392, 399
Stepanov, A.V., 261, 264
Stolurow, L.M., 4, 426, 448

T
Talyzina, N.F., 400

Teplov, B.M., 177
Tonge, F., 106
Trakhtenbrot, B.A., 108

U
Uspenskii, B.A., 394

V
Voishvillo, E.K., 442, 448
Vorobev, G.V., 393
Vygotsky, L.S., 207

W
Whorf, B.L., 207

Y
Yablonski, S.V., 442
Yudina, O.N., 444, 477

Z
Zadeh, L., 159
Zykova, V.I., 102, 261, 266

Subjects

A

Algorithm(s), viii, 54, 64, 77, 80, 85ff, 100, 193, 210ff, 220ff, 321ff, 337, 348, 418, 433
  design (construction) of, viii, 10, 341, 372

efficiency of, 88
instructional, 19
properties of, 108, 111
Algorithmic processes (prescriptions), 106, 146, 156, 193, 225, 435, 473
Algorithmoid process, 194, 433

Acknowledgments

The chapters in this volume are adapted from the following
original sources:
1. *Problems of Philosophy*, 1962, No. 9.
2. Paper submitted to All-Union Conference on Teaching
   Methods, 1961.
3. *Knowledge Is a Strength*, 1962, No. 10.
4. *Psychology of Education*, Poland, 1967, No. 5.
5. *Scientific Journal of Güstrow Pedagogical Institute*,
   Germany, 1966/67, No. 6.
6. *Ibid.*, No. 7.
7. *Foreign Languages at School*, 1968, No. 1.
8. *Problems of Psychology*, 1959, No. 3.
9. *Transactions of the APS of the RSFSR*, 1961, No. 115.
10. Moscow, 1965. Published by the Pedagogical Society of
    the RSFSR.
11. *Ibid.*, 1966.
12. *Ibid.*, 1969.